Bloomer Girls

SPORT AND SOCIETY

Series Editors
Randy Roberts
Aram Goudsouzian

Founding Editors
Benjamin G. Rader
Randy Roberts

*A list of books in the series appears
at the end of this book.*

Bloomer Girls

Women Baseball Pioneers

DEBRA A. SHATTUCK

University of Illinois Press

URBANA, CHICAGO, AND SPRINGFIELD

© 2017 by the Board of Trustees
of the University of Illinois
All rights reserved
Manufactured in the United States of America
1 2 3 4 5 C P 5 4 3 2 1
∞ This book is printed on acid-free paper.

Library of Congress Cataloging-in-Publication Data
Names: Shattuck, Debra A., author.
Title: Bloomer girls : women baseball pioneers /
    Debra A. Shattuck.
Description: Urbana : University of Illinois Press, [2016]
    | Includes bibliographical references and index.
Identifiers: LCCN 2016007026 | ISBN 9780252040375
    (hardcover : alk. paper) | ISBN 9780252081866 (pbk. :
    alk. paper)
Subjects: LCSH: Women baseball players—United States.
    | Women baseball players—United States—Biography.
Classification: LCC GV880.7 .S53 2016 |
    DDC 796.3570922—dc23
LC record available at http://lccn.loc.gov/2016007026

Cliff
I miss you so much
See you in a few minutes

Mom
I couldn't have done this without you

Contents

Preface

MOM WAS THE BASEBALL FAN in our family. As a young child I was vaguely aware that Mom regularly watched games on TV while Dad, an electrical engineer at NASA, pretty much ignored them. I tended to follow Dad's lead until the summer of 1970, when my ambivalence toward baseball changed after I received two free tickets to a Cleveland Indians game for finishing fifth grade with high marks. I will never forget walking up the ramp in old Cleveland Municipal Stadium and catching my first glimpse of a professional baseball diamond. Its size and beauty filled me with awe. I have no memory of who the Indians played that day or whether they won or lost, but I have never forgotten the sense of wonder I felt when I first saw that field.

From that moment on, baseball fever had overtaken me. I became a regular fixture on the couch next to Mom when the Indians were on TV. When they were not, I was in the neighbors' backyard mimicking my baseball heroes on my own Field of Dreams. The neighbor boy and I took turns impersonating Indians catcher Ray Fosse and ace pitcher "Sudden Sam" McDowell.[1] During our endless summer of fantasy games, we struck out scores of New York Yankee batters and propelled our beloved Cleveland Indians to our fantasy World Series. I lobbied my parents to take me to games whenever they could, and began devoting my nickels and dimes to bubble gum in hopes of obtaining baseball cards of favorite players. I distinctly remember the day Dad presented me with Ray Fosse's autograph. Returning from a business trip, he happened to be on the same airline flight as Fosse, and he asked Ray to scribble a few words to his star-struck fifth grade daughter. In the years that followed, I played street ball with the neighbor kids and did a brief stint as an umpire for the youth league in Vermilion, Ohio. I would have happily continued my umpire duties had both players and coaches not made it clear through snide and demeaning comments that I was not welcome on the diamond. Their vitriol caught me off guard. This experience served as an unpleasant introduction to the unlegislated law of the land that "baseball is for boys and softball is for girls."

My enthusiasm as a baseball fan never recovered after I was ostracized on the youth baseball diamond. I still watched occasional games on television but was more likely to listen to Herb Score and Joe Tait call games on the radio while I worked jigsaw puzzles or did homework. I no longer idolized players or tried to mimic them. The dream of becoming the next Ray Fosse or Sam MacDowell was over. I turned my attention to playing volleyball, basketball, and softball in high school and college, periodically revisiting my baseball memories and lamenting that there were no girls' teams. To me, this made no sense. I knew from my street ball days that the smaller-sized baseball was much easier to grip and throw than a softball, and I knew from personal experience that a softball did not exactly feel "soft" when it hit you or jammed your finger after a wicked hop. In my naiveté I thought that once girls demonstrated they were as capable as boys of playing (or umpiring) baseball, they would be welcomed into the sport. I did not yet grasp how intractable 150 years of history and cultural tradition could be, nor did I appreciate the power of myth in shaping that history. Once I understood this, I realized that if girls and women were ever going to have the opportunity to play baseball with no editorial strings attached, it would take more than merely proving their athleticism or winning access to dugouts through the courtroom. It would require determining the reasons for the deep-seated antipathy to girls and women playing baseball so these factors could be addressed and ameliorated. Thus began a historical and intellectual journey that has taken me from backyard pitching sessions to the shrine of the national game in Cooperstown—a journey that has enabled me to appreciate how closely tied baseball still is to our national psyche and why girls and women still find it difficult to gain acceptance on the emerald diamond.

Acknowledgments

THIS BOOK HAS BEEN IN WORK for almost three decades. It is impossible to convey fully the gratitude I feel toward the many people who have helped me along the way and who have created and maintained the archives, libraries, historical societies, and digital resources that make historical scholarship like mine possible. I am grateful to Dick Wentworth, former director of the University of Illinois Press, who first suggested to a young Air Force captain in 1990 that she write a book based on her research, and to his successor, Bill Regier, who allowed the now-retired scholar to pick up where she had left off more than a decade earlier, and who waited with supreme patience for the project to finish.

I collectively thank all of my professors at the University of Iowa for teaching me the craft of historical scholarship. I especially thank Susan Birrell and Tina Parratt, who encouraged and aided my application and acceptance into a UIOWA doctoral program. I am grateful to my primary advisors, Linda Kerber and Leslie Schwalm, and to PhD committee members Connie Berman, Tina Parratt, Chris Ogren, and Allen Steinberg. Linda, Leslie, and Allen provided invaluable assistance on my manuscript, as did UIOWA alum and scholar Barbara Handy-Marchello.

I have benefited immeasurably from the work of myriad colleagues in the fields of women's history and baseball history. Gerda Lerner, Kitty Sklar, and Tom Dublin introduced me to women's history at a critical juncture in my development as a scholar. John Thorn was the first to publish my research and is an irreplaceable mentor and font of baseball wisdom. David Block's *Baseball Before We Knew It* inspired me, and David's friendship and willingness to share his research has been of inestimable value. The same is true of Barbara Gregorich, whose *Women at Play* was one of the first books dedicated to revealing the hidden narrative of women's involvement with baseball. Like David, Barbara has generously shared her research and offered her encouragement.

I have received invaluable help from fellow baseball and sport historians at conferences of the North American Society for Sport History, NINE, and the Frederick Ivor-Campbell Symposium. I have benefited from the online camaraderie and expertise of members of the Society for American Baseball Research's Nineteenth Century Base Ball, Origins, and Women and Baseball committees—particularly Tom Altherr, Jean Ardell, Priscilla Astifan, Jerry Casway, Bob Cullen, Leslie Heaphy, Richard Hershberger, Dorothy Seymour Mills, Bob Tholkes, and the late Craig Waff. Special thanks go to Larry McCray for maintaining SABR's invaluable Protoball Chronology Web site. Countless individuals graciously shared articles, clippings, and photographs from their collections; those not already mentioned elsewhere include Randall Brown, John Dyke, David Kemp, Jeffrey Kittel, Joann Kline, John Kovach, Marty Payne, Mark Rucker, and Phil Zaret. Maria Brandt, Donna Burdick, Gloria Lundy, Susanne Stahovec, and J. Camilo Vera conducted research on my behalf. Of the many archivists and librarians who supported my work, I am especially indebted to Ken Cobb (New York City Municipal Archives), Julie Couture (Lebanon Historical Society), Gloria Gavert (Miss Porter's School), Joseph Gleason (George Sim Johnston Archives of the New York Society for the Prevention of Cruelty to Children), Lillian Hansberry (Penn State Abington Library), Nancy Logan and Linda Miller (Roanoke College Library), Janalyn Moss (University of Iowa Library), Rosemary Plakas (Library of Congress), Bill Rowan (Tri-State Corners Genealogical Society), Joyce Salmon (Punahou School), Tim Wiles (National Baseball Hall of Fame Library), Jeffrey Willis (Converse College), and Dot Willsey (Gerrit Smith Estate National Historic Landmark).

This book would never have come to fruition without the support of my family—particularly my mother, who accompanied me on countless journeys near and far in search of elusive clues to the forgotten history of women baseball players. She labored alongside me for years—examining endless pages of microfilm and digitized newspapers, typing hundreds of pages of transcripts, and proofreading hundreds of pages of text. She doggedly persisted in keeping me on track when I despaired of ever finishing. My sister, Sandye, helped with research and echoed my mother's encouragement along the way. My late husband, Cliff, and children, David, Kristen, and Katie, brought joy into my life and patiently endured the many absences and sequestrations my research necessitated.

I appreciate my John Witherspoon College colleague, Jamin Hübner, for pushing me through the last hurdle of discouragement with a timely quotation from Winston Churchill:

Writing a book is an adventure.
To begin with, it is a toy and an amusement;
Then it becomes a mistress, and then a tyrant.
The last phase is that, just as you are about to be reconciled
To your servitude, you kill the monster, and fling him out to the public.[1]

What a relief to finally fling the "monster" out into the public. I trust the adventure of reading it will prove as enjoyable as the adventure of writing it.

Finally, I pay homage to the gracious God who gave me life, redeemed me, and set my feet upon a Rock—the God who walks with me through life's darkest hours and fills my heart with joy unspeakable and a peace that passes understanding.

Bloomer Girls

Introduction

Women play baseball—after a fashion. Few play it well. The
"hardball" game is a man's sport and although members of the
fair sex have tried it since way back when and there are teams of
women players who still tour the country for exhibition games
against men's teams, their chief stock in trade is novelty. It is
decidedly unusual for a girl to be skilled in this sport.
—Arthur T. Noren, *Softball* (1966)[1]

What if we just admitted that softball and baseball are not, in fact,
"separate but equal" but entirely different sports? There is no
rational basis to claim that girls can't throw overhand, run 90 feet
between bases or handle a hardball. And there is no reason but
sexism to prevent them from doing so.
—Emma Span, *New York Times* (2014)[2]

BASEBALL HAS NOT ALWAYS been identified as a man's game despite
its boosters proclaiming it a "manly" pastime from the moment it coalesced
into a new sport from multiple bat and ball games in antebellum America. For
most of the nineteenth century, girls and women actively (although not always
consciously) resisted this gendered narrative by playing the game. Unfortunately,
the record of female involvement with the national pastime became significantly
distorted over the course of the nineteenth century; this intentional and uninten-
tional distortion helped create and perpetuate baseball's identity as a masculine
sport. Today, four decades after girls and young women filed more than twenty-
two lawsuits against the Little League Association and various youth and high
school leagues for the right to play baseball, most Americans still assume that
baseball is for boys and men and that softball is for everyone, but especially
girls and women.[3] Modern feminism, which so successfully opened the door to
countless opportunities for women in business, politics, economics, the military,
and sport, did little to open baseball dugouts to girls and women. Why is that?

"All play means something," says Johan Huizinga. It is a "special form of
activity" that serves a social function.[4] As the so-called *national* pastime, countless constituencies have used baseball for diverse social functions; these func-

tions have varied over time as sociocultural contexts evolved. Yet, despite the fluidity of context and constituencies, baseball remains strongly gendered as a man's game. How do we account for the current association of baseball with masculinity long after other previously gendered sports like distance running, basketball, and competitive skiing have become gender neutral? Why is the mantra "baseball is for boys and softball is for girls" still so deeply engrained in the collective consciousness of our twenty-first-century minds while news of women running corporations, ruling from the Supreme Court bench, presiding over cities, states, and universities, and commanding military units is considered passé?

The history of baseball bears little resemblance to the past, as John Thorn presciently reveals in his study of how baseball's early power brokers and boosters constructed false stories about their sport to perpetuate particular sociocultural narratives they wished to convey. In *Baseball in the Garden of Eden* Thorn concludes that "in no field of American endeavor is invention more rampant than in baseball, whose whole history is a lie from beginning to end."[5] One of the most invidious inventions from baseball's past is that the game is and always has been a man's game. This is simply not true; there were always "Eves" in baseball's Eden.

This study addresses a number of questions: How and why did the gender-neutral child's game of baseball become so fiercely gendered as "masculine?" Who were the historical actors (male and female) who consciously or unconsciously wielded the tools that gendered the sport? Why has this gendered identity persisted, and can it ever be deconstructed to return baseball to a game for everyone?

Sport and Gendered Identities

Sport is one of many tools human beings use to inculcate and express sociocultural identities like race, gender, social class, and ethnicity. Individual sports can be characterized as gender neutral (recreational swimming, tennis, golf, etc.) or masculine (football, baseball, cricket, etc.) or feminine (synchronized swimming, rhythmic gymnastics, etc.).[6] These categories are fluid; the characterization of games and sports as masculine or feminine changes over time, just as the ideals that people associate with masculinity and femininity change over time.

During the twentieth century, determined sportswomen successfully recast a host of previously gendered sports as gender neutral (or at least began the process toward that end). Marathons, decathlons, and triathlons, bobsledding, speed skating, and body building slowly lost their "men-only" identities as elite female athletes subverted their gendered narratives by proving that women could master them. This is not to say that demonstrated excellence automatically transforms a sport's gendered identity, or alters its hierarchical power structures, or changes its status within the broader culture. Demonstrated excellence does, however, problematize and challenge the gendered identities associated with particular sports, making it more difficult for groups to use those sports to perpetuate a particular gender ideal.

Transforming a sport's gendered characterization can take decades and is not a binary process. Gender ideals are fluid and influenced by factors like race, ethnicity, and class and they are jointly constructed by men *and* women.[7] Both men and women have used sport to model and perpetuate ideals of masculinity and femininity.[8] This study explores that process using baseball as an exemplar; it describes how the gender-neutral child's game of baseball became gendered as a man's game over the course of the nineteenth century and why female physical educators ultimately chose to create the separate game of "women's baseball" rather than continue to support a gendered counternarrative for the national pastime. Baseball is a useful example for this study because, unlike other sports, it was labeled the "national pastime" early in the nation's formative period. It was birthed and grew to adolescence at the same time the young United States was developing a national culture. As Jules Tygiel notes, the sport became highly popular precisely because its creators "fashioned it in their own image."[9] The drive to equate baseball with American (U.S.) identity and values was so strong it led to the fabrication of historical narratives about the sport that tried to erase links to British antecedents and that misrepresented women's participation.[10]

The history of women baseball players, like the origin of modern baseball, has been distorted by myth and misperception, leading to the erroneous belief that baseball has always been a man's game. Decade after decade in the nineteenth century, the popular press and baseball boosters perpetuated misinformation and historical amnesia about female players by labeling each new athlete or team as a "novelty." Novelty implies oddity—something not seen before—something without a history. Each new generation of players thought it was the first because it had no historical memory of preceding generations. The letters, diaries, and reminiscences of women players from the nineteenth century onward reflect their belief that what they were doing was out of the norm and "new." Because women players in succeeding generations were unable to establish strong links to previous generations of players, they were unable to alter the perception that they were interlopers in the masculine space of the baseball diamond. With each passing decade that journalists and social commentators labeled women players "novelties," baseball's reputation as a masculine sport became more deeply entrenched. Modern scholars unknowingly perpetuated this distortion by repeating the observations of past actors; they did not realize that what each generation of observers was reporting as novel was actually a continuation of past practice.

Scope and Methodology

To some extent, this study harkens back to the early days of women's history when scholars sought merely to insert forgotten women back into the historical record. Because no published resource to date thoroughly quantifies the numerical, temporal, and geographic scope of nineteenth-century women baseball players, a portion of this book is devoted to filling these historical gaps. In fact, the sheer number of previously unknown female players and teams caused me to constrain my study to the nineteenth century. The appendices provide details on specific teams and individuals that played (or planned to play) during the nineteenth century. The list will undoubtedly grow as more nineteenth-century resources are digitized.

Simply documenting the existence of female baseball players does not answer the questions about baseball's gendered identity—in fact, the existence of such a large number of nineteenth-century female players problematizes that history. Thus, this study also considers why girls and women (many of whom played baseball before the sport acquired the institutional power structures that ultimately perpetuated its gendered identity) were not able to prevent baseball's characterization as a masculine sport in the first place. I use Michael Messner's "trilevel conceptual framework" to explore the complex process through which baseball became gendered. In *Taking the Field: Women, Men, and Sports* (2002), Messner describes how institutional structures, culture, and social interactions collectively create a "center" for a particular sport—the locus of money, power, and elite athleticism—against which all participants and related endeavors are gauged.[11] I explore how baseball's evolving rules and institutions (its *institutional structures*), the narratives crafted and perpetuated by players, team owners, the media, and baseball boosters (its *culture* or *creed*), and the actions of baseball players—both male and female—(*social interactions*) influenced the development of a "center" of baseball that privileged male participation and accomplishments by mischaracterizing and marginalizing female participants. Each of Messner's categories has a broader application as well, and throughout the study I situate the discussion of the sport's institutional structures, cultural influences, and social interactions within the context of broader sociocultural issues like nationalism, women's rights, and shifting gender ideals.

This historical reclamation project is not without its challenges, both philosophical and methodological. Philosophically, the question looms about whether it is even possible to recover the past—to restore historical memory. Historian Dan Nathan writes: "History is a human construct, a starting point that challenges us to recognize the contexts and purposes for which it is written. ... [T]he past is always more ambiguous, complicated, and disordered than the prose used to describe and analyze it."[12] So, in one sense, we must begin by acknowledging that there is no single history of women baseball players to be restored—the best that can be hoped for is to construct a narrative that reflects more accurately the experiences of women baseball players than what has come down to us through the discourses crafted by others. That is much easier said than done. As Cahn reminds us, women's experiences are "not unmediated, not directly accessible, and certainly not universalizable."[13] Female baseball players came from varied social backgrounds and played in myriad temporal and physical spaces; they shared neither mental nor physical characteristics. Ultimately, groups of women baseball players had more in common with other subsets of women than they did with each other. Late-nineteenth-century female professional baseball players, for example, had more in common with female theatrical performers of the same era than they did with the women who organized pick-up teams and civic teams; female scholastic and collegiate players had more in common with their peers who played basketball and tennis than they did with female professional baseball players. Ironically, the one thing that nineteenth-century women baseball players did have in common was the one thing they lacked—an accurate sense of their place in the historical narrative of baseball.

Philosophical challenges aside, there are also numerous methodological hurdles to overcome as well—the most vexing of which involve the availability and nature of the primary documents needed to craft this narrative. Apart from a handful of diaries, letters, scrapbooks, and personal narratives of nineteenth-century women baseball players, everything we know about them is mediated through other (mostly male) eyes. Newspapers are, by necessity, used extensively in this reconstruction of female baseball history, but with the full understanding that they are, in the words of media critic James W. Carey, usually "tissue-thin slices of reality."[14] For historians of women's baseball, these "tissue-thin slices of reality" are sometimes all we have to work with but, if carefully analyzed, they can help us reconstruct the sociocultural context in which women played baseball even if they cannot necessarily tell us much about the players as individuals.

Another methodological difficulty is more basic: we do not know the true identities of many players because scores of them, particularly those who played for money, used "stage names"; others became invisible to historians when they married and took their husbands' surnames. We know these women existed in flesh and blood, but without their real names we cannot employ census records, city directories, and similar tools of the historian's trade to ascertain basic facts about them, such as ethnicity, social class, and family life, nor can we locate their descendants, some of whom may have access to firsthand documents or historical artifacts of their forebears' exploits on the baseball diamond.

The lack of historical artifacts poses another methodological challenge. There are few cultural repositories of memory for female baseball players.

There are no shrines to women players on par with the National Baseball Hall of Fame in Cooperstown; sportswriters of the late nineteenth and early twentieth centuries did not create national female baseball heroes for youngsters to emulate, nor did commercial businesses capitalize on baseball hero worship to hawk female baseball cards and memorabilia to eager fans to the extent they did for male players. There was no female counterpart to Henry Chadwick, whose standardization of baseball statistics facilitated record keeping and created, in Jules Tygiel's words, the "historical essence" of baseball.[15] Because detailed statistics of male baseball players were preserved decade by decade, today's historians can compare male players from one era to another, gaining insights into how the game and its male players changed over time. This statistical tool is largely unavailable to historians of female players.

Baseball scholars sometimes invoke the concept of a baseball "creed"—a shared sense of (primarily mythical) beliefs that emerged over time about the power of the game to shape individual and national morals. Steven Riess notes that there was always a disparity between the "idea" and reality of baseball. "The baseball creed constituted a cultural fiction," he writes, "and even though it was inaccurate, the conventional wisdom influenced the way people behaved and thought."[16] This baseball creed was (and to some degree still is) passed down from generation to generation—primarily from men to men—on a personal level from fathers to sons and on a cultural level from sportswriters, reporters, and philosophers to generations of fans. There is no feminine counterpart to the baseball creed that draws mystical, transcendent bonds between mothers and daughters and generations of women players. Women did not formally participate in "creating" the game of baseball nor did they shape its creed to any significant degree. Even though the creed was a cultural fiction, it nonetheless shaped the way men and women behaved and thought about the game and the game's relationship to society. From its earliest inception the creed's adherents held it sacred to such an extent that they went to great lengths to perpetuate it—verbally, and sometimes physically, attacking anyone (women, gamblers, detractors of all stripes) who tried to infiltrate their sacred spaces and tarnish the ideal image of baseball they were so meticulously constructing.

Despite the difficulties, this historical reclamation project is important if we are ever going to understand accurately the process through which baseball became gendered as masculine and why that identity has proven so resilient. This study is organized into five roughly chronological chapters, beginning in antebellum America and ending at the turn of the twentieth century. Most chapters begin with a description of baseball's development during a particular era, with an emphasis on how male players adapted the rules and institutions of the sport (its structure) to perpetuate particular gender ideals. Chapters describe the cultural context that shaped media discourse about baseball and public opinion about female players. To the extent possible, each chapter highlights the perceptions of female players, particularly as they saw themselves in the context of baseball culture and social ideals of gender. Chapter 1 focuses on the "birth" of baseball in antebellum America and early efforts to structure it as an adult male sport. It provides an overview of women's sporting heritage and explains how this heritage influenced girls in the United States to play baseball. Chapter 2 describes the continuing evolution of baseball's rules, its geographic spread after the Civil War, and the increasingly nationalistic tone of its proponents. It details the growing number of girls and women who played baseball in schools, colleges, and local communities between 1865 and 1879. Chapter 3 describes the professionalization of baseball between 1865 and 1879 and chronicles the emergence of professional female baseball teams that presented baseball as theatrical spectacle—provoking sometimes angry responses from those intent on establishing baseball as an exemplar of American civilization and masculinity. Chapter 4 explores the gendered narrative of baseball during the 1880s—a decade in which male boosters increasingly sought to use the sport to define and model idealized characteristics of white, native-born masculinity. It demonstrates that girls and women continued to problematize this narrative by playing baseball on community, school, and college teams. This chapter analyzes the ways in which men shaped the discourse about women players through the media, fiction, poetry, art, music, and other cultural forms. Chapter 5 focuses on the 1890s—a seminal era in the evolution of baseball's gendered narrative when the emergence of a new ideal for femininity (the bold, athletic "Gibson Girl") supplanted previous ideals of meek, fragile middle- and upper-class white womanhood and provided women with an opportunity to lay claim to the emerging center of baseball. It chronicles the varied types of girls' and women's baseball teams in the decade and describes how female physical educators ultimately chose to relinquish their claim for a voice in baseball's continued evolution by creating a separate baseball surrogate for girls and women.

What about Softball?

The sport of softball has little bearing on the gendered narrative of baseball in the nineteenth century; the name "softball" did not identify a baseball surrogate until 1926, and the sport itself was not officially codified with standardized rules until 1934.[17] Historians generally attribute the invention of softball to a group of men in Chicago who, in 1887, laid out a baseball diamond indoors in a gymnasium so they could continue to play during the winter months. In other words, contrary to a common misconception, softball was not invented as a game for girls and women so that they would stop playing baseball. It was invented by men for themselves and quickly became popular among men and women, who played it at YMCA gyms and colleges throughout the country. Almost immediately, male and female physical educators and recreation professionals recognized the game's potential to provide healthful exercise for girls and boys, and men and women of all ages and physical abilities. They moved the game outdoors and adapted the rules and equipment according to players' abilities and skills. Most of the games featured underhand pitching, smaller diamonds, and softer balls. By the early nineteenth century, softball precursors known by names like kitten ball, diamond ball, mush ball, and pumpkin ball were played on makeshift fields at tens of thousands of parks and schoolyards across the country. In the mid-1920s, amateur sportsmen and women and physical educators began creating the governing bodies and organizational hierarchy to standardize rules and promote play in communities, schools, and colleges. So, while softball would play a major role during the latter half of the twentieth century in helping sustain baseball's masculine reputation, it was not part of the process of creating that identity in the first place.

1. Creating a National Pastime

The game of Base Ball is one, when well played, that requires
strong bones, tough muscle and sound mind; and no athletic game
is better calculated to strengthen the frame and develop a full, broad
chest, testing a man's powers of endurance most severely.

—*New York Times,* September 27, 1856[1]

In the game of base ball as now played we undoubtedly have a
strictly national pastime. What cricket is to an Englishman, base
ball is to an American.

—*Quincy Whig,* July 13, 1868[2]

BASEBALL IS NOT A MAN'S GAME. It is a game. At its most basic level this game satisfies a deep human need to play—a need that led Dutch historian Johan Huizinga to suggest in 1938 that perhaps *Homo Ludens* (Man the Player) might be a more descriptive title for humankind than the popular appellations, *Homo Sapiens* (Man the Reasoner) and *Homo Faber* (Man the Maker).[3] Human beings have always played and, for thousands of years, they have played games with balls or with bats and balls. In the *Odyssey,* Homer spoke of the princess Nausica and her maids, who "threw off the veils that covered their heads and began to play at ball," and of Laodamas and Halius, who entertained Ulysses and the Phaeacians by dancing nimbly as they tossed a ball between them.[4] Paintings on ancient Egyptian temples and medieval castle walls depict men and women playing bat and ball games—sometimes together and sometimes separately. In these depictions of ball play from times past, whether literary or artistic, there is no hint of impropriety that women are among the players. This began to change in the late eighteenth and early nineteenth centuries as *Homo Ludens* began to harness more systematically play as a training ground for social and civic virtue and to carve out distinctive play spaces for men and women—labeling some games "female" and others "male." Myth, memory, and history combined to transform gender-neutral bat and ball games into our deeply gendered national pastime.

A National Sport Emerges in Antebellum America

Baseball was not "born" on a particular date in a particular place; it emerged over time and spread over geographical space (like "dandelions," says John Thorn) from a variety of informal bat and ball games played mostly by children. As early as 1734, the rules for Harvard College freshmen mentioned the accouterments of bat and ball games. In an era when college students were typically boys of fourteen to eighteen years of age, not only was a freshman forbidden to "intrude into his Senior's company" or "laugh in his Senior's face" or "ask his Senior an impertinent question," he was also expected to "find [furnish] the rest of the Scholars with bats, balls, and foot balls."[5] As adults in the 1760s, the young men who furnished bats and balls for their classmates at Harvard may have purchased copies of John Newbery's *A Little Pretty Pocket-Book, Intended for the Instruction and Amusement of Little Master Tommy and Pretty Miss Polly* for their children. Newbery's book, first published in England in 1744 and in the American colonies in 1762, contains one of the earliest print references to the term "base-ball." Accompanied by a woodcut of boys playing the game, the book gives a rhymed summary of the rules: "The Ball once struck off, Away flies the Boy, To the next destin'd Post, And then Home with Joy."[6] Newbery's book also includes illustrations and poetic descriptions of other bat and ball games like stool-ball, trap-ball, and tip-cat.

The sport we know as baseball emerged in antebellum America at a time when adults were exploring new ways to socialize children through play.[7] According to Howard Chudacoff, from the late colonial period onward, "the judicious selection of toys, games, and books," particularly in middle-class homes, "was intended to set children's play on a proper course."[8] Adults taught children that a well-ordered society required that each sex understand and carry out the responsibilities of its prescribed "sphere." Children learned that the masculine sphere encompassed public spaces where men created wealth and wielded power and that the feminine sphere harbored private, domestic spaces where women crafted tranquil refuges for men and where they exerted moral influence over children. In reality, the boundaries of these social spheres were always fluid, overlapping, and under negotiation; there was a continual stream of men and women stepping out of prescribed roles individually and en masse. These interlopers generated both positive and negative social commentary and catalyzed simultaneous retrenchment and reframing of existing boundaries.

The shift in attitudes toward play and the emphasis on strict social boundaries in antebellum America shaped baseball's gendered nativity. The adult men who organized ball clubs like the Magnolias, Gothams, Knickerbockers, and Jolly Young Bachelors in the 1820s, 30s, and 40s wanted to continue playing youthful ball games—but doing so opened them up to criticism that they were eschewing their proper adult responsibilities. They countered this criticism by recasting the evolving game as an inherently masculine, *adult* activity—one uniquely suited for imbuing practitioners with the physical and mental qualities essential to preserving a democratic and free citizenry. In 1823 a contributor to the *National Advocate* described "witnessing a company of active young men playing the *manly* and athletic game of 'base ball' in Greenwich Village" (emphasis added).[9] In 1837 the members of the Olympic Ball Club of Philadelphia justified their predilection for play by linking their version of baseball to other types of field sports and by emphasizing their "manly and athletic character."[10]

Bat and ball games were popular throughout the fledgling republic. By the 1830s and 1840s increasing numbers of adult men, reluctant to give up the games of their youth, organized fraternal sporting clubs to continue playing their favorite ball games. The choice of game varied by region. Round ball (also called base ball) and rounders prevailed in New England, except in Connecticut, where clubs preferred Wicket. Wicket spread to Connecticut's Western Reserve and into the territories that became Ohio, Michigan, Indiana, Illinois, and Iowa. Town ball was the game of choice in Cincinnati and in Philadelphia, where it competed for players with the popular British game of cricket. In September 1845, devotees of a New York variation of baseball organized the Knickerbocker Base Ball Club and codified rules that eventually evolved into the sport we recognize as baseball today.[11] As the New York game supplanted regional variations over the ensuing three decades, the organizational structures and creedal proclamations crafted to distinguish the sport from British antecedents and to validate it for adult play profoundly influenced the relationship of girls and women to the sport and shaped historical narratives about it.

Gender, Nationalism, and Baseball

Scholars of gender understand that concepts like "masculinity" and "femininity" are human constructs that change over time and are never universally defined. Michael Kimmel notes that it is more appropriate to speak of "masculinities" rather than masculinity because the concept means different things to different people based on factors like race, ethnicity, geography, and social class. Gail Bederman suggests that it is more useful to focus on the *process* through which gender ideals like "manhood" gain the status of "truth" rather than trying to precisely define a particular gender ideal at any given historical moment.[12] The process of gender formation is critical to this study because it was in the process of trying to define and redefine masculinity and femininity that nineteenth-century men and women transformed baseball from a gender-neutral game to a deeply gendered sport. As adult male baseball players transformed children's bat and ball games into a sport that could represent and inculcate their ideals for masculinity, women found themselves cast (along with children) as the antithetical "other" and increasingly distanced from baseball's shifting center.

The sport of baseball began assuming its modern form as the United States evolved from an almost exclusively agrarian society to a nascent urban-industrial one. Economic transformation wrought profound social changes as distinctions between public and private spaces became more pronounced and as men began defining their masculinity based on individual accomplishments rather than communal cooperation. E. Anthony Rotundo describes the resulting shift from an ideal of "communal manhood" in colonial America to an ideal of "self-made manhood" in early nineteenth-century America. According to Rotundo, as self-made men began to define their masculinity in terms of work roles rather than domestic roles, they placed a higher value on "ambition, rivalry, and aggression." Sport was one of the tools men used to carve out "all-male preserves" where they could reinforce and promote masculine identities—identities influenced as much by class, race, and ethnicity as by gender ideals.[13] Elliott Gorn describes how men of successive generations transformed the structure and culture of the ancient sport of boxing to suit their particular social, ethnic, and racial identities.[14] Though some men in the United States embraced prizefighting as the optimal platform for shaping and performing gender and class values, others turned to baseball.

Like boxing, baseball was contested ground between social classes. John Thorn has debunked the long-held baseball origins myth of "pristine amateurs cavorting on green fields for good fun and mild exercise," conclusively demonstrating that antebellum baseball teams reflected the ethnic, social, and moral diversity of the times.[15] Though cultural artifacts from immigrant and working-class teams are in comparatively shorter supply to those of native-born, middle-class teams, enough remain to demonstrate that saloon keepers, political hatchet men, and unskilled laborers were just as likely to consider baseball *their* game as the lawyers, bank clerks, physicians, and businessmen who organized the formal baseball clubs and associations that would ultimately shape the structure, culture, and historical narrative of the sport.

Structuring a Sport

As the forces of industrialization reordered the rhythms of life and imposed order and structure in the workplace, and as mass immigration and urbanization upset demographic norms and social class structures, middle-class men and women adapted to these changes by trying to impose order and structure in other areas of their lives—including leisure activities. Between 1830 and 1860, young men in the growing merchant and middling classes in Philadelphia, Boston, and New York began organizing formal sporting clubs that mirrored the structure of their workplaces. They submitted themselves to formal constitutions, codes of conduct, and written rules to govern their actions on and off the field.[16] The emergence of formal sporting clubs mirrored the emergence of other types of clubs and societies organized by middle-class men and women to promote particular activities. Baseball, town ball, round ball, and wicket clubs flourished alongside moral reform societies, missionary societies, and antislavery societies. Working-class men, plus boys, girls, and women of all social classes played bat and ball games too. Their teams were usually more loosely organized than those of middle- and upper-class male sporting clubs. Working-class men's contests, much to the chagrin of middle-class moralizers, were often marked by gambling, cursing, and overzealous competition that sometimes resulted in violence on and off the field.[17]

This chapter focuses primarily on the middle-class fraternal baseball clubs of New York City, for it was their determination to bring order and structured growth to their sport that ultimately enabled them to shape, codify, and control the future evolution of the modern spectator sport we know today. It was this commodified version of baseball that formed the "center" of the sport as Messner uses the term—a center that placed a premium on elite, adult male athletes and that valued financial profit over fraternal fun and camaraderie. This center coalesced even as schoolchildren and men and women of all ages and social classes continued to play the sport in all its forms—representing an alternate center whose viability and influence diminished over the course of the nineteenth century as the professional game for adult men gradually monopolized the cultural narrative of the sport.

The New York Knickerbockers were active in proselytizing their version of baseball. The club printed and distributed one hundred copies of their rules throughout the country during the 1840s and 1850s. The New York game also got a boost from publications like *Porter's Spirit of the Times* and the *New York Clipper*, which printed copies of the rules in 1856, and from businessmen and travelers who fanned out across the country from New York taking the game with them. By 1858 there were 125 baseball teams in and around New York and countless others scattered throughout the country.[18] *Porter's* commented that every empty lot within ten miles of the city was being used as a baseball field.[19] Most baseball teams in antebellum America grew out of informal social ties as boys and young men from the same school, neighborhood, or business got together for pick-up games whenever time permitted. There were, however, a growing number of formal sporting clubs, like the Knickerbockers, comprised of well-to-do businessmen and professionals whose members valued the long-term camaraderie membership brought them and who enjoyed hosting like-minded clubs for games and elaborate dinners afterward. Concerned about the chaotic development of the sport and what they perceived as the corrupting influences of working-class interests, these clubs banded together and created a formal structure through which they could manage the sport's future.

In 1857, the New York Knickerbockers called for a meeting of local clubs to standardize rules and lay the groundwork for an overarching structure to manage the sport. They also hoped to continue spreading the New York game to other parts of the country. Sixteen clubs attended the convention and, sensing value in unity, founded the optimistically named National Association of Base Ball Players (NABBP) the following year.[20] The NABBP grew quickly (it had one hundred member clubs by 1865) and was the first of many governing bodies that would shape baseball's center during the nineteenth century.[21] Codifying rules for play on the field and standards for player behavior off the field, the NABBP laid the foundation of the formal structure of modern baseball and began to shape its creed.

NABBP members understood that it was not enough to *proclaim* that baseball was a manly pastime—they had to transform its rules to make it more difficult so they could *prove* it was a manly pastime. One of the rules of the early New York game that undercut a masculine narrative was the one allowing fielders to put out a batter by catching a ball on the fly or after the first bounce. The Massachusetts game made no such allowance. Year after year, beginning in 1857, reformers in the NABBP tried to convince member clubs to change the "*boy's rule* of the catch on the bound" to make the game more "manly" (emphasis added). Henry Chadwick was particularly critical of the bound rule, noting that catching a ball after a hop was "a feat a boy ten years of age would scarcely be proud of."[22] The debate over the bound rule raged for seven years until 1864, when NABBP clubs finally voted to adopt the fly rule. The gendered narrative of baseball was firmly planted.

Shaping a Culture

No sporting structure can become foundational without the means to promulgate it and defend it from detractors. To shape the center of a sport, a sport's structure must become integrated into what Messner calls "dominant symbols and belief systems" to the extent that it can shape and influence the culture of that sport and even the day-to-day practices (social interactions) of all participants—not just those at the center of the sport.[23] Those crafting the structural foundation of modern baseball benefited from an urban-industrial transformation that catalyzed the rise of team sports and technological advancements that transformed the way information was shared in the United States. The steady expansion of canals, roadways, railroad lines, and telegraph networks enabled the rapid physical and electronic transmission of news and facilitated the development of a "national" culture that baseball boosters tapped into to market their sport. As the means of distributing news improved, so too did printing technologies and mass-production techniques—both of which contributed to an explosion in the number of inexpensive newspapers, periodicals, and books available to all classes of society. The "Penny Press" was born in 1833 with Benjamin Day's founding of *The Sun* in New York City. During the 1840s, "Flash papers" surreptitiously informed male readers in big cities where they could find brothels and local establishments where they could gamble on sports contests ranging from horse races to walking matches to dog fights. Other publications like William Trotter Porter's *Spirit of the Times* (1831) provided sporting news to upper-class readers.[24] As baseball gained in popularity, the editors of sporting periodicals and local newspapers across the country increasingly included stories about contests and players, which helped spark more interest in the game. By the late-1850s, just as the New York–area clubs were organizing the NABBP, editors like Frank Queen, who had founded the popular sporting and theatrical publication *The New York Clipper* in 1853, sensed the financial potential in baseball and began hiring dedicated sportswriters to cover the game. In 1858, Queen hired Englishman Henry Chadwick—the man who would play a pivotal role in shaping both the structure and culture of baseball for almost half a century. Newspaper editors and reporters became allies of players (and later, team owners) in creating a narrative for baseball that eventually solidified its status as a cultural icon alongside motherhood and apple pie and that gradually displaced women outside baseball's evolving center.[25]

To begin the transformational process of regulating their sport and elevating it to the position of respectability enjoyed by other British pastimes like cricket, yachting, and horseracing, NABBP clubs had to overcome two primary challenges—both required changing cultural attitudes about appropriate leisure activities. The first obstacle adult male ballplayers had to overcome was the widespread assumption that bat and ball games were childish activities; the second was the pious belief that wasting time on recreations was sinful and dangerous for the country. In the process of addressing these concerns, adult men crafted a structure for baseball that portrayed women, not as players, but as moral guardians who would protect baseball against evil excess.

Though gender ideals comprise a continuum rather than a binary, those trying to define them tend to articulate desired behaviors and characteristics in binary terms. They articulate an ideal alongside a contrasting "other." In the gender binary, for something to be manly, it cannot be feminine—nor can it be childish. In the case of baseball, the first "other" baseball enthusiasts had to address and vanquish was childishness. That was because, for most of the antebellum era, there was a general lack of appreciation in the United States for the relationship between physical well-being and exercise. Formal physical fitness programs like those popular in Germany, Denmark, Sweden, and Britain were rare in the United States despite the fact that German, Swedish, and British immigrants had established indoor and outdoor gymnasia in eastern and midwestern cities during the 1820s, 30s, and 40s.[26] Seeing little benefit in adult men exercising with Indian clubs and apparatus, most Americans perpetuated the sentiment put forth by the *Daily National Intelligencer* in 1822 that, though it was fine for boys to "buffet one another at schools, and amuse themselves with divers other gymnastic exercises," it was "unbecoming in men."[27] By 1846 Dr. John Collins Warren, who had helped found one of the first public gymnasia in the country in 1825, was decrying the fact that most gymnasia in the United States had fallen into neglect. He blamed the problem on a lack of understanding about the correlation between exercise and good health.[28]

Lacking widespread public support for gymnastic exercise and not yet attuned to the ways team sports could be leveraged for sociocultural purposes, the adult men who loved baseball in all its forms in antebellum America had to be willing to buck public opinion if they wanted to play. "It required 'sand' in those days to go out on the field and play as prejudice against the game was very great," notes Thorn. "It took nearly a whole season to get [enough] men together to make a team, owing to the ridicule heaped upon the players for taking part in such childish sports."[29] The disapprobation of adult men playing bat and ball games persisted. In March 1860, an observer commented that while school boys had been playing baseball "all over the land from immemorial time," until recently men had usually only played on holidays, and even then looked for an out-of-the-way place to do it.[30] Middle- and upper-class gender ideals that prioritized men's intellectual achievement and self-control over feats of physical strength and prowess exacted a high price. In 1856, the editor of *Harper's Weekly* observed that lack of exercise was turning American men into "a pale, pasty-faced, narrow chested, spindle-shanked, dwarfed race." Two years later, Dr. Oliver Wendell Holmes Sr. lamented that "such a set of black-coated, stiff-jointed, soft-muscled, paste-complexioned youth as we can boast in our Atlantic cities never before sprang from the loins of Anglo-Saxon lineage."[31]

Along with their general naiveté about the benefits of exercise for adult men and women, many citizens harbored a deep-seated suspicion of any activity that did not produce a tangible benefit to the community, the church, or the soul. The United States was a multifaceted collage of mixed races, tongues, and faiths long before millions of immigrants flooded into the country in the late nineteenth century. There was never a single, homogenous American culture or society, but there was a definite imprint of Protestant religious fundamentalism across the land during much of the nineteenth century. The response to early adult ball players must be understood in the context of a society where religious principles were not just promulgated in churches and schools, but were integrated into laws, popular literature, and social treatises. Adult men were not just criticized for playing children's games in antebellum America—they were criticized for playing, period. "[A] fowling piece, a fishing rod, and a ball club, have been looked upon as instruments of Satan," lamented a contributor to the *Rochester Union and Advertiser* in August 1858 as he explained the reluctance of many Americans to embrace "healthful and innocent amusements" as mitigation for the debilitating stresses of urban-industrial life.[32]

The adult male players who organized the NABBP in the late 1850s had to shape the rules and ethos of their game to make it compatible with social ideals of masculinity, adulthood, and religious morality. The optimal way to counter charges that baseball was a tool of the devil was to demonstrate that the sport contributed to building "American" (Protestant) civilization. Fortunately for individuals who relished the excitement and bracing competition of a vigorously contested baseball game, a growing number of physicians, clergymen, and educators began endorsing a new ideal of masculinity that valued physical strength and morality over intellectual achievement and wealth. The narrative of "muscular Christianity" rejected the premise that recreation and play were antithetical to Christian service; it taught men that they had to strengthen their bodies along with their morals so that they would have the physical stamina to protect the weak and spread the gospel.[33] The *New York Times* urged its male readers to get outside into "God's open air, where health, strength and manhood may be earned."[34] Advocates of muscular Christianity promoted team sports and games that required physical strength, dexterity, and courage; conversely, they disparaged activities that reflected effeminacy—if women could excel at a sport or game, it could not be considered a "manly" pastime. Women became the antithetical "other" in antebellum narratives of muscular masculinity; they found themselves distanced from baseball's developing center as baseball boosters like Henry Chadwick promoted the sport as both an "invigorating exercise" and a "manly pastime."[35]

The muscular Christianity movement of the 1850s enabled baseball players and boosters to link their sport more closely with ideals of manliness, morality, and robust health. The *New York Sunday Mercury* advocated in October 1853 that more be done to promote baseball because, like cricket, it could help "do away with pale faces, with emaciated frames . . . and premature demoralization and death."[36] Four years later, in an article describing the inaugural meeting of the NABBP, the *Spirit of the Times* urged schoolmasters and clergymen to "lend a helping hand" in making baseball "a great national institution" because so many young men were eschewing outdoor activities in favor of "the fumes of cellars and the dissipation of the gaming table."[37] The *Times* editor, like many reform-minded men and women of the day, believed there was a correlation between healthy outdoor sports, morality, and spiritual well-being. These men and women were the recipients of a reforming zeal birthed in the fiery preaching of the Second Great Awakening. Taught that they had a moral obligation to spread the gospel and correct social evils before Christ would come again, millions of men and women joined churches, missionary and Bible societies, temperance and abolition societies, prison and asylum reform organizations, and charitable concerns.[38] No aspect of life was untouched by the crusading zeal of Christian reformers—including leisure activities. The reformers who promoted baseball on the grounds that it would motivate players to "withdraw from the moral miasma of saloons and the enticements of rum" were invoking the prevailing spirit of moral reform. Narratives of manliness, reinforced by the broader muscular Christianity movement, enabled thousands of adult men to justify joining baseball, round ball, town ball, and wicket teams from California to New York, New Orleans to Canada between 1845 and 1860.[39]

Though many early rules changes (like the fly catch) were intended to distinguish baseball from childish pastimes, there was a subtle corollary that players could not have missed. In a culture that routinely attributed childlike emotions and physical weakness to women, advocates of the fly rule, longer base-paths, and (eventually) overhand pitching, must have realized that if their evolving game was not suited for children, then it was not suited for women, either. In 1860 Chadwick, the man Jules Tygiel credits with inventing baseball's "historical essence," identified the archetypal baseball player: "[P]layers must possess the characteristics of true manhood," Chadwick insisted. "Baseball to be played thoroughly, requires the possession of muscular strength, great agility, quickness of eye, readiness of hand, and many other faculties of mind and body that mark the man of nerve."[40] The gendered "others" in Chadwick's narrative are children and women because neither possessed the characteristics of "true manhood" as his contemporaries described it. In the process of crafting a new narrative for their game, baseball proponents indirectly (and later, directly) influenced women's relationship to the sport.

Shaping Social Interactions

Both players and media supporters recognized the possibility of leveraging baseball to promote ideals of manliness, nationalism, and middle-class Protestant respectability. As increasing numbers of men persisted in characterizing baseball as "manly" (in contrast to childish or womanly), they wove a narrative that gradually distorted the gender-neutral narrative of the sport. These men ignored or suppressed the fact that European girls and women had been playing bat and ball games for centuries and that American girls and women shared their foremothers' sporting heritage.

David Block, an expert on early baseball antecedents, includes several references to girls and women playing early bat and ball games in his path-breaking book, *Baseball Before We Knew It*. Block establishes that in eighteenth-century Britain, "youths of both sexes" played the bat and ball games that spawned American baseball and that, in fact, the game known as "base ball" in Britain was primarily played by girls or by boys and girls together.[41] Block also cites examples of adolescent and adult women playing bat and ball games in Britain. Historian Catriona Parratt has documented the wide variety of sports and recreations enjoyed by working-class women in eighteenth- and early nineteenth-century Great Britain. "At fairs and hirings and festivals, as well as on other occasions," Parratt writes, "girls and women played ball games such as cricket, stoolball, trap-and-ball, handball, and 'folk' football. They ran in footraces, and battled one another in prizefights, quarter-staff fights, and sword fights."[42]

Girls and women in the early republic and antebellum America would have had firsthand knowledge and shared memories of their own mothers' and grandmothers' sporting experiences and they would have been exposed to accounts of real and fictional sporting women, such as those described by Jane Austen, Mary Russell Mitford, Jane Marcet, and Joseph Strutt.[43] Strutt's work was particularly informative. In 1801, Strutt published a comprehensive study of the sports and pastimes of the British people; his book became a classic of sorts, going through multiple printings in Britain and the United States during the nineteenth century.[44] At a time when historians rarely included women's activities in any meaningful way or applied the lens of social class to their topics, Strutt did both. His work was widely distributed in the United States, and anyone reading it would have learned that, for centuries, British girls and women had been actively participating in a wide variety of sporting activities, including hawking, hunting, fishing, and ball games. Strutt included Homer's account of Nausica and her maids playing ball and, though it would certainly be an historical stretch to directly link ball-tossing girls in ancient Greece to baseball-playing girls in antebellum America, Strutt's description of medieval and modern girls and women engaging in early forms of tennis, handball, field hockey, and baseball establishes an important historical backdrop for this study of female baseball pioneers. It reminds us that baseball's gendering as a masculine sport was not predetermined—something had to intervene in the historical flow of the past to push women outside the coalescing center of the modern sport.

Strutt's book foreshadows the manipulation of cultural narratives that would ultimately recast baseball as a man's game. Immediately after a section in which he describes the coed game of club-ball in Britain, Strutt makes the following assertion: "From the club-ball originated, I doubt not, that pleasant and *manly exercise,* distinguished in modern times by the name of cricket (emphasis added)."[45] Why would Strutt call cricket a "manly exercise" right after describing its predecessor as a game played by men and women together? And why does he fail to mention female cricket players in his subsequent description of cricket? Strutt not only crafted a narrative describing cricket as a man's game but he suppressed the counternarrative that British women had been playing cricket for generations. It is inconceivable that Strutt, who was obviously well informed about the sporting activities of British women, did not know about Britain's female cricket players. Eighteenth-century British newspapers and sporting periodicals routinely published news about women's cricket matches to include information on challenges, outcomes, and gambling lines. Women's cricket was a normative activity—not an oddity—yet Strutt chose to describe the sport as "manly exercise" and to delete any mention of female players from his book.[46] By erasing women from the historical narrative of cricket, he helped establish cricket as a male-only space where manly attributes could be practiced and promulgated. Strutt's linkage of cricket and manliness presaged similar efforts by U.S. baseball players to structure their sport in such a way that women's participation would be discouraged and marginalized.

Girls and Women Problematize the Storyline

Gender ideals, like other cultural values, are constantly in flux. Anne Firor Scott notes that old and new social values "often exist not only side by side, but cutting across each other."[47] Such was the case with gender ideals and baseball's gendered identity throughout the nineteenth century. Even as the NABBP and adult male baseball players and their supporters in the media crafted and honed a masculine storyline for baseball that persists to present day, athletically inclined girls and women problematized that narrative by continuing to participate in a wide variety of outdoor sports and games, including baseball. Women baseball players and their supporters leveraged cultural narratives that validated their actions just as men were doing to validate theirs. So, for example, as men used the rhetoric of muscular Christianity to deflect criticism that playing baseball was impious, men and women used the ideals of muscular Christianity to argue that rigorous outdoor activities, like baseball, were good for women because they would force them to abandon the cumbersome clothing styles that rendered women virtual invalids. On June 18, 1859, the *Portland (Maine) Transcript* described a local men's ball club "enjoying the sport with great gusto." After wishing that more young men would choose "this manly game" over the saloons, billiard rooms, and club rooms they frequented, the editor agreed with another newspaper that "ball playing would prove as agreeable and useful to ladies as to gentlemen," with the added caveat: "No doubt, but then the ladies must adopt the bloomer costume. A ball once lost under the circumference of crinoline would be very difficult to regain."[48]

The Portland newspaper was just one of several that weighed in on the suggestion that women would benefit from playing baseball. A month earlier, the *Albany Morning Times* had stated: "An exchange says there seems nothing violent in the presumption that ball playing would prove as agreeable and useful to ladies as to gentlemen. Bosh! Just think of looking for the ball every minute or two under the circumference of crinolined players."[49] The next day, the *Troy (New York) Daily Times* reprinted the *Albany Times* article and retorted: "Humbug! As if a woman must at all times and under every circumstance, be arrayed in the stiff and conservative propriety of drawing room attire." The editorial continued: "We are no advocates of the bloomer costume, but we can imagine that there are occasions on which short dresses minus the outlandish pantaloons—in brief, a rig permitting the free and natural exercise of the lower limbs—would be both healthful and proper.—Why not, Mr. *Times*?"[50] Other papers reprinted the dialogue over the course of the next month.[51]

Despite suggestions in the 1850s that baseball could improve women's health, it does not appear that adult women played baseball in antebellum America. There is ample evidence, however, that school-age girls did. There was (and is) an age component to gender. Though children are often conditioned from a young age to begin emulating the gender ideals of their elders, adults frequently allow children latitude in exploring activities outside those prescribed boundaries. Fortunately for the girls who loved romping and playing outdoors with the boys while their peers stayed inside hosting tea parties for their dolls, some nineteenth-century parents believed that vigorous play was as beneficial to their daughters as it was for their sons.

Though most antebellum and postbellum books and periodicals on games and sport for children usually segregated activities by gender, young children often ignored these informal gender boundaries and played together. Newspapers and periodicals matter-of-factly reported on the girls and boys playing baseball and regional variants of bat and ball games together. Sally Tice of Warren County, Missouri, became a popular teammate for ball games at her school yard in the 1820s. According to county historians, Sally "was a splendid ball player, and played with the boys at school, who always chose her first, because she could beat any of them."[52] In December 1840, a non-native resident of Honolulu in the Kingdom of Hawaii commented that one of the most gratifying evidences of the "increasing civilization in this place" was that "native youth of both sexes" were playing the "same old games [including 'good old bat and ball'] which used to warm our blood not long since."[53] About the same time that Hawaiian boys and girls were playing an early form of baseball, "rosy cheeked girls" in Macon, Georgia, were serving as umpires at boys' baseball games.[54] Elias Molee, who attended school in Wisconsin in the 1850s, recalled boys and girls playing One Old Cat and Two Old Cat together at school during their twenty-minute recess period.[55] These primary sources, though rare, indicate general approbation of young girls participating in bat and ball games. While criticism and condescension toward adult women playing baseball would become increasingly common as the nineteenth century unfolded, the benevolent attitude toward juvenile girls playing persisted.

Education is a primary vehicle through which one generation perpetuates its gender ideals to succeeding generations. One aspect of the debate over the proper educational approach for girls was the question of how much and which types of physical exercise were good for them. Though most individuals advocated distinctive exercise regimens for boys and girls, a vocal minority argued that girls should be allowed to pursue the same vigorous activities boys did. Abolitionist and women's rights activist Frances Dana Gage saw a correlation between a mother's physical fitness and her ability to raise physically healthy children. "If the mother is physically effeminate, can her children be physically strong?" she asked. "Why not begin at the beginning of this great work, and make more strenuous efforts to develop the physical powers of our girls, encouraging them to more active exercise and athletic sports?" She challenged her readers: "Why shall they not have gymnasiums and boat clubs, and lay off their cumbrous dresses, on the play ground at least, and join their brothers in a game of base ball or cricket?"[56] Gage's emphasis on "strenuous efforts" and "physical powers" directly challenged proponents of muscular Christianity who sought to reserve these descriptors for men by positioning women as the antithesis. In the parlance of the day, effeminacy implied weakness while manliness connoted strength. Gage rejected the premise that society benefited by keeping women in a perpetually weakened condition.

Though many agreed with Gage that girls and women needed to be physically fit, not everyone agreed on the means to that end. Many insisted that girls and boys should engage in different types of physical activity tailored to their distinctive adult gender roles. Catharine Beecher was an influential advocate of this position. Daughter of the nationally known, socially active minister Lyman Beecher, Catharine enjoyed a ready-made public platform from which to espouse her viewpoints on education, physical fitness, and gender roles. In 1848, Beecher lamented the "deplorable sufferings" she saw among young wives and mothers whose physical health had been neglected by their parents when they were young. In an effort to reverse the dangerous trend, Beecher published a textbook for girls' schools: *A Treatise on the Domestic Economy, for the use of Young Ladies at Home and at School*. Arguing that parents should devote their "principal attention" to the "physical and domestic" education of their daughters while reducing the "stimulation of the intellect," Beecher urged teachers to give school children ample time to play outdoors during the school day.[57]

Although she encouraged girls to get outdoors and play, Beecher, like many devout Christians of her day, assumed a natural boundary between many feminine and masculine activities. While Gage argued that girls should be encouraged to join the boys in rowboats and baseball games, Beecher advocated gender-segregated recreational activities for girls and boys—things like making dolls and doll clothes for girls and building sleds and sledding for boys. Eight years later, in *Physiology and Calisthenics: For Schools and Families,* Beecher advocated that all children be trained in calisthenics and gymnastics (forms of exercise designed to promote "beauty and strength") but cautioned against allowing girls to engage in "those severe exercises that involve danger, either from excess or accidents" because those activities, while beneficial to the "stronger sex," were unsuited to the "female constitution."[58]

The antebellum girls who enjoyed the thrill of wielding a bat and chasing elusive spheres of yarn and leather with the local boys in the pastoral villages and burgeoning cities of antebellum America had no sense that they were problematizing a gendered narrative that adult men were trying to craft for their sport. Like their club-ball and stool-ball playing forebears in Britain, they simply loved to play. Some of these girls may have read Jane Austen's *Northanger Abbey* (written in 1798–1799 and first published in 1817) and were emulating her fictional heroine, Catherine, who had "a thin awkward figure" and "by nature nothing heroic about her," but who, nonetheless, preferred "cricket, base ball, riding on horseback, and running about the country at the age of fourteen, to books."[59] Athletically inclined girls had other literary role models like Agnes Fleming, a character in Louisa C. Tuthill's *The Young Lady's Home* (1839), who was not only fluent in Latin and well-read in the classics by the age of twelve but also enjoyed riding horses, playing "ball," pitching quoits, and rolling nine-pins with her father, who believed that active and athletic exercises would give "vigor" to her young mind and body.[60]

The girls fortunate enough to attend one of the many female academies and seminaries in the United States that utilized Jane Marcet's popular *Conversations on Natural Philosophy* (first published in 1819) would have found it perfectly logical for the book's female character to use a baseball analogy to explain the concept of inertia: "In playing at base-ball I am obliged to use all my strength to give a rapid motion to the ball; and when I catch it," explains the female student in Marcet's textbook. "I am sure I feel the resistance it makes to being stopped. But if I did not catch it, it would soon fall to the ground and stop of itself."[61] Schoolgirls across the United States had ample opportunities to read and emulate the engaging stories of British author Mary Russell Mitford, who included frolicking girls who loved outdoor games like baseball in her celebrated tales about village life in early nineteenth-century Berkshire County, England.[62] Mitford's sketches first appeared in 1819 in *Lady's Magazine* and were so popular that they were reprinted in newspapers and published in five volumes between 1824 and 1832.[63]

Though scholars continue to debate the genealogical linkages between bat and ball games like British base-ball, club-ball, cricket, stool-ball, Rounders, and American baseball, the fact remains that playing bat and ball games was a normative (not aberrant) activity for girls and young women in Britain for centuries. The same was true in the United States, where countless girls played outdoor sports and games (including baseball). In 1859, Francis Henry Guiwits, a twenty-seven-year old dentist living in Avoca, New York, wrote a letter to *Harper's Weekly* challenging a statement in a previous issue that baseball should not be considered the national sport because it was only played in a few eastern cities and not in the hinterlands. Describing baseball as he saw it played as a child, Guiwits asserted: "For twenty years (which is as long as I can remember about it) base-ball has been a 'popular game' wherever I have lived." He reported that it had been regularly played at "raisings" of buildings and "frames" in villages and rural districts of western New York and that it was still "*the* game (emphasis his) at our district schools during the intermission hours, and often engaged in by youths of both sexes."[64]

Schools provided an optimal location for girls and boys to play games together. Sometimes students organized teams for fun and recreation, independent of adult intervention; at other times, it was adults who organized the teams to promote the health and fitness of schoolchildren. Frances Gage lauded Eagleswood School, near Perth Amboy, New Jersey, as an exemplar of how coeducation and shared recreational activities could benefit both boys and girls. She noted that Eagleswood administrators provided girls with the same opportunities to exercise, row boats, and play "ball" that boys had. According to Gage, Eagleswood promoted the idea that running, rowing, riding, and jumping were not "unnatural for young ladies."[65]

Eagleswood School was a component of the Raritan Bay Union, a utopian community founded in 1853 by leading social activists, including nationally renowned abolitionists and women's rights advocates Theodore Weld, Angelina Grimké (his wife), and her sister, Sarah Grimké. The provisional charter for the Raritan Bay Union promised that education would be a "central object" of the Union and that its system of training would include "gymnastic, industrial, scientific, literary, artistic, social, and spiritual" pursuits. The goal of the program was to prepare students "for whatever sphere the tastes and abilities of the young, of either sex, seem best to qualify them."[66] The Raritan Bay Union quickly attracted intellectuals, artists, abolitionists, and women's rights supporters from across the country. Leading cultural figures like Louisa May Alcott, Henry Thoreau, Ralph Waldo Emerson, and Horace Greeley relaxed and shared ideas there. Theodore Weld served as principal of Eagleswood which, according to Gage, attracted the daughters of professors, ministers, merchants, and the "first families of Fifth avenue."[67] Gage reveled in the fact that these daughters of privilege were allowed to "toss back their curls under their boating hats, put their ungloved hands to their oars, and bear away with steady sweep into the current," rowing for miles. After their invigorating physical exercises, they could turn their attention to Greek and Latin studies just like their male counterparts at Cambridge and Yale.[68]

Eagleswood promoted an ideal for women that espoused healthy athleticism and rejected debilitating clothing styles and strictly ornamental education. The Springs, Grimkés, and Weld were actively resisting prevalent narratives about how "true womanhood" should behave and look in public. Athletic games like baseball were part of their strategy for transforming girls into vigorous, self-assured women. Gage was pleased with Eagleswood's emphasis on physical fitness for girls and hoped that other schools would follow its lead. She promised readers she would lobby the principal of New York's newly opened Dansville Seminary to allow girls to play baseball, ride horses, and pursue any other "feat[s] of physical endurance" that would keep them from growing "weak or rickety."[69]

Although schoolboys were generally free to pursue whatever athletic activities they chose, schoolgirls needed the support of administrators if they wanted to play "rough" sports and games. At schools where administrators believed such activities were beneficial, girls found a supportive environment in which to organize baseball teams. They benefited from time set aside by administrators for student recreation. In 1862, the *Sacramento Daily Union* reported that students at the Young Ladies Seminary in Benicia, California, were required to walk and exercise on the school grounds for two hours every day, between three and five o'clock. Among the activities they enjoyed were "games of ball."[70] School catalogues referenced students playing "games *at* ball" (emphasis added) at the Benicia seminary for many years and, though it is impossible to determine definitively whether "games at ball" meant baseball, it is likely since the sport was well established in California by the time Benicia residents established their Young Ladies Seminary.[71] Benicia, the short-lived capital of California,[72] was situated across the bay from San Francisco where, as early as 1851, newspapers were reporting that boys and men regularly played baseball on the town plaza. At least one used the term "play at ball" to describe their games.

Students at Benicia's Young Ladies Seminary benefited from the fact that school administrators believed in the importance of physical fitness for young women.[73] Mary Atkins had been born and raised in Ohio, where she graduated from Oberlin College—the first coeducational college in the United States. She was a strong advocate of balancing mental training with physical exercise, and when she became principal at Benicia in 1854, she established mandatory recreation periods for students. She also procured "swings, parallel bars and other gymnastic appliances" for the fenced playground where her female charges did calisthenics, played "graces," and indulged in "games at ball."[74] When Cyrus and Susan Mills took over the institution in 1866, they continued promoting healthy recreations like baseball.[75]

Whether they played in schoolyards, rural fields, or on city streets, many young girls enjoyed the thrill of running bases, swinging bats, and throwing balls just like their male peers. Unconcerned about broader issues of gender relationships, women's rights, and changing definitions of manliness, these youthful baseball players unwittingly contested the narrative that baseball was unsuited for children and best left to men. They embodied a counternarrative that would endure throughout the nineteenth century. Few begrudged them the opportunity to play the sport they loved, but their daughters, granddaughters, and great-granddaughters would enjoy a less favorable climate on the baseball diamond.

2. 1865–1879: Contesting a National Pastime

The Amateur Game

We hear on all sides of woman—of her rights and of her wrongs—
we hear of her from our pulpits, we read of her in our novels and
essays, we see her occasionally on the lecture—a speaker or at
the meetings of politicians, we find her demanding her rights as
a representative—and lately, some of the more favored portion
of our rural districts have beheld her as a practical advocate of
muscular Christianity and a player of base-ball.
—*The Days' Doings,* October 1868

UNION AND CONFEDERATE SOLDIERS carried regional bat and ball games (including baseball) with them wherever they went.[1] By the end of the Civil War, baseball was more popular than ever. There were at least two thousand teams in the United States in 1867, and the New York version of the game was beginning to supplant some of the regional variations.[2] *Oliver Optic's Magazine* informed its youthful readers that baseball was "the most popular [game] in the United States."[3] Baseball forever changed after the Civil War. Society was changing, and baseball along with it. Baseball remained primarily a game played by boys and men who paced off the boundaries of their diamonds in rural pastures and empty lots in America's growing cities, and who made their bats and balls out of materials at hand. But the game was beginning to lose its innocent idealism as a friendly social event during which rival teams vigorously competed on the field for bragging rights and a silver ball or trophy, and then sat down for a congenial dinner afterward. By the late 1860s, baseball had developed an alter-ego—a win-at-all-costs business for professional players whose win-loss records directly affected their future salaries. Just as women of the antebellum era had found themselves cast (along with children) as the "other" to adult men who wanted to play baseball, women of the immediate postbellum period found themselves further distanced from baseball's shifting center by professional interests whose narratives portrayed them, not as players, but as spectators and moral guardians of the bleachers.[4]

Structuring Baseball's Center in the Postbellum Era

Adult male baseball players had proclaimed the sport to be a "manly" activity during the antebellum era as a way to expand the sport's center to include them. They added a nationalistic subnarrative by changing rules to further distinguish the game from British antecedents and to make it more appealing to U.S. audiences. Having successfully recast the child's game as an adult activity, some entrepreneurs, players, and media supporters began to contemplate how they could turn pastime into profit. The postbellum period began with a new battle for the soul of baseball—one that pitted amateurs against professionals in a struggle for control of the structure and creed of the sport. This battle would ultimately shape a new governing structure and creed for baseball that would further marginalize women.

Economics and social class ideals were at the core of the contest between amateurs and moneyed interests. Those espousing amateurism considered amateurism a mark of gentility and upper-class morality; their narratives highlighted the fraternal nature of friendly contests between like-minded gentlemen. Amateurs looked down upon men who would eschew proper and honorable work in order to sell their services to a baseball club, and they predicted the sport would be irreparably tarnished once it became a vehicle for lucre. They likened professional baseball players to the "worthless, dissipated gladiator[s]" who fought for money in the back rooms of saloons or in secluded spaces.[5] Banning payments to players ensured that only (moneyed) gentlemen could play—gentlemen whose on-field actions could (theoretically) not be bought by unsavory characters and gamblers.

The battle was brief; the voices of amateurism were quickly drowned out by the purveyors of professionalism, who boldly proclaimed their passion to solidify the structure of the emerging national pastime by applying the same principles of capitalism and efficiency that were powering U.S. industrial growth. By 1870, the divisive issue had torn the NABBP apart; when seventeen of the twenty-seven member clubs in the association refused to support a resolution declaring the practice of paying players "reprehensible and injurious to the best interests of the game," the NABBP folded.[6] Within a year, the professional teams had formed a new structure for shaping the sport—the National Association of Professional Baseball Players (NA).

Numerically, the NA member teams constituted only a tiny fraction of the thousands of amateur civic, pick-up, school, college, semiprofessional,[7] professional, and factory baseball teams thriving across the country, yet these voices of professionalism (and the moneyed interests behind them) began wielding a disproportionate influence on the evolving structure and culture of the sport. At their first convention in March 1871, member clubs passed resolutions creating the framework for a national championship.[8] They stipulated that only member clubs were eligible to compete for the championship and that only games against other member clubs counted toward the final standings. By constituting themselves as the *National* Association of Professional Base Ball Players even though they represented only nine baseball clubs, and by restricting competition for the *national* championship to member clubs, NA members were, in essence, claiming the mantle of leadership over the development of professional baseball in the United States and the right to define what it meant to be an elite baseball team. Though this organization would be supplanted by another *National* league five years later, it pioneered practices that later leagues would copy and adapt as they sought to control the structure and culture of baseball.

It did not take long for newspaper and sporting periodical publishers to recognize that they could profit from promoting professional baseball teams. Countless editors added sports coverage to their newspapers, while entrepreneurs founded baseball-focused periodicals like *The Ball Players' Chronicle* (1867) and the *New England Base Ballist* (1868). By century's end, even small-town newspapers were routinely printing professional league standings and game results.[9] The disproportionate attention paid to professional teams and players helped solidify a cultural meaning for the sport that privileged the accomplishments of elite athletes and diminished those of less skilled players, including women. As the NA and follow-on organizations like the National League (1876), International Association of Professional Base Ball Players (1877), and American Association of Base Ball Clubs (1882) jockeyed to establish monopolies on professional baseball in key cities, they mandated rules that governed not only how the game was played on the field, but also who was eligible to play (whites, not blacks; men, not women, and so forth), and how fans had to behave in the stands.[10]

Professional baseball did not immediately capture the hearts and minds of the American people; for much of the 1870s and 1880s, most professional teams struggled to turn a profit, and voices of dissent continued to harangue professionals for ruining the (mythically) pure and healthful sport. Even though professional baseball lacked the national prestige it would one day enjoy, its power brokers still wielded enough influence to alter the historical narrative of the game. Even those who thought baseball was a perfectly acceptable activity for women increasingly began to make distinctions between legitimate players—that is, those who could make home runs—and everyone else. In 1867, after reporting that "Female Base Ball Clubs are being formed in some portions of the State," the *Utica (N.Y.) Morning Herald* pointed out that while women "have an undoubted right to play base ball," it was hard to imagine "a fair creature arrayed in all the paraphernalia of dress, hoop-skirts, and sun bonnet making a home run!"[11]

By the early postbellum period, the center of baseball had shifted enough that observers were beginning to internalize an increasingly rigid definition of what it meant to be a ball player. They also began to categorize games qualitatively along a hierarchy of value ranging from children's' play to "third-nine" games to "muffin" games to amateur contests to professional contests.[12] In 1866 the *Sunday Mercury* criticized as a "counterfeit affair" a game that used a female umpire and scorekeepers. The paper argued that the game should not have been labeled a muffin game, because only those who "by excessive weight, lack of experience, or by some physical incompetency are *unfitted for ball-players*" could comprise a "genuine" muffin game (emphasis added). The reporter equated "second-class" players as those who "have ceased to equal the high demands of the game in these days of improved play."[13] In this case, the reporter was not arguing that second-class players should not play baseball but that they should not represent themselves as belonging to a higher category of player. As the nineteenth century progressed, the general public increasingly regarded girls and women as the antithesis of "baseball player" and their games as child's play—not legitimate (valued) competition.

A *National* Pastime Begins to Take Shape

As the New York game displaced town ball, rounders, and other regional variations of bat and ball games in the early postbellum period, and as professional interests began their quest to commodify the sport, baseball began to show signs of becoming a truly national pastime. Between 1865 and 1879 the number of boys' and men's civic baseball teams, pick-up teams, muffin teams, business teams, school teams, college teams, and professional teams mushroomed.[14] One particularly exuberant observer gushed in 1871: "[Baseball] is the great game of the middle class. Every city has its favorite club that travels leisurely over the country every summer, paying its way as it goes, by the gate-money of its admirers. . . . [Baseball] has passed from city to town, from town to village, till it has overspread the nation."[15]

What has long been overlooked in traditional histories of baseball is that each type of boys' and men's team had a female counterpart. Despite practical and sociocultural deterrents, more girls and women took up baseball during this era than had in any previous period. They played on more than one hundred baseball teams located in twenty-one of thirty-eight states plus the Kingdom of Hawaii. (Eighteen of the states had not had female teams prior to 1860.)[16] Every region of the country had girls' and/or women's teams except the Southwest, and, like boys and men's teams, the girls' and women's teams sprang up in urban and rural communities, on school yards and college campuses and, occasionally, on factory grounds. Sometimes young girls and women played each other on all-female teams; other times they played with or against boys and men. Almost all female players were white, although there are a handful of cases where black women played together.[17]

Baseball's Many Forms

Pick-up teams and civic teams came in many varieties. Girls and boys, men and women organized pick-up teams. They existed for a specific timeframe (often only a single game) and purpose (fun or fund-raiser). Team names often reflected player characteristics ("Fats" and "Leans," "Marrieds" and "Singles," and so forth) more than geographic or cultural identity. Some muffin teams featured quirky competitions, such as those between one-legged and one-armed men, married and single women, or between teams on ice skates or waist deep in water.[18] Civic teams linked their identity to a location; they could be composed of paid or unpaid players. Amateur civic teams were privately organized, either by ad hoc groups of men and women or by members of a formal sporting club. Ad hoc civic teams were informal, (that is, members did not pay dues nor adopt a formal constitution and bylaws) and often short-lived. Teams associated with male sporting clubs were more structured and tended to endure longer. Some civic teams, like the Forest City Club of Rockford, Illinois, and the Nationals of Washington D.C., became closely associated with the fortunes of their cities and were increasingly funded and operated by city boosters and entrepreneurs anxious to capitalize on baseball's transformation to a saleable commodity. Though the majority of civic teams in the nineteenth century rarely played more than a few dozen miles from their home towns and existed merely to facilitate spirited but friendly competition for local bragging rights, the top echelon of civic teams (like the Forest City Club and Nationals) evolved into the major and minor league teams of modern Organized Baseball.

Business teams were organized either by the employees of a particular business or industry or, increasingly in the late nineteenth century, by business owners anxious to provide wholesome and healthy entertainment for employees to keep them out of trouble and loyal to their companies. School and college teams of the 1860s and 1870s were organized and led by students, not faculty or staff; they provided a fun, healthy diversion from studies and promoted school or class esprit de corps. Male collegiate players often sought opportunities to compete against their peers at other colleges or on local community teams; female collegians generally eschewed matches with outside opponents in favor of intramural competition. Professional teams could be either civic teams or one of a growing number of male, female, or coed barnstorming troupes organized to entertain spectators across the country.[19]

The wide variety of teams in the nineteenth century must be factored in to any discussion of women's relationship to baseball because girls and women played baseball in all its forms. Peter Morris points out that traditional histories of baseball tended to focus on the development of the professional game, ignoring entire categories of baseball teams (like the muffin teams) that proliferated in the 1860s and 1870s.[20] Morris notes that the men who played in muffin games were resisting narratives that professional baseball best represented the game they had played as youths. They continued to emphasize the camaraderie and social aspects of the game as it had prevailed in antebellum America.[21] Women, too, embraced baseball on their own terms and, like the muffin players, were gradually marginalized outside the center of the sport.

Reinforcing the Cultural Narratives of Nationalism and Manliness

It was no accident that baseball boosters increasingly spoke of their game as a *national* pastime despite that it attracted only a fraction of the spectators that flocked to other types of leisure activities. Far more citizens attended walking and boxing matches, horse races, and burlesque, vaudeville, and circus performances than attended amateur and professional baseball games during this era.[22] This inconvenient fact did not deter baseball boosters from spinning their nationalistic narrative in hopes of carving out a space for themselves in the burgeoning world of commodified leisure entertainment. In much the same way that the sporting press of the late nineteenth century would "create" the American game of football and turn it into a seasonal spectacle on college campuses, the sporting press of the mid-nineteenth century created the "national" game of baseball and used it to promote national values, idealized masculinity—and its own fortunes.[23]

Prior to the Civil War, a handful of editors at newspapers in and around New York City, like the *New York Clipper, Porter's Spirit of the Times,* the *New York Herald,* and the *Sunday Mercury,* had reported on local baseball teams, matches, and the evolution of the New York game. *Beadle's Dime Base Ball Player,* first published in 1860, had covered both the New York and Massachusetts forms of the game.[24] After the war, local and national publications increasingly focused on the New York version. Jules Tygiel attributes the popularity of the New York game to the fact that its practitioners adapted it to reflect American's growing appreciation for all things "modern" and "scientific."[25] Teams like the Washington Nationals and Cincinnati Red Stockings actively worked to spread the New York game—the Nationals making a tour of the West (Midwest) in 1867 and the Red Stockings heading east in the fall of 1868 for a series of games with elite clubs in Philadelphia, New York, Brooklyn, and Washington, D.C.[26]

The emerging narrative of nationalism left little room for women. The related ideals of modernism, science, and American "civilization" increasingly invoked by male baseball boosters related to public spaces, where men wielded power and authority. Women's relationship to these concepts was ancillary, not primary, and as male baseball boosters proclaimed their sport's ability to heal social ills, transcend sectional differences, and forge a national identity, they linked this power to masculine ideals. "There is no nobler or manlier game than base-ball, and the more it is cultivated the better for the country," asserted *Harper's Weekly* in June 1865.[27] Three years later the *Quincy (Ill.) Whig* reinforced the theme, celebrating the fact that so many southerners were playing baseball: "[P]robably nothing could have been introduced into the south better calculated to benefit the southern young men than this our national game." Because the sport required "courage, nerve, pluck and endurance to excel in it," concluded the unnamed author, southern youth would find in baseball "the very field for exciting sport which they had previously sought in amusements of a more objectionable character."[28] Where grapeshot and Minié ball had once subdued a generation of rebellious southern men, now wooden bat and horsehide ball would redeem and restore them to the national fold.

Some southerners resisted this baseball diplomacy; they had their own sporting pastimes. While northern youth grew up playing bat and ball games like Townball, base ball, One Old Cat, and wicket, southern youth played Chermany, Chumney, and Round Cat.[29] In 1874 George William Bagby, an unrepentant southern secessionist whose humorous (and autobiographical) "Mozis Addums" letters were much loved in the South, communicated through the fictional character his determination to continue to teach southern boys to play Chermany as a way to resist the encroachment of northern culture and values: "My aim was to supplant the vile pastimes of base-ball and billiards which befell the Commonwealth as part of the loathsome legacy bequeathed us by the war," Bagby's alter-ego intoned. "I could not, indeed, believe that these debilitating and abnormal sports would perpetually exclude the time-honored and patriotic games to which Virginians had been accustomed . . ."[30] Bagby's voice was easily overwhelmed by the reality of baseball's popularity in the South. In October 1868, the Ku Klux Klan club faced off against "nine Carpetbaggers" in Fayetteville, Tennessee, while teams from Macon and Savannah, Georgia, vied for bragging rights the same year.[31] From Texas to Virginia, Arkansas to Florida, baseball teams sprang up in every one of the former states of the Confederacy in the decade and a half following the war.[32] By 1879, New Orleans had so many baseball clubs that one observer noted that there were not enough names to go around.[33]

The narratives of nationalism and manliness were not uncontested. Advocates of amateurism continued to insist that the emerging professional game undermined, rather than reinforced, ideals of masculinity and nationalism. Some sought to enlist the aid of women in grounding baseball's center in middle-class values. In August 1867, the Reverend J. T. Crane complained in *The Ladies' Repository* that adults were ruining baseball by turning the "innocent, pleasant, healthful amusement" of his boyhood into a "ponderous and elaborate affair" in which grown men organized themselves into formal clubs with rules "as rigid as those which govern the proceedings of Congress."[34] Crane criticized baseball players who neglected their families and jobs to practice baseball and whose zealous drive to win games caused injuries and overexertion. He was particularly upset by the rapidly increasing number of players who were being paid to play. By appealing to his female readers' sense of morality and Protestant work ethic, Crane hoped to mobilize their support for restoring the national pastime to what he believed had been a purer game.

Crane prefaced his remarks by commenting that baseball "would seem so far out of the line of feminine pursuits that nothing need be said of it in the columns of the *Repository*" but added that because baseball was being "styled the national game" and women were regularly invited to attend contests, they did have a stake in the sport.[35] Crane's sense that he needed to justify addressing an article on baseball to women indicates the extent to which narratives of gender crafted by the NABBP and its supporters were beginning to gain traction. Efforts to restructure baseball's center to privilege elite adult male players were only partially successful, however; the cultural narratives being spun to reinforce the new gendered structure of the sport were being covertly and overtly challenged by scores of female teams and players.

The same year that Crane solicited women's aid in restoring baseball to its less competitive roots, newspapers in Michigan, Ohio, New York, and New Jersey reported that girls and women in their communities and in Pensacola, Florida, had organized teams.[36] That girls and women continued to play baseball, even as men tried to recharacterize the sport as masculine, indicates the extent to which the structure and creed of baseball remained contested throughout this era. News of the female baseball teams in Niles, Michigan, and Pensacola, Florida, gained nationwide coverage and eventually reached Henry Chadwick. On July 18, 1867, in his newly launched *Ball Players' Chronicle*, Chadwick quoted a statement from Delabere P. Blaine's *An Encyclopedia of Rural Sports*: "There are few of us, of either sex, but have engaged in base ball since our majority." Then Chadwick added skeptically: "Think of American ladies playing base ball!"[37] One week later, apparently apprised of the fact that American women *were* playing baseball, Chadwick reprinted an article from the *Albany Evening Journal* about the Niles and Pensacola teams.[38] By republishing the article about female baseball teams, whose existence undercut the masculine narrative he and others were trying to propagate, Chadwick gave legs to a story that might otherwise have attracted less attention. Between July 1867 and January 1868 newspapers in Michigan, Wisconsin, Indiana, Tennessee, Pennsylvania, New York, New Jersey, Washington, D.C., Kansas, and Missouri reported on women's baseball teams.[39] So many papers picked up the story about the team in Niles, Michigan, that the *Niles Weekly Times* quipped in September that reports of the team had been "circulated from Dan to Beersheba; told in Gath and published in the streets of Ashkelon, for aught we know."[40]

Analysis of articles about baseball in the postbellum popular press indicates the extent to which efforts to propagate a particular structure and cultural creed for baseball were beginning to bear fruit. As the narrative that baseball was a man's game began to resonate more forcefully in public discourse, women players began to elicit sharply contrasting reactions in the press. Though matter-of-fact reporting and friendly teasing about women players was common, an increasing number of reports included editorial comments either supporting or criticizing adult women players. In August 1867, the editor of the *Wellsville Free Press* made his support of women baseball players clear: "We go in for base ball among the women. It will give them what they so much need and so seldom get, a full breath of Heaven's bon-fresh air."[41] His perspective was not shared by the editor of the *Niles Weekly Times,* who did his best to refute the multiple reports popping up around the country that women were playing baseball in Niles. "It is totally incorrect," he asserted. "The young ladies of Niles have not been infected by the base ball mania. . . . There is no such association and no ladies ball club."[42] One month later, a number of newspapers across the country were quick to repeat the story about a "Miss Howard" of Allen's Prairie, Michigan, who had allegedly died three days after overexerting herself playing baseball. Several newspapers prefaced the story with the comment: "We have to record still another death from base ball folly."[43]

The reporters who considered Howard's death the result of "folly" may have internalized the gendered narrative of baseball emerging from the NABBP and its supporters, or they, like Crane, could have been expressing disapproval of the increasingly cutthroat (and dangerous) nature of baseball competitions in general.[44] As it turned out, Amaret (or Amorette) Howard, the twenty- or twenty-one-year-old daughter of prosperous farmers had not died because she had played baseball; she had succumbed to typhoid fever, which had swept through her family during the previous three months.[45] It is unlikely that newspapers outside the immediate vicinity of Allen's Prairie would have mentioned Howard's death had it not been for the report linking her death to baseball.

Another reason that postbellum articles about women baseball players began to include editorial comments was that efforts to recast children's bat and ball games as an adult male sport occurred simultaneously with the birth and growth of a major women's rights movement in the United States. U.S. women held their first formal women's rights convention in July 1848 in Seneca Falls, New York, just three years after young men in New York City organized the New York Knickerbockers—the club that would spearhead creation of the NABBP and standardization of rules for modern baseball. Over the ensuing decades, women like Elizabeth Cady Stanton and Susan B. Anthony founded countless women's rights publications and traveled the country vigorously lobbying for greater social, political, and economic opportunities for women. Like-minded activists organized scores of local and state women's rights organizations and banded together to found the National Woman Suffrage Association in 1869.[46]

Those anxious to recast baseball as a game best suited for men needed to portray women as physically and mentally unsuited for playing. Women's rights activism and women's success in previously male-only jobs and professions undercut their narrative of feminine ineptness, necessitating that they adapt their strategy to leverage fear of social upheaval. In the fall of 1867, papers across the country reprinted an article from the *Home Journal* entitled, "Sexual Assimilation."[47] The article argued that the once well-defined boundaries between the sexes were being blurred: "Female physicians are multiplying; civil offices are filled by women; occupations which have hitherto been considered exclusively masculine are usurped by them," the article reported. Women "become painters and sculptors; they pop the question and institute proceedings for divorce; they look forward to the female millennium of suffrage with an assurance that makes it a foregone conclusion," continued the unnamed author, horrified that "our New York girl *gamins* even are beginning to sell papers and polish boots."[48] After noting that women were "more out of doors" and mingling with men "in their hitherto exclusive amusements" such as driving and riding horses (astride), swimming, diving, hunting, fishing, walking, rowing, and gymnastics, the disgruntled author speculated that it was only a matter of time before "we shall hear presently of female base ball and cricket clubs."[49]

Apparently the author was unaware that baseball was already popular with girls and women. The composer of a new song about the sport recognized its broad appeal, including a reference to female players:

> The girls too, aping lordly men,
> Have taken up the chase,
> And with Bloomer pants, and gaiters high,
> They fly from "base" to "base"![50]

The unflattering dig at women "aping" men and running bases with their "gaiters high" mirrored contemporary descriptions of women's rights advocates.[51]

Though contemporaries sometimes attributed women's rights motives to female players, it is virtually impossible to ascertain their motivations because so few of them left personal accounts. What is clear, however, is that many of their contemporaries *assumed* they were motivated by factors other than sheer enjoyment of the sport. Reports of women baseball players in the 1860s and 1870s often appeared alongside articles about the women's rights movement. On September 15, 1870, for example, the Albert Lea, Minnesota, *Freeborn County Standard* mentioned girl baseball players in the same issue in which it published a lengthy article describing the first election in Wyoming in which women had been permitted to vote. Newspapers reported stories about women baseball players (and women athletes in general) in the same manner that they reported news about the emergence of women doctors, dentists, lawyers, postmistresses, railroad ticket agents, and telegraph operators. These women were newsworthy because they were engaged in activities traditionally defined as masculine or, in the case of baseball, activities being increasingly defined as masculine.

One of the best examples of the dichotomy in media coverage of female baseball as either normative activity or women's rights statement can be found in newspaper articles about two female teams that played in Peterboro, New York, in the summer of 1868. Peterboro (Peterborough) was a small community of about 350 individuals located sixty miles east of Seneca Falls on the banks of Oneida Creek in the rolling hills of picturesque Madison County.[52] The village, like many New York communities, had its own baseball teams. In 1859, fourteen-year-old Gerrit Smith Miller, grandson and namesake of the town's wealthiest and most respected citizen, organized the Bobolink Base Ball Club.[53] Nine years later, his then twelve-year-old sister Nannie served as captain of the senior nine of a girls' baseball club. According to some contemporary accounts, Peterboro's female baseball club had fifty members, who organized senior and junior nines in the summer of 1868.[54] The teams purportedly played a number of practice games "outside the town and away from the gaze of the curious" to hone their skills before staging an exhibition game "before a large and anxious multitude of spectators" on Saturday, July 25, 1868.[55] Nannie was the most prominent member of the club. Her family's long-standing leadership roles in social reform initiatives provided her with the latitude to engage in activities some might have considered inappropriate. Nannie's grandfather, Gerrit Smith, had served in the U.S. House of Representatives, ran for president, and helped fund John Brown's ill-fated 1859 raid on Harper's Ferry, Virginia. Smith was a vocal supporter of the women's rights movement and believed that "[e]veryone should be left at entire liberty to choose an individual sphere—a man to choose to knit or sew—a woman to choose to fell trees or to be a blacksmith."[56] Nannie's grandmother, Ann, was an active member of women's rights associations[57] and her mother, Elizabeth Smith Miller, had designed and introduced the "short dress" (later called Bloomers) to second cousin Elizabeth Cady Stanton and friend Amelia Bloomer in 1851.[58]

The female baseball club at Peterboro is the best documented of all the women's teams of the 1860s. At least twenty-six newspapers across the country reported its existence between August 6 and October 3, 1868. Students at nearby Hamilton College (where Nannie Miller's grandfather had graduated as valedictorian in 1818) mentioned the Peterboro club in their literary journal:

> We are happy to learn, that a Young Ladies' B.B. Club, has been organized in Peterboro. The honorable and responsible post of Captain, is held by Miss Nannie Miller, grand-daughter of the Hon. Gerrit Smith, of '18. How much more sensible a few hours daily practice on the Ball Ground, than weeks of weary experiment with the "Grecian Bend" now becoming so popular with the ladies. Should the charming athletes of Peterboro, wish to contest the palm with "Hamilton," the Senior Nine would be most delighted to receive a Leap Year challenge to a friendly game; surely the Young Ladies' would not be so inconsiderate as to dare us to a match, while we are alone and so far from our parents.[59]

All of the published reports about the Peterboro nines seem to be based on only two original sources—one written by Elizabeth Cady Stanton and another by an unnamed individual whose detailed description of the game and players indicates someone closely associated with the club or an eyewitness to its activities. Unfortunately for historians, these accounts contain conflicting details that make it difficult to determine what actually happened. Further complicating matters, two illustrations published in the *Sporting Times* and *The Days' Doings* portray erroneous information about the players.

On July 20, 1868, Stanton arrived in Peterboro for a three-week visit with her cousin, Gerrit Smith, and his wife Ann; Elizabeth and Nannie arrived about the same time to spend the summer. While in Peterboro, Stanton wrote three lengthy letters about her travels for *The Revolution*.[60] In her second letter, written on August 1 and published on August 6, Stanton described Peterboro and Gerrit Smith's home life at length before adding, almost as an afterthought: "We were delighted to find here a base ball club of girls. Nannie Miller, a grand-daughter of Gerrit Smith, is the Captain, and handles the club with a grace and strength worthy of notice. It was a very pretty sight to see the girls with their white dresses and blue ribbons flying, in full possession of the public square, last Saturday afternoon, while the boys were quiet spectators at the scene."[61] Note from this account that Stanton found the club already in existence when she arrived. It was a baseball club of "girls" (not women) who had recently (the reference to "last Saturday" places the game on July 25, 1868) played a public game in front of a number of boys who watched quietly; the girls' uniform consisted of white dresses and blue ribbons.

After Stanton's letter about the Peterboro baseball game appeared in *The Revolution,* multiple prominent newspapers reprinted her account almost verbatim. The earliest known reprint appeared in the *Cleveland Plain Dealer* on August 11, 1868. [62] This article specifically cited "Mrs. Cady Stanton's" letter as the source of its story. Over the next five days, a flurry of almost identical articles appeared in newspapers in New York and Ohio.[63] On August 17, the *Philadelphia Inquirer* reported simply: "There is a female base ball club at Peterborough, New York."[64] Reprints based on Stanton's letter continued to appear sporadically in newspapers throughout the remainder of August and into September, with the last known example appearing in the *Boston Investigator* on March 3, 1869.[65] The widespread publication of Stanton's account of the baseball club came to the attention of a distant relative, who wrote to Gerrit Smith on August 17 from Columbus, Ohio: "I see by the papers Mrs. Stanton is or has been at Peterboro. Her support of the girls base ball club has been widely copied throughout the West."[66]

The second, and more detailed account of the Peterboro club both supports and contradicts Stanton's description. The earliest known published accounts from this anonymous source appeared simultaneously in the *New York Clipper* and the *Chicago Daily Evening Tribune* on August 29. Two days later, an article identical to the *Clipper* article, minus a box score, appeared in the *Syracuse Courier and Union.*[67] According to the articles based on the anonymous source, the Peterboro baseball club consisted of about fifty "young ladies" who organized the club because they were "jealous of the healthy sports enjoyed by the more muscular portion of mankind." Unlike Stanton's account of the players wearing "white dresses and blue ribbons flying," the anonymous source reported that the girls wore "short blue and white tunics, reaching to the knee, straw caps jauntily trimmed, white stockings and stout gaiter shoes." It was the anonymous source who reported that the senior and junior nines had practiced outside the town before playing an exhibition game in front of spectators. This source also provided the first and last names of the players on the senior nine and the last names of the players on the junior nine. It identified Nannie Miller as the captain of the senior nine but made no reference to her relationship to Gerrit Smith, as all the articles based on Stanton's letter had done.

Other details from the anonymous source included: Mrs. J. S. Smith served as umpire; Miss Martin and Mrs. Benning (or Benny) served as scorers; a penny was flipped to see which team would bat first; the Juniors won the toss; the first batter was a player named Hattie Harding; she was out on a fly ball; the rest of the Juniors experienced a similar fate throughout the game and the

Senior nine won easily, 29–5. The detailed coverage of the game in the articles from the anonymous source was typical of that for men's games, including the editorial comments about individual players: "Bertha Powell gave six runs by outrageous muffs in the third and fourth innings. With this exception, however, the Senior nine acquitted themselves well, and nearly every member showed some particular points of fine play. But the Juniors were sadly beaten and have much to learn yet, especially in the choice of balls to strike at. Mary Sterns played at second base very well, and we shall not be surprised to see her one of the Senior playing nine next year."[68] Calling out a player for poor play was a common feature of baseball reporting during the era, but it was decidedly unusual for a young woman to be publicly humiliated in this way.

After the *Clipper, Daily Evening Tribune,* and *Courier and Union* articles appeared, another group of virtually identical articles was published, albeit condensed, and also based on the anonymous source.[69] Emily Howland, a women's rights activist from New York, pasted one of these articles from late August into her scrapbook.[70] The widespread coverage of the Peterboro baseball game eclipsed that of the female teams in Pensacola, Florida, and Niles, Michigan, the previous year. This attention may have stemmed from the connection of the team to Elizabeth Cady Stanton at a time when the women's rights movement was receiving extensive press coverage about a rancorous schism over whether to subordinate the fight for woman suffrage to that for black men's suffrage.[71]

Most articles about the Peterboro players were positive, indicating that baseball's gendered reputation was not yet solidified. "Ball playing is as good a method for developing the girls as it is for the boys," insisted the *New York Herald* when it reprinted Stanton's account of the game.[72] Two months later, in a lengthy article explaining why baseball was "now universally admitted to be the national game of America," the *Herald* reported matter-of-factly that not only were many upper-class gentlemen counted among the thousands of spectators who gathered to watch men's teams compete, but that "ladies often grace the scenes of contests in large numbers and even aspire—as in Peterboro, N.Y.—to wield the bat and sling the ball in a style remarkable and praiseworthy."[73] Clearly, the writer saw nothing untoward about women participating in the national pastime as spectators and players.

Two contemporary illustrations of the Peterboro game reveal the ways in which women's participation in baseball was mediated by observers. The two images stand in stark contrast to one another, and neither accurately reflects descriptions of the game in contemporary sources. *Sporting Times* published its illustration (fig. 1) on the front page on August 29. It depicts buxom players in provocative poses wearing frilly shorts and shirts, plumed hats, high-button heels, and earrings.[74]

FIGURE 1. "The Last Sporting Sensation—A Female Base Ball Club at Peterboro, New York." *Sporting Times,* August 29, 1868.

The *Days' Doings* illustration (fig. 2) appeared on October 3.[75] It shows neatly dressed women wearing knee-length pantaloons under short tunics, with hats and earrings. The field is ringed by a large crowd of well-dressed men in suits and top hats and a smaller number of women wearing hoop skirts. The crowd was not unlike those that attended men's games. Though the players in *The Days' Doings* illustration are wearing more clothing than those in the *Sporting Times* illustration, they are still scantily clad by the standards of the day—their legs are bare from knee to ankle and their tunics barely cover their hips.

Both illustrations of the Peterboro baseball game appeared in tabloid journals which, like their ubiquitous modern counterparts at grocery store checkout aisles, thrived on shocking their readers. Periodicals like *Sporting Times* and *The Days' Doings* used illustrations to attract (male) readers, not to accurately report news. The engravers who created the images were generally not eyewitnesses to the events they portrayed; they simply mixed a smattering of eyewitness details with liberal amounts of artistic imagination and editorial spin. Neither paper portrayed the female baseball players in a positive light. The *Sporting Times* impugned the moral character of the players by showing them in risqué cloth-

FIGURE 2. "The Last Illustration of Women's Rights—A Femele [*sic*] Base-Ball Club at Peterboro, N.Y." *The Days' Doings,* October 3, 1868.

ing and provocative poses. *The Days' Doings* illustration was less sexualized but still implied that women baseball players were manly—they wore pants, not feminine fashions, and they played in front of a mixed audience—something no respectable woman of the day would do.

Sorting out historical fact from fiction regarding the Peterboro baseball game is difficult given the conflicting details in newspaper accounts and illustrations. Were the players girls or adult women? Were there really fifty of them? Why did they organize baseball teams—were they playing for fun and health or were they firing another salvo in the ongoing battle for women's rights? It is impossible to answer the first two questions with certainty, but historical context provides insights into the meaning of the game to players and observers.

Strictly speaking, the Peterboro game was not staged by women's rights activists as part of their broader campaign for political rights. Stanton devoted only a few sentences to describing it in her lengthy letter to the *Revolution,* and neither she nor Elizabeth Smith Miller and other activists mentioned the game in their personal or public correspondence.[76] The absence of an overt declaration about the game's relationship to women's rights in Stanton's letter is significant. If the Peterboro players had meant the game to be "the last illustration of women's rights" as *The Days' Doings* asserted, Elizabeth Cady Stanton, one of the foremost advocates of women's rights at the time, would surely have articulated that motivation more forcefully in her letter to *The Revolution*.

On the other hand, the Peterboro game *was* part of the broader campaign for social change in the sense that the players embodied a key component of the women's rights movement—they were outdoors running and playing and embracing a vigorously healthy lifestyle. Women's health and women's rights were indivisible, and many understood the deleterious affects of corsets and bulky clothing. Concerned individuals had organized societies as early as 1835 dedicated to "putting down the wicked slavery to fashion, which destroys so many females" and, by the 1850s, newspapers and periodicals regularly published articles about the dangers of crinoline and corsets.[77] Gerrit Smith, his wife, and daughter were outspoken supporters of women's dress reform. Smith commented to Stanton in 1869: "I am amazed that the intelligent women engaged in the 'Woman's rights movement' see not the relation between their dress and the oppressive evils which they are striving to throw off."[78]

Stanton and many other women's rights activists understood that women could not hope to thrive in broader social roles if they were sickly and weak. She regularly appealed to women to engage in more vigorous outdoor work and recreation instead of being continually cooped up inside sewing, doing laundry, and keeping house. Stanton appealed to society more broadly to enlarge women's "sphere" for the good of the race: "These feeble men we see about us may trace back their paralyzed limbs and softened brains to sickly, silly mothers, shut up in what is called woman's sphere within four walls. As woman is naturally more nervous than man, how suicidal for the race to assign her all the employments that tax the nervous system, without giving her an opportunity for the development of muscle and bone."[79] At a time when women were ideologically and often physically relegated to private domestic spaces (unless in the company of a man), the energy and enthusiasm of the female baseball players in "full possession of the public square" in Peterboro was something to be celebrated. Immediately after describing the scene in which female ball players possessed the public square and boys watched quietly, she added: "We thought if the author of 'the Spirit of seventy-six' had ever visited Peterboro, she would not have postponed the good time of woman's redemption to quite so distant a future."[80] Lady Liberty herself would champion the liberation of robust, healthy women like the female baseball players of Peterboro, in Stanton's mind.

The connection between healthy exercise and women's rights was not lost on the unnamed author of the article accompanying *The Days' Doings* account of the Peterboro game, who wrote:

We hear on all sides of woman—of her rights and of her wrongs—we hear of her from our pulpits, we read of her in our novels and essays, we see her occasionally on the lecture—a speaker or at the meetings of politicians, we find her demanding her rights as a representative—and lately, some of the more favored portion of our rural districts have beheld her as a practical advocate of muscular Christianity and a player of base-ball. In the latter capacity, at least, she deserves our unqualified attention and commendation. Physical exercise is one of the needs of American men, especially of American women. The Grecian Bend, and other kindred absurdities, have had their day, (so let us devoutly trust) and in their stead attention is being directed to physical sports of a bracing and healthful character. Every well-wisher of woman—(and what man with a wife, sweetheart, sister or daughter is *not* such a well-wisher)—will wish our female base-ball clubs, and similar organizations, all success, and only wish that there were more of them.[81]

This writer did not feel threatened by the physicality evinced by the female baseball players and understood that the nation would be better off when women adopted healthier lifestyles.

Though it is impossible to establish definitively the motivation of most nineteenth-century female baseball players, it is safe to say that the majority benefited from the development of physical education programs for women in communities, schools, and colleges during the latter half of the century. Even women who opposed the broader political agenda of women's rights activism enjoyed the positive climate of support for exercise and good health it stimulated. They also benefited from the work done by women's rights activists to dismantle social and economic obstacles. In 1868, a time when women's property rights were still in dispute and few women had the opportunity to run businesses, one group of women in Kalamazoo, Michigan, had the financial means and the business savvy to establish a baseball and croquet club, procure their own playing grounds, and organize their own course of training.[82] That there were enough members in the Kalamazoo club to field two baseball teams indicates the extent to which women in Kalamazoo considered baseball a *feminine* activity—as appropriate for them as croquet. Baseball was not yet a *man's* game; girls and women did not yet have to assert a right to play—they could simply play.

Social Interactions and Baseball

Although cultural perceptions of baseball as a man's game had not yet solidified in the mid-nineteenth century, sociocultural norms and the emerging gendered narratives about the sport *did* influence the ways in which women interacted with baseball as players and/or spectators. There were doubtless many women who decided not to play baseball because sociocultural narratives about their supposed biological frailty and their idealized role as women deterred them.[83] The women who did choose to play baseball had another decision to make—whether to conform (or not) to prevailing gender norms. Some conformed—playing baseball in corsets and long dresses on smaller fields by modified rules; others wore bloomers (or even pants) and played on regulation fields by regulation rules.[84]

Most nineteenth-century girls and women conformed to prevailing gender norms while playing baseball, but some did so only reluctantly. In 1900, Jeannette L. Gilder, a former newspaper reporter and popular literary figure in and around New York City, wrote *The Autobiography of a Tomboy,* in which she recalled the fun she and other girls had had playing baseball in New Jersey in the early 1860s. "There were two clubs in Birdlington [Bordentown], composed entirely of girls," she wrote, "and we played a lively game."[85] As was the case with many of the games played by girls and women during the nineteenth century, Gilder and her teammates played on a ball field "within our own gates," to keep them private. Gilder also recalled that she and the others had played baseball for hours on end in the hot sun; so long, in fact, that she jokingly wondered how she was alive "to tell the tale!" Gilder related that her hands were as hard as the boys who played baseball, a fact of which she was proud. To her disappointment, however, while "there wasn't a boy in the village who hadn't a crooked finger" all of hers were perfectly straight. It was a "fly in my ointment," she related, that she had not broken a finger playing baseball.[86]

Writing thirty-three years after the fact, during an era when physical educators were adapting games like basketball and baseball to the "special needs" of women, Gilder wanted her readers to understand that the game she and other girls had played in the 1860s was "real" baseball. "I can assure you that we played with the hardest balls and seldom 'muffed,'" she insisted. She also reported that after a newspaper reporter in a neighboring town got wind of their games and published a wholly fictitious account of their playing (claiming they "knocked the ball into each other's eyes, punched one another's heads, and behaved in a generally outrageous manner"), they were forced to give up baseball and amuse themselves with activities appropriate for "well-regulated girls."[87] Gilder's account of her baseball-playing days may have been somewhat idealized after the passage of so much time, but that she recorded the activity in her autobiography indicates the importance she attached to playing baseball at a time when girls were expected to be "well-regulated." Gilder was proud that she had resisted societal definitions of proper gender boundaries, and wore the label "tomboy" as a badge of honor.

Observers sometimes mocked women who tried to play baseball while conforming to gender ideals. In 1869 the *New Orleans Daily Picayune* reprinted a story from the *New York World* about a fictitious baseball game between women's rights activists.[88] The roster of the "No. 7 Hose" (an allusion to their shared hosiery size) included women's rights luminaries Elizabeth Cady Stanton and Susan B. Anthony, while the roster of the Blue Stockings included sisters Alice and Phoebe Carey (sic: Cary), both of whom were famous in New York literary circles. (Phoebe was a staunch women's rights activist and served as editor of Stanton and Anthony's *The Revolution* for a time.) The anonymous author gave an inning-by-inning farcical account of the totally inept attempts of the women to play baseball while bedecked in the latest feminine fashions. The *New York World* writer seemed intent on demonstrating that women were incapable of exceling in any masculine roles, but the editor of the *New Orleans Daily Picayune* had a different take. Attributing the baseball game to feminists' efforts to strengthen themselves for manly tasks, he asked rhetorically: "[C]annot they, by a system of gymnastics—by out door exercise; by exposure to the changes and inclemencies [sic] of the weather—increase their bone and muscle? Cannot they, in fact, become as hardy and vigorous as their present rulers?"[89] His comment about women becoming as "hardy and vigorous" as their male "rulers" is key to understanding why so many mothers (and members of the general public) were reluctant to condone participation by young women in certain (masculine) athletic activities like rowing, boxing, and baseball. Even if the women who rowed, boxed, and played baseball held no grand aspirations for public life or upsetting gender roles, the fact that others imputed those motivations to them could be off-putting to aspiring female players.

Schoolgirls and Baseball

Children rarely considered how their sports and games fit into the grand scheme of gender relationships—that was their parents' concern. Across the country at countless all-female schools and coeducational schools, day schools, and boarding schools, young girls and teenagers played baseball throughout the nineteenth century. They played at places like the Prospect Hill School in Greenfield, Massachusetts (1874), Mount Holyoke Female Seminary in South Hadley, Massachusetts (1884), and the Mary A. Burnham School for Girls in Northampton, Massachusetts (1894).[90] They played in the schoolyards of urban common schools, rural grammar schools, elite private seminaries, and public high schools. It is impossible to quantify precisely the extent of schoolgirls' participation in the national pastime because scholars have only recently begun a focused effort to recover evidence about them. Fortunately, some of these past players are still speaking to us about their love of baseball through diary entries, school newspapers, yearbooks, and letters. A number of them stare out at us with serious faces from team photographs. Immortalized in these time capsules of albumen paper and silver nitrate, they pose with bats, balls, and sometimes gloves, proudly celebrating their camaraderie as teammates and staking a claim to a place in the history of the national pastime.[91]

Grace Aspinwall, a student at Miss Porter's School in Farmington, Connecticut, in the mid- to late-1860s recalled that she and her fellow students had organized a baseball club during her final year at the seminary—but only after persistent lobbying of the school's proprietor. "Baseball was introduced at Miss Porter's School while I was there,—I think my last year in the spring of 1867," wrote Aspinwall. "A group of girls, including myself, after many consultations, approached Miss Porter on the subject, and notwithstanding many hesitations on her part for a time, fearing we would 'attract too much attention,' she gave her permission, if we would select a field approached by going through other fields where there were no 'passersby'!"[92] Aspinwall felt deeply honored by her selection as pitcher and proudly reported the fact when she "talked over the latest baseball news" with her seven brothers.[93]

Twelve-year-old Charles Hurd, a student at the West Lebanon Academy in Lebanon, Maine, loved baseball, and he saw nothing unusual about playing with girls. On April 8, 1869, Hurd informed his uncle, Charles Berry: "The great excitement over here is base ball and jumping rope. The boys play at morning, noon and after school in the after noon and the girls play ball as well as the boys[;] them that are not large enough to play ball jump rope. The teacher likes it as well as we do[;] he sent after three or four base balls to day. . . ."[94] Annie Howes, Vassar Class of 1874, recalled that she had played "hop-scotch on the sidewalks in Boston, and baseball and prisoner's base with the children of the neighborhood."[95]

It was primarily the boys and girls of the nation's public and rural schools who played baseball together. The adolescent sons and daughters of the nation's elite were usually educated separately in institutions tailored to prepare them for their appropriate social and gender roles as adults. Wealthy boys generally attended elite college preparatory or military academies; their sisters went to finishing schools and seminaries. Even in communities where boys' and girls' academies and seminaries existed in close proximity, adults strove to ensure that students intermingled only under tightly controlled conditions with plenty of chaperones on hand.[96] Though girls and boys, young men and women, often found ways to rebel against the moral and social restraints imposed upon them by adults, it was more difficult for them to do so at boarding schools, where they were subjected to the round-the-clock hypervigilance of administrators and faculty acting in loco parentis. The financial solvency and reputation of boarding schools depended on administrators providing a safe and wholesome atmosphere that conformed to parental expectations.

Invariably, the students at female schools were subjected to more-intense scrutiny and control than young men; it was difficult for them to play baseball on school grounds without the approval of administrators and parents. Grace Aspinwall was fortunate to attend a school where the proprietor allowed female students to play baseball. It is evident from Aspinwall's account that Sarah Porter was initially hesitant to allow her students to organize baseball teams. Porter could rationalize that playing baseball was a healthful activity for her students, even as she anticipated backlash from those who believed baseball was either inappropriate (unladylike) or dangerous for young women.[97] Porter advocated a healthy lifestyle for her students that included mandatory daily walks and calisthenics, plus vigorous outdoor activities such as sledding and skating in the winter and horseback riding and rowing in the spring. Porter demanded feminine decorum from students yet she did not hesitate to deviate from social norms when they were counterproductive to her students' present and future well-being. She refused, for example, to allow her students to wear bustles and long trains on their dresses because she knew bulky clothing would limit their physical activity.[98]

Despite Porter's liberal attitude toward exercise for young women, she still had to be convinced to allow her students to play baseball. The persistent narratives of the sport as a physically demanding and manly pastime were beginning to influence women's perception of the game. Kate Stevens, captain of the student-organized Tunxis Base Ball Club at Porter's school, later wrote that her team had only played, "or tried to play," a few games before "sundry, rather preemptory letters from our parents put a stop to that somewhat strenuous exercise."[99] Note that parental criticism focused on how strenuous baseball was, not that it had a reputation as a man's game. In this case, the narrative of baseball as a game best suited to strong, vigorous adult men provoked fear in some parents, who agreed with then-prevalent assumptions that vigorous exercise for postmenarcheal young women could seriously harm their reproductive organs.[100]

Despite lingering concern over the safety of vigorous activities for young women, many found opportunities to play baseball. In 1870, the *Lancaster (Ohio) Gazette* reported that students at the South Senior and South Junior Grammar schools had formed baseball teams and were playing each other several times per week. The players ranged in age from twelve to sixteen and used balls and bats that had been adapted to suit them.[101] One hundred fifteen miles away, students at a school in Cincinnati organized the "Favorites" and "Mountain Maids" teams.[102] Baseball was popular with male and female students at the Punahou School in the Kingdom of Hawaii, where former New York Knickerbocker Alexander Cartwright enrolled his three sons.[103] Male and female students played baseball at Punahou before the school bell rang and during the one-hour noon recess. In May 1875, the school newspaper, the *Punahou Mirror*, reported: "The young ladies of Punahou play ball now. Their mothers played before them and their grandmothers before that period, probably, and why shouldn't they play . . . ?"[104] The article provides insights on contemporary attitudes about girls playing baseball. Note the challenge implied in the retort, "and why shouldn't they play?" and the comment that love of baseball was passed from mothers to daughters and sometimes even from grandmothers to granddaughters.

Like boys and men, girls and women used baseball as a medium for camaraderie and socialization. In April 1872, fourteen-year-old Alice Stone Blackwell, daughter of women's rights leaders Henry Blackwell and Lucy Stone, wrote in her diary: "At recess Sadie and the rest of us played catch, and she and Hattie Burdett planned a base ball party, which Sadie asked me to join, saying she was sure I should make a good player. Of course I said yes."[105] Blackwell's use of the term "party," rather than "team," implies that baseball was serving a social role for the young teenagers. Later entries indicate the extent to which Blackwell had internalized narratives about baseball's special place in the broader culture. Watching her school friends play a game at Harris Grammar School, she sadly realized that she was "absolutely and utterly ignorant of the game."[106] Blackwell learned to play baseball by watching her friends play. She and her schoolmates played baseball regularly at recess throughout the school term, whether it was cold and wet or "stewing hot."[107] The process of team selection for games was an opportunity for Blackwell and her peers to demonstrate social loyalties— loyalties that went beyond athletic ability. On May 4, Blackwell lamented to her journal that she was the last player team captain Mary Scholonbach selected, even though Blackwell's best friend Sadie kept urging her to choose Alice.

Alice Blackwell's journal is one of few personal accounts of nineteenth-century girls playing baseball. It provides important insights into how the players viewed what they were doing. Blackwell made more than a dozen references to baseball in her journal in 1872, and a handful more in 1873. Each was recorded in the same matter-of-fact manner in which she spoke about playing croquet (something she did frequently during summer months), rowing, swimming, and reading. For Blackwell, playing baseball was a natural activity for girls—it merited no special editorial comment. As the daughter of two ardent and vocal women's rights advocates, Blackwell grew up in a home where dismantling gender barriers for women was a priority. Steeped in social consciousness, if Blackwell had perceived that baseball was not a gender-neutral activity for school girls, she likely would have commented in her journal about how she and her friends were challenging social mores by playing. Baseball was not the central focus of Blackwell's life any more than it was for the thousands of girls and boys across the country who played. It was just one of many enjoyable diversions that filled time during the long passage of childhood. Blackwell played baseball frequently enough that her mother made it a point to mention it during a speech she gave at her daughter's graduation from Harris Grammar School as valedictorian, but it was not so important to Alice that she continued to play as an adult.[108]

During the 1970s, schoolgirls would have to sue for the right to play on Little League baseball teams but, a century earlier, girls like Blackwell and her friends could freely engage in the sport many were proclaiming the national pastime without fear of criticism or reprisal. Nineteenth-century school girls benefited from the fact that baseball's reputation as a man's game had not yet solidified, and that few baseball boosters considered them a threat to the emerging structure and cultural creed of baseball. As gender norms came under increasing attack from determined women's rights activists in the late nineteenth century, however, juvenile female baseball players sometimes became symbolic pawns in the ongoing battle over gender ideals and women's rights. In 1873, the *Woman's Exponent* announced: "Ohio girl students play base ball, and the newspapers talk of it. Well?"[109] The "Well?" in this Mormon women's rights publication reflects the readiness of adult women to defend youthful female baseball players from all who would question their motives.

Female Collegians and Baseball[110]

Even if they played baseball only for fun, and not to challenge gender mores, adult women were sensitive to how they might be perceived, and consciously sought to deflect potential criticism. Deference to public opinion was particularly common on college campuses. Whether they played at all-women colleges or coeducational colleges, female collegiate baseball players ignored the swelling chorus of voices asserting that baseball was a man's game and played anyway—but they did so in a way that tried to accommodate prevailing gender ideals. They often hid their games from the public gaze, navigated shorter base paths, and wore long dresses and even corsets on the field. Even if they only played for fun and tried to conform to feminine ideals, female collegiate baseball players were symbolically challenging evolving narratives about women's supposed biological frailty and baseball's function.

Only a small percentage of nineteenth-century women ever had the opportunity to attend college.[111] Not only did many consider college a waste of time for women, some believed higher education would kill or maim them. In March 1869, the director of physical culture at Vassar College observed that physicians and critics of women's higher education were convinced that four years of vigorous study would leave young women prepared only "for the physician or the grave."[112] Some women scoffed at such doomsaying; they understood that social custom, not biology, was the greatest obstacle to women's aspirations for higher education and success in politics, sports, and professions. Neither side knew for certain if it was right, however; consequently the first generations of women collegians understood that they were under intense scrutiny. Francis A. Wood, who joined Vassar's faculty as instructor of music in 1866 and remained on staff for more than forty years, remembered that it was "impressed upon the whole [Vassar] family that the higher education of women was an experiment, and that the world was looking on, watching its success or defeat. The good of the college was the watchword, and not mere gratification of individual preferences."[113] It was in this context of uncertainty that some collegiate women played baseball.

Several patterns emerge from an analysis of women's collegiate baseball, no matter when or where it was played. First, nineteenth-century players generally represented a cross-section of the student body at any given school at any given time. For example, of the thirty-six students at Vassar College whose names appear on the rosters of the Laurel, Abenakis, and Precocious ball clubs in 1866 and 1867, fourteen (39 percent) left school before the end of their second year, while eleven players eventually graduated. Seventy-two percent of the twenty-five players who never graduated were "special" or "preparatory" students—the same percentage of students enrolled in the special or preparatory courses at Vassar during the 1866–1867 school year.[114] There was nothing to distinguish baseball players socially, politically, or culturally from their fellow students. Marriage and childbearing rates for former players and nonplayers were indistinguishable, and the same percentage of players as nonplayers went on to work outside the home (or not). The vast majority of collegiate baseball players, like the majority of female collegians, were white. In fact, there is no evidence to-date of black women collegians organizing baseball teams—whether this is because they did not organize teams or because they lacked the means to preserve the records of their actions remains to be discovered through future research.

A second consistent pattern is that baseball was never the most popular sport on college campuses. Throughout the nineteenth century, would-be collegiate baseball team organizers sometimes struggled to field teams, especially after tennis, golf, and basketball appeared on campuses. From baseball's first appearance at colleges like Vassar, Smith, Olivet, and the University of North Dakota, it remained primarily a sport played only sporadically on student-organized teams, by a small percentage of the female students. Even after physical educators began offering baseball as part of their curricula, only a small percentage of students signed up. Lilian Tappan reported that only 25 of 338 (7 percent) students selected baseball as their optional form of exercise during the spring term in 1877. Only gardening, with 24 students, attracted fewer. The other options in their order of popularity were: walking (116), croquet (108), and boating (94).[115] Despite the relatively small numbers of nineteenth-century female college baseball players, it is clear from their surviving yearbooks, school newspapers, letters, diaries, and scrapbooks that those who did play thoroughly enjoyed it. A fair number considered their playing days such an important aspect of their collegiate experience that they fondly wrote about them decades later.[116]

A third pattern characterizing nineteenth-century female collegiate baseball is that the majority of players tried to conform to prevailing gender ideals about femininity while playing baseball. They hid their games from male spectators and wore the latest feminine fashions. "Men's sports were played before stands full of spectators; women's sports were played behind hedges," writes historian Pamela Dean. "The fields were carefully screened and 'no papas or even grand-papas' ever saw those bloomers."[117] Though Dean was referring to athletic games on southern campuses in the late nineteenth and early twentieth centuries, her comments apply throughout the nineteenth century. The baseball players at women's colleges had little difficulty segregating their activities from the male gaze because many of their colleges had been purposely constructed in secluded, rural areas. Female baseball players on coeducational campuses had a more difficult time avoiding the male gaze but could mitigate their circumstances by wearing feminine clothing and avoiding aggressive, overly athletic play. Newspaper articles about female college baseball games sometimes mentioned players stopping games to attend to stray hairpins or torn skirts. As late as 1901, Livinia Hart, a former collegian, recalled that students at several women's colleges had organized baseball teams "some years ago" but that none lasted a full season because players had found it an "utter impossibility" to play ball and "attend to the train."[118] On rare occasions, corsets and heavy skirts could protect female ball players. Minnie Stephens, who played on a baseball team at Smith College in 1880, recalled one such moment: "One vicious batter drove a ball directly into the belt line of her opponent," Stephens wrote years later, "and had it not been for the rigid steel corset clasp worn in those days, she would have been knocked out completely."[119]

Livinia Hart's comment about the short-lived baseball teams of the 1890s reflects another consistent pattern of nineteenth-century female collegiate baseball teams. Most teams lasted only a few weeks to a couple of months. For most of the century, women's college baseball teams, like most other sports teams, were organized and led by students. Students formed teams for pick-up games or competitions between "houses" (dormitories) or classes. Even after physical educators began integrating student sports teams into their programs, female baseball teams did not represent their institutions as men's sports teams did. Thus, team duration was tied to a set period in the physical education curricula, not to a season of intercollegiate competition. It was only after the turn of the twentieth century when "women's baseball" (and later, softball) became an official intercollegiate sport that colleges and institutions began fielding women's teams year after year. Baseball was just one of myriad new activities nineteenth-century female collegians could explore during their time at college, so it is not surprising that students did not devote themselves extensively to the sport.

Another reason female collegiate baseball teams were short-lived is that many of the collegiate players were not willing to endure the criticism sometimes heaped upon them by fellow students or by male peers convinced they were trying to emulate men or push a women's rights agenda. In the *Class Book* for 1878, an unnamed Vassar student recalled how difficult it had been finding enough students willing to play baseball:

> After hesitation on the part of some,
> Who feared it really couldn't be done
> With the prudence and propriety due
> From ladies, in Miss Terry's view;
> And some who feared the "cold world's" sneer,
> That is, the part of it which is here,
> and some who thought the Po'keepsie papers
> Would bristle all over with scandalous tapers,
> Our energetic captain succeeded
> In getting all the recruits she needed.[120]

Even twenty years later, Vassar students recalled how opposition to young women playing baseball deterred some students. In 1896 the *Vassar Miscellany* included a retrospective article about the Vassar Athletic Association. It noted that at one point students had organized class baseball teams at the prompting of the gymnasium instructor and were enjoying the game thoroughly. "The conservative world, however, looked upon this as a step beyond its ideas of propriety," lamented the anonymous writer, "and one by one the girls dropped out, influenced, doubtless, by the opposition of family and friends. Thus baseball was given up."[121]

By and large, female collegians did not play baseball to protest their exclusion from certain social and cultural spheres; they played baseball for the same reason male students did—because it was fun. Nonetheless, because cultural narratives about baseball were changing, female collegians had a different relationship to the game than their male peers did. Even commentators who seemed favorable to the idea of adult women playing baseball often teased them or likened them to children. In October 1869, the *Chicago Times* announced that students at the Northwestern Female College, at Evanston, had organized the Diana Base Ball Club. It printed a challenge to the team made by the "Baltics"—a junior (boys') team. The tone of the invitation was patronizing and dripping with gendered allegory: "Hoping that as ancient Diana was goddess of the chase, so may you, the modern goddesses, consent to become the protecting deities of our national game in this vicinity, and, with goodness that goddesses and the ladies, their equals, are famous for, accept this challenge."[122] The adult players declined the invitation, informing the *Times* that they were seeking an "older game" and would happily play any "regular senior organization." Baseball at Northwestern Female College was short-lived because, that same year, the trustees of Northwestern University decided to admit female students, and enrollment at the all-female institution declined sharply.[123]

The thirty-six students who had played baseball at Vassar in the spring of 1866 and 1867 had done so with the tacit support of administrators who believed in the importance of outdoor exercise for women. By the time baseball returned to Vassar in the fall of 1875, cultural attitudes toward the sport had changed to the extent that students had to consider the potential negative ramifications if they chose to play. In October 1875, *The Vassar Miscellany* asked its readers, "Could baseball be called improvements or the reverse? As mankind is divided on that subject, we will not enlarge on our advancement in that respect."[124] The student paper was responding to a sudden (but short-lived) surge of interest in baseball, promoted by Vassar's new resident physician, Dr. Helen Webster. With Webster's encouragement, students organized seven or eight baseball teams with names like the Sure-pops, the Daisy-Clippers, and the Royals.[125] In early November, Katharine Griffis wrote to her friend, Mary: "Ball playing is all the rage at present; there are a number of clubs. . . ."[126] Not only were students playing baseball at Vassar, but students were turning out in droves to watch them. The games became a highlight of the social scene on campus. "[T]he ball ground is the prettiest sight in the P.M. that you can imagine," Griffis continued. "All the clubs have different costumes & their crowds of girls with their bright shawls, pretty camp chairs, etc., go out to watch the games & it looks so cheerful & lively."[127]

The initial enthusiasm for baseball waned on campus after the 1875–1876 school year despite the fact that Lilian Tappan, Vassar's director of the Department of Physical Education, oversaw a mandatory physical fitness program that included baseball as one of the optional activities. *The Vassar Miscellany* reported in October 1876 that the baseball clubs had been "consolidated and reorganized."[128] In fact, Sophia Foster and others "who had learned the value of rigorous play" managed to reconstitute only two of the baseball teams. Foster's identification of the baseball players as students who had "learned the value of rigorous play" indicates the extent to which young women of her generation continued to worry about claims that they might kill or permanently maim themselves by overtaxing their minds and bodies. Foster and her teammates also had to consider the increasingly gendered reputation of the national pastime. The students who played baseball at Vassar in the latter half of the 1870s were challenging the emerging ideal that baseball was a tool for shaping masculine identity. Few students were willing to contend with the backlash that ensued when word got out about their games. Foster recalled that "the public, so far as it knew of our playing, was shocked" even though the students played on the secluded grounds of the campus. After a player injured her leg running the bases, Foster and the others who carried her to the infirmary were certain this would put an end to their games. They were surprised when Dr. Webster told them that they should keep playing even though the public would likely condemn the game as too "violent" for women. Parents had their say about baseball too. Foster believed the reason so few students continued to play baseball was because "there was too much pressure against it from disapproving mothers."[129]

It was not just mothers who deterred students from playing baseball—peer pressure played a role too. In January 1876, editors of the school newspaper observed: "After a senior class has indulged in base ball clubs, and spent the autumn in displaying its Gym suits and powers of running at match games,—after that, its reputation for dignity among the under graduates may be regarded as a minus quantity."[130] In July, the editors mentioned the "much condemned base ball clubs" and acknowledged that archery was far more popular because it "had a flavor of aristocracy that base-ball lacked."[131] Some of the peer pressure came from students at other campuses. Male students enjoyed poking fun at female students whenever they perceived those students were overstepping their gender boundaries. In 1880, for example, Princeton students joked about the athletic activities of Vassar students:

> Quoth he to chaff her, I've heard they row,
> Play base ball, swim and bend the bow,
> But, really now, I'd like to know—
> If they play foot-ball at Vassar?[132]

It required a good deal of self-confidence to continue playing baseball in the face of this kind of peer pressure.

Apart from the students at Vassar and the female colleges in Evanston, Illinois, there is no evidence of students at other women's colleges organizing baseball teams between 1865 and 1879. There is only one known instance of female students at a coeducational institution organizing teams during this period. That was in Salem, Iowa, where male and female students and teachers at Whittier College each organized their own baseball teams in the fall of 1873.[133] Annie Packer, who ran the female department and taught mathematics, was a member of the women's team; C. C. Picket, principal of the men's department, played on the men's team.[134] Whittier College was a Quaker school specializing in teacher training. It had succeeded the Salem seminary, which residents had founded in 1841 and opened to its first class of college students in April 1868.[135] It is uncertain how many students attended Whittier in 1873 when the baseball teams played, but the graduating class of 1874 had only eight students in it—three women and five men. The institution was quite isolated—accessible via a ten-mile stagecoach ride from the nearest railroad station in Mount Pleasant. The male and female baseball teams most likely scrimmaged each other rather than challenging teams from nearby communities. Their isolated play posed little if any challenge to the emerging cultural narrative about baseball as a sport best suited for adult men.

Though it might seem logical that women on coeducational college campuses would be more likely than students at all-female colleges to play baseball, considering they would have regular opportunities to watch male students play, there are several reasons why this was not the case. First, because women collegians were under significant scrutiny from critics convinced that higher education would "unsex" or physically harm them, most women collegians scrupulously sought to demonstrate that they could be both feminine *and* intellectual. This meant conforming their dress and behavior to the prevailing gender guidelines of their era. For women on coeducational campuses bold enough to try their hand at the increasingly masculinized sport of baseball, finding a place to play where male students could not watch was much more difficult than it was for those at women's colleges.

Another reason why female baseball players were not as numerous at coeducational institutions as they were at all-women schools was that relatively few women attended any given coeducational institution at any given time. While all-women schools like Vassar, Wellesley, and Smith had two hundred to three hundred female students *each* on campus in the 1870s, private and state schools of the time generally enrolled only a few dozen women at most. The University of Nebraska had one of the largest populations of female students in the 1870s; it fluctuated between a low of twenty-seven female students in 1873–1874 to a high of 123 in 1875–1876—the only academic year prior to 1880 when it enrolled more than one hundred female students. Michigan State University had ten or fewer women throughout the 1870s. Iowa State Agricultural College (the future Iowa State University), the first coeducational state college, welcomed its inaugural class in 1869—it had 173 students, only thirty-seven of whom were women. On the women's campuses, where young women were often encouraged to try their hand at nontraditional activities, only a small percentage of students ever expressed an interest in playing baseball; it would have been difficult to field a team of nine players at a coeducational institution where only small cadres of women attended at any given time.

Another deterrent to women's baseball teams on coeducational campuses was that many of the female students who attended them were commuters or lived off-campus in privately procured housing. It took decades before most coeducational institutions of higher learning provided dormitories for their female students. At the women's colleges, where the majority of students lived and dined together on campus, it was much easier for them to form social bonds, which then led to the creation of extracurricular clubs and teams. Women who commuted to coeducational institutions had more difficulty forming the strong social ties that bound other college students.

Most nineteenth-century female baseball teams at coeducational institutions did not debut until the 1890s, when enough women were attending individual institutions to make it possible to find enough willing to play. Another key factor in the growth of teams after 1890 was that thousands of women had attended college by then, decisively demonstrating that women were as intellectually capable as men and that college life would not kill or maim them. There do not seem to be any common threads between the coeducational schools where female students played baseball—some were secular institutions, others were denominational; some were located in the East and Midwest, others in the West and South. Some offered women degrees on the same basis as men; others allowed women to attend but only granted them diplomas or certificates, not full-fledged degrees. Some had dormitories for female students on campuses; others did not. The common factor at coeducational colleges, like that at all-women institutions, was that players tried to conform to feminine ideals while playing.

Adult Women and Baseball

While female collegians had little inclination (or opportunities) to play baseball on campuses during the 1860s and 1870s, there was no shortage of teenagers and adult women who played on civic and pick-up teams throughout the country. They found baseball to be an enjoyable and exhilarating activity. Girls and women organized more than fifty civic and pick-up teams between 1865 and 1879.[136] Because newspaper articles about these teams were usually exceedingly brief, it is often difficult to determine the ages of players. However, there is no question that adult women did play baseball during this era. Many, if not most, played simply for fun and exercise, although a pick-up game in Cincinnati between the Invincibles and Woman's Suffrage Base-ball Clubs in September 1869 may have been inspired by a major meeting of woman's rights activists, including Lucy Stone and Susan B. Anthony, that the city had hosted two weeks earlier.[137] Just like many of the amateur men's teams of the era, women's teams sported clever names like, "Longstockings," "Leap Year Winners," "Striped Stockings," "Young Independents," and the "Calicos."[138]

Most women's civic and pick-up teams of the 1860s and 1870s were located in the Northeast, East, and Midwest. This reflected the popularity of men's baseball in those regions. There is scant evidence of women organizing teams in southern or western states during the 1870s, even though men's teams were fairly common in those regions by the end of the decade. The only known western and southern states with women's civic and pick-up teams at this time were Kansas, Iowa, North Carolina, and Kentucky.[139] The lack of evidence of women's baseball teams in the West and South may be more to the relative paucity of digitized newspaper sources for those areas rather than to a lack of teams; time will tell, as historians explore newly digitized sources in those regions. It is possible, however, that there simply *were* fewer female baseball teams in the West and South owing to demographic and cultural differences in those regions.

One early women's civic baseball club in the Midwest garnered a fair amount of press despite the fact that players banned spectators from their only known game. The *Rockford Weekly Register-Gazette, Chicago Tribune,* and *New York Clipper* all carried articles about the game played by the "Marrieds" and "Singles" of Rockford, Illinois, on August 16, 1870 on the grounds of the local men's team; the Singles prevailed, 33–3.[140] The fact that the women barred spectators indicates that they were not trying to use the sport to openly challenge women's exclusion from many public realms—they were simply having a good time. The women who played on the Rockford teams had been afforded ample opportunities to watch quality baseball matches in their hometown before they organized their own teams. Rockford, a city of about 15,000 residents, was blessed with a talented men's baseball team—the Forest City nine. Some of the women had probably witnessed the game in which the sixteen-year-old future Hall of Fame pitcher, sporting goods magnate, and National League cofounder Albert Goodwill Spalding pitched the Forest City nine to victory against the visiting Washington (D.C.) Nationals in 1867—that team's only defeat during its midwestern tour.

Although most pick-up and civic teams in the 1870s were short-lived and played only intrasquad games, a handful of reports indicate that girls and women did sometimes play female teams from other cities or local boys or men's teams. In July 1871, a paper in Indiana reported that the *Louisville Commercial* was thinking about challenging the female baseball team of Crawfordsville.[141] There is no word on whether this game ever took place but, five years later, the *St. Louis Globe-Democrat* reported that the Leap Year Winners, a female baseball club in Virginia, Cass County, Illinois had recently "vanquished" a men's team in a match game.[142] In June 1877, a team of "young ladies" in Kinsley, Kansas, played a "spirited" game with the "Kinsley Free Booters." The following month a group of young ladies in nearby Fredonia defeated a team of young men (the paper alternately called them girls and boys) in a three-inning match, 28 to 9. The paper reported that the Fredonia "ladies" were planning a match against the ladies' nine from Neodesha in the near future.[143] Sometimes individual female baseball players challenged men in head-to-head competition. The *Elk*

County Advocate of Ridgway, Pennsylvania, reported in June 1875: "Reading has a beautiful female base ballist, who challenges 'Jhonny' Briton of Lewistown."[144]

Newspaper coverage of nineteenth-century women who played baseball with or against men differed based on the social class of the players. Reporters generally wrote matter-of-fact articles about middle- and upper-class women playing baseball in mixed company or in front of men; their unspoken assumption was that these women were only having fun—not challenging social mores about women's proper place. In contrast, commentators frequently excoriated the working-class women who joined barnstorming baseball teams and played in front of male spectators and (sometimes) against men's teams.[145] In this case, the assumption was that women who would accept money to play (or work) in mixed company were dangerously immoral.

Critiquing the Counternarrative

The public did not know quite what to make of female baseball players. Many believed that baseball was both fun and fashionable and that it was as useful for the physical health of girls and women as it was for boys and men. Others were not so sure. The cultural narratives about baseball being a manly pastime did influence public perceptions about the sport. Like *The Days' Doings,* which had associated the female baseball game in Peterboro, New York, with the women's rights movement, some began to assume that women's increasingly common participation in vigorous sports like baseball was really a covert tactic in the battle for equal rights. They believed women were using athletics as a wedge to open a breach in the male sphere through which women could pour to capture occupations and public roles previously reserved exclusively for men.

Depending on one's opinion about the impending rupture in gender role boundaries, some vociferously protested against athleticism in women, while others welcomed it. Both groups suspected that physically robust women could wrest away from men what verbal banter on the lecture circuit had failed to deliver—the vote. In July 1870, the *New York Times* described the "novel spectacle" of a group of young women from Pittsburgh competing in a mile and a half rowing competition. The reporter could not decide whether public exhibitions like rowing would improve women "mentally and morally, or even physically," but he was confident of one thing—if women continued to demonstrate their physical strength in public, they would be able to overcome male opposition to their demands for equal rights and suffrage. "No doubt it will take many boat-races *and base-ball matches* (emphasis added) to harden feminine muscles to successful competition with the monopolists of the ballot-box," he concluded, "[b]ut of this the champions of female suffrage may be sure: that they will find more account in one such victory as we have suggested than in a dozen triumphs of the rostrum."[146]

Many were appalled by the idea of physically robust women wresting the ballot from men and barging into masculine preserves en masse. A month after the *Times* article appeared, the *Morning Oregonian* of Portland reported that women in Detroit were learning to play baseball. "What with female ball clubs, female boat clubs and the like it would seem that the fair sex are likely to secure their 'rights' quite as rapidly as the most radical would desire."[147] In 1871, a male baseball booster named William R. Hooper erroneously reported that baseball was standing in the breech against further encroachments of women into the masculine sphere: "And not only is the game health-giving, but we point with pride to its moral influence," Hooper wrote. "It is the conservative power of American society. While woman is soliciting office and demanding the franchise, base-ball clubs are only accessible to men."[148]

Hooper's assertion that only men played organized baseball was wrong, but the fact he *believed* baseball was standing strong against the assaults of women's rights activists is important. He was relieved that while men were finding it increasingly difficult to justify denying women access to professions and the ballot box, they felt no pressure to admit women to their baseball clubs. "Whether this arises from that innate love of the graceful that would keep a woman from jumping loftily into air after a ball on the fly," he wrote, "or that catching in laps is forbidden by the rules of the game, or that the rapid running of the bases is inconsistent with the stability of chignons and waterfalls," he was not sure. Despite the undisputable reality that countless women still believed baseball was an appropriate *feminine* activity, Hooper held out hope that baseball would continue to be a safe haven for men: "Our female Canutes are told by the wave of base-ball now rolling over the land, 'Thus far mayest thou go, and no farther.'"[149]

Hooper's hope that baseball would continue to serve as a line in the sand against women's rights encroachments was a relatively rare perspective. Public opinion about female pick-up and civic baseball teams continued to be generally positive, although some reporters teased women for their lack of athleticism or belittled the idea of women engaging in serious athletic competition. The *Iosco County Gazette* commented that while some of the young women on the Amateur Base Ball Club in East Tawas, Michigan, were "quite proficient" at the game, most were poor batters.[150] James M. Bailey's comical tale about six inept female baseball players in Danbury, Connecticut, proved so popular in 1878 that Mark Twain incorporated it into his *Library of Humor* a decade later. Twain's reprint included an illustration showing grown women awkwardly trying to pitch and throw while another stands nearby fixing her hat.[151]

The use of humor to demean female baseball players was a tactic commonly employed by opponents of women's suffrage. Reporters frequently portrayed women's rights activists as either masculinized or overly concerned with their physical appearance to the point that it prevented them from giving proper attention to serious matters (like casting an informed vote).[152] As the structure and cultural creed of baseball began to take on a masculinized reputation, more and more commentators sought to discount or diminish women's relationship to the sport. In 1876, for example, papers in Michigan teased that players on the female baseball club in Manitowoc, Wisconsin, "stop when running the bases to fix their bustles" and the *New York Evening Telegram* reported that just because Gilead, Connecticut, had a female baseball nine "doesn't make it a femi-nine game, for all that. Gilead can't bamboozle the public mind that way."[153] The *Evening Telegram*'s comment indicates the extent to which the cultural center of baseball was shifting as increasing numbers of individuals internalized the narrative that baseball was a man's game. This unwillingness to acknowledge that baseball was as much a woman's game as it was a man's game would play a decisive role in creating the myth of baseball's gendered heritage. No matter how many girls and women played baseball, those who wished to reserve baseball for men could simply argue that just because women played did not make baseball a woman's game.

3. 1865–1879: Commodifying a National Pastime

The "Professional" Game

If those who really enjoy base ball as a sport desire to retain
for it the interest of the respectable classes, they must sternly
set their faces against the professional player. In every point of
view he is an eminently undesirable person, and he ought to
be peremptorily and completely suppressed.
—*New York Times,* March 8, 1872

About 1,500 people, including half-a-dozen ladies, assembled
at the ball grounds on Tuesday afternoon, attracted thither by
the announcement that two nines composed entirely of female
players would contend for the mastery. Those who attended
the game with the expectation of witnessing an exhibition of
low character were disappointed, for the women conducted
themselves with entire propriety, and paid no attention
whatever to the crowd, except to join now and then in the
laugh arising from some of their many errors.
—*Boston Post,* July 30, 1879

GEORGE E. VAILLANT ONCE OBSERVED that "the passage of time
renders truth itself relative. . . . It is all too common for caterpillars to become
butterflies and then to maintain that in their youth they had been little butterflies."[1] Today, Major League Baseball (MLB)[2] is a multibillion-dollar business
dominated by male players and team owners.[3] Over the years, many have assumed that the modern structure of the MLB is simply a larger-scale version
of early professional baseball. Nothing could be further from the truth; in fact,
there are few parallels between modern professional baseball and early professional baseball. Perhaps the most significant distinction between the two is that
the early professional game was gender-neutral—both men and women earned
their livings on baseball diamonds in the nineteenth century. This startling
fact is virtually unknown to modern audiences because, though both men and

women participated in the early commodification of baseball, it was men who ultimately constructed a structure for the professional game that marginalized and later erased women's involvement with the developing business. Although today's elite professional baseball players are often idolized as heroes, early professional players (male and female) were often condemned—the former for introducing filthy lucre into the supposedly pristine pastime, and the latter for subverting gender ideals of femininity by playing in public for money.

Scholars have written volumes about the evolution of professional baseball, but no one has yet highlighted the gender-neutral aspects of the nascent professional game. By applying modern definitions of professionalism (that is, elite athletes paid to compete at the highest levels of a sport) to the past, many scholars have misrepresented the early professional game and denied the mantle of professionalism to the myriad women who earned their living playing baseball in the nineteenth century. Technically speaking, neither male nor female baseball players met the criteria of "professionals" in the strictest sense of the word as it was defined in the latter half of the nineteenth century. Though eighteenth-century dictionaries granted the status of "profession" to any "calling, vocation or known employment," those published in the latter half of the nineteenth century linked the term to callings, vocations, and employments that required "a learned education."[4] This semantic distinction evolved during a period of social and cultural upheaval in the United States when the forces of industrialization, urbanization, and immigration were transforming society and cultural institutions. One of the ways the emerging middle class sought to distinguish itself from the masses was to develop more stringent credentialing requirements for "professions." Education became the locus of differentiation between respectable professionals and charlatans pretending to be respectable.

Dictionary definitions aside, however, the basic understanding of a professional in the nineteenth century was someone who earned money doing something—particularly something that required practiced skill. When members of the National Association of Base Ball Players (NABBP) began arguing about amateurism and professionalism in the 1850s and 1860s, no one claimed that paid players were not really professionals because they lacked a "learned education." A person who played baseball for pay was a "professional" as far as advocates of amateurism were concerned. Countless teenage girls and young women met this criteria.[5] However, because female professional baseball players did not organize themselves into professional players' associations or create enduring league structures as men did, scholars have tended to place them in a separate analytical category from male professional players based solely on gender. A different historical narrative emerges when this artificial distinction is removed and scholars shift the focus from gender to the early professional game itself. The new narrative reveals that male and female professional baseball players had more in common with each other than they did with those who championed amateur baseball.

Adult male players who sought to legitimize baseball as a scientific and godly recreational choice for adult men had successfully portrayed children and loafers as the undesirable "other" during the 1840s and 1850s. By the late 1860s, however, the line between male players and "other" became blurred as amateurs and professionals wrestled over the future of the sport. Supporters of amateurism reserved the mantle of respectability for themselves; their "other" was professionalism and they railed against those who would risk corrupting the game for personal gain. The girls and women who continued to play baseball on civic and pick-up teams and at schools and colleges were theoretically aligned with those upholding the amateur spirit of the sport; those who played baseball for money on barnstorming teams were squarely in the camp of the professional "others." They too were accused of corrupting the game for money, but they faced the added charges of perverting morality and undermining feminine virtue.

Professional baseball had to overcome significant cultural obstacles to become a multibillion-dollar business. During its infancy, both men and women played on teams whose managers had to craft marketing narratives emphasizing the exciting and respectable nature of their entertainment product in order to attract middle- and upper-class audiences. Managers tried to convince potential spectators that players' behavior was respectable on and off the field and that the entertainment product offered was suitable for women and children. The following quotations are from an 1889 advertisement for a women's professional game and from an 1882 advertisement for a men's professional game, respectively:

> These exhibitions are first-class in every particular, moral in every sense, free from every objectional [sic] feature, and can be visited by anyone, even the most refined and fastidious, and these games and pastimes by ladies have been endorsed by leading newspapers of the country, also by noted clergymen and the leading medical faculty of the country.[6]

> No beer, liquors or cigars will be allowed in the grand stand, where an attendance of ladies will be especially invited. The desire is to make this division of the ground so attractive and inoffensive that ladies will find it a pleasure, as they did some years ago, in patronizing the game.[7]

Despite these marketing strategies, many, if not the majority, of spectators at most male and female baseball games in the nineteenth century came from the ranks of the working class, and newspapers routinely noted the "rough" nature of crowds at women's contests.

Efforts to popularize early professional baseball were largely unsuccessful. Though championship matches sometimes drew tens of thousands of spectators, most professional games (male and female) were sparsely attended by today's standards. If success as professionals was measured in terms of fan interest, then women professionals actually held a slight edge over their male counterparts. In 1879, for example, six of the eight teams in the National League averaged fewer than one thousand fans per game. The Red Stockings and Blue Stockings professional women's teams (which traveled together playing games against each other) played in seven of the eight cities that had National League franchises, drawing an average of 1,130–1,335 fans—more than the NL team in each city.[8]

That these women's teams outdrew men's teams is particularly noteworthy because of the differences in how men's and women's professional teams scheduled games. Men's teams played approximately forty home games and forty road games—scheduled in advance. These teams could develop loyal fan bases because they repeatedly played in the same eight cities. Female teams did not have this luxury. The Red Stockings and Blue Stockings traveled more than three thousand miles and played at least twenty-eight games in twenty-seven cities between July 4 and September 1, 1879. Many of their games were scheduled on-the-fly, as advance men traveled ahead of them, negotiating terms with the owners of playing venues near the rail lines. Though numerical attendance figures are available for only twenty-three of the women's games, the total of 34,500 spectators for those games is more than attended all forty of the home games in five of the seven major league cities where they played. Only the pennant-winning Providence Grays and the second-place Boston Red Stockings attracted more spectators—and they needed forty games to do it.

Male and female professional baseball teams struggled to make money in the first decades of the professional game. Profit margins were exceedingly slim;

TABLE 1. Attendance for Red Stocking and Blue Stocking games in NL cities (1879)

National League Team	Final Standings	NL Attendance (40 Home Games)	NL Average (Total / 40)	Female Team Attendance in NL City
Chicago White Stockings	4	67,687	1,692	Did Not Play
Providence Grays	1	47,595	1,189	1,200
Boston Red Stockings	2	36,501	913	600–800 or 1,500
Cincinnati Reds	5	28,000	700	1,000–1,700 Game 1 4,000 Game 2
Buffalo Bisons	3	26,000	650	About 1,000
Cleveland Blues	6	25,000	625	800–1,000
Troy Trojans	8	12,000	300	1,500
Syracuse Stars	7	9,000	225	300

travel was difficult and inclement weather could (and did) wreak havoc with team finances. In April 1875, Harry Wright, arguably one of the most successful early professional players and managers, informed Boston Red Stockings treasurer Frederick Long that the team had run out of money in Washington, D.C. because of rain-outs; it needed an infusion of funds to pay the hotel bill and to purchase tickets to get to the next scheduled stop. Scholar Richard Hershberger notes: "The scary thing is, this was the Bostons: by far the most efficiently run club in the NA."[9] It was not unusual for professional men's teams to forfeit away games at the end of a season rather than incur the necessary expenses to travel to a distant venue. Many of the early women's professional teams collapsed for lack of funds midseason, leaving players to appeal to charity to get home.[10]

Professional baseball was the product of emerging social, cultural, and economic changes; it struggled for legitimacy for decades, while amateur baseball's popularity grew exponentially. Professional baseball was an unsightly caterpillar in the 1860s and 1870s, with little indication that it would one day transform into a butterfly. By the time it did, men had redefined what it meant to be a professional baseball player (white and male) and created formal governing structures (and informal "gentlemen's agreements") that excluded the undesirable others (blacks and women).

Baseball for Sale—the Emergence of Commodified Entertainment

The restructuring of baseball's center from an amateur pastime to a business operation occurred concurrently with the general transformation of leisure activities in the United States. The 1870s brought a confluence of factors that spawned a perfect storm of profitable prospects for entertainment entrepreneurs, including baseball team owners. A revolution in mass media production motivated newspaper editors in cities large and small to begin adding sporting and leisure sections; businessmen and women took advantage of lower costs to expand their print ads for a host of products, including theatrical and sporting events. Meanwhile, the same ever-expanding, interconnected web of railroads that made it possible to supply thousands of cities, villages, and hamlets with fresh food and inexpensive consumer products also streamlined the process for transporting theatrical troupes, sports teams, and circuses—thus expanding the customer base for those entertainment businesses. Most important, economic and demographic changes sparked by the industrial revolution, urbanization, and immigration created a mass audience with leisure time and expendable cash for entertainment entrepreneurs to woo. The leisure opportunities available in this decade were unprecedented in scope and variety, and millions of men, women, and children from every social strata and geographical region of the country surrendered their hard-earned nickels, dimes, and quarters to attend sporting events, circuses, freak shows, and a vast array of itinerant theatrical productions.[11]

The national sporting press and sensational publications like the *National Police Gazette* vaulted female baseball players, pedestriennes, rowers, swimmers, cyclists, and boxers onto a national (and international) stage, where they were alternately heralded as forebears of a new generation of healthy, robust women and derided as evidence of the moral decay of society. Pedestrianism was particularly popular. Huge crowds turned out to watch men and women compete to see who could walk the farthest without stopping. German pedestrienne Bertha Von Hillern drew crowds of ten thousand paying spectators to two walking exhibitions in Boston in January 1877, and thousands crowded New York's Pedestrian Hall in February 1879 to watch Florence Levanion and Cora Cushing compete in a race to see who could walk three thousand quarter miles in three thousand quarter hours.[12]

By the 1870s, showmen like P. T. Barnum and Adam Forepaugh were harnessing emerging transportation and communications tools to organize and transport the infrastructure and personnel needed to stage spectacular entertainment extravaganzas anywhere the railroads ran. In cities large and small, and in rural towns and railroad whistle-stops, residents were periodically assailed with gaudy and bellicose promotions for circuses, carnivals, minstrel shows, variety shows, and theatrical productions. Every newspaper and magazine advertisement, colorful handbill, and sign plastered on buildings and fences in the community promised citizens an exciting, one-of-a-kind show they would never forget. When the big day arrived, promoters staged grand parades through town centers to heighten anticipation and draw even more spectators to the main event.

Baseball boosters joined the emerging entertainment business. Novelty and excitement were the hallmarks of successful entertainment enterprises, and baseball aficionados experimented with a number of schemes to promote one or both. Town boosters staged comical muffin games while politicians, businessmen, and media interests joined forces to begin promoting professional civic teams and entertainment entrepreneurs began experimenting with barnstorming baseball teams of various sorts. Some of the civic teams would eventually evolve into the modern major- and minor-league teams of Organized Baseball, but in their infancy their commercial success depended on the same factors common to other entertainment forms. Novelty and excitement sold tickets, whether the entertainment product being hawked was men's and women's baseball, balloon ascensions, boxing, sharpshooting, weightlifting, long-distance cycling, or bearded ladies.

Some scholars have recognized the links between early professional baseball and other entertainment forms. James E. Brunson III notes that, by the end of the 1860s, baseball had already become "an ideal object of minstrelsy and professional entertainment," and he identifies strong ties between a number of successful "minstrel barons" and professional baseball clubs like the Forest Citys of Cleveland and the Philadelphia Athletics.[13] Benjamin Rader writes that "colorful pageantry was a conspicuous part of the early pro game" as teams rode through city streets in horse-drawn omnibuses to parks festooned with brightly colored pennants and flags, while brass bands entertained spectators with team songs and popular ditties as vendors hawked scorecards and food. Teams wore gaudy uniforms, like the bright red stockings of the Cincinnati Reds and yellow silk jerseys of the Baltimore Canaries of the National Association.[14]

Virtually all of the pioneering female professional baseball players, and many of their male counterparts, understood that their livelihood depended on entertaining fans, not just playing the game well. Many early female professionals came from the ranks of theatrical performers and could make the transition to "performing" baseball with relative ease. Male players, who relied on athletic skill to obtain their spot on team rosters, had to find creative ways to stand out from the crowd. Michael Joseph "King" Kelly became a fan favorite in the 1880s in large measure because of his antics on (and off) the field. In his autobiography, *Play Ball,* Kelly wrote that he made it a point to engage in "kicking" during games because he knew the crowd loved it. "People go to see games because they love excitement and love to be worked up. . . . The people who go to ball games want good playing, with just enough kicking to make things interesting thrown in."[15] Rader contends that the professionalization of baseball in the late 1860s led to the rise of a new class of professional players "whose roles resembled more the actors and actresses of the day" than the boys and young working-class and white-collar men who had played for fun and fraternity in the previous decades.[16]

Rader's description of players as "actors" is particularly relevant to a study of early professional baseball because it is this link to the entertainment business that blurs lines of distinction between female and male professional baseball players. Early female professional baseball players were not elite athletes, nor did they develop a formal structure to promote competition, as men did. They did, however, work in the same criticized profession as male players and they shared the same financial uncertainties. Their erasure from historical narratives about the early development of professional baseball mirrored that of women in general, whose place in history has only recently been reestablished. For female baseball players, the structure of Organized Baseball and modern cultural ideals about athletic professionalism have hindered their reintegration into the historical record.

The Early Structure of Men's Professional Baseball

By the late 1860s, it was no secret that many NABBP teams were paying players under the table; a common practice was to hire (and pay) men for jobs that did not actually exist in exchange for their services during baseball matches. As baseball competitions and championship victories became more important to communities, town leaders began luring players from other teams to join theirs. Soon, elite players began "revolving" from team to team as new financial opportunities presented themselves. Revolving was so common by 1867 that the NABBP adopted a rule requiring players to wait thirty days before playing a game with a new club. The rule had minimal effect, as players and teams found creative ways around it in their quest for victories.[17] In 1868, recognizing that they had little hope of halting the covert practice of paying (and stealing) players, and concerned that uncontrolled professionalism would irreparably subvert the narrative they were trying to sustain of baseball as a healthful and morally uplifting sport, the majority of delegates to the NABBP voted to support a measure that authorized member teams to begin openly paying players.[18] They hoped to end the financial subterfuge and bring stability to member teams. The Cincinnati Red Stockings were the first openly professional team to take the field under the new rules. During the fall and winter of 1868–1869, manager Harry Wright recruited the best players he could find, creating a baseball powerhouse that amassed a perfect record of sixty-five wins and zero losses in 1869. The positive press the Red Stockings generated for Cincinnati in newspapers nationwide led scores of city boosters and entrepreneurs throughout the country to organize professional baseball teams to attract attention (and businesses) to their locales. The genie of professionalism was out of the bottle and nothing would put it back in. Shrewd businessmen moved quickly to restructure the sport for maximum efficiency and profit.

As advocates of amateurism lamented what they considered the corruption of *their* pastime, professional baseball became a commercial success—not for teams initially, but for ancillary businesses. While the financial fortunes of even the most successful professional baseball teams swung wildly from boom to bust throughout most of the nineteenth century, the men who manufactured and sold sporting goods, produced the newspapers and periodicals that promoted baseball, and operated the other businesses that catered to baseball fans consistently enjoyed the fruits of the new baseball business.[19] By 1870, two baseball manufacturers in Natick, Massachusetts, were producing almost 400,000 baseballs a year; a company in New York added another 162,000. Others produced tens of thousands of baseball bats, uniforms, spiked shoes, rulebooks, scorebooks, and many other baseball-related products. Sporting goods stores multiplied in large cities and smaller communities to hawk the new products.[20] As profits accrued for ancillary businesses, and as successful teams enjoyed the occasional lucrative payoff, supporters of professional baseball sought to apply scientific techniques of business management to the sport to structure it for long-term growth and success.

The National Association of Professional Base Ball Players (NA) that had succeeded the NABBP in 1871 was ill-equipped to manage the development of the professional game. The NA was a cooperative—not a corporation; member clubs were primarily interested in regulating competition between teams in order to determine an annual champion; they were not focused on turning baseball into a commercially successful business. That fell to Chicagoan William Ambrose Hulbert who, as president of the NA's Chicago White Stockings team, was becoming increasingly concerned about the immoral reputation professional baseball had developed. Newspapers routinely reported on players throwing games for gamblers, and on other illicit activities occurring on and off the field. As a wealthy coal merchant and member of Chicago's Board of Trade, Hulbert understood that, if professional baseball was ever going to get on solid financial footing, it had to be well regulated and free from the taint of immorality that was driving away middle- and upper-class customers.[21] Hulbert's motives were not entirely idealistic—he was also fed up with powerhouse teams in the East, like Boston, stealing the best players from other teams. He knew that the loosely affiliated NA structure would never be able to regulate baseball the way it needed to be regulated if it was going to become a profitable and stable business.

In 1876, Hulbert, with the assistance of star pitcher Albert Goodwill Spalding, organized the National League and promptly set out to restructure baseball for the future. Hulbert saw to it that NL member teams were run like stock companies, with leadership clearly invested in team owners, not shared among investors and players. This was the foundation of the business model known as "Organized Baseball" that would come to dominate cultural narratives and social interactions related to the sport. Hulbert and other NL team owners controlled which cities could have NL teams. A key component of Hulbert's plan to regulate development of the sport was to limit the size of the NL. Whereas the NA had welcomed any team that could pay its $10 entry fee, Hulbert stipulated that only teams in cities with a population of 75,000 could join the new league. He also guaranteed each club a monopoly in a particular territory by requiring prospective new teams to get permission from existing members before joining the league, and by preventing any city from having more than one league team. To stabilize finances, Hulbert specified that NL clubs could only play other NL clubs and that host teams were required to pay the visiting team half of the base admission collected. In an effort to distance the NL from the immoral reputation of the NA and professional baseball in general, Hulbert also saw to it that the NL banned Sunday games, gambling, and liquor sales in its parks.

In an effort to promote attendance by middle- and upper-class patrons, the NL set admission prices at fifty cents a game—double the price for NA games.

The National League commenced its inaugural season in 1876 with eight teams located in Boston, Chicago, Cincinnati, Hartford, Louisville, New York, Philadelphia, and St. Louis. Though the intentions of team owners were good, because they did not yet have clear legal standing, it proved difficult for them to regulate the development of the sport or the behavior of players and spectators. The drive to win trumped most other objectives, and some member teams routinely ignored league rules or found ways to skirt them when it was in their individual best interest. NL overseers could not prosecute unruly players or teams that failed to enforce rules against drinking and gambling. Most important, the NL held no influence over the myriad unaffiliated professional baseball teams that continued to operate throughout the country. The public judged professional baseball as a whole—not just baseball as envisioned by Hulbert and others who wanted to package it in a morally appealing way. In 1877, eighteen professional baseball clubs organized the International Association of Professional Base Ball Players. The IAPBBP was just one of many leagues that would be formed during the nineteenth century to try to exert control over the evolving center of baseball.[22]

It took a quarter of a century for the National League to solidify its status as arbiter of "organized" baseball. During the twentieth century, it had to make peace with another upstart league, the American League (est. 1903). Together, these two organizations, along with a commissioner of baseball, would come to dominate the structure of baseball in such a way that they ultimately influenced its place in the broader culture.[23] None of this was yet settled in the nineteenth century, however, and the would-be power brokers of professional baseball in the 1870s, 80s, and 90s had to contend with the proliferation of organized leagues and men's and women's professional baseball teams—each seeking the opportunity to profit from baseball's commodification as a leisure entertainment product.

Women's professional baseball teams were especially irksome to those trying to package baseball as a sport in which elite male athletes competed on behalf of a community. Not only did women baseball players undercut the evolving narrative of the game's inherent masculinity, but they represented direct competition for spectators' leisure dollars. The men who organized professional women's baseball teams in the nineteenth century were not interested in duplicating the formal structure of groups like the NL and IAPBBP in order to promote and govern the development of women's baseball. They were independent entrepreneurs who engaged in cutthroat competition with one another and with purveyors of men's professional baseball teams as they sought to cash in on an emerging entertainment and leisure culture.

Women's Professional Baseball—Burlesque al Fresco

The earliest professional women baseball players *performed* baseball. Their games were theatrical productions announced by elaborate advertisements and parades and staged with costumes and circus-like spectacle. Though professional men's games featured some of these same theatrical aspects, there was a marked difference between the male and female game on the field. Women's teams promised fans a competitive match, but early female professional players lacked the practiced, athletic skills to deliver it at a level the men did. The theatrical trappings of female professional baseball games *were* the entertainment, whereas the theatrical trappings of men's professional games were merely adjuncts to the serious competition on the field. The most successful men's professional teams were the ones that consistently dominated the competition through physical skill and "scientific" play. Lacking the experience and practiced athleticism of male players, professional female baseball players found other ways to attract and entertain spectators. They put on a show for fans—mimicking male players' mannerisms while adding their own feminine twists. They "kicked" at umpires, stopped on the base paths to fix their hair, caught balls in their skirts, formed "bucket brigades" to relay balls from the outfield, and even downed glasses of beer while seated on the bench during games.[24] Their antics entertained crowds and helped direct attention away from their often poor playing skills.

Early professional female baseball teams grew out of a theatrical form known as burlesque. Burlesque had arrived on American shores in August 1868 when Lydia Thompson brought her "British Blondes" to New York City. Thompson's burlesque troupe set multiple attendance records in New York's fashionable theaters as it played to sold-out, middle- and upper-class audiences for a year before departing on a tour of some of America's largest cities. Early burlesque featured biting, sarcastic comedy—not striptease and Cooch dances; those came later. In early burlesque, women played men's roles and performed song, dance, and dialogue to lampoon politicians, celebrities, and social customs. As Robert Allen explains in *Horrible Prettiness: Burlesque and American Culture,* "Initially dominated by women writers and producers as well as performers, burlesque took wicked fun in reversing roles, shattering polite expectations, [and] brazenly challenging notions of the approved ways women might display their bodies and speak in public."[25]

The popularity of Lydia Thompson's burlesque troupe sparked the creation of home-grown burlesque troupes. These theatrical companies lampooned U.S. politicians and social movements, such as woman suffrage. Not surprisingly, the initial good humor and acceptance of burlesque by middle and upper classes soon gave way to scathing criticism of the art form as the wealthy increasingly found themselves the butt of jokes and as female performers began displaying more and more skin on stage. According to Allen, by the mid-1870s, burlesque was increasingly shunned by the nouveau riche and embraced by the working class. As the target audience changed, so too did burlesque. Thin, petite female leads performing dialogue or songs gave way to silent actresses whose performances were limited to modeling their voluptuous bodies. By the late 1870s (the same period in which several female professional baseball teams were organized), burlesque was all about "sexual titillation for the common man," as Allen put it.[26]

Though most nineteenth-century female baseball teams did not overtly market "sexual titillation" to attract audiences, critics insisted that this was what they were covertly promising. Middle-class moralists railed against the working-class women who performed on theatrical stages for mixed-sex audiences. These women ignored social mores about proper feminine behavior; by symbolically trading the security of the home for the public space of a theatrical stage, they were making themselves sexually available. The women who took their performance outdoors to ball fields where theater walls no longer shielded them were doubly guilty. Women's professional baseball in the 1870s was burlesque al fresco—performance removed from an enclosed wooden stage onto a pastoral, grass-covered diamond, and gender roles reversed. Women ran the base paths and men cheered (and leered) from the grandstand at the players' gaudily costumed bodies.

A key indication that male organizers of professional female baseball troupes were influenced by the rise of burlesque as a distinct entertainment form is the fact that burlesque troupes were already incorporating female baseball skits into their shows before the first professional female baseball teams were organized in 1875. The first known female baseball burlesque act debuted at Tony Pastor's Opera House in New York City in September 1868 (just one month after Lydia Thompson's British Blondes arrived). Pastor, whom theatrical historians would later christen the "Father of Vaudeville," promoted his new show in the local papers, announcing: "A new sensation to suit the times, called BASE BALL or the CHAMPION NINE, in which the great match game between the Female Base Ball Club and Tony Pastor's Club for a Prize Bat, [will be] played by a full nine on each side."[27] These types of indoor female baseball burlesque acts continued to be staged around the country well into the 1880s. The Theatre Comique in Cleveland advertised a "Female Base Ball Nine" in February 1872 and "the Forest City Female Base Ball Club" in May 1878.[28] In Brooklyn, Hank Darley advertised for performers to stage his female baseball club act in August 1875—the same month Frank Myers's Springfield Blondes and Brunettes began practicing for their outdoor baseball performances.[29] Out west, theaters in Los Angeles, Denver, Central City (Colorado), Salt Lake City, and Reno featured female baseball clubs and "Beauty at the Bat" in burlesque acts between 1876 and 1879.[30]

Another indication of burlesque's influence on professional female baseball is the fact that early teams, like Frank Myers's Blondes and Sylvester Wilson's English Blondes, adopted names reminiscent of Lydia Thompson's troupe. It is impossible to determine whether the promoters of women's professional baseball teams consciously sought to leverage the popularity of burlesque to attract spectators, but it is clear that middle-class critics of women's professional baseball frequently accused women's teams of making a burlesque of the sport. Male professionals were chastised for exposing baseball to gambling and corrupting influences, but female professionals alone bore the charge that they were subverting baseball's manly character. On July 8, 1879, the *Baltimore Sun* printed an article entitled, "Women at the Bat—A Base Ball Burlesque in Baltimore." Two days later, the same paper reprinted news about the teams' game in Washington D.C.: "Everyone enjoyed the exhibition except those who are up in the 'thirty-third degree' of the sport, and they are very much shocked at what they called a burlesque on the national game."[31] In mid-August, the *Detroit Tribune and Post* continued the theme, remarking about the teams' game there: "It was the worst burlesque upon the national game imaginable, and not even funny."[32] Even newspapers that did not specifically call the female baseball games burlesque frequently depicted women as "performing," rather than "playing," baseball and wearing "costumes" as opposed to "uniforms." They printed announcements of games in the "Amusements" column, rather than including them with the sporting news.

Blondes and Brunettes (Springfield, Illinois)

In late July 1875, the *Chicago Daily Inter Ocean* notified readers that female baseball clubs from Boston and Montreal were negotiating to reserve Dexter Park for a game that September.[33] Apart from this notice, there is no evidence that these teams existed. The inquiry for the venue likely originated with twenty-eight-year-old Frank Myers of Springfield, Illinois who, along with five associates, had recently organized a "National Amusement Association" and recruited women in Chicago to join a troupe of female baseball players that would barnstorm the country later that summer.[34] Like managers of other barnstorming entertainment troupes, Myers and his associates tried to schedule performances months in advance of launching a tour. Claiming that their teams originated in Boston and Montreal was a way to heighten interest and attract spectators. Rebuffed by Chicago venues, Myers and his partners organized the Blondes and Brunettes of Springfield, Illinois, in August 1875. These are the earliest known female professional baseball teams.

Newspapers identified Myers as the business manager and treasurer of the National Amusement Association and Lewis Rosette as "President." Rosette was an attorney in partnership with his brother, John, who had moved to Springfield in 1855 at the request of Abraham Lincoln. The other men affiliated with the female baseball enterprise were Seth B. Brock, Thomas Halligan, Frank Simmons, and "Reddy" Stevenson. Brock was justice of the peace in Springfield; local papers did not specify his role in the organization but the *New York Clipper* credited him (and Thomas Halligan) with conceiving the idea of the female baseball troupe in the first place. Halligan had lived with Myers's family since at least 1869 and was a longtime employee at Myers's store. Twenty-five-year-old Frank Simmons ran his own business selling books, stationary, and periodicals; he also sold tickets for the Blondes and Brunettes games. "Reddy" Stevenson worked for the *Springfield Daily Journal* and was a member of the local men's team, the Watch Factory Nine. He helped teach the Blondes and Brunettes to play, ensured they got plenty of coverage in the local media, and occasionally served as scorekeeper for games.[35]

Four years before helping found the first women's professional baseball teams, Frank Myers inherited the thriving mercantile operation his father had built up in the Illinois state capital. A shrewd businessman in his own right, Myers expanded the family business until it became one of the largest retail stores in central Illinois. He knew the value of advertising in promoting a business, and in early September 1875 he and his partners launched a media blitz in Springfield and surrounding towns to promote the Blondes and Brunettes. In marketing his female baseball enterprise, Myers established a pattern that would be duplicated by most professional women's teams from the 1870s to the era of the All-American Girls Professional Baseball League in the 1940s. He promoted female baseball as a "novelty," emphasized the femininity of the players, and advertised games as wholesome family entertainment—suitable even for proper "ladies" and children.

On September 2, 1875 the *Illinois State Register* included a short account of a practice game played the previous day by the Blondes and Brunettes and included the teaser: "The female ball tossers wear striped hose." The next day it printed another teaser: "Jacksonville is filled with envy, because of Springfield's female base ball tossers."[36] Within days advertisements and articles about the team appeared in numerous papers throughout Illinois and, within a week, in Missouri, Indiana, Ohio, New York, and Georgia.[37] Several of the papers identified the teams as the "Diamond Garters" and the "Lace-Top Stockings." On September 9, 1875, the *Illinois State Register* formally introduced the teams to the public, announcing them as the "Sensation of the Age."[38]

Unlike many organizers of subsequent women's professional teams, who were more interested in making a quick buck (even if it meant stealing players' wages), Myers tried to field a quality, enduring business enterprise. This required a significant financial investment. Not only did he purchase fancy "costumes" for his players, he also paid to have a special canvas fence built to enclose the diamonds wherever his teams played.[39] Though men's professional baseball teams played "home" and "away" games on fields with permanently fixed infrastructures, female professional teams had no home fields. They had to carry canvas enclosures and (sometimes) grandstands everywhere they went in order to protect their entertainment product from the unwanted gaze of freeloaders. Not only did managers have to purchase them, but they also had to pay for additional train cars and laborers to transport, assemble, and disassemble them. Operating a professional female baseball team was not cheap—or easy—as Myers and his partners quickly learned.

The Blondes and Brunettes (sometimes called Blue Stockings and Red Stockings by journalists) played a private practice game on September 1, followed by five public games (all in September). Three of the games took place in Illinois and one in St. Louis, Missouri. The location of the fifth game may have been New York City, but that has not been definitively established. Games were preceded by a parade. The Blondes and Brunettes played their first public game in front of two hundred to five hundred spectators on Saturday, September 11, 1875 in Springfield. On the thirteenth and fourteenth they played their second and third games in Decatur and Bloomington, Illinois. The crowd in Decatur was described as "not large" while the Bloomington paper described the spectators in their city as "a motley crowd of some two hundred or more gentlemen who paid their half dollars for admission, and several hundred more deadbeats who took reserved seats on fences, and wagons, and trees, and stole their amusement at the expense of a discouraged manager."[40] (Canvas fences were no match for determined freeloaders.)

Myers scheduled two games in St. Louis for Saturday and Sunday, the eighteenth and nineteenth but, after the first game, law enforcement officials threatened to arrest the players if they tried to play again. Local papers in St. Louis, which had provided favorable announcements about the upcoming games, were incensed once the first game took place. The *St. Louis Republican* called it "a revolting exhibition of impropriety" and the *Globe-Democrat* called it "a disgrace to the city."[41] Moral reformers demanded that police step in and prevent the teams from desecrating the Sabbath. (The *Daily State Journal* noted sarcastically that the ban on Sunday games apparently did not apply to men's teams, two of which entertained one thousand of the five thousand spectators who had shown up for the women's game on Sunday.)[42]

Myers had envisioned a European tour following a U.S. tour.[43] That dream quickly evaporated. The disappointing size of audiences at the first four games and the harassment from law enforcement officials in St. Louis necessitated that he scale back his expectations. Player attrition also contributed to his decision; it was a constant problem. There were seventeen players on the team rosters for the first game in Springfield on September 11. Two days later, Myers had added an eighteenth player plus two substitutes for the game in Decatur. The following day, he was scrambling to replace seven of those players for the game in Bloomington on the fourteenth. Ultimately, he managed to field only sixteen players, four of whom had not appeared on previous rosters. Bloomington reporters observed that the names "Blondes" and "Brunettes" no longer applied because so many players had been injured in the first two games that the teams now consisted of a hodge-podge of players with different hair colors and complexions.[44] By the time the teams arrived in St. Louis, Myers again had to augment the rosters with local actresses.[45] After police halted the second game, a number of players left the troupe to return to their former variety shows; the Chicago-based players pawned their luggage to buy train tickets back to the Windy City.[46]

Despite the rocky first week of operation, Myers was unwilling to abandon his plans to promote a profitable baseball enterprise; he consolidated his remaining players into a single team and headed east. Newspaper coverage leading up to the team's fifth game is sketchy, making it difficult to determine precisely where this game was played. The *Syracuse Daily Courier* reported on September 20 that the Blondes and Brunettes would play in Syracuse soon, and the *New York Times* announced the next day that the teams would play a game on Union Grounds "in about two weeks."[47] No articles about a game at Union Grounds have come to light, and it is possible the consolidated troupe never made it all the way to New York City. It did play one final game somewhere out East. On September 30, the *New York Varieties* carried a story subtitled, "The Blondes and Brunettes' Take to the Field—A Friendly Contest with a 'Picked Nine' of the Male Persuasion." The article included an illustration (fig. 3) and reported that a women's team had defeated a men's team, 11 to 10; it does not specify when or where the game took place.[48]

Unlike the illustrations of the Peterboro game, the *New York Varieties* image seems to be fairly accurate. It shows the women wearing knee-length pantaloons, short-sleeved blouses, caps, and high-topped shoes. Their legs appear to be bare, however, even though descriptions of the Blondes and Brunettes uniforms from various newspapers indicate that the women's legs were covered by striped stockings. The *Bloomington Pantagraph* noted that the Blondes wore a "jaunty white hat, blue pants trimmed with white, reaching a little below the knee, blue jackets, similarly trimmed, confined at the waist with a black belt, and white hose striped with blue." The Brunettes wore the same hat but their suits were white, trimmed with blue, and their stockings were white striped with red. Several accounts mentioned that the players wore light leather gloves. (Some

THE RED STOCKINGS AND WHITE STOCKINGS MUST YIELD THE PALM TO THE STRIPED STOCKINGS—THE "BLONDES AND BRUNETTES" TAKE TO THE FIELD—A FRIENDLY CONTEST WITH A "PICKED NINE" OF THE MALE PERSUASION.

FIGURE 3. Illustration of a Springfield Blondes and Brunettes game. *New York Varieties,* September 30, 1875. Courtesy David Block.

male players were just beginning to adopt gloves too.) One paper described their outfits as "Zouave" style, and the *Boston Investigator* added that the women were "attired in fashion not often seen off the stage . . ."[49] It was highly unusual at the time to see women wearing anything resembling pants unless they were performing in a variety show or circus.

The Springfield Blondes and Brunettes apparently did not play again after their fifth game, although numerous newspaper accounts in October and November published misleading information that the teams were preparing to set out on tour or were still playing. On September 30 a paper in Buffalo reported that a "New York female nine" would play there during the first week of October. A St. Louis paper reported the same day that women in Buffalo were organizing a team. No record of this team or game exists; both of the articles were likely referring to Myers's organization, which was still out East at the time. On October 2, almost three weeks after Myers's troupe departed Springfield, *The Days' Doings* mistakenly informed readers that two female baseball nines were practicing in Springfield in anticipation of departing on a playing tour. In mid and late October, papers in Missouri and Illinois stated that Springfield had two female teams—the "Diamond Garters" and the "Lace Top Stockings." The last reference to the Springfield teams appeared in Michigan's *Jackson Citizen Patriot* on November 20. It erroneously identified the teams' home city as Springfield, Ohio and noted that the teams had "recently" played their first public game.[50]

Myers's National Amusement Association was short-lived, playing all of its games in a two-week period. By late September, Myers and his associates realized their female baseball enterprise was not the profitable gold mine they had envisioned and pulled the plug on the Blondes and Brunettes. The following spring Myers became president of Springfield's first men's professional baseball team, the Liberties.[51] The remaining partners and players went their separate ways.

Public opinion about the nation's first professional female baseball troupe ran the gamut from supportive to brutally negative. Those who understood that the games were intended to be theatrical entertainment, not athletic contests, were generally supportive; those who viewed scantily clad women performing in public as immoral were brutally negative. The *St. Louis Globe-Democrat* asserted that the residents of Springfield were "not at all ambitious" to have the teams identified with their city, but the Springfield papers did not reflect this opinion.[52] After the teams' first public game in Springfield, the *Daily State Journal* (where Reddy Stevenson worked) politely minimized the poor quality of play and emphasized the entertainment value of the exhibition. It observed that the players had been quite nervous at first but had improved as the game went on. It emphasized that "no immodest act—save female base ball playing be so considered—obtruded itself, nor was their other objectionable features."[53] The *Illinois State Register* agreed, reporting that everything was done "decently and in order" and that "the contest seemed to be greatly enjoyed by the spectators." It added that the women were not particularly good players but that "there was nothing, save, perhaps, the exhibition of female anatomy, to which exception could be taken, and even that is frequently discounted in first-class theaters."[54] Supportive editors generally agreed that there was "no indecorous action or language on the part of the players," despite their unorthodox profession.[55]

Despite favorable reports in Springfield, Decatur, and Bloomington papers regarding the morality of the entertainment product Myers was selling, other papers were not buying the storyline. The *Harrisburg (Pa.) Telegraph* commented that no matter how people differed on this issue of baseball's influence on young people, "there is no room for doubt as to the impropriety of women engaging in it."[56] The *Inter-Ocean* reported that, after the teams' "performance" in Bloomington ended, "a crowd of roughs gathered around and insulted the girls by abusive language."[57] After the teams played in St. Louis, the papers excoriated them. The *St. Louis Globe-Democrat* railed: "This is an age of fraud, and if the stereotyped remark was ever applicable to any community it is to St. Louis." The "fraud" alluded to was the Blondes and Brunettes baseball game, and the paper identified the thousand spectators who had attended the event as "victims" who were "mourning the loss of their misspent half dollars."[58] The *St. Louis Republican* was even more blunt in its derision: "The whole affair was a revolting exhibition of impropriety, possessing no merit save that of novelty, and gotten up to make money out of a public that rushes to see any species of semi-immorality."[59]

The criticism of the Blondes and Brunettes in many newspapers reflected two trends—one fairly new and another well established. The new trend was the growing perception of baseball as a man's game. The *Harrisburg Telegraph*'s assertion that "there was no room for doubt" that it was improper for women to play baseball was disingenuous considering that scores of women's civic and pick-up teams were receiving favorable press from other publications. The real basis for most criticism about nineteenth-century professional female baseball players related to the long-standing assumption among middle- and upper-class moralists that most women who performed in public for money were sexually promiscuous. Those who earned money playing a sport that was closely associated with gambling and drinking were particularly suspect. Though Myers and his associates in Springfield seem to have been respectable members of their communities, the reality was that many nineteenth-century managers of professional female baseball teams were exactly the type of men that Victorian moral reformers worked tirelessly to thwart—they were indeed unscrupulous charlatans who exploited young women for personal gain.

English Blondes and American Brunettes (New York City)

Within a year after Myers's operation collapsed, businessmen and theatrical managers in various parts of the country tried their hand at organizing professional female baseball operations. In February 1876, a newspaper in Bristol, Pennsylvania, reported that a ladies' baseball club had been organized in Philadelphia. A few days later the *St. Louis Republican* commented that the "speculative genius" who was responsible for the new team was "unmindful of the fate of a similar enterprise in St. Louis last year"—a likely reference to Myers's troupe.[60] In March, the *St. Louis Globe-Democrat* announced: "Look out for the Female Base Ball Club, for it will soon make its appearance."[61] It is uncertain whether the St. Louis paper was announcing that the Philadelphia team would play there or that someone was organizing a new female team in the city. There was a tantalizing clue published in the *St. Louis Globe-Democrat* three years later that the female club in Philadelphia in 1876 may have been the brainchild of Sylvester Franklin Wilson. The newspaper reported that Wilson was preparing to launch a new baseball operation in New York City in the spring of 1879 and added: "He does it every spring."[62]

Sylvester Wilson was an on-again, off-again newspaper publisher, theatrical manager, and petty criminal who was intimately familiar with courtrooms and jails. By the time he moved from Cincinnati to Philadelphia (and then to Camden, New Jersey) in April 1876 to seek his fortune during the nation's Centennial Exhibition, he had already been arrested at least three times in Nebraska and multiple times in Cincinnati for blackmail, slander, impeding justice, impersonating a U.S. marshal, and assault.[63] The baseball team mentioned in the newspapers may have been one of his planned money-making schemes for the year; it was not unusual for him to begin issuing press releases and advertising for players during the winter. The 1876 team never materialized, and Wilson spent his time running a railroad ticket–forging operation and publishing *George Francis Train's Paper*. He also added assault and fraud to his already lengthy rap sheet.[64]

Wilson's connection to the wealthy and eccentric Train dated back to the early 1870s when he had served as editor of Train's *People's Paper* in Nemaha, Nebraska.[65] Train was a fierce advocate of the working class and of women's rights—he had traveled to Kansas with Elizabeth Cady Stanton in 1867 to battle for woman suffrage and he funded her publication, *The Revolution*.[66] In 1873 Train was indicted for his "obscene" publications; Wilson moved to Cincinnati and carried on Train's work there, publishing a small newspaper called the *Train League* that advocated Train's "free love" doctrines.[67] Train became a household name in the 1870s after making the first of several trips around the world and running for president multiple times. He lived with Wilson in Camden for several months in the winter of 1876–1877 and made several speeches on Wilson's behalf during his ticket-forging trial in Philadelphia. The pair kept in touch for years.[68]

In March 1879, Wilson launched a media campaign to market the English Blondes and American Brunettes—two female baseball teams he and business partner William B. Powell organized under the auspices of the "Ladies Athletic Association." He sent press releases to papers throughout the country. The *Chicago Tribune* printed one but noted wryly that Wilson was "particularly reckless in the use of capital letters."[69] The *Lowell Daily Citizen* reported that Wilson's teams were "handsomely costumed in silk and woolen," and would depart on a world tour after playing two games a day for one week in New York City beginning on May 5. The *Harrisburg Daily Independent* reported that the troupe would be accompanied by a brass band.[70]

Wilson and Powell knew that financial success depended on attracting middle- and upper-class spectators to their baseball exhibitions. They sent gilt-edged invitations to physicians and clergymen in the city in hopes that their attendance would motivate other upper-class clientele to turn out.[71] Leveraging changing attitudes toward women's physical fitness, Wilson designed a marketing campaign that portrayed himself as a great benefactor to women: "[M]y object is to start a new thing, to develop women of America. I am going to open here a field for their physical perfection. There is to be base ball, lacrosse, archery, polo, walking, running, velocipede riding and everything. Ponies are now in training. . . . It is going to work a revolution in this country and world. These ladies are all cultivated women, who, off the field, are able to grace any drawing-room. I tell you that it is the biggest thing that has ever occurred for the women of America."[72] In a trope he would revisit continually during his decade-plus career as a female baseball showman, Wilson reminded the public that the ancient Greeks had encouraged their women to participate in "open-air Gymnastics" and that this was how they had produced those "beautiful and graceful figures" that artists immortalized in marble.[73]

Anyone reading Wilson's press releases would have thought that he and his players were the scions of high society. In reality, Wilson was a serial scam artist who tried to swindle the baseball-loving public the same way he swindled countless other marks over the course of his three-decades-plus criminal career. He launched his baseball operation from an area in New York City that had a decidedly unsavory reputation owing to its abundant gambling dens, rat pits, and seedy businesses. Wilson felt right at home in the city one contemporary labeled "The Great Maelstrom of Vice."[74] He boarded at Hamilton House in the heart of the "Tenderloin District" where saloons, lowbrow theaters, and brothels abounded. At least one of his players, outfielder Mary Callahan, lived in the same area. The New York Society for the Prevention of Cruelty to Children (NYSPCC) reported that Wilson's baseball headquarters at the Hamilton House had been the scene of "midnight carousals, can-can dances, etc. [that] surpassed the high revels of any dive in the Bowery."[75] Wilson's players were not the demure damsels of drawing rooms he claimed they were. Most were veteran entertainers and street-wise teenagers who earned their livings working in the theaters, saloons, and dance halls that moral reformers decried. The captain of the Brunettes had previously starred in theatrical productions and two of the Blondes had performed in Barnum's hippodrome. Other players were female trapezists, singers, and dancers. At least two were runaways.[76]

For a few weeks in April and early May 1879, the press dutifully parroted Wilson's marketing narrative, helping him erect a façade of respectability around his enterprise. When the English Blondes and American Brunettes first faced off on May 10, reporters generally treated the affair positively. They understood that Wilson was marketing a theatrical performance staged as a stylized competition. An article in the *New York Herald* on May 13 was typical: "One of the most picturesque and graceful exhibitions ever given in New York was witnessed by those who assembled yesterday afternoon to attend a game of base ball played by eighteen young ladies trained by Mr. Sylvester F. Wilson, at the Athletic grounds [on the] corner of Madison avenue and Fifty-ninth street."[77] Though Wilson's media campaign was carefully tailored to put his entertainment commodity in the best possible light, no amount of flimflammery on his part was going to lure residents of New York's grandest neighborhoods to his makeshift baseball diamond even if he did claim it was located at "the very center of the aristocratic part of the metropolis."[78] A large crowd did turn out for the first game, but reporters noted that the audience was definitely not composed of the "clergy and medical faculty" Wilson had sought to entice with the embossed invitations.[79]

The large crowd that attended Wilson's baseball exhibition did enjoy the show. The *Washington Post* described how "eighteen young women pranced about, essaying base ball until the audience roared itself hoarse."[80] It described the "picturesque" changes of innings when a "cloud of blue skirts and a forest of blue legs" would advance to the shelter tent while "a flock of red legs and caps soared out over the field."[81] It also reported that when the band struck up a waltz, the first and second baseman of the Brunettes began waltzing around the bases, and that when it played "Killarney," four of the fielders kept time with their feet.[82] Other reporters playfully highlighted the competitive theme of the entertainment, describing the antics of the "Jennies, and Gracies and Josies" on the field.[83] Most reports ended with a line score and roster, just as was done for men's games.

All told, Wilson's teams played six games between May 10 and May 17. Reporters noted that crowds at three of the first four games were large. The contests ranged from seven to nine innings—the English Blondes won four of six games. Wilson seemed to have found a winning entertainment formula, but three days later his baseball enterprise came to an abrupt end when officers of the NYSPCC arrested him and Powell for "engaging girls under sixteen years of age for the purpose of taking part in immoral performances," having sexual relations with two of their players, and for abducting one of the players from her home.[84] Newspapers around the country carried the sensational story.[85] Wilson and Powell were arraigned in police court on May 24, where the judge set bail at $1,000 each—a huge sum in 1879. Their case came up in the Court of Special Sessions a week later. According to NYSPCC records, a grand jury indicted both, but neither was tried owing to lack of evidence.[86]

Many of the women who made their living in the entertainment business in the nineteenth century were routinely exploited by unscrupulous managers. Wilson's players, some of whom were as young as fourteen, were particularly victimized. One player described her ordeal to a sympathetic reporter three months after she had joined a new baseball troupe in Philadelphia. The sixteen-year-old informed the reporter that she had answered Wilson's advertisement in May for "pretty and well-formed ladies" to learn to play baseball. She and twenty others were hired and told to return the next day to pick up their "costumes," the cost of which would be deducted from their salaries. The costumes consisted of a "tight-fitting bodice, a pair of short pantaloons, a kilt skirt, high-cut shoes, and striped stockings." When asked whether she enjoyed playing baseball, she informed the reporter that it had been an ordeal. The majority of the young women had never played baseball and were quickly black and blue with bruises. They were so sore and lame that they could only practice twice a week. The girl noted that they had played a public game but that they had done much better in "rehearsals." Adding insult to (literal) injury, the players never received a penny of their salaries.[87]

Though both male and female professional baseball players faced economic exploitation by team owners and managers, only female players faced sexual exploitation as well. Male players chafed under the reserve agreements that bound them to a particular club and kept them from selling their services to the highest bidder.[88] They protested the fees team owners charged them for uniforms and travel expenses, but they did not have to contend with lecherous employers who routinely demanded sexual favors from them, as their female counterparts did. The players on the English Blondes and American Brunettes teams were just the first in a long line of female professional baseball players whose ability to earn a livelihood on the diamond was interrupted by the arrest of their employers. While Wilson and Powell sat in jail, some of the players returned to the theater while others joined a new baseball team forming in Philadelphia. Powell disappeared from the historical record of women's baseball after his release, but Wilson began planning his next women's baseball operation almost immediately. By October he was managing another women's baseball troupe in Chicago under the alias U. S. Franklin and making plans to send two more teams on the road.[89]

Lady Nine of Baltimore and Lady Nine of Boston (New Orleans)

Not all paid female baseball players played on barnstorming teams; there are a few examples of men paying women for single exhibition games. Beginning on May 27, 1879, large ads in the *New Orleans Times* announced businessman H. E. "Abraham" Hezekiah's plans for the "First Grand Female Base Ball Festival Ever Exhibited in the South." The ads promised readers that if they showed up at the fairgrounds on Sunday, June 15 they would witness a female baseball game, a pony race, a mule race (with female baseball players riding the mules), and a contest of blind man's bluff featuring "fat men, 200 pounds and over." Afterward they could enjoy an evening of dancing under electric lights, competing to win a beautiful fan (for the best lady waltzer) and a walking cane (for the best male waltzer). Cost to attend the festival was fifty cents (free for children under twelve).[90]

Hezekiah was trying to cash in on the baseball mania sweeping New Orleans. "The epidemic of base ball playing has broken out in this city with great virulence," observed the *Times* on May 1. By the twenty-eighth it notified readers that teams were organizing and reorganizing so quickly that it could no longer print details about clubs, only game scores.[91] Like Myers and Wilson before him, Hezekiah targeted the sophisticated elements of society with his marketing campaign. He used the local media, particularly the *Times,* to portray himself as a "gentleman" concerned about citizens' health and welfare. (Hezekiah promised to donate 10 percent of the proceeds of the festival to the newly organized Auxiliary Sanitary Association.)[92] He claimed his teams were from cosmopolitan cities in the North and assured the public that his players would uphold the strictest standards of feminine decorum.[93]

Hezekiah was marketing a lie. The "ladies" he employed were not recruited from across the country or even from Boston and Baltimore. The "Lady Nine of Baltimore" and the "Lady Nine of Boston" were home-grown teams; players were likely recruited through ads in theatrical publications and word-of-mouth solicitations in saloons, theaters, and brothels. This fact alone, if known to the general public, would have dissuaded many from attending. No self-respecting southern belle would ever play the manly game of baseball in public, especially while wearing a short skirt, baseball cap, and brightly colored silk stockings. By the same token, no self-respecting southern gentleman or lady would financially support such an affront to southern gentility.

Hezekiah enjoyed a brief period of support from local media, but that faded when the true nature of his enterprise came to light. On June 13, Hezekiah staged a grand procession through the city to promote the festival. Newspapers described the parade (and its unintended consequences) in detail.[94] Though he was merely following standard practice for advertising baseball games and other entertainments, Hezekiah's gaudy procession (which featured the players wearing their baseball "costumes") incensed some of the local citizens, who complained to the acting mayor (Mr. Isaacson). Hezekiah nearly lost the opportunity to stage his festival when Isaacson discovered he did not have a permit from the city. Fortunately for Hezekiah, he was able to obtain the permit after numerous "gentlemen of standing" and several local newspapers endorsed the event.[95]

The Female Base Ball Festival was held as planned on June 15. The *Times* reported that about one thousand people attended "and seemed to enjoy the entertainment immensely." The mule race, which featured three of the female baseball players, and a horse race went off without a hitch. The baseball game got off to a rocky start when some of the players struck for their wages, which had not been forthcoming. The game was delayed an hour while management and labor negotiated a settlement. Eventually Hezekiah found an acquaintance willing to put up a stake of $10 per player, and the women took the field.[96] The temporary work stoppage foreshadowed the chaos to come. Although he reportedly took in $594 for the event, Hezekiah was unable to satisfy all his creditors, who were vociferous in their displeasure. The *Times* detailed the mayhem that descended on Hezekiah the next day as "female base ballers, gate keepers, boys, trainers, flunkeys and others yelled in unison for their lucre."[97] The *Picayune* joked: "Whom the gods would destroy they first make organize a base ball club" and happily reported three days later that "female base ball games have come to a short stop."[98]

Female Blue Stockings of Philadelphia and Female Red Stockings of New York

A week after Hezekiah's festival, Philadelphia's Grand Central Theater owner William Gilmore watched his Female Blue Stockings of Philadelphia and Female Red Stockings of New York play their first practice game at Oakdale Park.[99] Gilmore and his associates recruited their players from Philadelphia and New York City (where some had played on Sylvester Wilson's English Blondes and American Brunettes teams).[100] The men had the financial means to launch their teams on an ambitious cross-country tour that covered thousands of miles, eleven states, and the District of Columbia. At a time when most professional men's teams averaged fewer than one thousand spectators per game, Gilmore's baseball operation scored a stunning success when it drew five thousand spectators to its first public exhibition game on July 4, 1879 in Philadelphia. So many men swarmed onto the field that it took a squad of police officers wielding baseball bats to push them back.[101] Three days later, the female teams drew a "crowd of thousands" to a match in Baltimore, earning $1,400 in gate receipts. On July 9, they played in front of three thousand to five thousand people (including "officers of the government great and small") in Washington D.C.[102] It seemed that Gilmore had finally figured out how to field a financially successful professional female baseball franchise—something most purveyors of the men's professional baseball product were still unable to do.

The players in Gilmore's troupe were not sharing equally in the profits they were generating on the baseball field. When not on the road, they were forced to supplement their earnings by performing a baseball act in Gilmore's theater, after which they had to serve as companions to men who purchased special fifty-cent tickets for the postshow "grand promenade." Gilmore's theater was of the decidedly "lowbrow" type. One reporter who attended the baseball show and "grand promenade" described the experience for readers. He noted that the preliminary performance was a standard variety show "generously interlarded with base ball playing by a number of gaudily dressed but somewhat awkward young women." When it ended at 10 o'clock, the theater quickly "metamorphosed" into a "typical concert saloon" featuring a well-stocked bar just offstage. As soon as he sat down, one of the sixteen-year-old baseball "players" tripped over to him and boldly asked to be treated to a drink. Making herself comfortable, she gave him the backstory on the female baseball troupe.[103]

The teenager explained that two weeks after her troupe in New York (Wilson's former team) collapsed, she and other players received an offer to travel to Philadelphia to join Gilmore's. They were promised $10 per week plus expenses (including free board) but had to pay an agent's commission plus train fare and baggage costs themselves. That left them with $7. Then the nickel and diming that was so rampant in the theatrical business began. The agent informed the women that he had been mistaken when he told them their board would be paid—they would have to pay $5 per week for lodgings. Additionally, until they reached a high enough level of proficiency on the baseball diamond that managers could launch a road tour, the players would be expected to help with other facets of the operation. That meant hawking drinks at the midnight promenade concerts. Once on the road, players would receive only $7 per week plus expenses. The girls and young women who had traveled from New York to join Gilmore's theatrical company quickly realized that they were trapped. With only $2 left from the original $10, they did not have enough money to return home. They had no choice but to stay. The young woman told the reporter that when some of the players fell behind on board payments, managers turned them out into the streets. They also informed the remaining players that their salaries were being cut to $5 per week (only enough to cover board) but that they could earn extra money giving "promenade midnight concerts" like the one the reporter was attending.[104]

The teenager's account provides a rare behind-the-scenes glimpse into the challenges of working-class women employed in the entertainment industry. Unscrupulous managers used promises of fame and riches to entice them to join their companies and then found ways to manipulate their earnings to the point that they became completely dependent on them. Gilmore cut players' salaries yet still required them to purchase their costumes (white shirts, pink sashes, sailor hats, and fancy slippers) out of their remaining meager pay. He pressured them to supplement their income by using their sexual allure to cajole men into spending money at his bar. The commissions the players earned hawking drinks at Gilmore's midnight "concerts" became their primary source of income. The young women were virtual prisoners. Any rebellion or violation of company policies meant instant ejection. One player demanded that theater doors be unlocked so she could leave prior to one of the midnight concerts; Gilmore immediately kicked her out of the company. The remaining players pooled their money and bought her a return ticket to New York. Soon afterward, the baseball troupe began its first tour.[105]

Life on the road posed a new set of challenges for troupe members. Twenty-three of them, accompanied by Gilmore and three other men, traveled more than eight hundred miles in twelve days after their initial exhibition on July 4. The crowds the women entertained were "composed chiefly of the rougher element," as one newspaper put it.[106] Two weeks later, in New Haven, Connecticut, Gilmore barred police from the grounds and hired his own security to manage the crowd. It was a mistake; they could not keep order. A group of ruffians drove people from the stands, attacking a black woman in the process. They surged onto the field and pelted the players with stones and mud as they made their escape in a wagon. To add insult to injury, Gilmore abandoned the players almost penniless at the hotel.[107] The players managed to keep their engagement in Providence, Rhode Island, two days later, but when a tornado halted their game after two innings, they straggled back to Philadelphia, leaving a number of unpaid bills behind them.[108]

Gilmore's baseball operation was on shaky financial ground. Reviews were mixed, but mostly negative. One paper described the baseball troupe as nothing more than "a party of broken down variety performers."[109] After their game in Washington, D.C., one reporter claimed that the audience had thoroughly enjoyed the game, while another pronounced the affair "simply disgusting."[110] Gilmore was encouraged by the size of crowds that had turned out for some of the exhibitions and decided to regroup and launch another tour. The second tour covered almost 2,500 miles and lasted just over a month.[111] The young women played games back-to-back-to-back while traveling almost continuously.

TABLE 2. Initial Schedule of the Female Blue Stockings of Philadelphia and the Female Red Stockings of New York, 1883

Date	Place	# of Fans
Fri., July 4	Philadelphia, PA	5,000+
Mon., July 7	Baltimore, MD	approx. 5,000
Tues., July 8	Baltimore, MD	approx. 250
Wed., July 9	Washington DC	3,000–5,000
Thurs., July 10	New Brunswick, NJ	300+
Sat., July 12	Jersey City, NJ	1,200+
Mon., July 14	New Haven, CT	600–1,000
Wed., July 16	Providence, RI	1,200

Crowd sizes in Massachusetts were smaller than those on the initial tour, and players found themselves again victimized by Gilmore as he, his wife, and two team agents jumped off their train as it departed the Worcester station, leaving them without tickets or money to get to Pittsfield.[112] Somehow the troupe and remaining managers managed to continue their journey. They initially planned to make their way back to Philadelphia, but the $100 gate receipts at Pittsfield and the arrival of a new manager (possibly Sylvester Wilson) convinced them to continue.[113] The games in New York were fairly profitable and would have been more lucrative if heavy rain and the threat of thunderstorms had not dissuaded fans from attending in Buffalo.[114]

As was the case with the previous tour, players were subjected to taunting and jeering during performances and sometimes faced physical harm. By

TABLE 3. Schedule for Second Half of Blue Stockings and Red Stockings Season

Date	Place	# of Fans
Mon., July 28	Boston, MA	Unknown
Tues., July 29	Boston, MA	600–800 or 1,500
Wed., July 30	West Lynn, MA	500+
Thurs., July 31	Lowell, MA	approx. 1,000
Fri., Aug. 1	Lowell, MA	Unknown
Sun., Aug 3	Manchester, MA	Unknown
Tues., Aug. 5	Worcester, MA	approx. 300
Wed., Aug. 6	Pittsfield, MA	400
Thurs., Aug. 7	Albany, NY	"large crowd"
Fri., Aug. 8	Troy, NY	1,500
Sat., Aug. 9	Utica, NY	1,100–1,500
Tues., Aug. 12	Rochester, NY	1,200
Wed., Aug. 13	Buffalo, NY	1,000
Thurs., Aug. 14	Syracuse, NY	300*
Fri., Aug. 15	Rocky River, OH	800–1,000
Sun., Aug. 17	Detroit, MI	"a large crowd"
Tues., Aug. 19	Fort Wayne, IN	Unknown
Thurs., Aug. 21	Logansport, IN	"large number"
Fri., Aug. 22	Lafayette, IN	Unknown**
Sat., Aug. 23	Indianapolis, IN	Unknown**
Mon., Aug. 25	Louisville, KY	1,200
Tues., Aug. 26	Cincinnati, OH	1,000–1,700
Aug. 28, 29, or 30	Columbus, OH	Unknown**
Sun., Aug. 31	Cincinnati, OH	4,000
Mon., Sept. 1	Springfield, OH	approx. 1,000
Wed., Sept. 3	Wheeling, WV	Game cancelled
Unknown	Pittsburgh, PA	Game cancelled

* Syracuse paper stated game had been cancelled; others said it had been played.
** Game may not have taken place.

eschewing their "proper" place in the social hierarchy, these women had for-feited the cultural protections available to "ladies" in the nineteenth century. In Pittsfield, Massachusetts, young men crowded around the bench where players sat awaiting their turn to bat and verbally abused them until police intervened. Three other toughs laid down in the base paths and leered as the players ran past; they too were ejected by police.[115] In Rocky River (where newspapers erroneously reported that five men had drowned in Lake Erie while sailing to the game) fans behaved well for two innings and then surged close to the diamond while police did their best to hold them back.[116] The same scenario was repeated in Louisville, where police could not keep the "roughs" in the crowd subdued. The game was called early and players escaped in their omni-bus amid a hail of stones.[117] The worst violence occurred in Springfield, Ohio, where manager "Frankhouse" (possibly Wilson) and a friend got into a fight with a group of black men who were verbally abusing the players. Frankhouse struck Ben Hayes on the head with a board, inflicting what some newspapers erroneously reported was a fatal blow.[118] The violence continued later that night when Frankhouse and his companion were being escorted to jail. A mob intervened and the pair escaped.

After narrowly escaping incarceration, Frankhouse called it quits. The be-leaguered manager bought train tickets for the players to Columbus and then skipped out with the remaining funds from the $250 gate money. Stranded in Columbus, many of the players walked hundreds of miles east before they were able to obtain help from politicians and charities in various cities along the way to get train fare home.[119] The Female Blue Stockings of Philadelphia and Female Red Stockings of New York, who had begun their season with such promise just two months earlier, were permanently defunct.

The Social Interactions of Professional Female Baseball

For the most part, during the latter quarter of the nineteenth century, proprietors of male and female brands of the professional baseball product faced the same obstacles when trying to expand their customer base by attracting middle- and upper-class audiences. Both had to overcome the unsavory reputation of a sport still associated with hard drinking, gambling, and carousing players. Propri-etors of women's professional baseball had the added burden of overcoming significant antipathy to women who performed for audiences for money. Neither group of baseball entrepreneurs was particularly successful at expanding the demographic base of their fans. Working-class men consistently made up the majority of spectators at nineteenth-century professional baseball games despite the fact that male and female promoters consistently offered reduced (or free) ticket prices for women and children and advertised special grandstand seating to isolate them from the "rougher" elements in the crowd. The presence of large numbers of women in the stands was so unusual at both men's and women's professional games that reporters generally commented on it.[120]

The working-class men (and smaller numbers of women and children) who attended men's and women's professional baseball games in the nineteenth century were openly resisting middle-class moralists' efforts to steer them into more "acceptable" leisure pursuits. Reading rooms and public health lectures were unappealing substitutes for dance halls and female baseball burlesque shows. Middle-class moralizers sought to distance themselves from the working classes who frequented professional female baseball games by asserting that such games only attracted lecherous men (so-called "bald heads") and the dregs of society. "Police Commissioners and ex-Commissioners were sandwiched in with pimps and thieves," claimed the *St. Louis Globe-Democrat* after a game in its city, "while bank burglars and garrotters might have been seen in proximity to city and county officials in various parts of the field."[121]

National League moguls and their media allies recognized that women's professional baseball teams posed direct competition for a limited fan base; consequently, they worked tirelessly to distinguish the male baseball product from the female product. They hyped the competitive nature of the men's professional game while belittling the physical abilities of women to deliver the same quality product. After watching the Red Stockings and Blue Stockings play in Detroit, a reporter concluded that the players' "awkward antics demonstrated that while there are many things a woman can accomplish, playing base ball is not one of them."[122] The *St. Louis Globe-Democrat* reached a similar conclusion, commenting: "Girls will never play base ball to advantage. Their collar bones are too long, to say nothing of other impediments."[123] These types of reports resonated with many readers who were upset by the efforts of women's rights activists to revise gender roles. Activists doggedly chipped away at political, economic, and legal restrictions on women while women entered the workforce in unprecedented numbers as government departments, businesses, and industries expanded across the nation. By emphasizing women's physical shortcomings, critics of female baseball were implying their unsuitability for other "manly" occupations as well.

Some critics tried to link the new professional women's teams to the women's rights movement. In September 1875, the *Bloomington Pantagraph* chose the headline "Female Ball Catchers: The Divine Right of Woman's Suffrage Extended to the Green Diamond" for its report on a Blondes and Brunettes game. The *Baltimore Sun* reported in 1879 that some who supported professional female baseball "hoped she might begin to enlarge her sphere and gain victories on the diamond field akin to those which she has won in law, medicine and theology."[124]

The strategies of male baseball boosters to disparage the physical abilities of female players and to link them to the women's rights movement were ultimately successful. By the 1880s, increasing numbers of individuals were calling baseball a man's game. This gendered characterization solidified as interest in men's professional baseball grew. Though the promoters of men's professional baseball were eventually able to heighten interest in the men's game, they were unable to put their female competitors out of business. Women's professional baseball teams continued to multiply in the 1880s and 1890s. Male managers of these teams had a ready pool of players to choose from. Despite the hardships of life on the road and not infrequent abuse at the hands of unscrupulous male managers and cruel crowds, scores of young working-class women, and a few rebellious middle-class teenagers, continued to seek opportunities to practice their chosen profession—"performing" and playing baseball. For them, "the show must go on" was more than a trite phrase—it was their ticket to adventure and a livelihood away from mind-numbing factory work, demeaning domestic service, or life in the gilded cage of feminine propriety. While these women sought their livelihood on professional female baseball teams, the purveyors of the male game adopted a new strategy to thwart them. While continuing to disparage their morality and their physical abilities, these men increasingly tried to erase them from cultural narratives about the game.

4. The 1880s: Molding Manly Men and Disappearing Women

The now national field-game of the United States known as
base-ball was evolved from the old English school-boy game of
"rounders" which is almost obsolete. Beyond the fact that the
form of the field on which both games are played is similar, there
is scarcely any resemblance between them, the original sport being
a mere boyish pastime, while the American game of base-ball is a
sport requiring the trained skill of manly athletes to excel in it.
—*Appletons' Annual Cyclopaedia* (1886)[1]

Why shouldn't the girls play ball? It was originally a woman's game,
and the men have stolen it from them. Go to any country school,
and at noon you will see the girls playing ball with great vim and
relish. It is the best sport they could engage in.
—*Pittsburg Dispatch,* September 23, 1889[2]

BY THE 1880s, unprecedented numbers of girls, boys, women, and
men were playing, watching, and following baseball—blacks and immigrants
of every stripe among them. References to the game appeared in books, poems,
theatrical skits, songs, games, cartoons, cigarette cards, and many other cultural
forms. Both amateur and professional versions flourished, though players and
promoters of the latter still found it a challenge to secure consistent profits.[3]
Those who manufactured and sold the accouterments of the game and those
who launched baseball-related periodicals or incorporated regular coverage
of amateur and professional games into their existing publications reaped ever
larger profits as the sport spread. Baseball was so popular that many believed it
was protecting American "civilization" from fracturing as successive tsunami-
sized waves of immigrants poured into the country. In 1889, reflecting on the
meaning of the sport to the nation, poet Walt Whitman waxed eloquent: "It's our
game: that's the chief fact in connection with it: America's game: has the snap,
go, fling, of the American atmosphere—belongs as much to our institutions,
fits into them as significantly as our constitutions, laws: is just as important in
the sum total of our historic life."[4]

This was a decade in which native-born, middle- and upper-class citizens began contemplating a role in the world beyond their national borders. Flushed with nationalistic pride about industrial and technological advancements and exuding Social Darwinist–fueled confidence in the superiority of the Anglo-Saxon "race," countless missionaries and businessmen launched crusades abroad to harvest souls and plumb new markets. As they watched the European powers carve up Africa and force their way into Asian markets, some recommended baseball as a tool of foreign diplomacy and commerce. In 1888, Albert Spalding, whose last name would become synonymous with a global sporting goods empire, led the nation's premier players on an ambitious six-month-long world tour of baseball to showcase the game and, he hoped, spread its popularity.[5] Sports journalists across the country covered the tour in detail, fully expecting that "America's game" would soon be "known in every civilized part of the globe fully as much as cricket is."[6] The team returned home to a hero's welcome. National League president A. G. Mills lauded the players as "gladiators" who were "covered with their American manhood."[7]

During the 1880s, the oft-repeated mantra about baseball inculcating masculinity took on new prominence as Americans' worries about floods of immigrants and the emasculating nature of office and factory work grew. With the issue of professionalism versus amateurism largely settled (both were clearly there to stay), narratives of "otherness" increasingly focused on women, blacks, and immigrants. With Anglo-Saxon manhood and American civilization seemingly under assault from every side, both amateurs and professionals had a stake in portraying baseball as a morally pure, culturally uplifting sport capable of inculcating masculinity in its practitioners. Those who controlled the structure of professional baseball went a step further and portrayed the game as one best suited to white, Protestant, Anglo-Saxon manhood. Alan H. Levy notes that by the 1880s, major and minor league teams were slowly forcing black players out, reflecting a shift in team owner, fan, and (white) players' racial sensibilities. Newspaper coverage reflected the change. "Races began to be more emphasized," Levy writes, "and the emphasis was often decidedly vicious—former phrases like 'that dark-skinned receiver' were sometimes replaced by words like 'that N_____ catcher.'"[8] Though it was relatively easy to incorporate Jim Crow into organized baseball, it proved impossible to profit without immigrants. With middle- and upper-class citizens still not wholeheartedly embracing the professional game the way they would in the twentieth century, professional team owners had to rely on working-class spectators to fund their bottom line. As teams began hiring talented first- and second-generation immigrant players, these players developed loyal and enthusiastic fan bases that boosted team revenues.[9]

Women had not yet played with men on their professional teams (that would occur sporadically in the ensuing decades),[10] but it was nonetheless the men's professional teams (or more precisely the structure of organized baseball and the cultural hegemony it established over the sport) that led to the "disappearing"[11] of women from historical narratives about baseball, and that ultimately solidified its gendered heritage as a "man's" game. Girls and women who played baseball for fun on school, college, and other amateur teams posed little threat to narratives of elite athleticism and manliness that organized baseball boosters were crafting because social convention deterred most women from pursuing the elite form of athleticism that characterized male professional players. Professional women baseball players *did* pose a threat to professional baseball, however. Their teams competed for fans in major and minor league cities and their association with working-class burlesque entertainment forms visibly undermined narratives of middle-class morality that leaders of organized baseball were trying to promote.

It was difficult for purveyors of the men's professional game to gain traction with a marketing strategy that portrayed professional baseball matches as exciting, family-friendly spectacles of elite, manly, "American" athleticism when teams of working-class women, blacks, Chinese, and other un-elite, un-manly, and purportedly un-American counterfeits continued to hawk their brand of baseball across the country.[12] By and large, the threat to organized baseball posed by black and ethnic muffin teams was minimal; black teams tended to cater to black audiences and the ethnic teams were relatively few in number. As women's professional teams continued to proliferate, however, and to draw thousands of spectators who might otherwise have spent their scarce leisure dollars on men's baseball, the men whose livelihoods were bound up in the evolving structure of organized baseball felt compelled to do something to undermine the appeal of the women's teams, or to at least make it clear that they were not *real* baseball teams and that their members were not *real* baseball players.

Some newspaper editors—particularly those whose fortunes were tied to the success of men's professional baseball—made it their personal mission to use their publications to shape public attitudes about women baseball players. Francis C. Richter was one such man. Born and raised in Philadelphia, Richter had enjoyed playing amateur baseball as a young man. As an adult, he stayed connected with the game by helping organize the American Association in 1882. A year later, he helped organize the Philadelphias as a new entry for the National League and launched a new sporting periodical called *The Sporting Life*. The masthead read: "Devoted to Base Ball, Trap Shooting and General Sports." Richter's paper found a ready audience. Subscriptions soared from 2,800 to 21,000 in less than a year. After three years, the publisher was distributing 40,000 copies a week across the United States and Canada.[13] Richter's financial fate was tied to the success of men's organized baseball, and he was determined to promote the game. Through his association with both the structural and cultural sides of baseball, Richter became one of the most influential advocates for professional baseball (and fiercest opponent of professional female baseball). His was a narrative that helped solidify baseball's identity as a man's game.

For more than two decades Richter followed the fortunes of dozens of professional female baseball teams as they crisscrossed the United States. He printed frequent accounts of their failings and editorial comments about the inappropriateness of baseball for women. Richter was a thorn in the side of men like Sylvester Wilson who tried to make their living selling women's baseball. In the inaugural issue of *Sporting Life* (April 15, 1883), Richter cited advertisements Wilson had placed in March for an investor to help him start another female baseball team. Richter kept a wary eye on Wilson's operation, predicting in August that the venture would fail just like all previous female baseball troupes.[14] He was only partially correct. Before it collapsed, Wilson's new baseball organization attracted tens of thousands of spectators to games in eleven states.[15] Meanwhile, men like Richter continued to work hard to establish a solid business model for the professional game.

Codifying the Structure to Control the Game

William Hulbert and his associates in the National League were still struggling to achieve their grand vision for baseball. They had structured the league to try to ensure profit to all member clubs by providing a full season of competitive matches for fans, adapting rules to make the game more exciting for spectators, and by marketing a narrative of middle-class morality. None of their objectives had been fully realized. Most league clubs, particularly those that languished far back in the standings for most of the season, had trouble turning a profit. Competitive parity remained elusive; last-place teams finished twenty to forty games back in the standings and only two or three teams were still in the running for the league championship late in the season. Uneven competition and financial problems caused a revolving door of clubs into and out of the National League.[16] The challenge of controlling the structure and culture of professional baseball grew even more difficult after 1882 when other aspiring baseball entrepreneurs formed two new professional leagues—the American Association (1882—six teams) and the Union Association (1884—twelve teams).[17]

The American Association (AA), in particular, undermined NL influence over the structure and culture of baseball; AA leaders had an entirely different vision for the future. While most NL club owners at least paid lip service to the idea of upholding Victorian morality at their ballparks, AA club owners chafed at restrictions on alcohol and Sunday baseball. Owners of the Cincinnati Reds led the charge to organize the rival league after NL leaders expelled them after the 1880 season for playing nonleague games on Sundays and for trying to overturn the league's ban on alcohol. The new "Beer and Whiskey League," as the AA would come to be known, represented a rival to the NL's claim on the center and soul of professional baseball.[18]

The power structure of professional men's baseball shared many of the characteristics of emerging business corporations and trusts. League owners worked to ruin competitors and to exert hegemonic control over their workforces. Baseball's laborers (the players) found themselves financially squeezed and without a voice in league decisions. Player resentment grew over the reserve rule, blacklists, and gentlemen's agreements that bound them to specific clubs, burdened them with fees, and artificially depressed their wages.[19] Eventually, rival league officials recognized that there was strength in numbers and, while still at odds with one another over the culture of the game, they allied against the players. In 1883, NL owners signed an agreement with AA and Northwestern League (a minor league) officials to respect each other's reserve rules and blacklists. Players fought back when team owners announced a salary cap in October 1885; a group of them organized the Brotherhood of Professional Base Ball Players and, within a year, 90 percent of NL players had joined. Frustrated in its attempts to curb owners' growing power, the Brotherhood established the Players' League in 1890 but it folded after only one season.[20]

When these birth pangs of "Organized Baseball" ended, the structural center of baseball was firmly in the hands of management. The soul of baseball was still up for grabs, however. Organized Baseball owners could control the structure of their business model, but they could not wield autocratic authority over the culture of baseball—that belonged to baseball players and fans writ large. Every boy, girl, man, and woman (no matter their race, ethnicity, or social status) who played and watched the sport had a share in the evolution of baseball culture. That did not deter the power brokers of men's professional baseball from trying to shape the ideological center of the sport as a man's game and symbol of American "civilization." Their campaign to control the meaning of baseball encompassed an array of strategies—from "disappearing" and disparaging women players to shaping cultural imagery about them. Professional female players were particular targets of efforts to recast baseball as a man's game, but no female player was completely insulated from the fallout of attacks on her professional peers.

Crafting a *Manly* Culture—"Disappearing" and Disparaging Women Players

Efforts to "disappear" female baseball players predated the 1880s. After reporting on the existence of the Springfield Blondes and Brunettes professional teams in September 1875, the *Utica Morning Herald* instructed:

Now, if Springfield regards this female ball club as discreditable, it must not undertake to write it down. Women who take to base ball, minstrel performances, bloomer costumes or suffrage advocacy, are not to be written down. They exist on adverse criticism; they thrive on opposition and newspaper protest. The only effectual way of inducing them to observe the sex line is to let them alone. Calling names will do no good. Denunciation will, sad to say, only excite curiosity, and keep alive the evil. And, after all, playing ball is a part of 'women's rights.' We are not sure it is not the least objectionable feature of their assertion.[21]

Three years later, the *Chicago Tribune* took a similar approach, denying that there was any such thing as a real female baseball team: "Now, as a matter of fact, there never was such a thing as a female base-ball nine except in a show,—and, more, there never will be."[22]

Attempts to erase women baseball players from the historical record continued during the 1880s. In 1888, John Montgomery Ward, an elite player in the NL and founding member of the Brotherhood, published a book for aspiring baseball players and fans.[23] Ward wanted to popularize the sport, and he especially wanted to squelch the long-lived and annoying assertion that America's national pastime was really just an offshoot of an earlier British game of the same name. With nativism and nationalism at a fever pitch, it simply would not do for America's national pastime to be a British import. So Ward, born and raised in Pennsylvania, joined an increasingly vocal group of baseball businessmen and journalists who rewrote baseball's history. They created a myth that the game was a wholly American invention and, in the process, pruned many of the feminine branches off baseball's ancestral tree.

Ward had a distinctive approach for proving that baseball was an American invention. While others focused on differences in rules between American baseball and British games like baseball, cricket, and rounders, Ward argued that because *girls* had played British baseball, it simply could *not* have been the precursor of the American game. He cited three references to British girls playing baseball. The first was the letter Mary Lepel (Lady Hervey) had written in 1748 that mentioned the Prince of Wales playing baseball indoors with both male and female family members during chilly winter days. The second was Jane Austen's inclusion of a female baseball player in her novel *Northanger Abbey,* and the third reference was a comment in the 1852 edition of Blaine's British encyclopedia of sport that "there are few of us of either sex but have engaged in base-ball since our majority."[24] Based on this evidence, Ward concluded: "The fact that in the three instances in which we find the name [baseball] mentioned it is always a game for girls or women, would justify the suspicion that it was not always the same game, and that it in any way resembled our game is not to be imagined. Base-ball in its mildest form is essentially a robust game, and it would require an elastic imagination to conceive of little girls possessed of physical powers such as its play demands."[25] In one brief paragraph, Ward acknowledged that women *had* played the British game of baseball, while he simultaneously "disappeared" hundreds of American girls and women who had been playing American baseball for decades. Ward's verbal slight-of-hand aimed to preserve both the masculine reputation of his "robust" game *and* its homegrown ("Made in the USA") credentials.

John Ward was a highly educated man; he graduated from Columbia Law School in 1885. He certainly would have read newspapers and the popular press; it is inconceivable that he did not know that American girls, like British girls, played baseball. By 1888, when he wrote his book, newspapers and periodicals across the country had already published countless articles about girls and women playing baseball in school yards, on college campuses, on local civic and pick-up teams, and on professional barnstorming teams. Ward likely had knowledge of at least some of the more than 150 different baseball teams in twenty states and four territories that girls and women had organized since his birth in 1860. Perhaps he had missed newspaper coverage of the Female Blue Stockings of Philadelphia and Female Red Stockings of New York when they staged an exhibition game in Providence, Rhode Island, in July 1879 while he was away on a road trip with the Providence Grays. But, surely, he could not have missed the extensive reporting on the Young Ladies' Base Ball Club four years later when it played three exhibition games in front of thousands of people in New York City in September 1883 while he was a member of the New York Gothams, who were hosting the Chicago White Sox for a series. Ward suppressed information about female baseball players that undermined his narratives about baseball's relationship to American exceptionalism and masculinity; in the process he perpetuated the myth that baseball was, and always had been, a man's game.

While some sought to "disappear" women from baseball history, others manipulated the narrative of baseball by distorting imagery of female players in popular culture. Baseball was not just a game played in physical space; it was also an ideal in peoples' imaginations—part of the cultural triad of "baseball, motherhood, and apple pie." Baseball transcended emerald diamonds and wooden grandstands; it found its way into poetry, literature, songs, theatrical performances, and novels. It spawned board games, card games, cigarette cards, and countless other collectibles. By the late 1860s, enough women were playing baseball that they generated cultural references in jokes, advertisements for consumer products, and in songs, poems, books, and theatrical productions. Many of the references were fairly innocuous, but many were covert efforts to advance and reinforce the false message that baseball was, and needed to remain, a man's game.

The gendered references in cultural artifacts targeted both women and men. Those aimed at women invoked prevalent perceptions about women's innate physical weaknesses and capriciousness. The subliminal message was that, even though they might play *at* baseball, they could never truly *be* baseball players. If, by some chance, they achieved the proficiency of male players, they did so only by surrendering their femininity—becoming "unsexed" Amazons. Gendered references targeting men implied that, because they had failed to uphold traditional boundaries between the social spheres—allowing women to make inroads into male professions and public spaces—they were to blame for the increase in the number of women baseball players. The implication was that if they would reassert their manly prerogatives and actively keep women off the ball field, out of colleges, and away from male occupations, social ills would cease and life would get back to "normal."

Jokes

Female baseball players were integrated into jokes as early as 1870. Quips about them (ostensibly crafted merely to entertain) reinforced gender stereotypes:

"New Lisbon, Ohio, has a female base ball club. One of the girls recently made a 'home run.' She saw her father coming with a big switch." (1870)[26]

"Mercersburg has a female base ball club. They want a young man for catch 'er." (1878)[27]

"Women are too easily put out to play baseball successfully." (1879)[28]

"The female Base-ball Clubs are coming West. Shoo! Shoo! And have we escaped cholera to come to this?" (1879)[29]

"There are sixteen female base ball clubs in Kansas. Just imagine eighteen angry and excited females engaged in a discussion with one poor, unprotected umpire." (1889)[30]

"A Texas baseball club has a pretty young female pitcher, with a figure of perfect mold. Of course everybody gets onto her curve." (1897)[31]

These quips reached a broad audience, often appearing in multiple newspapers across the country over a period of many months and sometimes years. The joke about a female player making a "home run" when she saw her father (or mother) coming with a "big switch" ran in dozens of papers across the country between 1870 and 1871.[32]

Photographs and Illustrations

The most effective tool for shaping cultural attitudes toward female baseball players was to propagate false images of them. The fictionalized illustrations of the female baseball players in Peterboro, New York, published by the *Sporting Times* and *The Days' Doings* in 1868 are examples of gender marking through visual media.[33] The strategy continued throughout the century. A particularly egregious example of how men used photography to control public perceptions of female baseball players was the introduction of cigar and cigarette cards depicting female players as either masculinized or sexualized. Sporting goods companies had been using baseball imagery on "trade cards" since the late 1860s when Peck and Snyder first used them to advertise products.[34] In the mid-1880s, tobacco companies began leveraging new printing technologies and color lithography to publicize their products with ever more elaborate, colorful, and creative means. Allen & Ginter of Richmond, Virginia, was particularly innovative, producing more than eighty sets of cigarette cards between 1885 and 1890 covering themes as diverse as birds, fish, animals, actors and actresses, U.S. presidents, flags, pirates, military decorations, and racing colors of the world.[35] It also produced three sets of nine cards purporting to feature the players of two different female baseball teams—the "Black Stocking Nine" and the "Polka Dot Nine" (fig. 4). (No such teams existed at the time, although Sylvester Wilson organized a troupe called the Black Stocking Nine in 1890.)

The Allen & Ginter cards depict the female players with serious faces in the act of catching, running, hitting, or sliding just as similar sets of male baseball cards did. That is precisely why these images were so detrimental to perceptions about female baseball players. They propagate a lie. The few women who dared wear pants in public in this era were excoriated and sometimes even arrested; there are no known examples of female baseball players wearing this type of uniform at the time. In fact, the women depicted in the baseball card sets were not even baseball players—they were actresses hired by photographers to pose for themed pictures.[36] While male baseball cards featured actual players like John Ward, female baseball cards depicted nameless women mimicking male activities and dress. The female baseball cards proved so popular that Allen & Ginter issued several additional sets in subsequent years.

Other companies incorporated women baseball players into their card sets as well. Because tobacco companies purchased photographs from dealers, a number of women from the Allen & Ginter card sets appear on cards issued by Pacholder Tobacco, a major competitor (fig. 5).

The Pacholder cards have different captions and feature its cigarette brands, but the backdrops and uniforms of the players are identical to many of those used in the Allen & Ginter cards. Images produced by S.W. Venable, another tobacco

FIGURE 4. Allen & Ginter tobacco cards (1884–1886). Courtesy The Rucker Archive.

FIGURE 5. Pacholder tobacco cards (1886). Courtesy David Block.

company, in the late 1880s and early 1890s were full-color drawings, not photographs. They were extremely risqué by the standards of the day (fig. 6). Each card included a month-long schedule for men's major league baseball on the back and advertisements for the company's products.[37] The players' uniforms were more appropriate for a vaudeville show or circus than for a baseball diamond.

The S.W. Venable female baseball cards mirrored sexualized images of women popular at the time. In July 1887, newspapers across the country reprinted an expose written by a Boston-based reporter about the proliferation of nude photography. The reporter classified indecent photographs into three categories, the first, and "least objectionable" of which depicted "the cigarette girls, with skirts pulled up to their knees, and *the female baseball players*" (emphasis added).[38] He noted that these images were "printed by thousands" at a

FIGURE 6. S.W. Venable tobacco card (c. 1890s). Courtesy Legendary Auctions.

local "fashionable" studio "for the edification of morbid erotomaniacs whose sexual appetite is stimulated by views of thick ankles and striped stockings." The second category comprised the "gross" and disgusting variety of pictures sold surreptitiously in bar rooms, and the third included nude and seminude images of women posed like the women in classical paintings and sculptures. The reporter noted that not all the women who posed for these types of photographs were disreputable; many factory workers or "young girls of good reputation" sought the work because it paid so well—up to five dollars an hour.[39] The implication that female baseball players would demean themselves to appear in photographs targeted by moral reformers like Anthony Comstock undermined efforts by female players to control perceptions about themselves.[40]

Cigarette cards were not the only visual medium used to distort perceptions about female baseball players. On July 18, 1885, the *National Police Gazette* published a satirical illustration of a female batter and catcher purportedly playing a game at Wellesley College; both players are dressed in exceedingly short skirts, long stockings, and caps (fig. 7). Well-dressed male and female spectators look on. The caption reads: "Maidenly Muffs. The Freshmen of Wellesley Female Seminary Organize a Baseball Nine Like Real Little Men."[41]

Images of female baseball players created by players bear little similarity to those produced by their critics. The photograph of a baseball team at Allegheny College in Meadville, Pennsylvania (fig. 8)[42] stands in stark contrast to the image of Wellesley players published by the *Police Gazette*. The young women's appearance conforms to prevailing ideals of femininity; each player's hair is neatly coifed, and all have the waspish waists associated with the ideal female physical form of the day—several players appear to be wearing corsets. If it were not for the baseball bat and ball included in the image, the photograph could be interpreted as a group of young women getting ready to attend a chapel service or a social event with a group of young men. Team photographs of female collegiate baseball players (and nonprofessional, civic teams) reflect the social bonds players shared and the pride they felt in what they were doing—a pride that motivated them to preserve tangible reminders they could revisit when their playing days were over. Photographs invariably show players wearing either long dresses or approved female gymnastic uniforms—an indication that players were visibly contesting the notion that femininity and baseball were incompatible.

The distorted imagery of female baseball players on tobacco cards and fictitious illustrations of them in newspapers and pulp serials negatively influenced attitudes about them. Apart from the professional baseball players, who were often forced to wear sexualized clothing and *had* to play in public, the vast majority of nineteenth-century female baseball players tried to conform to prevailing gender ideals; they wore feminine clothing when they played and often

FIGURE 7. Purported illustration of Wellesley students playing baseball. *National Police Gazette*, July 18, 1885.

tried to keep their games hidden from public view. Yet, the proliferation of the female baseball cards contributed to a growing perception that women who played baseball were engaging in a masculine activity that would inevitably masculinize or "unsex" them.

Poetry and Fiction

Not all cultural imagery of female baseball players merited the attention of moral reformers, but even innocuous references in poems and novels still influenced readers to perceive female players and the sport of baseball in a certain way. Though entertainment of an audience was the primary objective of these cultural artifacts, they provide clear evidence that the history of baseball cannot be divorced from the history of gender roles in the United States. This poetic verse described one woman's attempt to find her niche in life:

> I've tried to make boxes; I can't.
> A sewing-machine run? I shan't.
> I've stood as a model for cloaks;

FIGURE 8. Team photo (1890), Allegheny College Archives. Courtesy Wayne and Sally Merrick Historic Archival Center, Pelletier Library, Allegheny College.

I don't like the ton's pointless jokes.
I've sung in the chorus—small pay!
Sold needles and pins for a day.
I've canvassed for books for a week,
But, alas, was too awfully meek;
I've worn a white cap, watched the kid,
N. G., very tame, and I slid;
I've been a wall-flower upon hire,
I aspired to something much flyer;
A female base-ball club I tried,
I never could learn how to slide;
I'm told that my form's very neat,
I know I have got pretty feet.
Thank heaven! A chance yet remains
Where I can get paid for my pains:
In a cigarette-factory I'll pose,
And the charms of my ankles disclose.
—H. S. Keller (1886)[43]

Horace Keller's message seems to be that the type of woman who would consistently seek her livelihood outside women's traditional roles of homemaker and mother was the type of woman who would demean herself as a cigarette card model to make a buck.

Women's relationship to baseball comprised a major plot element in Mary Prudence Wells Smith's novel, *The Great Match* (1877).[44] In the novel, civic rivalry between Milltown and Dornfield is played out on the baseball diamond. Milltown is wealthier than Dornfield and has an all-important branch on the railroad line. Dornfield residents console themselves with the knowledge that their baseball team can beat Milltown's team even though Milltown businessmen are paying their players. Smith employs common gender stereotypes throughout her story, particularly as they related to the proper relationship of men and women to the national pastime. In her book, men are expected to woo their women and uphold the honor of the town by joining and exceling on the local baseball team. Those who do not are ostracized. In one scene, Smith's heroine, Miss Molly Milton, chastises the aptly named Dick Softy for refusing to join the local baseball team. Annoyed by Softy's excuse that he does not want to go through life "with only one eye, and fingers like potato-balls," Milton blurts out: "If I were a man, I'd play my part; and if base ball were the part, I would play until all my fingers were as crooked as an eagle's claw."[45] Molly talks boldly about playing baseball herself but knows her place in the gender order. At the grand baseball fête, the elegantly dressed Molly tosses a baseball to various players but coquettishly ducks behind team captain Ned Black each time the ball is thrown back.[46] Smith's novel used baseball to reinforce the gender order of her day.

Like Smith's portrayal of Molly Milton as a girl who feigned fear of a tossed baseball, many of the short poems and quips about female baseball players in the 1880s and 1890s emphasized their incompetence as athletes. "Young ladies pitch base ball and *occasionally catch* [emphasis added] at Asbury Beach," wrote the *Titusville Herald* in 1887.[47] The *Saginaw Evening News* printed "The Maiden Base Ballist":

> There was Mary and Katie and Nan,
>   Mollie and Josie and June;
> Maud and Carrie and Fan,
>   But they couldn't hit a balloon.[48]

Sporting Life sarcastically pointed out that Cora Tenner's new play, "One Error" was not about "the performance of a female base ball club."[49] The *Ogdensburg Daily Journal* observed: "Lillian Nordice, it is said, hammers the life out of a piano once a month. If she ever loses her voice, she ought to make a capital pitcher for a female base ball club."[50]

The Social Interactions of Women's Baseball—
Contesting the Coalescing Center

Scores of girls and women across the country ignored criticism and continued to play baseball on civic and pick-up teams, factory teams, and school/college teams. Four states (Alabama, Colorado, West Virginia, and Maryland) and four future states (Montana, New Mexico, South Dakota, and North Dakota) got their first female baseball teams during the 1880s. As in the past, the majority of the scores of female baseball teams organized during the 1880s were short-lived—enduring for only a few days or weeks.

Despite the abundance of female players, the myth that women could not understand or play the game continued to pervade press coverage. In March 1880, the *Chicago Tribune* informed readers that Sallie Van Pelt, editor of the *Dubuque Times*, had reported on more than sixty baseball games for her paper in 1879. The *Tribune* then gushed: "She is the only lady in the United States who understands every point of the game and is able to report on them. She is also considered the best authority in Dubuque on the National game."[51] Though the *Tribune* may have been correct about Van Pelt being the only woman regularly reporting on baseball games in 1880, it was mistaken about Van Pelt's singular status as a student of the game. From the earliest days of the modern game, when men first began displacing boys on baseball fields, men's teams of all stripes (social and competitive, amateur and professional) had encouraged women to attend games. Baseball matches were not just athletic contests; they were part of a complex tapestry of social rituals through which men and women defined the roles and hierarchies of gender, race, and social class. Male baseball players, black and white, enjoyed performing feats of masculine strength and virility for the "weaker" sex, and many women enjoyed attending the games to witness these displays of masculinity and to reciprocate with complementary displays of femininity.[52]

By the 1880s, thousands of women across the country were avid baseball fans and understood the game's finer points. In August 1885, Francis Richter observed that the "base ball boom" in New York had so affected local women that they were regularly attending games at the Polo grounds. Richter noted that the women were as invested in the game as much as male spectators, noting: "they bring out their score cards and pencils, argue over the merits of the coming players, and consult their little diaries, in which they have entered records of past League games." Hundreds of them "stood on the seats and screamed and waved their handkerchiefs and brandished their fans in ecstasies of applause."[53] Though it is doubtful that women attended games to deter immoral behavior of players and fans, the fact that they *did* attend invariably strengthened the narrative some team owners were perpetuating. Connie Mack, who spent sixty-six years in professional baseball, wrote in his memoirs that when he first began playing baseball in the mid-1880s it was not as respectable as it became; he attributed the improvement to women—"a powerful moral influence in raising its tone."[54]

Even as some newspaper editors recognized the existence of competent and enthusiastic female baseball fans, many continued to dismiss the notion that women could and did *play* baseball. In his article about female fans in New York, Richter insisted that "none of them ever play it" even though he knew full well that girls and women regularly played baseball. Like Ward, Richter was "disappearing" female baseball players.[55] Nineteenth-century journalists routinely made sweeping assertions about women's interests and capabilities based on cultural assumptions rather than on careful research or unbiased observation. In the process, they perpetuated those (frequently false) assumptions. When it came to women's relationship to baseball, journalists freely employed adjectives like "unique," "novel," and "only." By reporting assumption as fact—even in the face of obvious evidence to the contrary—they grafted another gendered twig onto baseball's ancestral tree, distorting its history in ways that caused (and still cause) persistent problems for girls and women who wanted (and want) to play baseball.

Baseball for Schoolgirls in the 1880s

While adult female baseball players were increasingly criticized in the 1880s, school girls continued to receive favorable press as they organized scores of baseball teams across the country—mostly in the Midwest and the East. Bridgton Academy in Maine had five boys' baseball teams and two female teams in 1884; two years later in New Hampshire, Concord High School's newspaper reported that a number of female students were "quite expert in the national game."[56] As increasing numbers of female students began attending high schools in the 1880s and 1890s, more of them had the opportunity to play baseball. Female students at Tallmadge High School in Ohio practiced regularly for a game at the end-of-term picnic in 1885, while the *Washington Post* noted in 1889 that a team of girls at the Pittsfield (Mass.) high school was planning to play a factory team in Poughkeepsie.[57]

It is often young people who catalyze social change; their desire to distinguish themselves from their parents' generation often emboldens them to openly contest established norms to carve out a new social space for their generation. One of the most obvious signs of change in the late nineteenth century was the number of young men and women who eschewed the single-sex activities of their parents' generation in favor of heterosocial leisure pursuits in which groups of young men and women played croquet, tennis, golf, and, even baseball together. In July 1883, a group of nine young women in Huntsboro, Alabama, defeated a male nine, and the following year the Good Girls' Base Ball Club and the Good Boys' Base Ball Club played each other at Punahou School in Honolulu. In 1887, the *Wichita Globe* reported: "In Galt, Cal., all the high-school girls play ball with the young men."[58] Though doubtless exaggerating the number of girls playing baseball in Galt, California, the *Globe*'s report that male and female high school students were playing ball together reflected changing social mores about gender, and the newfound confidence of many young women in their athletic abilities.

Baseball at Colleges in the 1880s

The women fortunate enough to attend college in the 1880s benefited from new understandings about the relationship between physical fitness and women's reproductive health, and from the fact that a generation of female graduates who preceded them had survived the rigors of higher education. Women arrived on college campuses to find newly constructed gymnasia and professional physical educators and/or physicians waiting to teach them the latest scientific methods of health and hygiene. Though most collegiate physical fitness programs in the 1880s continued to focus on calisthenics, walking, and individual activities, some promoted team sports like baseball. Whether they played on teams in physical education classes or on informal student-organized teams, female collegians found in baseball an activity that reflected and solidified social bonds.

Students at Smith College organized "house" (residence) teams as early as 1880. "We have formed two Base Ball nines," Evelyn Jean Forman, a resident of Hubbard House, confided to her journal on April 27, 1880. "Ella Flynt, Minnie Stephens, Florence Harrison, Ella Stetson, Mame Clarke, Anna Morse, Mame Van Ausdal, Mira [Hall—Forman's roommate] and I are the members of one nine. And the 'other set' have a nine. We are going to play match games after we have practiced longer. We have heaps of fun playing nights after supper."[59] The social nature of the Smith house teams comes through clearly in Forman's journal. As was the case with many of the early men's baseball teams, the Hubbard House teams grew out of social ties that prefigured athletic ties. (The "other set" to which Forman referred were fellow residents of Hubbard House, led by team captain Mary P. Winsor, who became their chief opponents on the baseball diamond.) Few of the women on Smith's earliest baseball teams had any experience playing the sport. Mary H. A. Mather, a member of Winsor's team, described the organization of her team in her memory book. She related that only four of the "nine unsophisticated maidens" who first met behind Hatfield Hall "knew anything about the mysteries of 'Base Ball.'" It was not long, however, before their "revered captain" had "initiated them into the secrets of 'batting + bases' and the playing began in ernest [sic]," she wrote.[60]

Mather's narrative and Forman's comment about the "heaps of fun" she and her teammates enjoyed playing baseball make it clear that the students reveled in their "mysterious" sport and were delighted with the new physical sensations they experienced as a result. "Ah! What tales could be told of 'hands' and 'stiffness,'" Mather noted gleefully. "[A]t the breakfast table a prevailing remark was—'Are you stiff today?' But the nine played on and the stiffer they became, the more they played. Soon 'nines' became the fashion."[61] Baseball's masculine reputation was well solidified by the 1880s, however, and not everyone was enamored with the idea of cavorting around a baseball diamond, even when pressed by friends to do so. In May 1880, Smith College freshman Mabel Allen informed her mother: "Two ball-nines have been formed here. They practice half an hour every night after supper. I was asked to join one of the nines, but refused."[62]

Those players who did enjoy their brief foray into the male sporting sphere seemed rather proud of the attention they were attracting. Mather noted that during a match between her team and Stephens's team, "the neighbors were much edified—and tramp[s], carriages, and small boys also appreciated it." She went on: "The paper of Springfield noticed the fact that the Smith students had invested in numerous balls and bats and would soon enter the field of national competition. So much has our club done. Long may it wave and may its acts be worthy of mention."[63] As long as the players were discreet about their activity, Smith College administrators tolerated the sport on campus. Once their activities became public, however, school officials banned the sport on campus. Minnie Stephens recalled: "We were told . . . the game was too violent, and also there was great danger in breaking the windows in Hubbard House, so we were politely ordered to give it all up." According to Stephens, "the fire of the base ball club still smouldered [sic]" within the former players but the twelve players from the Hubbard House teams who returned to Smith the following year did not reorganize their teams.[64] It was more than a decade before students began regularly organizing House teams and Class teams.

In 1884, while administrators at Smith were temporarily squelching baseball on their campus, 9 of 287 students enrolled at Mount Holyoke Female Seminary in South Hadley, Massachusetts, organized the "Mount Holyoke Nine" and posed for two team photos. The players, ranging in age from seventeen to twenty-one, came from Massachusetts, Connecticut, Vermont, and Maine. Seven went on to graduate, although none earned "official" college degrees because those were not issued until after the institution gained its college charter in 1888. The players posed for two team photographs and continued to play baseball until 1886, when a number of them graduated.[65]

Female Civic and Pick-up Teams of the 1880s

Whether on campus or off, baseball was a vehicle for social interaction and fun for most nineteenth-century female players. This was true no matter what social class or geographic region the players came from. It is often difficult to determine the social class of female baseball players, but enough evidence exists to indicate that players came from all social classes. In May and June 1882, newspaper reports about the Striped Stockings and Fancy Stockings of Quincy, Illinois, made it a point to inform readers that the players on those teams were "society girls."[66] The *New York Clipper* mentioned female workers at a Philadelphia shoe factory organizing a baseball club, and the *Brooklyn Daily Eagle* described the arrest of two black women baseball players who had assaulted a man with a bat.[67]

Baseball became increasingly popular in the West, where several states and territories got their first homegrown female teams. In addition to the inaugural female team in Glendive, Montana Territory in 1884, young women in Denver, Colorado and Blunt, Dakota Territory organized their first baseball teams too, while their counterparts in Utah played townball.[68] Young women in the future state of North Dakota established its first female baseball team in November 1886 in Bismarck, and the New Mexico Territory got its first female team in August 1888. A Rochester, New York, newspaper reported that the latter team was planning to barnstorm through Colorado, New Mexico, and Texas. It is uncertain if this ever occurred, but a group of women in San Antonio, Texas, discussed organizing their own team—the state's first—in April 1889.[69] In 1886 nine young women organized a team and immortalized it in a formal photograph taken in Lansing, Iowa (fig. 9); three years later, Pocahontas, Iowa, had a team too.[70]

In 1889 one newspaper reported that there were sixteen female baseball clubs in Kansas, but this may have been an exaggeration sparked by a flurry of articles about female teams in Haddam, McPherson, and Colby.[71] The previous year the *Nicodemus Cyclone,* an African American newspaper in Kansas, reported that women in Hope had organized a team.[72] It is uncertain whether this team was organized by whites or blacks.

Even as male baseball moguls strengthened their monopoly over the sport's formal structure, and as others propagated cultural imagery of baseball as a masculine game, middle- and upper-class gender traditionalists continued to embrace the sport. On September 24, 1886, a group of married and single women held a game in Gilmore, Pennsylvania, to raise money for local churches. Six hundred spectators turned out for the game in which the married women defeated the single women, 25–17 in seven innings. All of the players wore long dresses.[73] Young women played baseball at a resort on Asbury Beach in As-

FIGURE 9. Team photo (c. 1886), Red Apron Nine, Lansing, Iowa. Courtesy Joann Kline.

bury Park, New Jersey, in 1887, and in 1888 girls and women organized teams in Nyack, Utica, and Elmira, New York. The young women in Utica had the financial means to purchase matching "costumes" of blue and white and to play on an "admirable" diamond with a "neatly marked" field and well-manicured grass.[74] In July 1889, the *Manistee (Mich.) Democrat* reported that baseball was becoming quite popular with the young ladies in that town. The young women had organized two teams and were practicing and scrimmaging regularly on a vacant lot near Oak and Fifth streets. The paper teased that the site had been renamed "Crinoline park"—a likely reference to the traditional feminine garb the players were wearing.[75] In October 1889, nine young ladies, "well known in the society of Mount Washington" (near Baltimore) established a team.[76] This is the earliest known female team organized in Maryland.

One of the best publicized of the upper-class female civic teams of the 1880s was the one created by society women in Norwich, Connecticut. The *Boston Daily Globe* described the players as "cultivated, wealthy and refined members of the old-time families of Norwich" and reported that they practiced regularly on the lawn of a local farmer, Hezekiah Rudd, a "wealthy gentleman of leisure." The newspaper claimed that the women had taken up baseball because they were tired of the "flavorless feminine diversions" of croquet, tennis, and tea parties.[77] As was the case with most upper-class women's teams of the nineteenth century, the women in Norwich tried to keep their activity out of the public eye. Rudd's yard had a thick wall of hedges around it; nonetheless, a few "wicked boys and wickeder young men" occasionally managed to catch a glimpse through the foliage of the women playing.[78]

Keeping their activities hidden from public view was a key strategy female baseball players employed to contest narratives that they were trying to mimic men or encroach on their sporting spaces. This strategy was not available to the women hired to perform baseball for money. By their very existence, these players provided a potent tool that shapers of baseball's masculine creed could use to misrepresent female players in the public's mind.

Women's Professional Teams of the 1880s

The gap between men's and women's professional baseball grew exponentially during the 1880s for a number of reasons. First, as the popularity of amateur baseball grew, men's teams had access to an ever-expanding pool of talented male players and thus could increasingly market competition rather than theatrical spectacle to sell their product. Women's teams had to continue marketing novelty and theatrical-style entertainment because it was difficult for managers of women's professional teams to find (and keep) women willing to endure social humiliation to play baseball in public for money. Though managers did sometimes find talented female athletes, for the most part they had to continue filling rosters with anyone they could find.

A second widening distinction between men's and women's professional baseball was that as male entrepreneurs focused on building an enduring, formal baseball business structure that mirrored contemporary business models, the men who organized women's teams continued their short-term focus. They wanted to make as much money as possible as quickly as possible without encumbering themselves with long-term legal responsibilities and relationships. Rather than joining forces to promote and legitimize women's professional baseball, managers engaged in cutthroat competition for players and fans.

A third distinction between men's and women's professional baseball related to the relationships between labor and management. Male league officials had to deal with players who did not hesitate to express their dissatisfaction with management decisions or to organize themselves to gain leverage over their conditions of labor. Though there were a handful of incidents when female players took managers to court or refused to play until they were paid, by and large, purveyors of women's professional baseball rarely faced concerted resistance from players. They were conditioned by social mores to defer to men and to their elders.

The final, and perhaps the most significant difference between men's and women's professional baseball, was the fact that men's professional baseball (and men's baseball in general) enjoyed the loyal support of an ever-expanding network of media outlets and ancillary businesses whose financial fortunes were linked to baseball's growing popularity. Newspapers, periodicals, and sporting goods stores profited when baseball proliferated. The print media, in particular, played a major role in shaping public opinion about sports, culture, and gender roles. Once the majority of newspaper editors bought in to the narrative that men's professional baseball was a good thing (and that women's professional baseball was not), they solidified the gendered future of the sport through consistently positive coverage of the former and consistently negative coverage of the latter.

There were at least two dozen professional women's baseball teams organized during the 1880s. The majority of teams were comprised entirely of white players but, in 1883, John Lang, a white barber living in Philadelphia who had already organized several black men's teams and a Chinese nine, organized three teams of black women—the Dolly Varden No. 1, the Dolly Varden No. 2, and the Captain Jinks club.[79] As in the past, some women's professional teams were short-lived while others, like Sylvester Wilson's Young Ladies Base Ball Clubs, played entire seasons and reconstituted annually. Most female barnstorming teams continued to market theatrical entertainment but, by decade's end, some promoted competition against men's teams as an added attraction.

No matter how managers of women's professional teams tried to market their teams, the overwhelming message of the media was that professional women's baseball was an abomination—an affront to the idealized prestige of the national pastime. The parallel message was that female professional players were hopelessly inept, unfeminine, and immoral. Players on Lang's black women's teams faced the added burden of racist coverage. Though black men, like white women, had been playing baseball since its earliest inception, and though scores of highly talented black players had made their mark on white teams or all-black teams from the 1860s forward, the white press of the 1880s frequently lampooned both black and female players. The myth undergirding their narrative was that blacks and women were baseball novices who could offer spectators only comic relief, not serious athletic competition.

In a typical article about black male ballplayers in the white press, the *New York Times* described an "amusing" game of baseball played by the Orions of Philadelphia and the Washingtons of Long Branch in September 1882. Though conceding that the quality of play was "better than what was expected," the paper marginalized the black men by describing the "mirth-provoking spectacle" of their uniforms and the entertainment value of their "misplays."[80] Coverage of the Dolly Varden and Captain Jinks teams followed a similar pattern, with newspapers focusing on the gaudy and mismatched clothing of the players and employing racist slang to represent players' speech patterns.[81] In an era when spectators craved novelty, the teams of black women were doubly novel—they were women and they were black. Having already organized a barnstorming black men's team and a Chinese men's nine, Lang must have hoped to capitalize on novelty to attract spectators to the black women's games, but the venture quickly fizzled.

While Lang's efforts to profit from novelty baseball acts had little impact on broader narratives of baseball, the same cannot be said of Sylvester F. Wilson, whose persistent involvement with women's professional teams did more to harm perceptions of female baseball players than any other factor in the nineteenth century. Wilson organized female baseball troupes in at least ten of the twenty-four years between 1879 and 1903. (He was in prison or on trial for eight of the remaining fourteen years.)[82] Wilson had the talent to be a successful businessman—he was able to manage the logistical operations of multiple teams simultaneously, he was a skilled marketer, and he had no problem finding investors (although he frequently cheated them). Even Francis Richter, who loathed him, noted that Wilson's perseverance was "worthy of a better cause" and that if he would put the same energy into an honest calling he would be well-to-do.[83]

Wilson was a theatrical genius to some extent—he recognized the potential for professional women's baseball teams to attract tens of thousands of spectators annually, and shrewdly invoked classical tropes and contemporary themes of health reformers to market his baseball product. But Wilson also had serious character flaws, including an insatiable desire to surround himself with teen-age girls and young women, with whom he routinely took sexual liberties. In modern parlance he was a pedophile and sexual predator, and more than 130 girls and young women came under his control during the years he ran baseball teams.[84] Instead of going down in history as the man responsible for helping solidify women's professional baseball as a praiseworthy and respectable profession, Wilson tarnished the image of professional women players for more than a decade, making it exceedingly difficult for the managers who followed him in the 1890s to distinguish their legitimately talented and morally upstanding professional female teams from Wilson's. That he rose to infamy at the same time that men like William Hulbert were building a solid structure for Organized Baseball was particularly unfortunate, because an honest businessman who sincerely cared about the future of women's professional baseball might have changed the fortunes of women players considerably.

Apart from damaging the reputation of professional female players, Wilson solidified the gendered narrative of baseball as a man's game by promoting his women's teams as highly competitive even though they were not. This gave critics ample opportunity to use professional female baseball players as exemplars of women's inherent physical and mental weaknesses. Rather than focusing on the lack of talent of specific players on Wilson's teams—as reporters covering men's baseball did—critics of women's baseball made blanket statements about all women. Had Wilson hired talented female athletes, it would have been more difficult for critics to use women's baseball to reinforce gender stereotypes and roles.

In August 1883, Wilson and his business partners signed seventeen girls, ranging in age from fifteen to twenty-five, to contracts to make a lengthy tour throughout the East and South giving baseball exhibitions. The majority of troupe members were variety actresses; two had graduated from the Normal School of Philadelphia.[85] Encouraged by the number of individuals who sneaked glimpses through the fence enclosing the first scrimmage game, Wilson began charging a twenty-five-cent admission fee to practice games (the same price American Association teams charged); he admitted women for free and gave children a reduced rate of fifteen cents.[86] Wilson (using the alias H. H. Freeman) was so confident his venture was going to succeed that he began publicizing plans for the tour in newspapers across the country and sending letters to managers of men's teams in southern and midwestern states asking them to commit to games.[87]

As in the past, Wilson worked to craft a public image for his teams that would attract middle- and upper-class spectators. He designed advertisements that emphasized the "Elegant and Appropriate Costumes" of players and that touted the "Revival of the Ancient Greek and Roman Open-air Gymnastics for Ladies." He claimed that the "open-air exercises" they promoted were "indorsed by the Press, Pulpit and leading Medical Faculty of the country" and insisted that their "entertainment is first class in every particular, moral in every sense, and free from any objectionable feature, and can be visited with propriety by any one, even the most refined and fastidious."[88] He had yellow handbills containing the same message printed and distributed at games and in cities where he hoped to schedule games. The *New York Tribune* noted that this practice "threw a classical air" over exhibitions.[89]

Though Wilson had only slightly more success than he had had in 1879 convincing middle- and upper-class men and women to attend his games, he did still attract large numbers of spectators—including many women. Several thousand individuals attended the games at Merritt Grounds in Camden, New Jersey, on August 28 and at Jumbo Park in Philadelphia the following day. There were nearly one thousand women at the latter game—almost a third of the audience.[90] When Wilson took his teams on a quick out-and-back to Atlantic City on September 2, they drew another three thousand spectators.[91] The women played another series of games in Camden and West Philadelphia between September 3 and 5 and then ventured out on a short trip to Chester, Pennsylvania, and Baltimore, Maryland. Half of the eight hundred spectators in Chester were women, a number of whom brought their infant children with them. Almost four thousand men and women surrendered their quarters and dimes to watch the newly styled "Belles of the Bat" and "Queens of the Emerald Diamond" play at the Oriole Ball Ground on September 8.[92]

Though Wilson's troupe did not outdraw men's major league teams as Gilmore's 1879 teams had done, it did attract approximately twenty thousand more spectators than the 1879 teams. Approximately 37,000 spectators turned out for the twenty-one games of the Young Ladies' Base Ball Club for which attendance figures are available in 1883. The average of 1,762 per game exceeds by 262 the average number of spectators who had attended women's professional games in 1879. If the 1883 average holds true for the sixteen games for which no attendance figures are available, that means that approximately 65,200 spectators in eleven states saw Wilson's teams play their thirty-one games in 1883—23,000 more than the 1879 teams had drawn to their twenty-eight games.[93]

Richter followed the progress of Wilson's female baseball troupe throughout the 1883 season and occasionally published his comments. On September 10 he reported on the "comical playing" of the players. Two weeks later, no doubt disturbed by the fact that the women had attracted more than ten thousand spectators to their games in just over a month, he printed his strongest attack to date on the "miserable burlesque of the National game" perpetrated by Wilson's troupe. "These women cannot play a little bit," Richter emphasized. They "depend upon the vulgar curiosity of the mob to draw. The spectacle of eighteen faded, awkward women, in their ungraceful garments, is a positive disgrace and should be frowned upon by all lovers of the game." Three pages later, in the same issue, Richter insisted that the teams, which were trying to arrange games in Cincinnati, were unwelcome there. "This miserable aggregation should disband and the members thereof go back to their original avocations," he wrote.[94]

Richter wanted professional women's baseball teams to fail; he considered them an embarrassing sideshow that was hurting the reputation of his beloved national game. He must have been supremely disappointed when a huge crowd of four thousand to five thousand Cincinnatians turned out to see the women play on November 11 despite his insistence in late September that they were not welcome there. Richter was pleased when Wilson and his partners inexplicibly changed their route after the Cincinnati game to head west instead of south to New Orleans as they had planned, because the detour proved financially disastrous.[95] Bad weather and brutally negative press in St. Louis drastically curtailed crowd sizes and, by the end of the month, railroads and hotels were seizing the troupe's property for debts. By early December, individual players were seeking public charity to get back to Philadelphia, and Richter gleefully announced: "This settles female base ball clubs for good."[96]

It is clear from his coverage of nonprofessional female baseball players that Richter did not believe women could be legitimate baseball players. In 1892, he reprinted a lengthy article from the *Boston Globe* about a baseball game played by upper-class women against young men at a resort in Sconset (Siasconset), Massachusetts. The article was written by a "girl" who wrote an account detailing the silly antics and muffin play of the participants. Richter prefaced the article with the comment that the game represented "[n]ot such a game as the sporadic traveling female base ball combinations play for filthy lucre, but a real ladies' game."[97] Clearly the game was not "real" in any sense—players used a tennis ball, sat on bases, allowed some batters ten strikes and as many balls. By calling it a "real ladies' game" Richter was diminishing the accomplishments of truly talented girls and women who played baseball on school and college, civic and pick-up teams around the country. Even when Richter came across the highly talented Lizzie Arlington in 1898, the best Richter would allow was: "For a woman she did nicely."[98] Richter reached tens of thousands of readers with his periodical; his spin on women's baseball likely swayed some opinions about female players and undoubtedly reinforced even more.

Wilson quickly disproved Richter's assumption that female baseball was "settled for good." Confidence and bravado are the hallmarks of any gifted scam artist and huckster, and Wilson had both in spades. Within a week of Richter's pronouncement on the demise of women's professional baseball, Wilson (using his H. H. Freeman alias) was in New Orleans trying to organize another team.[99] Initially unsuccessful, he headed north, casting about for a lucrative theatrical gig. On January 24, Richter wrote that Wilson and his partner had put on a "snide entertainment" in Harrisburg, Pennsylvania; by April the pair was in Buffalo advertising for players to join "The One and Only Young Ladies' Baseball Club."[100] The advertisement specified that applicants had to be "young, good looking, active and of good form." They were to send photographs "and all particulars, age, height, color of hair and eyes" to "Freeman and Phillips."[101] With the plight of the 1883 team still fresh in their minds, numerous newspaper editors responded with anger that Wilson was trying to resurrect the traveling women's baseball teams. The *Cleveland Herald* wondered why the Buffalo police were not intervening. The *Quincy Daily Journal* urged that the "female base ball nuisance" be "suppressed."[102]

Wilson and Phillips had apparently been working behind the scenes with a new partner, Edward E. Everett, to gather players even before their advertisements appeared in newspapers in Buffalo and Philadelphia because, on April 5, teams of women called the "Blondes" and "Brunettes" played a game in Manayunk, Pennsylvania—scene of the 1878 game between male and female factory workers.[103] Four days later Richter lamented, "Not satisfied with last year's experience, the female base ball nines will again be in the field this year."[104] The game in Manayunk proved something of an aberration; Wilson, Phillips, and Everett struggled to find enough women to sign on for a full season of touring. They had to cancel games scheduled in Richmond and Chester, Pennsylvania, in late April—a large crowd had already gathered at the field in Chester before word spread that the troupe was a no-show. A similar scenario was repeated in Watervliet (West Troy) on May 9 when one thousand spectators showed up at the gate before the local hotel proprietor received a telegram from Newburgh cancelling the troupe's accommodations.[105] Wilson's troupe played in Kingston instead. Still short of players, the teams failed to keep an engagement in nearby Poughkeepsie on the twelfth. In anticipation of the trip to Poughkeepsie, Wilson had sent them press releases claiming that more than thirty thousand people had seen the teams play during their first week in Philadelphia.[106] This was a complete fabrication; there is no mention of Wilson's teams playing in Philadelphia in early 1884, let alone drawing thirty thousand spectators.

Back in New York City, Wilson partnered with Emile Gargh, another theatrical entrepreneur, to send multiple female baseball teams on the road in two troupes with Gargh, Phillips, and Everett. Both troupes played on May 17—one in Poughkeepsie for three hundred spectators and the other, eighty-two miles south in Newark, New Jersey, for four hundred spectators.[107] Everett proved to be as unscrupulous as Wilson—running off with his team's gate money ($92.40) after the Newark game. He justified his actions in a letter to Richter's *Sporting*

Life by claiming that he only took what was owed to him and that he knew that Gargh had the financial means to get the players home.[108] Once again, female baseball players had to appeal to charity for transportation back to Philadelphia.[109] Learning that a number of the stranded players had been with Wilson's 1883 troupe, Richter commented that they had not "profited by experience" before adding: "Females cannot play base ball even a little bit, and all attempts to organize and run such clubs must end in disaster and disgrace."[110]

As the summer baseball season got into full swing, Wilson tried to arrange another western tour. He contacted managers in Auburn and Oswego, New York, and in Atchison, Kansas, in early June.[111] The *Atchison Globe* reported on June 9 that the "Female Mastodon Base Ball Club of Philadelphia" would play the local Delmonicos sometime in July.[112] The 1884 season of the Young Ladies' Base Ball Club was rocky throughout. Managers struggled to keep eighteen players on their rosters and never raised sufficient capital for the western tour. Six weeks after Everett abandoned his players in Newark, Emile Gargh could muster only fourteen players for an exhibition on July 4 at the Oriole's ball grounds in Baltimore. The five hundred to six hundred men and boys who turned out for the game were a far cry from the nearly four thousand who had shown up the previous September; receipts were not nearly enough to pay expenses. When the teams staged a follow-up game the next day at Baltimore's Monumental Park, only thirty-two spectators turned out. Rather than deal with the creditors, Gargh simply abandoned the penniless players who, once again, had to appeal to the mayor and local charities for help getting home.[113]

After a number of disappointing forays into New Jersey and Maryland, Wilson decided to play a series of games in and around Philadelphia. Audience turnout was low and interest waned throughout the summer. Newspaper reports were sparse until September, when the *St. Paul Daily Globe* printed a much delayed account of the Baltimore fiasco. Calling female baseball players the "crude fruit" on the baseball tree, the *Globe* reprinted a scathing editorial from an unnamed paper excoriating female baseball as a "public nuisance."[114] A new flurry of articles accompanied Wilson and his players as they set out on another road trip beginning seventy-eight miles northwest of Philadelphia in Lebanon, Pennsylvania, on October 9. Originally billed as an exhibition between two female teams, Wilson had only enough players to field a single nine against a local men's team.[115] The troupe drew a respectable crowd of four hundred, but its fortunes took a quick downturn in Allentown and Easton, Pennsylvania, where it earned only $10 and $5 in gate receipts respectively on the thirteenth and fourteenth. Wilson found himself lacking funds to pay for meals and lodging; he pawned his watch while a group of railroad employees collected enough money to feed the players and send them home.[116] This pattern of financial "boom and bust" was a hallmark of professional female baseball well into the 1890s.

Undaunted as always, Wilson pressed on with plans to take his "Great and Only Young Ladies Base Ball Association of Philadelphia" on a southern tour to New Orleans. He had informed his wife the month before that he was leaving her for good. As his distraught and penniless wife packed up her belongings and took their eight-year-old son to live with her sister in September 1884, Wilson began contacting baseball team managers in numerous cities along the planned route to New Orleans. He booked a game in Mountain City, Maryland, for October 23 and arranged two games in Washington, D.C., on the twenty-fifth and twenty-sixth.[117] Two weeks later, the *Wilson (N.C.) Advance* reported that Wilson's team had played a men's team from Henderson at the Weldon Fair on November 12. The reporter lauded the fair organizers for keeping gamblers off the grounds that year but decried the "shameful scene" and "indecency" of the baseball game. He was relieved that "no Southern women have yet descended to such depths."[118] Wilson was undeterred by the initially poor reception in the South, taking his teams back to New Orleans several years in a row.

Wilson and his players arrived in New Orleans on the nineteenth and scheduled a series of games with the Bachs for Christmas week. They made a brief foray, 186 miles north to Jackson, Mississippi, for a game with the Mutual Base Ball Club on the twenty-third, returning home to rainy weather that forced cancellation of their Christmas games.[119] Richter had been relatively quiet about Wilson's embarrassing affronts to the national pastime for most of the 1884 season. In late November, however, he redoubled his efforts to discredit professional women's baseball by exposing Wilson for the criminal he was. On the twenty-sixth Richter informed his readers that he had received a postcard "over the signature of that notorious deadbeat and swindler, H.H. Freeman" containing a "lying and scurrilous" attack on him and his paper. Addressing Wilson by his real name, Richter warned the "ticket scalper" that if he returned to Philadelphia he would charge him with criminal libel and have him returned to Moyamensing prison.[120] On Christmas Eve 1884, Richter took the "scamp Freeman" to task for nauseating the public with the spectacle of his "tramps" playing baseball.[121]

The pot of gold Wilson hoped to find in New Orleans while the World's Industrial and Cotton Centennial Exposition was in town never materialized. The *Daily Picayune* noted in early January that the players were "drawing fairly at the Sportsmen's Park" but that two of the nine players had quit.[122] By the middle of January, Wilson was in a battle for players with a rival named P. S. Tunnison. Tunnison stole five of Wilson's players and put them in the field with four local amateurs for a game at Sportsmen's Park on Sunday, January 11. He called the troupe Tunnison's Texas tour team, and began planning exhibitions in Texas.[123] As the number of professional female baseball teams increased in the late 1880s and 1890s, competition between managers for players and spectators became more heated. Unlike the magnates of professional men's teams, managers of female teams never banded together into leagues to manage competition. Worried that he might lose spectators, Wilson assured the *Daily Picayune* that he had retained the best four players and that more were on their way from Philadelphia to fill out the roster.

Two weeks after losing most of his players, Wilson announced he was planning to take his team to Havana.[124] The trip never happened; instead Wilson tried to organize a major western tour. When his abandoned wife contacted him by letter in New Orleans asking him how she was supposed to support herself and their son, he responded that he was heading for San Francisco and that she would never see him again. He advised her to do what other women in her situation do—go out and find another woman's husband.[125] Wilson's depravity knew no bounds.

Wilson abandoned his plan to go to California and informed the *New York Clipper* that his reorganized troupe would play in Florida, Texas, Arkansas, Tennessee, Kentucky, Louisville, and Cincinnati instead.[126] This tour was fraught with endless financial problems and difficulties for the players, and the team disbanded in Hot Springs in late May. Only pitcher and catcher Pearl Emerson and May Lawrence remained with Wilson as he headed north to reorganize the troupe in Cincinnati.[127] Emerson and Lawrence were Wilson's most loyal (and talented) players; both had been with him since 1883 and would continue to play for him on future teams. Wilson hired the pair out for an exhibition game with a men's amateur team in Memphis on May 15—Richter claimed that "a more disgusted audience could not be found anywhere."[128]

It took Wilson almost a month to reorganize his baseball troupe, but he apparently obtained some significant funding because he was able to launch the new teams on an impressive tour that covered more than three thousand miles in three months with stops and planned stops in more than fifty cities in ten states—Ohio, Indiana, Illinois, Michigan, Wisconsin, Minnesota, Iowa, Kansas, Nebraska, and Missouri.[129] Shortly after departing Cincinnati, the team stopped in Kokomo, Indiana, where they played a game and were measured for "new suits." Descriptions of the players' uniforms varied, depending on the point editors hoped to make. The *Kalamazoo Gazette* reported that the players wore "exceedingly short skirts and phenomenally long stockings" while the *Wisconsin State Journal* was enamored with their "shoes of every variety, from the neat-fitting button boot to the most dilapidated run-down-at-the-heel slipper." It was also captivated by the first basewoman's "diamond ear-drops" and "almost buttonless shoes." The *Eau Claire Daily Free Press* gave the most complete description, noting that the players wore "short knee skirts of striped red and black material, black and red stockings, small baseball shoes or light slippers, black jerseys and little red caps."[130]

At some point in the season, Wilson had enough money to hire a private rail car to transport his large troupe, which consisted of twenty-four women, nine of whom played baseball. The other women comprised the "Imperial Cadets" (also known as "Amazonian Cadets")[131] and gave military drill exhibitions after ball games beginning in September. Two, and possibly four, of the women on the 1885 team had played on Wilson's 1884 teams.[132] According to a reporter who visited the troupe at its railcar in Omaha, the majority of players were from Chicago; some were married and enjoyed occasional visits from their husbands as they traveled.[133] One of the new players, Elsie James, joined the team in Indianapolis in late June; her season almost ended as soon as it began. Her father, a well-to-do citizen of that city, was furious about her decision and tried to head her off at the team's game in Fort Wayne in early July. James caught wind of his intentions and fled to Chicago, where she laid low until she could rejoin the troupe. James was still with the team in mid-August for games in Wisconsin.[134]

Now in his fourth season as a manager of female baseball troupes, Wilson added a new twist to his show—he had his teams play men's teams rather than each other. Not only did the audiences enjoy the sense of competition a "battle of the sexes" brought, but the new format reduced the number of women Wilson had to find who were willing to stick with the baseball troupe for months on end. It also gave him the flexibility to occasionally split his teams when advance men scheduled two games in one day.[135] Any hint of genuine athletic competition was lost as soon as the first pitch was thrown. Reactions were mixed once the audience and male players realized that few of the women were skilled players. Most of them adjusted quickly. The male players adopted the role of entertainers and most of the audience settled in to enjoy the baseball burlesque performance. Some, however, expressed outrage at the deception and demanded their money back.[136] Newspapers captured the gamut of emotions the female players evoked. The *Milwaukee Sentinel* noted that the "peculiar antics of the fair athletes . . . afforded considerable amusement to the spectators" and added that "few felt that they had not received entertainment commensurate with the money expended for admission."[137] A report from Oconto, Wisconsin, called the game the "most disgusting" ever played there, noting that the "'ladies' are not at all what they are advertised to be" and that some of the spectators "became so disgusted" they asked Wilson's players to leave the field.[138]

The women on Wilson's 1885 troupe experienced the same exuberant highs and embarrassing lows that characterized other seasons. Things began on a high note. Attendance in Indiana, Ohio, and Michigan numbered in the hundreds for games in July and early August. Things got even better in Wisconsin and Minnesota. The troupe's first game in Milwaukee on August 15 drew 2,800 persons—among the largest crowds ever assembled there on a weekday—and another large crowd turned out the following day when the women played a different team.[139] Large and "immense" crowds filed into the team's canvas enclosure at fairgrounds in Oshkosh, Waukesha, and Madison, Wisconsin, the following week. The game in Waukesha was staged at the annual military encampment of veterans of the 1st Wisconsin Regiment. Almost the entire regiment, five hundred to six hundred strong, turned out for the game. On August 28, Wilson's players entertained the biggest crowd that had ever played on the ball grounds in Eau Claire.[140]

On August 29, the troupe crossed into Minnesota where either three thousand to four thousand men or seven hundred men and eight women (depending which newspaper article got its facts straight) watched them play "a scrub team of homely Minnesota boys" on the grounds at the corner of Nicollet Avenue and Lake Street in Minneapolis.[141] On Sunday, August 30, Wilson took his team twenty-four miles northeast of Minneapolis to Stillwater, where cold, wet weather had forced cancellation of many planned events during the first three days of the Washington County Fair. On the fourth and final day of the fair, Wilson's team attracted an impressive crowd of 1,200 to 1,300 men, women, and children. A reporter for the *St. Paul Daily Globe* observed that the entire police force, minus its chief, had turned out to keep order but that the crowd was well behaved. The team cleared a respectable $300 for the event. Wilson had apparently not yet acquired the special railroad car employed later in the season; instead the team stayed at the Sawyer Hotel, where the players spent part of the next day at the windows flirting with male passersby.[142] The team's good fortunes continued in nearby St. Paul where they drew 1,500 fans, including "quite a number of ladies" to the old ball grounds for a match against a picked nine of men. The day was marred by some violence as five or six policemen tried in vain to hold back the crowd of men who tore down the team's canvas fence as it was being erected around the diamond. The atmosphere remained uncomfortable; all of the women in attendance left after only one inning, and Wilson called the end of play after just four innings.[143]

Wilson's team had mixed success after leaving Minnesota and, apart from a successful showing in the Nebraska state capitol on October 23 where the baseball team defeated a "scrub nine of boys" in front of an "immense crowd of statesmen and others," the 1885 troupe never again matched the financial success it had enjoyed in Wisconsin and Minnesota.[144] Perhaps emboldened by their proximity to so many legislators and legal authorities, the women in Wilson's troupe chose their visit to Lincoln as the place to try to force Wilson to pay them the $200 he owed in back salaries. They had local law enforcement seize the troupe's equipment and a share of the previous day's gate receipts until he paid them.[145]

Wilson somehow managed to scrape together enough money to settle the players' claims and the troupe continued its travels, playing games in St. Joseph,

Missouri, on the twenty-ninth and in Severance and Atchison, Kansas, on the thirtieth. Wilson split his team for the games in Severance and Atchison and augmented them with young men dressed in female clothes—a fact not lost on a reporter for the *Atchison (Kans.) Daily Globe,* who commented that a number of the players on the female team looked like they needed a shave.[146] By the time Wilson's two baseball teams reunited in Kansas City on November 1, its fate was sealed. Though Wilson confidently announced games for November and December (including a trip to Havana and a tour of Texas), it was clear that the troupe was in trouble. On November 2, Wilson had his assistant Charles Sporr (or Spoor) and advance agent Jules Lyons arrested, claiming they had stolen the $125 gate money from the game in Leavenworth and that they had been trying to lure his players away to form another group. Sporr claimed that the money was rightfully theirs for back salary and notified the press that H. H. Freeman was really Sylvester Wilson, the notorious ticket scalper from Philadelphia.[147] The legal battle between Wilson and Sporr caused a rift among troupe members. Twelve of them marched up Main Street in formation and made a neat flanking movement into the courtroom to give their testimony on Wilson's behalf; the others supported Sporr. The judge sided with the latter and released Sporr with no punishment.[148]

Wilson and Sporr went their separate ways, each taking players. Wilson tried to arrange some games in and around Kansas City to obtain enough funds to resume travels. He placed ads announcing games against a team in the Commercial League at Kansas City's League Park for November 8 and 9 and against the "fat men's base ball nine" of Independence, Missouri, for the following week.[149] On November 11, apparently unaware of the team's situation, Francis Richter informed his readers that "the female base ball club is ravaging Nebraska."[150] At some point, Wilson received an infusion of cash. Newspapers in Charleston, South Carolina, and Sherman, Texas, reported that a female baseball team had played local men's teams on November 21 and December 25, and a newspaper in Nebraska reported that they had played in Denison, Texas, on the twenty-sixth. Anxious to make up for lost revenue, Wilson increased ticket prices in Charleston to fifty cents each and was handsomely rewarded when 1,700 individuals passed through the ticket booth. Unfortunately for Wilson, another seven thousand freeloaders watched the game from nearby housetops, telegraph poles, and fences.[151]

On New Year's Day 1886 Wilson's team played a game in Dallas, after which they headed to Waxahachie, Waco, and Lampasas.[152] In Waco, Wilson's baseball team and military drill company staged indoor performances that sparked a physical altercation between the local promoter and a rival who had placed a notice warning women not to attend the disreputable shows.[153] On January 20 Richter, who had informed readers a month earlier that Wilson's baseball team was "ravaging" Nebraska, now informed them that the team was "ravaging" Texas. He added that Texans probably hoped its recent blizzard had "stiffened those female base ball cranks."[154] The *Oswego Daily Times* was more sympathetic, observing that the players were "forced to suffer continual abuse from the rougher element" who were attending their games.[155] On January 27, Wilson and his troupe arrived in San Antonio for a five-night engagement at the Fashion Theater, where they headlined with M. Bertrand, "the champion trick skater of the southwest," and several other song and dance acts. A local paper lauded the expertise and precision of Wilson's drill company.[156]

After wrapping up their engagement in San Antonio, Wilson and his troupe headed east for games in Seguin, Houston, Brenham, and Galveston. They drew a large crowd of 1,200 in Galveston on February 28 before disappearing from the historical record for almost two months.[157] In April, the *New Orleans Daily Picayune* reported that Wilson's teams were playing again but that four of its best players had left the troupe. Wilson soon got the team back up to full strength; on April 25 they were ready to play again.

The renewed season got off to an inauspicious start when, during the team's first game at Spanish Fort, a young man ran out of the crowd, grabbed the third basewoman by the back of her neck, and dragged her off the field, yelling that she was his sister and he was taking her home. Richter was just one of dozens of editors who reported the story over the next seven months.[158] The startling incident was a precursor of what was to come. On May 4, New Orleans police received a request from Cincinnati police to detain two of Wilson's players (Ella Burke and Fannie Crambert) because they were runaways. Wilson had provided the girls with train tickets from his base in New Orleans. Ticket broker Martin Mercer later testified that he had lent Wilson the money for the tickets and that Wilson had beaten him up when Mercer voiced second thoughts about how the money was being used.[159] As the negative press about Wilson and his operation mounted, Wilson began taking to the stump in Beach Park to make loud rants about "lying and blackmailing newspapers" to anyone who would listen.[160] The brash offensive was Wilson's modus operandi whenever he felt threatened.

As legal authorities dug further into Wilson's background and that of the twenty girls working for him, they recognized Wilson for the predator he was. The majority of his players were minors. Investigators discovered that five of the girls were from Chicago, one was from New York City, one hailed from Detroit, two were from Philadelphia, two were from Cincinnati, and at least two, Lizzie Clifford and Florence Harris, hailed from New Orleans. Harris's father was a deaf mute who became upset when he learned that she had joined the baseball club. He intended to pull her off the team but, after Wilson cajoled him, he agreed to let her drill with the military company. All of the players had suffered many privations under Wilson. Judge Davey released the older players but sent the minors to the House of the Good Shepherd until their parents or guardians could collect them. He bound Wilson over for arraignment the next day on charges of vagrancy and being "a dangerous and suspicious character."[161]

Never one to miss an opportunity to fulminate for the press and legal authorities, Wilson pled his cause loudly in the courtroom. Davey was not swayed by Wilson's portrayal of his high moral character and innocent intentions, nor was he moved by the copious tears shed by five of Wilson's players who attended the hearing to support him. Davey ordered Wilson to pay a fine of $25 or serve thirty days in jail. Unable to pay the fine, Wilson was remanded to the local jail. Within days Wilson had obtained a reprieve from the mayor in exchange for his promise to leave the city by May 8. He initially planned to head for Mobile, Alabama, but immediately began lobbying the mayor for more time so he could regroup his troupe for a trip to Pensacola. On May 14, still in New Orleans, Wilson wrote the mayor asking him to provide armed protection for him and his troupe so they could depart without molestation from law enforcement. Judge Buisson, acting on the mayor's behalf, ordered the chief of police to escort Wilson and his players to the train station and make sure they got on board.[162]

Wilson got into trouble again almost immediately. Still angry about his perceived persecution in New Orleans, he began publicly slandering Judge Davey and New Orleans's law enforcement officials as soon as he arrived in Pensacola. He was arrested but managed to escape while out of jail on a writ of habeas corpus. Wilson headed north to Birmingham with the nine players who had stuck with him after the debacle in New Orleans. These young women were devoted to Wilson and trusted him when he promised that their fortunes would improve. This pattern of devotion continued with future players too, some of whom testified at Wilson's abduction trial in 1892 that they loved him and that he had always treated them like a father—(a father who routinely molested them!).[163] The remaining players eventually had to petition Birmingham legal authorities to force Wilson to pay the three months back salary he owed them. Wilson was arrested for the third time in a month—not only for failing to pay his players but also for failing to pay his lodging bill.

Wilson again fled prosecution, abandoning six of the players penniless in Birmingham. One of the players, a fifteen-year-old from Detroit, was taken in as a servant by a sympathetic family. Her mother eventually learned about her location from newspaper articles about Wilson's arrest and sent money to bring her daughter home.[164] For parents whose daughters fell prey to Wilson's silver-tongued promises of riches and ran away with him to seek their fortunes, national publications offered one of the few avenues they had for tracking down their daughters. Fortunately for them, editors like Francis Richter kept close tabs on Wilson. On May 26, O. P. Caylor, one of Richter's regular correspondents in Cincinnati, provided an update on Wilson, reminding readers that he had once been run out of Cincinnati for inciting anarchy and that he had abandoned his wife and children in Camden. He concluded: "The penitentiary will never be a success till all such as he are pulled into it."[165]

After the rocky 1886 season Wilson decided to take a temporary hiatus from women's baseball. He and his star pitcher Pearl Emerson settled in Kansas City in early 1887; he passed Emerson off as his niece.[166] Wilson ran several scams in Kansas City in which he collected thousands of dollars from individuals in exchange for jobs with his newspapers and a promised future return on their investment. In each case, Wilson severed the partnership on false pretenses and the dupes were left with nothing. In the fall of 1888, Emerson decided to return home to Philadelphia—she had been on the road with Wilson almost continuously since she joined his original Young Ladies' Base Ball Club of Philadelphia in August 1883.

With funds running short, and eager to find another female companion to replace Emerson, Wilson scammed enough railroad passes and money to travel to Philadelphia and Washington, D.C., in grand style. In Philadelphia he conned the widowed mother of fourteen-year-old Elizabeth Brady into allowing him to take her with him to Kansas City. He represented himself as a wealthy, western newspaperman who wanted to adopt Brady and give her a fine home and education. Back in Kansas City, Wilson moved from boardinghouse to boardinghouse with "daughter" Brady, whom he passed off as Sylvia Wilson. Though he always rented an adjoining room for her, landlords grew suspicious and tipped off the Kansas City Humane Society, which rescued the young girl and sent her to the House of the Good Shepherd in Philadelphia.

Other Female Baseball Hucksters

While Wilson took a hiatus from female baseball, others filled the void. In January 1886, Victor E. M. Gutmann, a man described by one newspaper as a "champion dead beat," organized the Blue Stockings of Frisco and the Red Stockings of Chicago female baseball teams.[167] The teams debuted in public on Sunday, February 14, attracting several thousand spectators in San Francisco's Central Park; a week later they drew approximately 1,200 spectators to Sacramento's Agricultural Park.[168] The *Sacramento Daily Record-Union* noted that many of the spectators were prosperous doctors, businessmen, and lawyers who left during the first inning when they realized what type of show they had paid to see.[169] As he watched embarrassed spectators streaming out of the park during the game in Sacramento, Gutmann must have realized that he was not going to be able to make enough money to pay the salaries and expenses of his female baseball troupe on a regular basis. He abandoned the enterprise and went on to his next "nefarious catch-penny scheme."

Gutmann may have headed south to try to duplicate his initial success in Los Angeles. In August 1888, the *Los Angeles Times* reported that a man named "E. Gaudin" had recently arrived from San Francisco and announced that he was going to organize a female baseball nine to compete against a nine already organized by Sam Devilbiss. The *Times* warned its middle- and upper-class readers about the true nature of Gaudin's and Devilbiss's teams, reporting that many of the players had recently been employed as "beer-jerkers" at the White Elephant saloon and that the types of "macs, prostitutes, disreputables and cut-throats" who would attend female baseball games would make the usual crowd at a prizefight seem to be a Sunday-school picnic.[170] Apparently, the bad press was enough to deter Gaudin and Devilbiss from attempting to rent a venue for their proposed exhibitions; there is no evidence their teams ever played.

On July 4, 1887, professional mesmerist "Professor" E. G. Johnson staged a baseball game between the "Queens of the Diamond" and "The Climax" (a team of boys aged ten to eighteen) at the South Side baseball grounds. Johnson, who had impressed two hundred students and faculty at Chicago's Rush Medical College four years earlier with a demonstration of his talents, had organized the teams specifically for the event, which he hoped would prove profitable. Jokingly advertised as a demonstration of women's rights, the game drew five thousand of the thirty thousand Chicagoans who celebrated the Fourth of July at special events throughout the city. Many attendees were put off by the brevity of the skirt of the red-white-and-blue uniform worn by the female players which, according to one reporter "was not long enough to be on speaking terms with [their] knees."[171] Scores of disgusted spectators left the game early, including one thousand who were lured away in the second inning by a fight that began in the stands and then spilled outside the park onto Portland Avenue.

Wilson Returns

After spending two-and-a-half years running scams out of Kansas City, Wilson decided to return to female baseball. Employing a new alias—W. S. Franklin—he moved to Chicago in May 1889 and began advertising for players to form two female baseball teams. Employing his favorite classical trope in the advertisement he placed in the *Sporting and Club House Directory*—a publication that prided itself on guiding subscribers to the best whorehouses and gambling dens in the city—he announced: "Young Ladies Base Ball Club and Revival of the Ancient Grecian-Roman Open-Air Pastimes for Women. Wanted, at all times, young and handsome girls who can play ball. Liberal salary and all expenses to the right people."[172] By June, Wilson was instructing amateur and youth baseball teams to contact him at the Cosmopolitan Hotel on Clark Street to schedule games with his "ladies" club. On the twenty-first, he announced three games at three different venues in Chicago for the twenty-ninth, thirtieth, and July 1.[173] The day before their Chicago debut, Wilson took his new female team thirty-six miles northwest to Elgin, where they lost to the Elgins, 14–11.

Local papers do not seem to have reported on the women's early games in Chicago but, by July 3, Francis Richter had discovered that Wilson was back in the baseball business, and he was not pleased. "Chicago is about to inflict another female base ball team upon a long-suffering public," he wrote. "Female teams have been sent tramping over the country before, but all efforts to make these ventures pay proved a merited failure, and the same fate will surely await the present contemplated venture, so why degrade these women and disgrace the game anew?"[174] Two weeks later, the editor of Chicago's *Daily Inter Ocean,* who had been dutifully printing Wilson's notices in his paper, echoed Richter's tone when he asserted: "The female base-ball club should be suppressed."[175]

Ignoring his critics as he had so many times in the past, Wilson left Chicago with his team for a lengthy tour of Illinois, Michigan, Ohio, Canada, and New York between July and mid-September. After a game in Detroit on August 18, the troupe crossed over into Canada, where they played a series of games as they headed east toward a game scheduled in Buffalo on September 7. During this period, the troupe traveled more than two thousand miles and attracted crowds ranging in size from a few hundred to almost five thousand in Cleveland, Ohio.[176] Discounting Wilson's exaggerated claims that six thousand and eight thousand fans had witnessed games at Maroon Park in Chicago on June 30 and July 4, there is no question that the 1889 female baseball team was routinely drawing large crowds.[177] After reentering the United States, the team remained in New York for two weeks playing games in and around the Finger Lakes region.[178] Many of the spectators in New York were women—including half of the audience of eight hundred who attended the game in Oswego on September 9. After a successful run in New York, Wilson headed for Pittsburgh, hoping to take advantage of the crowds gathering in the area for an exposition. Two days after his team's arrival, Barnum's Circus drew fifteen thousand customers to performances in Allegheny on the twenty-third and twenty-fourth. Wilson must have been salivating at the possibilities for his club.

Wilson never stopped recruiting players. While the team played games in Pittsburgh and Allegheny on the twenty-first and twenty-third, he placed ads in local papers seeking twenty young women, aged sixteen to twenty, to join his "show company." The *Pittsburgh Dispatch* reported that twelve aspiring actresses had visited Wilson (W. S. Franklin) at the Hotel Crescent, thinking he was promoting a theatrical company. In reality, he was trying to organize a second team. The *Dispatch*'s coverage of Wilson's attempts to secure more players provides useful insights into his overall strategy. He freely informed the reporter that he always paid attention to how applicants looked because he wanted them to make a "good appearance" on the field. He did not want girls who were too skinny or too fat. He acknowledged that some of the players had theatrical backgrounds but stated that players came from all stations of life and backgrounds. Some still lived with their parents while others had held jobs outside the home. The majority of applicants had never played baseball but, occasionally, he found some with a lot of experience. He claimed it was not difficult to teach the rest how to play.[179] (Wilson had no intention of fielding a highly skilled team. His idea of teaching the rest "how to play" no doubt meant simply ensuring they understood the basic rules of the game, where to stand on the field, and how to bat and run bases. This, indeed, was not difficult to do but it certainly did not prepare the players to live up to the billing he gave them as superior players.)

The stop in Pittsburgh marked the beginning of a new phase in the 1889 season. Having learned from past mistakes about trying to prolong a season into late fall in northern climes, Wilson charted a route that headed east across Pennsylvania, and then south through Virginia, North Carolina, and Tennessee to Atlanta, Georgia, between early September and late November. One of the most unusual games of the season took place in Williamsport, Pennsylvania, on September 27 when the women played an exhibition game with a picked nine of "gentlemen of color."[180] This is the first and only time that a nineteenth-century women's professional baseball team is known to have played a black men's team.[181]

In late October, the *San Antonio Daily Light* reported that Wilson had been planning to bring his team to town for a series of six games in early December but that he had rescheduled the visit to November 5 to 15 to synch their visit with the International Fair. The *Silver City (N.M.) Enterprise* reported that the women would play there on December 19.[182] Clearly, Wilson intended to prolong the 1889 season indefinitely. Instead, southern audiences continued to resist Wilson's brand of entertainment, and his troupe came to another inglorious end in Atlanta on December 2. As the team traveled south into Virginia and North Carolina, they found it difficult to cover expenses. The *Shenandoah (Va.) Herald* described the players' pregame parade in Winchester as "demoralizing" and their conduct on the field as "disgusting." It noted that the exhibition the players gave "along the road" in Woodstock as they passed through the town en route to Staunton was "just the kind that southern people don't care to witness."[183] Reviews were no better in North Carolina. The *Biblical Recorder,* the official organ of the Baptist State Convention of North Carolina, described the female baseball team as an example of the "downward progress" of society. "Years ago no sane person in the South could have imagined such degradation possible," it lamented. Asserting that "female lecturers, female preachers, &c., have had their natural effect on the humbler classes of women in the South," it concluded: "The bottom is not yet reached."[184]

Gender and religious traditions were powerful forces in the postbellum South, and Wilson's troupe of scantily clad female baseball players presented little appeal to southern audiences. The team canceled a game in Goldsboro, North Carolina, on October 29 when they collected only $8 at the gate despite the fact that there were four hundred men milling around the venue.[185] Recognizing that he was not going to be able to support the troupe if he continued farther south, Wilson turned west hoping that audiences in Tennessee would be more welcoming. They were. The team had a good turnout in Greeneville on November 5 and drew at least two hundred to its game in Knoxville on the sixth.[186] After playing another game in Athens, Tennessee, on November 7, the troupe disappears from newspaper accounts until December 3, when the *Atlanta Constitution* reported that the "Ladies' Champion Baseball Club is no more. It died a painful and unnatural death yesterday. The struggle was long—it lasted more than a week, but . . . to-day the members will hit the grit for other fields."[187] Wilson was not in Atlanta when his team collapsed. He was on the road with a second club billed as the Philadelphia Female Baseball Club. That club failed too. Undeterred as always, Wilson organized still more female baseball teams in the 1890s. They proved his downfall, but not before his depravity became national news—news that Francis Richter happily published.

5. The 1890s: New Women, Bloomer Girls, and the Old Ball Game

What are our American girls coming to? The next thing I suppose we shall be having "lady" jockeys on our race tracks. "Ladies' Baseball League," indeed? In many other lines of business ladies are being introduced, and with the best of success, but surely the men are able to take care of this peculiar branch.

—Anonymous Woman, *Sporting News,* September 20, 1890[1]

The new woman is coming to the front in the most unexpected directions. Century runs by bloomer girls are as common as dirt, and female base ball, foot ball and tennis enthusiasts are found on every hand.

—*St. Louis Globe-Democrat,* October 1896[2]

THE 1890S WERE WATERSHED YEARS for the final gendering of baseball as a man's game. Though the fault line separating "men's baseball" from "women's baseball" (and later softball) would not be specifically demarcated until 1929 when physical educator Gladys Palmer published *Baseball for Girls and Women* to standardize and promote an official "women's" version of the sport, it was during the 1890s that baseball's road not taken most clearly presented itself.[3] The decade afforded women a previously unparalleled opportunity to stake a decisive claim on the national pastime just as tens of thousands of female cyclists and smaller numbers of golfers, swimmers, tennis players, and other athletic women were doing in other sports.

Baseball was more popular than ever in the 1890s. Unprecedented numbers of Americans of all social classes were embracing the game as a uniquely American, fun, and wholesome activity that had the ability to inculcate manliness in participants. As the final decade of the nineteenth century approached, the *Marquette Daily Mining Journal* observed: "Almost every class of persons has its representative base ball club in this country, demonstrating the great favor in which the game is held by Americans and its right to the distinction of being called the national game."[4] Newspapers in sprawling metropolises and tiny rural hamlets regularly carried stories about civic and collegiate teams as they faced off for local bragging rights. Baseball games were regular features at Sunday school picnics, county fairs, and Independence Day celebrations. Baseball was no longer the national pastime in name only, and more women than ever followed the fortunes of their local teams or tried their hand at playing themselves.

The context in which women played baseball in the 1890s differed from previous decades. Few living in the United States during the turbulent years preceding the dawn of the twentieth century were unaware of (or untouched by) the seismic shifts occurring in the nation's sociocultural landscape. Many of the unsettling changes centered on gender roles and ideals. The anonymous woman who wrote to *Sporting News* in 1890 wondering, "What are our American girls coming to?" sensed that something had changed. The *St. Louis Globe Democrat* recognized that "new woman" was reshaping the cultural landscape.[5] "New Women" seemed to be everywhere. Clad in Bloomers, business attire, or the latest French fashions as circumstances warranted, and exuding confidence, robust health, and a progressive vision to solve social ills, talented, ambitious, athletic white, middle- and upper-class women redefined femininity, sweeping away ideals of frail, tightly laced Victorian ladies as the model for "true womanhood" in America.[6] Unprecedented numbers of girls and women eagerly enrolled in high schools and colleges and countless women assumed leadership roles in colleges, governments, professions, and progressive reform organizations. By 1900, 20 percent of U.S. women were in the workforce and 40 percent of college students were women.[7]

Every generation has had its own version of the 1890s "New Women" (women unwilling to settle for less than they believe they can achieve and who refuse to conform to prevailing gender conventions) but the sheer number of women who embraced the waves of gender transformation sweeping over the country in the late nineteenth century caught the attention of social commentators and inspired the sobriquet, "New Woman." Joseph Dana Miller captured the mood of the times in 1896: "Ignore it as we will, deplore it as we may, the status of woman in society is undergoing, by the action of irrepressible forces, an astonishing and formidable change," he wrote.[8] As cultural commentators like Miller described the phenomenon of the New Woman in print and speeches, graphic artist Charles Dana Gibson gave her a face and a name—the Gibson Girl.[9]

Gibson's name became irrevocably associated with New Women, but it was Bernarr Macfadden who taught her that athleticism could be beautiful and that it was, in fact, a prerequisite for beauty. "[T]here can be no beauty without fine muscles," Macfadden counseled feminine readers of *Physical Culture,* his newly launched periodical on health and fitness.[10] Inspired by the example of British strongman Eugen Sandow, who wowed crowds at the World's Columbian

Exhibition in 1893, Macfadden transformed himself into a muscular, healthy man and made it his life's work to teach men and women how to find happiness and beauty through physical fitness. Sandow and Macfadden were influential in transforming ideals about physical beauty—Macfadden in particular helped free women from the idea that "true" women were weak and helpless.[11]

Macfadden's success was made possible by a confluence of trends that had been building in the United States for more than a decade. The growing influence of Social Darwinism was particularly important, as it drove innumerable reform impulses, one of which was to improve the physical health of white, native-born, middle- and upper-class men and women on whom the future of American civilization ostensibly depended. The belief that physical health and vitality were prerequisites of social stability and financial success helped spur the professionalization of physical education and the development of "scientific" programs aimed at teaching everyone how to live healthier lives. As educators at all levels began integrating physical education into their formal curricula, adults and children internalized new ideals about physicality.

It was not long before "new" women simply became "women" as new behaviors displaced traditional ideals. Commenting on the transformation in 1895, *Godey's Magazine* observed: "Ten years ago a woman who rode a bicycle, played golf or football, was supposed to be without the pale of decent society. Now the most modest women in the land amuse themselves in this way, and independence has got to be such a feature of the new woman that no one dreams of finding it unwomanly."[12] Social transformation is never a painless process because most people view change as a zero-sum proposition. One group's sense of progress and achievement is generally mirrored by another group's sense of loss and regression. For every New Woman who proudly enrolled in college, earned her credentials as a doctor or lawyer, wheeled freely about the countryside on her bicycle, or marked her ballot in school board and state elections, there were men and women watching with alarm—convinced that New Women were unraveling the fabric of society and threatening civilization itself.

Newspapers and periodicals were full of articles either lauding or condemning New Women. As concerns over "race suicide" multiplied, some blamed her desire to attend college for the fact that birthrates for white native-born women were plummeting while those of immigrant women soared. Herbert Spencer attributed the "deficiency of reproductive power" of upper-class women to "overtaxing of their brains."[13] Others pointed to the millions of women who entered the workforce instead of fulfilling their responsibility to stay home and direct well-ordered families. The fact that the rate of women entering the workforce during the 1890s exceeded the birthrate was cause for alarm for those who believed American civilization itself was at stake.[14] Occasionally, social commentators cited female baseball players as proof of the ongoing transformation in gender roles and ideals. "We are going very fast," observed Charles Dudley Warner in a frequently reprinted article. Society has "ceased to be astonished at finding women in unexpected places." In fact, he concluded, it had been "more shocked some years ago by the appearance in the field of female baseball clubs than it would be now by the advent of female football teams."[15]

New Women and the Old Ball Game

Society had "ceased to be astonished" by female baseball teams in the 1890s, not only because gender ideals were changing but because girls and women were organizing baseball teams in unprecedented numbers. There were scores of schoolgirl and adult female baseball teams in the 1890s in at least twenty-five states, including five (Arizona, South Carolina, Georgia, Wyoming, and Nebraska) that had never had homegrown teams previously.[16] More than forty professional teams barnstormed the country at various times during the decade, playing in the majority of states in the continental United States. Players came from all social classes and ranged from school-age children to middle-aged matrons. Factory workers in Rockford, Illinois, enjoyed baseball, as did the city's upper-class women who staged a well-publicized baseball game between married and single women as a fund raiser for their Ladies' Aid Society.[17] Black women's teams from Fort Valley and Atlanta, Georgia, were the featured entertainment at a Fourth of July celebration in 1894, while upper-class young men and women routinely organized coed baseball teams at various colleges and vacation resorts throughout the decade.[18]

Owing to Americans' growing acceptance of vigorous physical activities for women and the increased emphasis on physical education in schools and colleges, many female baseball players of the 1890s demonstrated impressive skills on the diamond—so much so that some were hired to play for men's teams as a way to attract spectators to those contests.[19] Professional women's baseball teams, which had counted on theatrical spectacle and novelty to sell tickets in the 1870s and 1880s, increasingly turned to marketing genuine competition to draw spectators. Though many of the teams continued to hire only marginally talented players, a growing number of "Bloomer Girl" teams were able to deliver the promised competition because they made it a priority to hire talented female athletes—and because they were not above having "toppers" (men in wigs and dresses) play key positions (pitcher, catcher, and shortstop).[20]

The more talented female professional teams and players tended to receive favorable press in the 1890s,[21] but the theatrical teams continued to generate so much criticism that civic players sometimes took pains to distinguish themselves from those teams.[22] In July 1891, a group of "society" girls in Washington Court House, Ohio, traded tennis racquets for baseball bats and challenged a team of local boys to a game. In an effort to differentiate themselves from the much-condemned troupes of working-class female baseball players touring the country challenging men's teams, the society women assured the press that they would not "play in public or travel" and that their game would be umpired by a prominent Presbyterian minister. Despite players' efforts to be discreet, word of their game appeared in newspapers in Georgia, Tennessee, Illinois, and Pennsylvania. Francis Richter conveyed his disapproval by subtitling his reprint of the article: "Respectable Ladies to Spoil Their Hands at the Sport."[23]

The thousands of girls and women, and boys and men playing baseball on civic and pick-up, school and college, factory and barnstorming teams throughout the decade had the potential to influence the culture of baseball and to restore its natal gender-neutral character. That they were unable to do so owed, in large measure, to the disproportionate influence of the powerbrokers of organized baseball.

The Enduring Structure of Organized Baseball

The "old ball game" fell on hard times in the 1890s—at least at the elite level. The *Utica Saturday Globe* declared 1890 to be "unquestionably, the most disastrous year, financially, the national game has experienced since 1876." The following year, noting that only one or two minor leagues expected to finish the 1891 season, it wrote: "Never in the history of the national game has disaster been so rife in minor league circles as this season."[24] Things were no better at the major league level. Both the American Association and Players' League collapsed in 1891, and two years later the owners of the twelve National League teams found themselves struggling to fill seats during a debilitating national economic depression. NL owners continued to battle the players over the reserve rule and other management decrees. Desperate to shore up their dwindling finances, most NL owners dropped their bans on Sunday games and relaxed their vigilance against gambling, drinking, and rowdiness in the stands. The result was predictable. The league "acquired a notorious reputation for brawling, both on the field and in the stands," writes Rader, and concerned observers lamented that the violence and obscenity was deterring "respectable women" from attending.[25]

Despite the travails of individual professional teams and leagues, the structural foundation of organized baseball laid by the National League in 1876 was secure and would endure. Major league team owners firmly controlled the evolving rules of the game and they were the de facto leaders of the professional baseball business. By the end of the 1880s, they had driven blacks out of the major leagues; in the ensuing decades they would exert pressure on professional and semiprofessional teams to withhold contracts from female players too.

Their vision for a stable business model for professional baseball was finally bearing fruit, and their influence over the culture of the game was reinforcing its gendered character.

When Cultures Collide: Women, Men, and Baseball

Throughout the nineteenth century, baseball had been a contested space where narratives of gender, race, ethnicity, social class, economics, and cultural practices played out on rural and urban, amateur and professional diamonds across the nation. By the 1890s the sheer number of women baseball players (and the tens of thousands of "New Women" invading colleges, law libraries, medical schools, businesses, and polling places) caused some to abandon their attitude of benevolent tolerance toward female players. These concerned individuals worried that the fabric of society was unraveling and that masculinity itself was under assault. When humor and sarcasm failed to stem the tide of New Women and female baseball players, some critics began putting down their joke books and picking up their poison pens.

Those who viewed baseball as a vehicle for conferring masculinity on its practitioners and for promoting American exceptionalism abroad incorporated a number of themes into their commentaries about female baseball players. Some of the themes focused on the role men needed to play in upholding male prerogatives, while others targeted female baseball players and any women who aspired to excel as athletes.

Women's Baseball = Women's Rights

This theme equated professional women baseball players with women's rights activists and the legions of "new" women who were unsettling gender traditions in the 1890s. "The equal suffragists in Kansas should approve the female base ball club," noted the *Atchison Daily Globe* in 1892. "Equal rights means an equal right to dress up in stripes and tear over a field after a ball, as well as it means the right to vote."[26] A year earlier the *Sioux County (Iowa) Herald* had observed: "The efforts of women to break into the national game and into Yale College are met with continual discouragement."[27] The *Herald*'s comment reflected the growing numbers of individuals who saw no difference between a woman who insisted upon invading the sacred halls of an Ivy League college and those who invaded the sacred spaces of the national game. In 1893, thousands of visitors to the World's Columbia Exposition flocked to exhibits on the Midway Plaisance featuring "primitive" people living in "authentic" villages; meanwhile, thousands of women attended a World's Conference of Representative Women held at the Exposition. The *Chicago Times* unkindly wondered whether the "short-skirted reformers" attending the Congress were part of the midway exhibits or members of a female base ball club.[28]

Hold the Line, Men

This theme targeted men, urging them to hold the line against encroachments of women into their traditional social spaces. On September 18, 1890, a female reader in St. Louis wrote a letter to *Sporting Life* decrying the proliferation of professional female baseball teams. She enclosed a copy of one of the advertisements Sylvester Wilson had placed in a New York newspaper the previous week promising excellent salaries to fifty "good looking" young women who would join his new baseball league. Unimpressed that talented female athletes could earn a lucrative salary playing baseball, and making a clear distinction between women's entry into other previously male professions, "M.S." wrote: "Ladies' Baseball League, indeed? In many other lines of business ladies are being introduced, and with the best of success, but surely the men are able to take care of this peculiar branch." Issuing a final challenge to professional male baseball players "who are not in favor of women's rights," she asked, "Are you going to say nothing while the 'ladies' take your places on the diamond, in the sporting world, etc.?"[29]

Stay on the Pedestal, Ladies

For centuries, a common theme used to justify women's subordinate status in political, legal, economic, and social realms was to argue that the often corrupt, brutal, and winner-take-all nature of associated activities would tarnish women's purity and expose them to unnecessary mental stresses that God (or nature) had not equipped them to handle. Many believed that women were divinely or naturally endowed with superior moral purity. Critics of barnstorming women's baseball teams insisted that players besmirched the inherent moral dignity of *all* women, not just themselves. The *Cedar Rapids Evening Gazette* said as much after a barnstorming team entertained spectators there in August 1892. Its reporter conceded that the players had done nothing, either through their behavior or speech, that could be considered vulgar, but insisted that such exhibitions should not be encouraged because they "can not fail to have the effect of lowering the dignity of woman and removing her from her natural sphere."[30] The *Dorchester (Md.) Democrat-News* agreed. After complimenting the members of the Young Ladies Base Ball Club of New York for their "gentle and quiet" behavior, the editors nonetheless admitted that they still regarded the exhibition as "demoralizing and as a step far downwards from the eminence upon which we love to place feminine modesty and true womanly character."[31]

Say It Ain't So

For some men, the best way to prove that baseball was too rigorous and scientific for women to master was to vigorously and repeatedly deny that there was any such thing as a talented female baseball player or a knowledgeable female fan. This was the approach John Ward had taken in 1888 when he claimed that American baseball could not possibly be linked to any English predecessors because girls had played English baseball. With girls' and women's teams proliferating all around them, it must have been difficult for men like Ward to sustain the narrative that the game was too difficult for women—but that did not stop them from trying. In 1895, the *Evening Post* of Denver reviewed the brief history of female baseball in Denver, acknowledging that a few female clubs had been organized. It then claimed, however, that the girls quickly gave it up when they discovered they could "make better and surer hits with a pretty hat than a ball club."[32] The following year, the *Philadelphia Ledger* simply denied that the city had any female players: "Rival cities are never tired of petty flings at Philadelphia. The latest calumny on this city is that it is the home of the female baseball player."[33] With girls and women playing on numerous school and civic teams in Philadelphia in the 1890s, the *Ledger*'s denial was completely false—but that did not stop numerous newspaper editors across the country from reprinting it in their papers.

It's Not You, It's Them; If It Is You, You're a Freak of Nature

This strategy alternately targeted men and women, telling men that if they did not play well against female teams, it was not their fault, and telling women that if they did play baseball well it was because they were freaks of nature. The *Quincy Herald*'s description of W. P. Needham's Boston Bloomer Girls players as "female freaks" was typical.[34] As newspaper articles about talented female baseball players proliferated, it became more difficult for critics to assert that women were physically and mentally ill-suited to play baseball well. Those determined to disparage female players sometimes claimed that women's baseball teams had an advantage over men's teams because the latter could not concentrate on playing when they had to compete against women or because social custom dictated that they not embarrass the women by beating them. In June 1895, the *New York Herald* claimed that the Hackensack Giants had been helpless against the "petite plump pitcher" of the All Star Ladies' Baseball club during a recent game because the male players were too distracted by the "curves" her bloomer uniform revealed.[35] In July the Minneapolis *Penny Press* titled its story about Lizzie Arlington's team's victory over a picked nine of local amateurs, "Were Too Polite to Win," and concluded: "The boys could have won if they so desired."[36] The theme of male gallantry in the face of female presumptuousness pervaded reporting on bloomer girl games—the persistent message was that female baseball players might be brazenly challenging social convention, but male players would maintain the high moral ground by treating them like ladies anyway.

Even those who acknowledged the athletic talents of select female baseball players sometimes refused to concede the possibility that women as a group could become talented baseball players. Instead, they propagated a narrative that the occasional woman who managed to mimic the skills of a male player was simply a freak of nature. The *Daily Register Gazette* of Illinois put it this way:

> Once in a while nature turns out in the way of a female physique something of a prodigy, just as she turns out freaks for the side shows. Occasionally a woman is seen who can hold up several hundred pounds in her teeth, or strike a sledge hammer blow, or perform on the trapeze or row, or ride, or swim, or do a variety of things that men usually do, much as men do these things, but at the best they are imitators of the feebler sort. Nature rarely turns out a woman who can throw a ball with a reasonable certainty of hitting a side of a barn at 10 paces, and therefore there never was and never will be a female ball team that can play ball.[37]

The *Des Moines Register* agreed, qualifying its statement that the team that visited Des Moines "play a very good game" with the caveat, "when the fact is taken in mind that it is an absolute and natural impossibility for a woman to play base ball."[38]

Are You a Woman or a Man?

The most effective and prolonged strategy employed to deter women from playing baseball was (and is) to convince them that athleticism and femininity are incompatible. Though some critics continued to cling to the biological argument that "women were never intended for baseball players," by the 1890s their words began to ring hollow as talented and athletic women golfers, archers, swimmers, sharpshooters, boxers, sprinters, cyclists, jockeys, tennis, basketball, and baseball players proliferated across the country.[39] As the argument that rigorous athletic activities were dangerous for women weakened in the face of overwhelming evidence to the contrary, critics slowly adapted their argument. Instead of claiming that athletics were dangerous to women's reproductive health, guardians of the gender status quo increasingly claimed that athleticism, femininity, and beauty were mutually exclusive characteristics. Women could not have it both ways, they argued; sportswomen had to choose between athleticism and femininity/beauty.

Who Would Doubt That I'm A Man?

VERSE 1:

If any meddling person should perchance suspect my womanhood,
I simply would assert that I can catch a ball when on the fly;
And you know well that no one can bring better proof that he's a man.
And you know well that no one can bring better proof that he's a man.
Where is the lady who would snub a member of a baseball club?
And where's the man who don't attach importance to a baseball match?
Judicious people all support this most exhilarating sport.
Judicious people all support this most exhilarating sport.

VERSE 2:

When I am standing in the field The luckless batsman's fate is sealed.
If he should chance to bat his ball, So that within my reach it fall;
I'd make a point without a doubt, I'd catch his ball and put him out.
I'd make a point without a doubt. I'd catch his ball and put him out.
I'll catch, I'll pitch, I'll bat, I'll run. I'll play as well as anyone.
Just look! ah, ah, that hurts! that pains! But he's a coward who complains.
Here is the ball! 'Tis surely fun to catch a high fly on the run.
Here is the ball! 'Tis surely fun to catch a high fly on the run.

VERSE 3:

But now I'll have to take the bat, I am expert and skilled at that;
I grasp it firmly with my hand; a high or low ball I demand.
No ball! No ball! That is no strike! Strategic pitching I dislike!
No ball! No ball! That is no strike! Strategic pitching I dislike!
But that's a go! with matchless grace I ran from home to centre base
A most extraordinary run! A noble manly deed well done!
I scored a run! And well I run! Now who would doubt that I'm a man?
I scored a run! And well I run! Now who would doubt that I'm a man?

CODA:

Admired, ay envied and renowned. Are heroes of the baseball ground!
And I? Have I no right to claim that I've just won a startling game?
Well, Mr. Umpire, tell me now, to your decision I shall bow.

FIGURE 10. "Who Would Doubt That I'm A Man?" Song lyrics and sheet music (1895). Library of Congress Collection.

M. Straube's song, "Who Would Doubt That I'm a Man?" (1895)[40] captures the essence of this challenge to athletic women (fig. 10). The lyrics describe a self-confident woman who not only loves attending baseball games but also fancies herself a superb player. An expert on batting, catching, and throwing, she likens herself to the "heroes of the baseball ground" who are "admired, ay envied and renowned." After slugging a double and gracefully running to second base, she celebrates this "noble manly deed well done." In Straube's song,

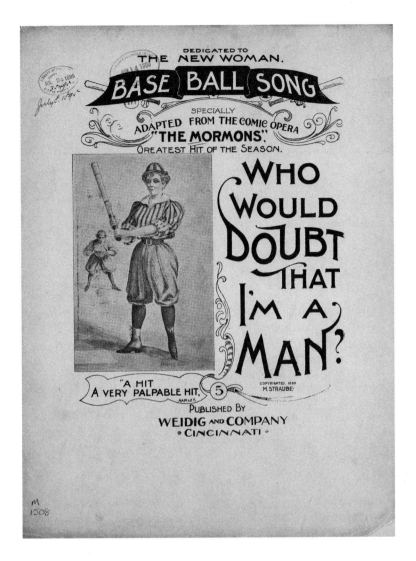

baseball is a metaphor of masculinity—for "no one can bring better proof that he's a man," than to "catch a ball when on the fly." The songwriter, rather than celebrating the athleticism of the New Woman and her mastery of the national pastime, seems intent on reminding her that her victory in the "startling game" has come at the cost of her womanhood. By arguing that skill on a baseball diamond epitomizes masculinity, the songwriter repeats a persistent theme of the nineteenth- and twentieth centuries that baseball is a zero sum game when it comes to gender. It cannot be used to reinforce both masculine and feminine qualities. If women want to play, they must forfeit any claims to womanhood.

Performing Masculinity and "Americanism" Through Baseball

There was a reason men like Straube sought to shame women into giving up supposedly masculine activities; masculinity seemed under assault. As women displaced men or crowded alongside them in countless occupations, colleges, and sporting venues, social commentators increasingly fretted about the "feminization" of the age.[41] It was hard not to worry with scientists like Alpheus Hyatt warning that if women gained suffrage, equality of education, and access to the same professions as men, it could inaugurate a period of "retrogressive evolution." Men would become "effeminized" and women would become "virified," he predicted.[42] While Hyatt approached the social issues of his day through the lens of the physical sciences, other critics of gender transformation focused on demographics and history. In 1893, historian Frederick Jackson Turner argued that the disappearance of the domestic frontier threatened the future development of the country. According to Turner, the process of "crossing a continent" and "winning a wilderness" had shaped American institutions and government. The steady and repetitive progression of civilizing the "savage" spaces of the eastern, midwestern, and then western frontiers had created "a composite nationality for the American people" that Europe would never have.[43]

Turner's association of the frontier with the nation's ability to sustain and spread democracy while absorbing and assimilating millions of immigrants was a clarion call for the men and women who were already preoccupied with worry over the perceived feminization of society. Reading between the lines of Turner's essay, these individuals concluded that the frontier had been a proving ground for masculinity—a place where strong, courageous, "civilized" men had conquered all manner of perceived and actual dangers on behalf of weak, innocent women and children. With no domestic frontiers left for men to conquer, some began transforming sporting arenas into surrogate frontiers where gender roles could be reinforced and displayed. Influential psychologist and educator G. Stanley Hall argued that the seemingly passive role played by fictional and real-life women on the sidelines of sporting contests was not passive at all—it was an active service nurturing masculinity. "The presence of the fair sex gives tonicity to youth's muscles and tension to his arteries to a degree of which he is rarely conscious," Hall wrote in 1906. "[A girl] performs her best service in the true role of sympathetic spectator rather than as fellow player."[44]

It was during the 1890s that the American Physical Education Association spearheaded the integration of formal physical education programs into academic curricula at grammar schools, high schools, and colleges across the country. It was also during this decade that scores of colleges organized athletic departments and supplanted many student-led sports teams with highly structured programs, "scientifically" managed by experienced coaches and professional physical educators.[45] More than ever before, Americans transformed sport into a vehicle of social change just as they had once transformed the untamed frontier into a civilized, "Americanized" space. Baseball was one of the sports harnessed to spread "American" civilization.

For those who viewed baseball as a tool for conferring masculinity and symbolizing American exceptionalism, the possibility that New Women might undermine its important social function sparked renewed efforts to shore up the game's gendered narrative. As increasing numbers of girls and women played baseball on civic teams, school and college teams, and on barnstorming teams in the 1890s, guardians of baseball's narrative of masculinity pushed back. "Woman is nowhere on earth more out of place than on a base ball diamond," insisted Francis Richter in 1890. "The formation of female base ball clubs should be discountenanced."[46] The editor of the *Haverhill (Mass.) Bulletin* concurred. "Base ball is a game requiring skill, agility and athletic qualities of the highest sort," he insisted. "It is not a ladies game and the fair sex have never succeeded in solving its mysteries. Neither is it a game which should be burlesqued. . . ."[47] In April 1892, a group of women in Huntington, Long Island, New York contacted the Society for Prevention of Vice to try to halt a series of games featuring female players. The following year the mothers of the male players on a Bloomfield, New Jersey, team that was scheduled to play the all-women Cincinnati Reds tried to prevent the game. Both groups of women were unsuccessful and the games went on as planned. The *Newtown Register* of Queens praised the women in Huntington for their effort, urging "people everywhere, parents especially" to follow their lead and to "set their faces as a flint against this outrageous business." The paper considered it "a shame to our civilization" that anyone would encourage female baseball teams to challenge men.[48]

Gender role transformation is a complex process of cultural negotiation. Even as some women and men decried the shifting sociocultural landscape they perceived, others embraced it. Women continued to play baseball for fun or wages, and thousands of male baseball players on teams across the country accepted the good-natured challenges of barnstorming and civic female baseball teams and joined them on the diamond for friendly competition. Sometimes this meant directly opposing parents, spouses, clergymen, and friends. The men who took the field on Long Island in 1892 to compete against a female baseball team did so despite the outcry against it from a number of local citizens. The captain of the boys' nine in Bloomfield, New Jersey, insisted that his team (comprised primarily of members of the local Y.M.C.A.) was going to play the female Cincinnati Reds even if "all Christendom turned out to protest."[49]

Social Interactions—Female Baseball Players of the 1890s

Baseball remained a popular sport among women of all social classes and backgrounds in the 1890s. As in the past, women in the East and Midwest continued to organize teams; they were joined by increasing numbers of women in the West. Southern women remained in the minority of female players. The female baseball teams of the 1890s mirrored those of the 1870s and 1880s, with the majority comprising civic and pick-up teams. Factory teams appeared, but not in great numbers. The biggest increase came in barnstorming female teams, but far more women played on school, college, civic, pick-up, and business teams than played on the professional teams. For nonprofessional players, having fun and maintaining good health inspired them to play. Many of the articles that reported on new civic and pick-up teams specifically addressed the players' motivations in this respect. An article in the *Grand Rapids (Mich.) Press* in August 1894 was typical. It reported that the group of young women in Brooklyn who were practicing baseball at least three days a week were not "playing ball to attract attention" and would not challenge other teams. They played solely "for the fun and healthy exercise the national game affords."[50]

Women Playing on Men's Teams

The majority of female baseball players in the 1890s played on all-female teams; some played on mixed teams of men and women or boys and girls, and a few played as the only female on otherwise all-male teams—a trend that would continue after the turn of the twentieth century. It is an irony of history that the growing influence of the narrative of baseball as a man's game actually opened up opportunities for women like Lizzie Arlington, Maud Nelson, Ruth Egan, Carrie Moyer, Alta Weiss, and Myrtle Rowe to earn a living or achieve renown by playing baseball on boys' and men's teams in the late nineteenth and early twentieth centuries.[51] When it came to making money, some men used the masculinized narrative of baseball not to isolate the game from women but to temporarily invite selected women in. These men had no intention of transforming the gendered narrative of baseball; they sought only to leverage it for personal gain.

Lizzie Arlington was not the first female baseball player to join a male team (a baseball club in Texas had a "pretty young female pitcher" in 1897),[52] but she was the first to garner prolonged national attention as an elite female player. Arlington enjoyed a decade-long career as the star of her local civic team, marquee athlete on numerous female barnstorming teams, and as the featured pitcher for a number of men's teams in Philadelphia and in the Atlantic League during the Spanish-American War. Arlington was born Elizabeth Stride on August 31,

1877.[53] She grew up in Mahanoy City, about forty-three miles north of Reading in the heart of Pennsylvania's anthracite coal region. Her parents, Henry and Mary Stride, had emigrated from Great Britain; Lizzie was their youngest of six children. Henry made his living operating a hotel but also enjoyed athletics. When he and his sons played baseball, raced horses, and did competitive shooting, they included Lizzie. She was a natural athlete, becoming the first girl in town to learn to ride a bicycle and, by age eleven, was giving roller skating exhibitions. Lizzie played polo, raced horses, and became an amateur champion shooter.[54] She also pitched for the local Mahanoy City baseball team at the tender age of thirteen; her brother, Harry, was the catcher.

On June 20, 1891, two months shy of her fourteenth birthday, Lizzie and her brother took the field as the battery for the Mahanoy City team against the visiting Cincinnati Reds—one of two professional women's baseball team barnstorming through the area.[55] After just one inning, the Red's manager, Mark Lally, announced that his pitcher was injured, and he recruited Lizzie and Harry to play for his team. With Lizzie pitching, and Harry catching, the Reds won the contest 20–11 despite the poor play of its regular players. Lally knew a good thing when he saw it, and immediately signed Lizzie to join the Reds. Within days, newspapers in nearby Hazleton and Freeland, Pennsylvania, were praising Stride's skills after she homered in games in both towns.[56]

Lizzie initially played for the Reds under her real name; however, by August 1891 she was using the stage name "Lizzie Arlington." She was a featured player on the Cincinnati Reds for three seasons. During her second season with the Reds, Lizzie was joined by another rising star on the female baseball circuit, Clementine Brida, who alternated the pitching duties with her. The earliest evidence of the two playing together is a roster published in the *Bedford (Ind.) Mail* on July 8, 1892.[57] It lists Arlington as catcher and Maud Bradi (Brida) as pitcher. The two played together on the Reds during the 1892 and 1893 seasons. Lizzie and Maud had known each other for about five years by the time they began traveling together with the Reds. Brida and her family had settled in Mahanoy City in 1887 after arriving in the United States from the Austrian Tyrol aboard the USS *Noordland*. Maud listed her occupation as "servant" on the ship's manifest and may have worked for Henry Stride at his hotel.[58] Brida, who was five years older than Stride, adopted the stage name Maud Nelson for the 1893 season. Nelson would eventually surpass Arlington as the premier female baseball player in the country, enjoying a four-plus-decade career that included owning and managing her own female baseball teams, and sometimes pitching for men's teams. In 1892, the nineteen-year-old Italian immigrant was just beginning to make a name for herself as a ball player (fig. 11).

Arlington and Nelson's baseball careers diverged in 1894 as Lizzie joined the Young Ladies Base Ball Club of New York and Maud joined the Young Ladies

FIGURE 11. Earliest known image of Maud Nelson in uniform.
Courtesy Joann Kline.

Champions of the World Base Ball Club. Arlington played for the other Young Ladies Base Ball Club of New York (also known as New York Stars) team in 1895 before disappearing from newspaper accounts for the next two years.

The year 1898 marked a milestone for Arlington (and women baseball players) as she became the first woman paid to play baseball for professional men's teams. NL and minor league teams were struggling financially owing to the Spanish-American War and unseasonably bad weather.[59] The twenty-two-year-old Arlington was at the peak of her game, and newspapers frequently lauded her play. Her talents attracted the attention of sporting and theatrical promoter Captain William J. Conner, who convinced Arlington to sign a contract with him. He promised to arrange exhibitions for her to pitch for men's teams and to pay her $100 per week—a tremendous sum at the time.[60] Conner negotiated with Edward G. Barrow, president of the Atlantic League (and future general manager of the New York Yankees), to hire Arlington to pitch for Atlantic League teams. He also hoped to convince Barrow's counterparts in the New York State League and Western League to feature Arlington in games.

Atlantic League president Ed Barrow was a showman at heart who knew how to fill seats at league ballparks. In 1897 and 1898, Barrow periodically featured professional boxers James J. Corbett and John L. Sullivan in league ball games as a way to boost attendance.[61] While other teams struggled during the war, Barrow's Atlantic League held its own. Barrow believed that a talented female pitcher would keep turnstiles spinning, so he signed Conner's female pitching star to a minor league contract to pitch for different teams in the circuit that season. On July 1, the *Philadelphia Press* broke the news that Arlington would debut with Atlantic League teams the following week and that she would play for the New York State and Western leagues after that.[62] The latter games never materialized, but Arlington did appear in numerous games with Atlantic League and nonleague men's teams that summer, including a game on June 25 in which she pitched for Norristown against Pottstown.[63]

On July 5, 1898, Lizzie Arlington became the first woman to play for a professional men's team in organized baseball when she pitched the ninth inning for the Reading Coal Heavers, who defeated the league rival Allentown Peanuts 5–0. Arlington gave up two hits, but no runs. She had an assist in the field but did not get to bat.[64] Arlington went on to pitch in scores of other games for men's teams, but she lost the opportunity to play in official Atlantic League games because the Hartford Cooperatives' managers balked at Barrow's money-making scheme for fear that the female pitcher might cause his team to lose an official league game.[65] Barrow and team managers compromised by featuring Arlington in exhibition games instead.

At some point in 1898, Arlington began wearing a distinctive uniform that marked her status as a woman and as a baseball player (fig. 12).[66] Contemporary newspaper articles about Arlington repeatedly referred to her as the *only* female professional baseball player in the country. This was incorrect. She was the only female baseball player paid by a men's league, but she was not the only woman who made her living playing baseball. Arlington had scores of contemporaries who played baseball professionally on the barnstorming female teams that crisscrossed the country from the late 1870s on. The number of teams and the number of female professionals only increased as the nineteenth

FIGURE 12. Lizzie Arlington in uniform (c. 1898). Courtesy Robert Edwards Auctions Collection.

century gave way to the twentieth. That newspapers were ill-informed (or willfully ignorant) about Arlington's female professional counterparts indicates the extent to which contemporary accounts of female baseball players skewed reality and strengthened the myth of baseball's gendered identity. As long as baseball boosters could label female players as novelties, they could continue to protect the myth that baseball was a "man's" game.

Characteristics of the Barnstorming
Female Baseball Teams of the 1890s

Female professional baseball teams continued to benefit from the public's interest in novel entertainment spectacles and their fascination with New Woman feats of athleticism.[67] More than forty female baseball teams barnstormed around the country during the 1890s, many of them operated by Sylvester F. Wilson under various aliases. While the 1890s saw its fair share of burlesque al fresco baseball troupes, it was also the decade that saw the origin of professional female baseball teams featuring talented athletes who competed head-to-head against men's amateur and semiprofessional teams across the country. These teams were the precursors of the long-lived, competitive Bloomer Girl baseball teams of the 1900s to 1930s. It is often difficult to differentiate between the two types of teams because of the widely divergent press accounts of female baseball in general during this period. Reporters sometimes disparaged the playing of the competitive teams in the same terms used for the burlesque al fresco teams simply because they opposed the idea of women traveling around the country playing baseball. An effort is made in the following sections to differentiate between teams organized strictly as burlesque troupes and those organized with a view toward fielding truly competitive female teams.

It is also challenging to trace a particular female baseball team through a season or series of seasons. Newspapers in various locales often gave different versions of a team's name—if they bothered to name it at all. In 1890, for example, newspapers covering one of Sylvester Wilson's teams called it alternately "The Young Ladies' Base Ball Nine of Chicago," a "female aggregation," "a Cincinnati female base ball club," "The Young Ladies Athletic Club of Cincinnati," "champion young ladies base ball club," "Black Stockings," and "the Young Ladies Base Ball Club of Cincinnati." Wilson himself called the team "my No. 1 club, the Chicago Black Stockings" in advertisements, and labelled it "Young Ladies' Base Ball Club No. 1" in a team photograph. It appears that Wilson fielded two teams simultaneously at times using the names interchangeably. He also used advertisements calling the teams the "Belles of the Bat" and "Queens of the Emerald Diamond."[68]

The difficulty tracking teams is compounded by the fact that managers sometimes had multiple teams on the road simultaneously or would split a single troupe into two groups for games in a particular region and then merge them back together. They also employed team names that had no relation to where teams originated. W. P. Needham organized his long-lived "Boston" Bloomer Girls team in Chicago in 1892; at least six female barnstorming teams in the early 1890s used variations of names linking them to New York City, even though some of the teams originated elsewhere. William C. Clyde and Robert Bey organized their New York Champion Ladies Base Ball Club in St. Louis in May 1894.[69] The two had also been affiliated with Joseph Bruckner's New York Champion Young Ladies Base Ball Club in 1892.[70] That team does seem to have originated in New York City and was alternately called the Young Ladies Base Ball Club of New York and the New York Champion Young Ladies (or Female) Base Ball Club in newspapers throughout the season. Between 1891 and 1894 there are newspaper reports about the New York Champion Young Ladies Base Ball Club, the Young Ladies Champions of the World Base Ball Club, the New York Giants, the New York Brunettes, and the Young Ladies Base Ball Club of New York. Rosters and travel schedules indicate that the teams were distinct, although it appears that the New York Champion Young Ladies Base Ball Club of 1894 was really just a new name for the Cincinnati Reds.[71]

Sylvester Wilson's Continuing Involvement With Women's Professional Baseball

After Wilson's 1889 baseball troupe collapsed, he returned to his old haunts in Cincinnati and began advertising for players in early May. He had a new team on the road by May 20.[72] Known alternately as the Black Stocking Nine and the Young Ladies Base Ball Club No. 1, the team was composed of players from Cincinnati and Chicago, including veteran players May Howard and Kitty Grant. Before they departed on tour, Wilson hired a professional photographer in Cincinnati to make postcards of the team that could be sold at games and distributed by advance men to promote the team (fig. 13).

One of the postcard designs listed the name of each player along with her position, and identified "W. S. Franklin" (Wilson) as manager. Most of the players' stage names (Effie *Earl*, Rose *Mitchell*, May *Howard*, Annie and Kittie *Grant*, Nellie *Williams*, and Alice *Lee*) and the poses they strike—leaning on bats, slouching, lying down, sitting with legs apart, and so forth—connote masculinity. The use of masculine surnames and poses is striking considering Wilson's persistent efforts to market the femininity and morality of his players. In August 1890, as he made plans to organize "The American Young Ladies' Baseball League for the 1891 season, Wilson publicized some of the rules he claimed governed the players:[73]

> Rule 7.—Any "kicking," quarreling or demonstrative complaints while traveling, or about rooms at hotel, will subject offending party to 20 cents fine for each offense.
>
> Rule 8.—"Flirting," "mashing" or making the acquaintance of gentlemen on trains, steamboats, at depots or hotels, or permitting the least familiarity, will

FIGURE 13. Sylvester Wilson's Black Stocking Nine (c. 1890).
Courtesy The Rucker Archive.

subject each offending member to a fine of 25 cents to $1 according to the gravity of the offense.

Rule 17.—No notes from dudes or would-be "mashers" will be permitted to be sent to the rooms of the lady members of the company.

Rule 25.—The proper place for lady members of the company at hotels is in their rooms or the ladies' parlor, and in no case should they make a habit of running through or occupying the office of the hotel or the gentlemen's sitting or waiting room; 25 to 50 cents will be imposed for violating this rule.

Rule 26.—No lady member of this company will be permitted to enter, either day or night, any saloon or bar room where intoxicating drinks are sold, under fifty cents to $1 for each offense.

Considering that Wilson's advertisements for the new league invited aspiring players to report either to the Dramatic Agency or to his personal residence between the hours of eight and ten P.M., it is likely these rules were for public consumption only and not actually enforced.[74]

Wilson's 1890 season was his most successful ever despite his usual run-ins with the law. He and his players were arrested in Danville, Illinois, on June 8 for playing a game on a Sunday, and the following month officials in Akron, Ohio, seized players' luggage until the home team received its promised share of the gate money Wilson had withheld.[75] Wilson and his players traveled more than eighteen hundred miles between mid-May and late August, drawing more than twenty thousand spectators to thirty games in Ohio, Pennsylvania, New York, and Canada.[76]

Emboldened by the success, Wilson launched his greatest scheme yet—a league of professional female baseball clubs. In August 1890 he placed advertisements looking for enough experienced young women baseball players to organize four to nine clubs for "The American Young Ladies' Baseball League" for the 1891 season.[77] A female baseball league would have posed at least a symbolic challenge to the monopoly organized baseball magnates held over the structure of professional baseball. Wilson's plan to organize a female baseball league is the first and only known time that someone contemplated doing so during the nineteenth century.

Wilson's league never materialized, but just the thought that it might provoked sharp criticism from Francis Richter, who headlined an article on the subject: "A Disgraceful Move: Introducing Females Into Professionalism."[78] Hoping to prevent Wilson from profiting further from his unsavory profession, Richter wrote: "No reputable base ball club should degrade itself and the game by renting these female ball players and their managers their ballpark to play in. Instead, all should imitate the example of President Charles Byrne of the Brooklyn Club who refused to lease his grounds for such a disgusting exhibition at any price whatsoever."[79] Richter reprinted one of Wilson's advertisements for players and reported that Wilson had already received a large batch of letters and numerous in-person applications. Wilson told Richter that many of the applicants were "too fat" or "not well developed" or, worse yet, "too old" but that he had signed twelve of them to a contract to play an upcoming game at Monitor Ball Park in Weehawken, New Jersey.[80] Wilson was lying about having hired new players for a new team. All of the women whose names appear on the roster of the Weehawken game had been with Wilson's team for at least six weeks—seven of them were in the photograph taken in Cincinnati at the start of the season.[81]

Richter's condemnation of Wilson's scheme did little good; he was an influential publisher, but even he could not control public opinion about female baseball. The day after Richter's article appeared in *Sporting Life,* Wilson enjoyed his greatest triumph ever as a female baseball manager when a huge crowd of seven thousand to ten thousand spectators turned out to watch his Black Stocking Nine play the Allertons at Monitor Park in Weehawken, New

Jersey. Wilson had been planning the event for some time, working with future Tammany Hall leader Charles Murphy, who managed the venue.[82] Though profitable, the game mirrored the rough and tumble nature of professional baseball at the time. The exhibition was marred by violence from the start as five hundred to six hundred "hoodlums" tore boards off the fence or climbed over it to gain entry to the park. Hundreds of spectators trampled the inner fence surrounding the diamond and surged closely around the field while the game was in progress. The teams managed to get in seven innings of play while two policemen struggled to keep unruly fans under control. Eventually, the unmerciful harassment from the hundreds of young men crowded around the diamond got to the female players, and some of them began punching offenders, setting off a series of fights among the crowd. As brawling fans surged onto the field, Nellie Williams grabbed a baseball bat and began swinging it to clear a safe haven for her teammates. She continued brandishing her bat in the carriage that whisked the players off to safety as a group of young toughs chased after them on foot.[83] It was an inauspicious conclusion to an otherwise historic day for women's baseball.

The size of the crowd at the game in Weehawken—a record for female baseball in the nineteenth century—must have been supremely satisfying for Wilson. After a decade of planning and scheming, setbacks and triumphs, he finally seemed to have found the winning formula for making it big in the entertainment business. The guardians of social morality, gender traditions, and the sanctity of the national pastime were mortified by Wilson's newfound success. Added to the chorus of warnings from moral watchdogs were the voices of professional baseball aficionados, who noted with horror that Wilson's teams were outdrawing at least one of the professional male leagues. "The attendance at the female base ball games down East makes the Brotherhood managers look sick," one wrote.[84]

Anxious to build on the success of the Weehawken exhibition, Wilson ramped up efforts to recruit players (and spectators) for his female baseball league. He launched a bold advertising campaign that included a full sheet broadside with the large headline: "COMING! THE CHAMPION LADY BASE BALL PLAYERS OF THE WORLD!" Claiming to be one in a series of weekly periodicals entitled the *Young Ladies' Athletic Journal,* with a daily circulation of one thousand to six thousand, the publication is a perfect showcase of Wilson's talent for blarney and bluster. "Immense Crowds Everywhere: Draws As Many People As a Circus!" he boasted. He bragged that the beautiful red, white, and blue canvas wall his operation employed enclosed more ground than the "mammoth tents" of Barnum and Forepaugh combined and that as many as a fourth to a third of audiences in many venues were women.[85] Ironically, just as Wilson seemed to have finally discovered the formula for making money from women's baseball, his narcissism, hubris, and flagrant disregard for morality and decency finally brought him down.

One month before his Weehawken triumph, Wilson had passed through Binghamton, New York, with his Chicago Black Stocking Nine and an entertainment troupe called the "Little Countess." While there, the forty-year-old Wilson became infatuated with fifteen-year-old Elizabeth "Libbie" Sunderland. Spinning tales of the riches she could earn and the beautiful dresses she would wear, Wilson convinced Sunderland to join his Little Countess troupe. Sunderland was Wilson's constant companion from that point on. Some newspapers reported that she was a sort of "mascot" for the team, selling score cards and photographs of the players, rather than playing. Others stated that she became an expert player and played shortstop on occasion.[86] As he had done in Kansas City to avoid attracting the attention of child protection agencies, Wilson kept Sunderland on the move between various boardinghouses. On March 4, 1891, Sunderland's sixteenth birthday, Wilson presented her with a diamond engagement ring. Five months later, officers of the NYSPCC finally tracked him down and arrested him. Along with Sunderland, they found five hundred photographs of nude women in his room.[87]

Though Wilson's fate was sealed from the moment he conspired to bring Libbie Sunderland to New York City, the arrest that would set the stage for his final downfall remained a year in the future. He and his team finished out the 1890 season playing in New Jersey, New York, Canada, Pennsylvania, and Washington, D.C.[88] In late March 1891, Wilson began planning for the season; he had two teams on the road by April 25.[89] They regularly drew crowds of one thousand or more. As he had done in the past, Wilson hired a photographer to produce team postcards that could be used to promote games and earn extra money. This time, he posed with his players, proudly displaying his distinctive "Dundreary" whiskers (fig. 14).[90]

It is difficult to track Wilson through the summer of 1891; one of his teams made a circuit of Iowa and the Midwest in June; another played in Pennsylvania, and one team played in Massachusetts, New York, New Hampshire, and the Canadian Maritimes. Francis Richter reported that Wilson had spent most of the summer in New York City, busying himself "obtaining fresh material for his ball clubs" and working various theatrical operations. At some point in late July or early August, Wilson joined the team touring New England. When he returned from Boston in mid-August, NYSPCC officials arrested him.

Wilson's arrest and trial captivated the nation. Newspapers in at least two dozen states and territories and in Canada kept readers apprised of progress in the case. Richter covered Wilson's trial in detail in the pages of *The Sporting Life*.[91] On August 22 he headlined one report: "In Jail at Last: A Disgrace to Base Ball Probably Now Ended—A Notorious Manager of Female Base Ball

FIGURE 14. Sylvester Wilson and his Chicago Black Stocking Nine (1891).
Courtesy Joann Kline.

Clubs Now at the End of His Rope."[92] Unable to raise bail, Wilson sat in New York City's Tombs prison throughout the fall of 1891 while NYSPCC agents worked to strengthen the legal case against him. On August 28 they introduced Justice Meade to Sylvester F. Wilson Jr., the eleven-month-old son of Wilson and one of his players, Annie (Ella) Long. Long was fifteen years old when she joined Wilson's Young Ladies' Base Ball Club in Philadelphia in 1889. She played under the stage name Lottie Livingston and traveled with Wilson until she became pregnant. She went home to Philadelphia, where her son was born at her parents' home in September 1890. Long turned him over to "Mrs. La Burt," who ran one of many unlicensed "baby farms" in the city, and returned to baseball.[93] Wilson made weekly payments to La Burt for his son's care until his arrest.

As Wilson's case progressed through the court system, the public learned the sordid details of his criminal behavior and sexual exploitation of his players. James W. Cameron, who had answered one of Wilson's advertisements for a business partner in February 1891, reported that he had seen Wilson in bed with Sunderland on numerous occasions. He testified that he had told Wilson that he considered his team "a traveling house of prostitution."[94] Mrs. J. W.

Davenport, who lived on the floor above Wilson's flat on Seventh Avenue, heard him say things to Sunderland that were "too disgusting to repeat."[95] The most damning evidence against Wilson came from Libbie Sunderland herself. Sunderland provided graphic details about how Wilson had engaged in sexual intercourse with her on or about Christmas Day, 1890. She reported that he continued to have sexual relations with her regularly until the second week of January 1891.[96] Assistant District Attorney McIntyre introduced a series of letters into evidence that Wilson had written to Long. Even Wilson's attorney admitted later that the letters were "vile and filthy" and that the man who wrote them "merits the severest condemnation."[97]

The shocking details of the players' exploitation at the hands of their manager provide insights into the economic context of the times. Countless thousands of families lived in poverty in America's cities, with little hope of bettering themselves and with few options when circumstances turned dire. Parents would (and did) turn their daughters over to men like Wilson on the promise that he would feed, clothe, educate, and employ them. Wilson lived in an era when attitudes toward childhood, marriage, and sexual crimes little resembled our own. Child labor laws were rare and ineffective. Child protective laws were relatively new and enforcement agencies, like the NYSPCC and its counterparts, were in their infancy. Financially destitute parents sometimes gave young daughters in marriage to older men or sent them out to find whatever work they could. The abduction law Wilson had broken reflected the social context of the times; it stipulated that the kidnapper had to have intended to have sex with a girl *under the age of sixteen* for a crime to have been perpetrated. Had Wilson waited until Sunderland's sixteenth birthday in March 1891 to have sex with her, he would have been innocent in the eyes of the law.

Escaping desperate circumstances, many of the teenage girls and young women on Wilson's teams considered themselves fortunate to be part of a family with Wilson as their patriarch. Despite Sunderland's sworn testimony that Wilson had molested her, she insisted that Wilson had always acted as a kind father to her and had given her a better life than she had ever had in Binghamton.[98] When her teammate, sixteen-year-old Sadie Burnell, took the stand, she affirmed Sunderland's assertion that Wilson always treated his players kindly.[99] Many of Wilson's players (victims) loved him and stayed with him for years even though they hated what he did to them. Trial transcripts and depositions make it clear that the girls took care of one another—teaching each other rudimentary birth control techniques and giving each other hints on how to avoid Wilson's sexual advances.[100]

On October 16, 1891, the jury in Wilson's case delivered a guilty verdict after less than ten minutes of deliberation. Newspapers trumpeted the news.[101] Shocked by the outcome of his trial and facing a $1,000 fine and five years in

Sing Sing, Wilson wrote a letter to Judge Martine from his cell in the Tombs the next day begging to marry Sunderland in return for dismissal of the case and promising to support Ella Long and her child until she could marry "someone worthy of her."[102] Wilson also reached out to his ex-wife, asking her to send an affidavit to the court that he had not abandoned her. Kate Giles, who had married Dr. Willis H. Hunt of Camden, New Jersey, several years earlier, gave a public statement to the press that Wilson *had* deserted her and had failed to support her and his son when they were married.[103]

On October 21 Judge Martine gave Wilson the maximum sentence. Accustomed to exoneration or slaps on the wrist for previous crimes, Wilson was "thunderstruck" by the verdict and rendered speechless.[104] Richter was delighted: "The sentence of Sylvester Wilson . . . will likely put an end to all the female base ball clubs," he exulted on October 31. "For this relief much thanks."[105] Richter celebrated too soon. For the next fourteen months, Wilson and his attorneys exploited numerous legal loopholes as they filed appeals with courts and judges in multiple boroughs.[106] As the courts rendered conflicting judgments and argued over jurisdiction, Wilson managed to stay one step ahead of detectives who were trying to bring him in. On December 23, 1892, his luck ran out. As he and George Francis Train walked into Koster & Bials Concert Hall to celebrate a recent legal victory, Detective John J. O'Brien placed him under arrest.[107]

On Christmas Eve 1892, New York City detectives accompanied Wilson on his long-delayed trip to Sing Sing. His prison intake form recorded that Wilson was forty-one years old, weighed 179 pounds, was 5' 9-1/2" tall, had a light complexion, gray eyes, thinning brown-gray hair (bald at the crown of his head), heavy beard, high forehead, large ears, and a fairly good set of teeth. It stated that he smoked, wore size nine shoes, walked with a limp, and had a small mole on the front of his neck and a small scar on the back of his left thumb. The flamboyant narcissist had been reduced to a set of bland descriptors.[108]

Wilson was imprisoned at Sing Sing from December 24, 1892, to September 11, 1896 (part of his sentence was reduced for "good behavior"). He then languished in New York City's Ludlow Street Jail for almost two years because he could not pay his $1,000 fine. On August 2, 1898, Wilson finally convinced Justice Newburger to release him owing to ill health.[109] NYSPCC officials immediately began tracking Wilson's movements again. Over the course of the next four years, Wilson was in and out of jail and prison. He continued to prey on young girls and on gullible marks. Shortly after Wilson organized his female baseball team in May 1899, the parents of a nine-year-old girl reported to the NYSPCC that Wilson had tried to talk them into letting him become her guardian so he could give her a "superior education."[110] In August 1899, the Philadelphia Society for the Prevention of Cruelty to Children had Wilson arrested after the parents of Lena Goldfriend complained to them that Wilson was "annoying" their daughter.[111] Wilson was sentenced to a year in Moyamensing prison.[112] In January 1903, he reappeared as Frank Hartright in an advertisement in New York City newspapers soliciting a partner to put up $500 to help fund a female baseball team. On April 29, NYSPCC officials spotted an advertisement in the *New York Herald* for "Girls for stage; young, small, stout; experience unnecessary; salary." The ad instructed applicants to report to "Hartright" at the stage entrance of Bon Ton Music Hall, a seedy theater located at 112 West 24th Street. The same issue included an advertisement for a young man to help coach a girls' basketball club. He was to report to the same location.[113] NYSPCC officials immediately suspected that Wilson was behind the ads.[114] They were right. After another trial revealed that Wilson had molested or tried to molest his players, aged thirteen to eighteen, and had shown hard-core pornographic photographs to some of them, he was sentenced to nine years in Sing Sing.[115] He did not realize at the time that it was actually a life sentence. Wilson spent the next several years lobbying judges and governors for clemency.[116] None assented and Wilson disappeared into the faceless crowd of inmates at Sing Sing and the State Mental Hospital in Dannemora, where he was transferred sometime before 1910.[117] On December 7, 1921, more than eighteen years after he had entered Sing Sing to serve his nine-year sentence, Wilson died at the age of sixty-nine.

Sylvester Wilson represented the dark side of women's professional baseball. Men's professional baseball had a dark side too, but it revolved around gambling, fixing games, drinking, smoking, and cursing. Those were moral indiscretions that the power brokers of organized baseball were ultimately able to control in large measure. There were no power brokers for women's professional baseball—there was no governing body to protect female players from managers who sexually abused them, frequently cheated them out of their promised wages, and occasionally abandoned them on the road. On March 4, 1892, as Wilson's appeals process dragged on, one Democratic state legislator in New York did try to end the exploitation of female baseball players. William Edward McCormick introduced a bill in the New York Assembly entitled, "An Act to Prohibit Female Base Ball Playing." Targeting only professional female baseball, it read:

—"No female shall be hired or employed to play base ball."
—A person who shall hire or employ any female for the purpose of playing base ball shall be guilty of a misdemeanor.
—This act shall take effect immediately."

If McCormick intended his bill to be taken seriously by his fellow representatives, he was disappointed. Accounts of the legislative session indicate that

McCormick's bill caused general laughter and a proposal from Representative O'Conner that the bill be referred to the Committee on Fisheries and Game."[118] The Committee on General Laws got the bill and had more fun with it, reporting back on March 25 that members favored the bill but with amendments. Its revised bill banned only hiring "red-headed" female baseball players, exempted Kings county and the village of Black Rock, and set the enactment more than a century in the future—January 1, 2009.[119] The New York Assembly never outlawed professional female baseball, but that it had even considered doing so highlights the range of emotions professional female baseball players evoked in the nineteenth century.

Women's Baseball Causes an International Incident

A year after William McCormick introduced his bill to ban professional female baseball in New York, Joseph Bruckner and his Cuban partner Edwardo Laborde took out an advertisement in *Sporting Life* looking for twelve "young lady ball players" to travel to Cuba to play baseball for six weeks. Interested women were to send their information, including position played, to Laborde at the Spanish Hotel in New York City.[120] America's national pastime had been played in Cuba as early as 1868.[121] It was particularly popular among middle- and upper-class men, who organized teams as social clubs, just as predecessors in the United States had done during the sport's formative years. Cuban baseball clubs fielded a variety of teams based on the skill level of the players. By the late 1870s, the senior nines of the Havana and Almendares clubs were dominating their rivals and had established reputations as the "Yankees of Cuban baseball."[122] U.S. teams occasionally traveled to Cuba for baseball games, and Laborde and Bruckner believed the novelty of a female team challenging the top Cuban men's teams would prove lucrative.

The managers found only ten women willing to make the trip; at least two of them, Lottie Livingston (real name: Annie Long) and Bertha Gordon (real name: Mattie A. Myers), had played professional baseball previously.[123] On February 25, Bruckner, LaBorde, and the American Female Base Ball Club departed New York City aboard the steamer Yucatan for Cuba.[124] They arrived in Havana on March 1. The team's first exhibition game was scheduled for Sunday, March 5, with the men's nine in Almendares.

Approximately ten thousand Cubans turned out to see the game. As was the case at playing venues in the United States, the crowd was comprised of individuals from all social strata. Wealthy citizens of Almendares and surrounding communities occupied the grandstand seats while poorer whites, blacks, and mulattoes occupied the cheap seats behind a fence that separated players from fans.[125] The majority of Cuban spectators were likely unfamiliar with the burlesque al fresco troupes in the United States, and many expected to see a competitive contest—not a mix of baseball and theatrical entertainment.

When they realized how poorly the women played, some of the spectators became infuriated. Several hundred men tore down the fence in front of their seats and swarmed onto the field demanding a refund and shouting that they had been duped into paying for a "farcical" baseball game. Within minutes, the unruly mob of malcontents sparked a general riot. Some spectators destroyed their wooden seats and set fire to the grandstand, reporters' stand, and the fences surrounding the club's grounds. Another group rushed the ticket stand and stole the gate money. While some of the fans turned their ire on the physical infrastructure of the Almendares club, others began physically assaulting the female players—tearing off their clothes and team badges, and ransacking their possessions on the bench. Mattie Myers reported to U.S. Consul General Ramon Williams that the mob had damaged her baseball "costume," and stolen her coat, silk muffler, and two valuable rings that had been in her coat pocket. She estimated her losses at $100 dollars gold, including her lost salary for the cancelation of the six-week engagement.[126]

The Almendares players and some of the spectators tried to protect the women; temporarily beating back attackers, the rescuers led them to a nearby house. The mob pursued closely and beat on the walls with sticks and fists. Police and soldiers belatedly arrived and dispersed the crowd. When calm was restored, the women sent a messenger to their hotel to retrieve clothing from their luggage. They were finally able to leave their refuge at 6:30 that evening.[127]

Professional female baseball players in the United States had faced angry crowds before, and had occasionally been pelted with rocks and sticks. The riot in Almendares exceeded any previous and subsequent incidents in both scale and danger. There was a social class component to the Almendares riot; the poor play of the female players may have been the initial spark that set off the riot, but rioters quickly expanded the target of their anger to include the physical infrastructure of the upper-class Almendares club grounds—evidence of underlying animosity between the poor and privileged in the city. Newspapers implied the class component of the riot when they commented that the majority of spectators were "respectable and well behaved" but that some came from "the lowest dregs of society." They also stated that the Almendares baseball club was composed of "young men of good class." The official report of the incident compiled by Consul General Williams for the State Department confirms these descriptions.

Disappointed spectators in the United States had verbally harassed professional female baseball players and sometimes threw projectiles at them, but they had never threatened their lives. The female players and the men who protected them were in very real danger as they struggled to get away from the rioters. Newspapers reported that some of the male players were "severely wounded" and that at least one of the female players was wounded.[128] Consul General Williams does not mention this in his official report to U.S. Assistant Secretary of State William F. Wharton, or in his letter to the Governor General of Cuba. Nonetheless, the fact that the women had to have someone retrieve clothing for them before they could leave the house where they had sought shelter indicates the extent to which they had been manhandled and roughed up by the crowd.

The riot at the Almendares baseball game caused an international incident. Many in the United States were incensed by the way the women had been treated, particularly when word spread that the mob had destroyed an American flag the women's team carried with them. Consul General Williams, who had previously served as vice consul general in Havana from 1874 to 1884, and who was an outspoken advocate of Cuban independence, wasted no time laying blame for the riot on Spanish authorities. In his official report to Assistant Secretary of State Wharton, Williams noted that the government had ordered the police to guard polling places that day—neglecting to provide the kind of security to the ballpark that would normally have been available at such a large gathering of citizens. He cited the absence of police as the "most probable cause" of the riot. Williams assured Wharton that the American Female Base Ball Club had paid the appropriate taxes and obtained the required license from local authorities for its exhibition. He emphasized that "there was nothing in the appearance and conduct of these young and harmless American girls to incite the acts of violence" perpetrated upon them. Williams enclosed a copy of a local Cuban newspaper report containing photographs of the American Female Base Ball Club and the damaged Almendares club grounds in his dispatch. He also included transcripts of the testimony female players had given him the day after the riot and a copy of the letter he had sent to the governor general of Cuba on March 10 demanding that the Spanish government compensate the women $725 gold for the loss of their personal property. This letter stated that the United States would seek additional compensation for "damages" at some future date.[129]

The Almendares riot provides insights on the relationship between the United States and Spain at a time when the United States was beginning to assert its military and diplomatic influence abroad. Relations between the United States and Spain over Cuban sovereignty had been tense for more than a decade; the riot in Almendares was one of many skirmishes in the ongoing battle of national wills that eventually exploded into all-out war in 1898. The *Salt Lake Herald* led its story about the baseball riot with the statement: "Cuba is getting ready for annexation."[130] Joseph Bruckner wasted no time leveraging the diplomatic tensions by filing formal charges against the Spanish government as soon as he and the players arrived back in New York City aboard the steamship *Yumuri* on Monday, March 13, 1893. He gave a special power of attorney to Vice Consul Joseph A. Springer in Havana empowering him to collect damages on the team's behalf.[131] (There is no record whether the Spanish government ever reimbursed Bruckner or the players.) Meanwhile, by spreading a highly sensationalized version of events, Bruckner appealed to U.S. nationalism to fan the flames of public outrage against Spain. He claimed that the Spanish government had failed to protect the women from the Cuban "hoodlums" who began verbally harassing the players from the moment they arrived at the field. He also claimed that it had allowed rioters to pull down, trample, and destroy the American flag the team carried, and to steal $5,000 in gate money.[132] Bruckner reported that he and two of the female players had drawn revolvers from their pockets (a shocking claim in and of itself) and exchanged gunfire with their attackers. He stated that a policeman and fireman had been killed trying to protect them and that almost all of the players were hit with bricks as they raced to the gatekeeper's house. He claimed they arrived at the house with "hardly a stitch of clothing left."[133]

Bruckner's version of events is highly suspect, as it differs markedly from Myer's official testimony to Consul General Williams and from Williams's report to the State Department. Williams makes no mention of the mob tearing down an American flag, of gunfire, or of deaths. Most newspapers helped Bruckner spread his narrative by reprinting his claims with little or no editorial comment, but at least one U.S. and one Cuban newspaper openly challenged his account. On March 17, the *Rocky Mountain News* "declared untrue" Bruckner's claim that rioters had destroyed the U.S. flag. It offered no evidence to support its report.[134] A week later, the *Omaha World Herald* reprinted a translation of an article from a Havana-based newspaper. The *Diario de la Marina* refuted Bruckner's version of events and shifted blame back onto him and his players for the riot: "We consider the claims of the female base ball players to be greatly exaggerated," the reporter announced. "The girls appeared here, according to the advertisements, as professional players, and even ventured to increase the ordinary charges of admission to their games on the ground that they were professionals." (This statement supports Bruckner's claim that rioters stole $5,000 from the team. Female barnstorming teams normally charged $.25 admission but, apparently, Bruckner charged the Cuban audience $.50 each.) Anxious to uphold the honor of the Cuban people and to diffuse tension between the two countries, the article continued: "Evidently the public was cheated, and revealed its disgust by the hostile attitude assumed against the pretended professional ball players."[135]

Though Bruckner hoped to invoke U.S.-Spanish tensions to increase his potential financial remuneration, Francis Richter concluded that no international "complications" were likely to arise from the incident. Noting that it was "not pleasant to have the American flag suffer indignities at the hands of foreigners," he quipped in *Sporting Life* that when "the Stars and Stripes gets tangled up with female base ballists it is in bad company and must take its chances." He predicted that the incident would soon blow over and that the men's team Larry Laffin hoped to take to Cuba in the near future would face none of the problems the women's team had endured.[136]

Richter was correct in predicting that little would come from the incident in Cuba; however, he did report that Cap Anson refused an invitation from a Cuban team to come to Havana with his Colts for a game in April 1893. Anson reportedly told the *Chicago Herald*: "This is a deadly conspiracy, but they don't trap old Popper. Why it isn't a month since they mobbed that female base ball nine over there, and if they'd mob them girls I guess they'd kill my Colts."[137] The mob in Cuba did prematurely end the 1893 season of the American Female Base Ball team, but it did not hamper baseball in Cuba, nor did it end the proliferation of barnstorming female baseball teams that continued to crisscross the country as the nineteenth century came to a close and a new century began. Fortunately for aspiring female professional players, the increasing appreciation for female athleticism in the 1890s motivated genuine sportsmen to begin organizing barnstorming female teams. Eventually these sportsmen (and occasional sportswomen) outnumbered the theatrical entrepreneurs, and female athletes were given the opportunity to join teams whose managers treated them with respect and built lasting "Bloomer Girl" franchises.[138]

Here Come the Bloomer Girls

Though baseball historians often mention Bloomer Girl baseball teams when they discuss women's involvement with the sport, it was actually *bicycles* and bloomers that were first linked in the public's mind.[139] For most people in the 1890s, a "Bloomer Girl" was a woman who rode her bicycle while wearing voluminous pantaloons or split skirts, not a woman barnstorming around the country playing baseball games against men's teams. The Boston Bloomer Girls, Chicago Bloomer Girls, and short-lived Trilby Bloomer Girls baseball teams debuted in the 1890s, but it was not until the first decade of the twentieth century that Bloomer Girl baseball teams like the Star Bloomer Girls, New England Bloomer Girls, Maximo Bloomer Girls, American Bloomer Girls, New York Bloomer Girls, and Kansas City Bloomer Girls began to proliferate.

With criminals like Sylvester Wilson bringing discredit upon professional female baseball, Bloomer Girl team managers initially found it difficult to distinguish their teams from the burlesque al fresco troupes. They also occasionally had to distinguish their teams from similarly named salacious entertainment troupes like "The Bloomer Girl Big Burlesque and Minstrel Company."[140] By the mid- to late-1890s however, teams like Mark Lally's Cincinnati Reds, W. P. Needham's Boston Bloomer Girls, and the various iterations of the Young Ladies Base Ball Club of New York were featuring at least a few highly talented female athletes (like Lizzie Arlington and Maud Nelson) who *played*, rather than performed, baseball, and reporters noticed. "The Boston Bloomer Girls surprised every one," wrote a reporter for the *Daily Statesman* of Austin, Texas. "[T]hey really know how to play ball and some of the plays they made would have been creditable to men. Their batting and fielding were excellent."[141]

Unlike their theatrical counterparts, Bloomer Girl team managers marketed athletic competition. By fielding teams of talented female (and male) athletes to provide audiences with an exciting and quality contest, these managers established a winning formula for women's professional baseball that endured into the twentieth century. Scores of Bloomer Girl baseball teams played in the early 1900s, providing hundreds of women the opportunity to earn a living playing baseball.

Hardships of Life as a Bloomer Girl

Life as a female professional baseball player was exceedingly difficult, even for those who worked for honest and conscientious managers. Travel was grueling; players traveled thousands of miles on trains, wagons, and other conveyances during the season, often not knowing when and where the next game would be held as advance men tried to arrange games on the fly. Maintaining personal hygiene and clean uniforms in an era before air conditioning, plentiful modern sanitation facilities, and coin-operated laundries was particularly challenging. The long seasons took their toll; newspapers sometimes commented on the sunburned and weather-beaten visages of the players or on how tired the players looked.[142] When the Boston Bloomer Girls played in Rock Island, Illinois, in early August 1895, a reporter noted that the game ended after only five innings because the "Beantown girls became fatigued."[143] Six weeks later, their exhaustion was even more apparent to a journalist in Little Falls, Minnesota, who reported that only the pitcher and first basewoman played well. The rest "seemed too tired to even try."[144]

Injury and illness were ever-present risks for barnstorming female baseball players. A paper in Raleigh, North Carolina, reported in August 1895 that a local doctor was attending a seriously ill player from the visiting Young Ladies Base Ball Club. When Maud Nelson's Boston Bloomer Girls visited San Francisco in October 1897, catcher Nelly Bly was unable to play owing to a "charleyhorse, tonsillitis, or some other, ailment," and Gustie Habeck was out with an undisclosed illness (her time of the month?). The team's male manager played for the injured Bly while Habeck worked the ticket gate.[145]

Illness was usually a short-term problem; injuries could be more serious. Whether athletes or theatrical performers, professional female baseball players were subject to a range of injuries ranging from charley horses, dislocated fingers, and sprained ankles to concussions and broken limbs. In June 1891, Agnes Carman of the Cincinnati Reds broke her collarbone in four places when she collided with the opposing first baseman. Two months later, one of her teammates was hit in the mouth by a swiftly pitched ball in Little Falls, New York. During the same game, two other players suffered black eyes from ground balls, and the catcher left the game with "puffed hands." The injury-plagued season continued the following month when Lizzie Arlington, who had joined the Reds after Carman was injured, was disabled during a game in Watertown from a "blow on the leg." Eight days later she was knocked unconscious for twenty minutes by a pitched ball. She was removed from the field in an ambulance.[146]

The Cincinnati Reds were not the only team to lose players to injuries. In June 1892, "Miss St. Joe" of Denver's barnstorming team suffered a broken nose when she collided with a male opponent during a game in Cheyenne. Two years later, Maud Nelson's teammate, Lizzie Haines, suffered a season-ending injury in Cedar Rapids, Iowa, when she was struck over the eye by a pitched ball. Haines remained "delirious" in a local hotel while the rest of her teammates departed for their next game.[147] The show had to go on. On rare occasions, female baseball players caused injuries to male opponents. The pitcher of the male nine in Rushville, Indiana, lost several of his teeth when he was struck in the face by a line drive hit by one of the Boston Bloomer Girls.[148] On July 9, 1898, twenty-three-year-old first baseman Frank Winder of Olathe, Kansas, collapsed during a game against the Bloomer Girls. The coroner attributed his death to heart failure. The *Denver Evening Post* unkindly announced in its headline: "Fell Dead on the Ball Field: Crossing Bats With the 'Bloomer Girl' Team Was Too Much for Winder."[149]

Players adopted various strategies for mitigating the hardships of the road and the threat of illness or injury. The women on Denver's barnstorming team of 1892 sat in a covered wagon when they were not in the field, drank water with oatmeal in it (for their complexions), and carried sponges soaked in water to help prevent heat-related illness.[150] Some players refused to slide or field sharply hit balls. The athletes among them wore protective gear such as catcher's masks and gloves to prevent injury as much as possible. The New York Champion Young Ladies Base Ball Club provided its catcher with an inflatable "breast protector," but she refused to wear the bulky appendage.[151] Owing to the nature of their business, players sometimes had to protect themselves from physical assaults; they used all available means to do so. At least one player in Cuba had protected herself with a gun; Sylvester Wilson's player, Nellie Williams, had wielded a bat during the brawl in Weehawken, and four years later, a player on W. P. Needham's Boston Bloomer Girl club knocked a male spectator down with a bat after fans in Anderson, Indiana, stoned them after a game.[152]

Dollars and Cents

The Bloomer Girl teams of the 1890s and beyond were generally well-financed and well-managed businesses that marketed competitive sport as entertainment. Because Bloomer Girl organizations fielded a more competitive team than their predecessors, they were able to develop loyal fan bases. This enabled teams to play profitable doubleheaders and to visit the same locations year after year. Bloomer Girl teams became so popular that charlatans sometimes tried to foist counterfeits on an unwary public. In 1894, a large crowd that had gathered for a female baseball game in Fresno became incensed when the female team turned out to be a group of children dressed in women's clothing.[153] Boston Bloomer Girl manager W. P. Needham took to calling his team the "original" or "only genuine" Bloomer Girl team as counterfeits (and legitimate competitors) multiplied.

The size and complexity of professional female baseball operations varied. Those on a shoestring budget had nine or fewer players plus a manager and a single advance man. The best-funded operations carried a full roster of women and substitutes, several managers, and multiple advance men plus canvas fencing, grandstands, and other equipment designed to deter freeloaders and make paying spectators comfortable. Some of these teams traveled in customized Pullman cars that served as mobile hotels. Those troupes that incorporated other types of entertainment into their programs had to transport and fund even more people and specialized equipment. The New York Champion Young Ladies' Base Ball Club of 1892 traveled with twenty-four people—four men, ten female baseball players, and ten female band members who played for pregame parades and during games.[154] Needham's Boston Bloomer Girls traveled with a bullfighting act and a band of Mexican musicians for part of the 1899 season.[155]

Working-class women were especially attracted to barnstorming baseball teams because they could earn more money playing baseball than they could in most other jobs open to them.[156] At a time when working women made only about $4.50 to $8.00 per week, Maud Nelson was earning $18 a week for the Boston Bloomer Girls.[157] Not all players earned as much as Nelson but, given the choice, many working-class women found traveling the country playing baseball far more appealing than mind-numbing, exhausting work as domestics, waitresses, farm hands, machine operators, or clerks.

Player Demographics

It is difficult to analyze the demographic composition of nineteenth-century barnstorming female baseball teams because even the talented athletes of the Bloomer Girl teams often used stage names, as their predecessors had done. Newspaper accounts rarely mentioned the race or ethnicity of players, a number of whom, like Maud Nelson, were first- or second-generation European immigrants.[158] Immigrants comprised the majority of working-class families in large urban areas like Chicago, New York City, St. Louis, and Philadelphia, where baseball entrepreneurs advertised for players.[159] Irrespective of ethnic origins, almost all nineteenth-century professional female baseball players were white. Newspapers invariably identified individuals as "colored" if they were black; apart from the short-lived Dolly Varden and Captain Jinks teams of 1883, no other reference to black women playing on barnstorming baseball teams has come to light.

Bloomer Girl Legacy

The Bloomer Girl teams of the 1890s paved the way for the Bloomer Girl teams of the twentieth century. They also spawned other female barnstorming athletic organizations such as a traveling female soccer team in San Francisco in 1893.[160] Talented female baseball players inspired countless girls and women to try their hand at baseball. It was no coincidence that teams sprang up in numerous communities in Canada after Sylvester Wilson's female baseball teams staged exhibitions there in the early 1890s.[161] The young women of Cherokee, Iowa, organized their team in August 1895 after learning that the Boston Bloomer girls were coming to town.[162] In April 1898, young women in Morris, New York, organized a baseball team and began practicing daily to "rival the record of the famous Cincinnati Reds of several years ago."[163]

More than a century has passed since the New Woman burst onto the scene in her voluminous bloomers—straddling her bicycle, swinging her tennis racket, and sliding into bases. We have the benefit of hindsight to know that she did not destroy the nation or emasculate men, but her contemporaries did not possess this long view. For them, New Women posed a dire threat to the survival of American "civilization" and "manly" men. Fortunately, as increasing numbers of talented, athletic female baseball players crisscrossed the country in the 1890s, earning the praise and respect of spectators and opponents, and as schoolgirls, college women, and civic baseball players decisively demonstrated that athleticism improved rather than harmed women, the general public began to embrace what it had once feared. The changing attitude about the value of vigorous physical exercise for women gave thousands of girls and women from all walks of life the opportunity to play baseball during the final decade of the nineteenth century.

Baseball for Schoolgirls

Many youthful ball players became quite talented. A classmate of Elizabeth Virginia Wallace (the future first lady, Bess Truman) recalled that Wallace was "the first girl I ever knew who could whistle through her teeth and bat a ball as far as any boy in the neighborhood."[164] Wallace played third base and was the "champion slugger" for her brother's sandlot baseball team in Independence, Missouri, almost a century after schoolgirls in the United States had mimicked characters in Austen's, Mitford's, and Tuthill's stories. Goodridge Wilson Jr. remembered male and female students playing all sorts of games together at his rural school in Virginia in the 1890s. He related that boys often chose girls first for teams, not from "motives of chivalry but because they were better runners" and he noted that the girls who enjoyed running races, playing townball, wrestling, and holding jumping contests at schools had grown up doing the same things on their farms and lawns with male and female playmates.[165]

Upper-class students played baseball at places like Mrs. Hazen's Suburban School for Girls in Pelham Manor, New York, and the Mary A. Burnham School in Northampton, Massachusetts.[166] Baseball was particularly popular among students at the Ogontz School in Philadelphia. Originally known as the Chestnut Street Female Seminary, the school was located in the heart of Philadelphia's most prestigious neighborhood. It took the name of Jay Cooke's luxurious forty-acre rural estate when it relocated there in 1883.[167] A rare action photograph of nineteenth-century girls playing baseball shows students playing at Ogontz circa 1890 (fig. 15). Another photograph depicts eleven serious-looking young women posed for a team shot with bats, balls, and a catcher's mask. Several of the players sport military rank on their sleeves, designating their status in the girls' military drill company.[168]

Baseball thrived for many years at Ogontz. In April 1895, the school newspaper reported: "The craze for ball playing this spring has broken out violently. Two base-ball nines have been organized, and the cries of the enthusiastic players assail the ears of the drowsy inmates of the house at absurdly early hours." After listing the names of the twenty-six students comprising the managers, players, and substitutes on the team rosters, the paper concluded: "The exercise thus gained will be highly beneficial, and it is to [sic] hoped that no bad bruises will be received in the zeal for feats of strength and for fun."[169] Ogontz School baseball players hailed from Colorado, Minnesota, Ohio, Pennsylvania, New York, Connecticut, and New Jersey. They used regulation baseballs, and bats that were only slightly lighter than those used by men.

FIGURE 15. Rare action shot of nineteenth century female baseball game. Ogontz School, Philadelphia (c. 1890). Courtesy of the Penn State University, Abington College Library, Ogontz School for Girls Archive Collection.

By century's end, adults were playing a more active role in student athletics; some advocated interscholastic competition for girls, but this was relatively rare. Dr. Milo S. Walker, who taught chemistry at Chicago's West Division High School, was a proponent of indoor baseball for girls and helped establish an interscholastic league.[170] Indoor baseball for girls debuted at West Division High School in 1895; Joseph Medill High School organized its team soon after. Initially students played only intrascholastic games, but beginning in the winter of 1899, they trained for interscholastic competition against area schools. By 1903, Chicago and Cook County physical educators were operating a scholastic indoor baseball league.[171]

The female students in Chicago initially used the same official indoor baseball rules that men did—a fact that concerned some gender traditionalists. Soon after the female students at West Division High School began playing the sport, the *National Police Gazette* printed an unflattering illustration, depicting them as buxom and scantily clad damsels in short pants and short-sleeved blouses (fig. 16).[172] Like the 1868 images of the Peterboro girls baseball team in *The Days'*

FEMALE STUDENTS PLAY BASEBALL.
FASCINATING GIRLS IN BLOOMERS AND SWEATERS PITCH, BAT AND MAKE RUNS, AT CHICAGO, ILL.

FIGURE 16. Purported illustration of Chicago-area high school students playing indoor baseball. *National Police Gazette,* March 16, 1895. Courtesy David Block.

Doings and *Sporting Times,* the *Police Gazette* image bore little resemblance to the reality taking place in Chicago-area high school gymnasiums; its purpose was to scandalize.

Even those who supported vigorous physical activities and team sports for girls often did so within the constraints of prevailing gender ideals. Walker advocated interscholastic competition for indoor baseball players but he also promoted special rules for girls. He experimented with a "lighter, softer and quite elastic ball" supplied by A. G. Spalding & Bros. and banned sliding, which he believed introduced "certain roughness entirely out of harmony with the true sport."[173] The modified equipment, diamond size, and rules that Walker and other male and female physical educators promoted to meet the "special needs" of girls and women eventually evolved into separate baseball games for women, thus solidifying the narrative of baseball as a man's game.

Though countless schoolgirls played baseball in the United States during the nineteenth century, they comprised only a small minority of their peers. In 1895 and 1896, J. R. Street conducted a survey to determine what sorts of recreational activities young men and young women had enjoyed as schoolchildren. Of his 183 respondents, mostly from Massachusetts and Maine, 160 were women. While fourteen of the twenty-three young men who responded reported that they had played baseball as schoolboys, only fifteen of the 160 young women had—in fact, baseball was at the bottom of their list of eleven activities. Favorite games of the girls were Hide and Seek, Croquet, Tag, and Tennis in that order. Dolls, House, and Cards ranked just above baseball.[174] Street's findings confirm that schoolgirls in the late nineteenth century generally conformed to prevailing gender expectations. By embracing gender-appropriate leisure activities they, too, helped solidify the gendering of baseball as a boys' and man's game. The girls who persisted in playing the game they loved despite criticism or teasing understood that their days of carefree cavorting with the boys on baseball fields would be fleeting. The bonds of womanhood awaited them.[175]

Baseball for Female Collegians in the 1890s

The third generation of young women who attended the nation's colleges after 1890 benefited from the pioneering work of predecessors who had demonstrated that women *could* engage in rigorous intellectual study without physically harming themselves. Even as late as 1897, however, female college students sensed that not everyone wished them well: "As women, and at a woman's college, the criticism to which our every act lies exposed, is invariably severe, and might even with justice be called unfriendly," commented an unnamed student in the Bryn Mawr yearbook."[176] Fortunately for this student and her peers, enough Americans were embracing the image of exuberance and athleticism embodied in the "New Woman" that it opened up new opportunities for them to explore their athletic potential. In 1897, Wellesley alumna Millicent Peirce Potter (Class of 1895) confidently asserted: "The purely intellectual woman, so prone to nervousness and despondent views of life, has at last given place to the *normal* woman, who has or who strives to have an abundance of good spirits as well as muscle to balance her developing thought [emphasis added]."[177] Potter attributed the new harmony between mind and body to the "growing influence of athletics" on her campus.

Most of the female baseball teams on college campuses continued to be organized by students. They organized house and class teams at Wellesley, Smith, Mills College, the University of Arizona, and the Women's College of the Western Reserve in Cleveland, Ohio, for example. Even southern students tried their hand at the national pastime. Baseball was one of the most popular sports played by students at the all-women Converse College in Spartanburg, South Carolina, during the 1890s. Students proudly posed for team photographs (fig. 17.).[178]

FIGURE 17. Team photo (1899), Class of 1901 baseball team at Converse College, Spartanburg, South Carolina. Courtesy Mickel Archives and Special Collections, Converse College.

Though most female baseball teams on college campuses in the 1890s were organized by students, a growing number of colleges began incorporating athletics and team sports into their official physical education curricula. Professionally trained physical educators encouraged their female students to take up sports like tennis, rowing, basketball, and baseball. Baseball was never the most popular sport on college campuses in the 1890s, but the young women collegians who played the national pastime thoroughly enjoyed themselves. Because baseball's center had, by this point, begun to coalesce around the ideal of the elite, professional male game, students understood that to play baseball was to tacitly resist gender ideals. Like the first generation of female collegiate baseball players, students in the 1890s often wore the latest female fashions while they played and frequently hid their practices and games from outsiders. They also jokingly disparaged themselves so not to appear to be overtly challenging the superiority of male athleticism. In June 1891, for example, Mount Holyoke College seniors who had brought baseball back to the college memorialized their experiences in their class book: "Baseball has had its victories, and several stock companies have been formed," they wrote, "and the skillful way in which eyes are blackened and fingers bruised is only one more additional evidence as to the inability of a woman to throw."[179]

Some female collegians of the 1890s were willing to play baseball with or in front of male students. In May 1893 the *Grand Forks Herald* reported that the female students at the coeducational University of North Dakota played baseball "every evening after supper" and were determined not "to be surpassed by the boys this spring." This was an interesting claim considering that three of the players on the female team were male students.[180] That same month the *Kalamazoo Gazette* reprinted an announcement from Ann Arbor that the "*co-ed* base ball team" (emphasis added) was hosting a "Grand Ballet."[181] In 1897, numerous female and coed baseball teams appeared at Olivet College in Michigan; two female boardinghouse teams welcomed men to a game they played as a fund raiser.[182]

The Road Not Taken

By century's end, men held almost exclusive control of the structure of "official" baseball, while women created a parallel structure for the baseball surrogate known as "women's baseball." The new sport of women's baseball grew out of the professionalization of physical education in the latter quarter of the nineteenth century. When schools, colleges, and communities began spending large sums of money to train and hire professional educators, these professionals began using sports, particularly team sports, to inculcate social values and to reinforce gender ideals. Eventually professional physical educators and coaches took control of what had previously been student-led collegiate athletic programs; they blazed sharply divergent paths for men's and women's athletics. Male athletic directors created a tiered structure of competitive athletics that featured clear divisions between elite athletes and everyone else; female physical educators developed athletic programs that emphasized equal participation for all and that adapted sports to meet the "special needs" of women.[183]

Feminist scholars sometimes decry that female physical educators chose the path they did. They lament that these women did not seize the opportunity to undermine stereotypes about women's supposed biological inferiority by encouraging and celebrating mental toughness and physical athleticism in girls and young women. In the context of late-nineteenth-century feminism and collegiate sport, however, their vision for women's athletics made sense. Biological determinism and Social Darwinism were powerful influences at the time. Rosalind Rosenberg notes that the "ancient belief in feminine uniqueness" was so pervasive that "liberation could only be conceived in terms of it." Thus even women trying to expand women's social roles did so while "defending the traditional conception of her nature."[184]

The majority of late-nineteenth-century feminists understood that physical fitness was essential to women's continued social advancement yet, like their predecessors, they could not agree on the best way promote that objective. Should athletic and recreation programs for girls and women mirror those of boys and men, or should they employ different objectives and strategies? Ultimately, the professional female physical educators who developed the formal structure of female physical education and athletic programs in the early twentieth century rejected the pattern of elitism and commodified competition that was beginning to characterize men's athletic programs. They focused on creating fitness and recreational programs that *all* girls and boys, women and men could enjoy no matter what their level of fitness.

Put off by what they saw as overemphasis on competition in men's programs and convinced of biological distinctions between men and women, female physical educators adapted the rules for sports like basketball, football, and baseball to minimize running, jumping, and physical contact. (Ironically, they simultaneously embraced and promoted the English sport of field hockey, which required a great deal of running.) Occasionally, physical educators invented new sports for girls and women as alternatives to popular competitive sports. In 1894, renowned physical educator Dudley Sargent introduced "Battle Ball." It combined features of bowling, baseball, cricket, football, and tennis. Within a year, advocates were touting it as a more socially appropriate substitute for football for women.[185] Physical educators also promoted baseball surrogates. In 1896, the *Washington Post* described "Lang Ball" as a cross between kickball and baseball. Players hung from a parallel bar at home plate and put a six-inch diameter rubber ball into play by kicking it. Pitchers could put the "batters" out by throwing the ball past them. The *Post* lauded Lang ball as "just the game for women" because, while including "all the health-giving features of baseball," it posed no risk of knocking them senseless or hurting their "pretty fingers."[186]

Lang ball did not catch on with female collegians, but they did play baseball in increasing numbers. By 1929, so many college women were playing so many different forms of baseball that physical educator Gladys Palmer published *Baseball for Girls and Women*. The book symbolically marked the decisive split between men's baseball and women's baseball—there were now two sports where there had once been one. Two sports, divided by gender.

Conclusion

BASEBALL DID NOT BECOME GENDERED as a man's sport overnight, nor did any single group dominate the cultural metanarrative of baseball as it matured from infancy to adolescence during the nineteenth century. Baseball has never been simply a sport; it has always been a means to an end. It has provided recreation, excitement, income (for some), exercise, and social bonding. It has been used to inculcate and symbolize "Americanism," middle-class, Judeo-Christian values, and "manliness." Urban boosters have employed it to build civic pride; armies have leveraged it to entertain troops and to mollify former enemies; health-care professionals have used it to pacify mental health patients; social reformers have employed it as an antidote for urban stress and a vehicle for assimilation; and physical educators have used it to promote health and fitness. This book has focused primarily on the gender leitmotif woven into the whole cloth of baseball narratives. Over the course of the nineteenth century, the twisted braid of the gender-neutral thread slowly unraveled so that male and female threads stood apart from one another. By century's end, men held almost exclusive control of the narrative of "official" baseball, while women controlled a parallel narrative for the baseball surrogate called "women's baseball." Their game was precursor to the new "official" game of softball that would emerge in the 1930s.[1]

The sport we call baseball today evolved from a diverse mix of children's bat and ball games; these games were, for the most part, a gender-neutral "blank slate" upon which adult men and women wrote their gendered narratives and then taught those narratives to their children. Upper class, middle class, and lower class, native-born and immigrant, white, black, Asian, and Hispanic, men and women, adults and children, gamblers, tradesmen, politicians, white-collar professionals, and theatrical entrepreneurs all embraced the sport and crafted their own unique narratives to reinforce the sociocultural and gendered identities they valued. In the process each contributed to baseball's elevation in status to national pastime and to its gendered identity as a man's game.

Not every group had equal influence on the ultimate character and culture of baseball, however. Early in its history, a small minority of white, male businessmen and elite players seized hold of the sport from children and adult amateur players (male and female) and constructed an enduring organizational structure that attracted the support of publishers and other businessmen who saw in the structure opportunities to expand their own influence and profits. Gradually the voices promoting baseball's professional structure drowned out the voices of the nameless millions who played the game for fun and other reasons unrelated to financial gain. The culture of the game these baseball power brokers developed was highly gendered and hierarchical.

Every decade of the nineteenth century saw more girls and women playing and watching baseball than in previous decades. Yet the narrative of baseball as a man's game gained momentum in each successive decade well into the twentieth century. By 1909, former semiprofessional baseball player (and soon to be nationally renowned adventure writer) Zane Grey could confidently assert: "All boys love baseball. If they don't, they're not real boys."[2] Grey's comment made perfect sense to a generation coming of age at a time when professional physical educators were harnessing play to inculcate gender values in children. William A. McKeever echoed baseball's gendered theme in 1913, insisting: "No boy can grow to a perfectly normal manhood today without the benefit of at least a small amount of baseball experience and practice."[3]

The men who organized Little League Baseball in 1939 perpetuated the gendered theme, writing a charter that reflected their determination to use the sport to develop "citizenship, sportsmanship, and manhood" in boys.[4] Tens of thousands of boys played Little League Baseball in the first half of the twentieth century, and the men who coached and mentored them valued their shared experience as men. The male-only space of the Little League diamond served such a powerful social function that when girls began suing for the right to join Little League teams in the 1960s and 1970s, the emotional outcry across the nation was widespread and intense—particularly after a New Jersey court ruled against Little League Baseball's ban on girls in 1972.[5] Sportswriter Frank Deford concluded that the angry response to the court's decision was sparked by the belief of some that girls who tried to get into Little League were not just "monkeying with men's baseball but with men's childhood."[6]

For decades most modern scholars of sport assumed that baseball was and always had been a man's game. They unwittingly perpetuated the gendered narrative introduced in the nineteenth century by men with a financial stake in shaping the game for their own purposes. Even feminist scholars who railed (and rail) against the exclusion of girls and women from scholastic, collegiate, and Organized Baseball structures and teams generally assumed that baseball had always been a man's game and that women never had a chance to alter that reality because of patriarchal structures of power. The truth about baseball's gendered past is far more complex.

Baseball began as a gender-neutral sport; its gendered future was neither inevitable nor quickly solidified. Men *and* women shaped the gendered narrative of baseball, and a large majority of both groups ultimately acceded to its characterization as a man's game. This characterization was continually contested as girls and women played. Some consciously contested the narrative of masculinity by arguing that baseball could benefit all who played it, including girls and women. Most women expressed their confidence in baseball's gender-neutral benefits simply by playing it. Theirs was a lived, not a verbal or written, counternarrative. There is virtually no evidence that nineteenth-century women viewed baseball's masculine reputation as an oppressive symbol of their exclusion from other facets of public life. Women's rights activists brought no lawsuits against Organized Baseball as they would in the twentieth century, nor did they mount a concerted campaign to end discrimination against female baseball players, as they did to end other types of discrimination against women.

Baseball's reputation as a man's game became solidified in the 1920s and 1930s with the invention of women's baseball, the popularity of softball, and the founding of Little League Baseball, but this gendered identity remains under negotiation today. There is evidence that the separate narratives of male and female baseball are beginning to reconverge—the ancestral tree of baseball is beginning to assume the less-gendered form of its youth. The International Baseball Federation has been organizing a Women's World Series since 2001; seventeen countries, including the United States, the Netherlands, Venezuela, Cuba, Australia, and Chinese Taipei have competed. Groups like Baseball for All, Girls Play Baseball, the USA Baseball Women's National Team, and Little League Baseball are providing opportunities and support for girls and women who want to play baseball instead of its softball surrogate.[7] SABR's Women in Baseball Committee is facilitating research on female baseball players, and women's vintage baseball teams are reminding women that they have an historical link to the national pastime. The gendered narrative of baseball is still evolving—time will tell what it becomes.[8]

Appendix

States without Identified Homegrown Female Baseball Teams in the Nineteenth Century

Arkansas	Mississippi	Tennessee	Virginia
Delaware	Nevada	Utah	Washington
Idaho	Oregon	Vermont	

Future States without Identified Homegrown Female Baseball Teams in the Nineteenth Century

Alaska	Oklahoma

Female Baseball in the 1850s and 1860s

Date	Place	State/Terr.*	Type of Team	Comments
late 1850s	Steuben County	NY	Public Schools	Baseball is "*the* game at our district schools during intermission hours, and often engaged in by youths of both sexes."[1]
1859	Perth Amboy	NJ	Coed Private School	"We are glad to record that there is one school in this country . . . where girls are encouraged to take vigorous physical exercise; where boys and girls are educated together; where the girls have boat clubs and play ball, . . ."[2]

Date	Place	State/Terr.*	Type of Team	Comments
1862	Benicia	**CA**	Private Girls' Seminary	Students at the Benicia Young Ladies' Seminary played "games of ball" as part of their regular daily exercises.[3]
1864–65	Benicia	CA	Private Girls' Seminary	School catalogues for the Benicia Young Ladies' Seminary state that students play "games at ball."
Nov. 1865	Harrisburg	**PA**	—	"Already we hear faint whisperings of a Ladies' Base Ball Club, and next summer will probably launch the Spinsters' Barge Club on the Schuylkill . . ."[4]
Spring 1866	Poughkeepsie	NY	Women's College	First- and second-year students at Vassar College organized the Laurel and Abenakis baseball clubs.[5]
Spring 1867	Poughkeepsie	NY	Women's College	First- and second-year students at Vassar College organized the Precocious baseball club. None had played on the Laurel and Abenakis teams in 1866.[6]
	Farmington	**CT**	Private Girls' School	Students at Miss Porter's School organized the Tunxis baseball club.[7]
July 1867	Dowagiac	**MI**	Civic	"A young ladies' base ball club is being organized at Dowagiac."[8]
	Saranac	MI	Civic	"The *Cassopolis Democrat* says a base ball club has been organized at Saranac in this State . . . . The ladies are also organizing a base ball club."[9]
	Niles	MI	Civic	"A young ladies' base ball club has been organized at Niles, Mich."[10]
	Pensacola	**FL**	Civic	"The Baseball Disease has attacked the women, the young ladies of Pensacola, Fla., having organized a baseball club."[11]
Aug. 1867	Hallsport	NY	Civic	"We are informed the Ladies B. B. C. of Hallsport, indulged in a spirited practice game Saturday afternoon last. Will they please send us an invitation to witness a game; or the score of one to publish? . . ."[12]

Date	Place	State/ Terr.*	Type of Team	Comments
Sept. 1867	McConnelsville	**OH**	Civic	"Some of the ladies of this place have organized a female Base Ball Club. The married members are said to be good 'catchers,' and are instructing the unmarried."[13]
	Bordentown	NJ	Civic	"In Bordentown, base ball is rampant. There is hardly a man, woman, or child, who is not more or less interested in one or more of the clubs. The enthusiasm on this subject has reached the female persuasion, and two base ball clubs have been organized among the young ladies."[14]
Oct. 1867	Allen's Prairie (Coldwater)	MI	Civic	"We have to record still another death from base ball folly. In Allen's prairie, Michigan, there is a ladies' base ball club. One day last week they played a game. Miss Howard was made ill by the over-exertion, and died in three days thereafter."[15]
	—	NY	Civic	"Female Base Ball Clubs are being formed in some portions of the state. . . ."[16]
1868	Kalamazoo	MI	Civic	"A number of ladies of this place have organized a base ball and croquet club.—They have secured grounds and are putting themselves through a thorough course of training. . . ."[17]
Mar. 1868	Boston	**MA**	—	". . . . I never sees girls play base-ball, but they say they do in Boston. . . ."[18]
July 1868	Peterboro	NY	Civic	"We were delighted to find here a base ball club of girls. Nannie Miller, a grand-daughter of Gerrit Smith, is the Captain, and handles the club with a grace and strength worthy of notice. . . ."[19]

Date	Place	State/Terr.*	Type of Team	Comments
Sept. 1868	Brooklyn	NY	Civic	"Following in the example of the 'Gushing Girls' of Peterboro, a movement is on foot in Brooklyn to organize a Club of female base ball players. They are to discard hoops and skirts utterly, and appear in a genuine Arab rig. Most of them are undergoing physical discipline, and all of them are making preparations for a match."[20]
Nov. 1868	Plymouth	**IN**	Civic	"The young ladies of Plymouth are organizing a base ball club."[21]
Apr. 1869	West Lebanon	**ME**	Coed Academy	"The great excitement over here is base ball . . . and the girls play ball as well as the boys."[22]
Sept. 1869	Cincinnati	OH	Pick-up	"A Match game of base-ball was played on Monday last between the Invincibles and Woman's Suffrage Base-ball Clubs, on the Relief grounds, which resulted in a bad defeat for the Invincibles, with the following score: . . ."[23]
Oct. 1869	Evanston	**IL**	Women's College	Students at the Northwestern Female College organized a base ball team.[24]
	Sedamsville	OH	Civic	"We fear that the religious war going on in Cincinnati is extending its demoralizing effect to the neighboring townships inasmuch as a telegram mentions the fact that a squad of female base ball players were engaged in their favorite pastime, near Sedamsville, Ohio, *last Sunday*." [Emphasis original.][25]

* **Bold font** indicates first year state/territory is known to have had a female baseball team or player.

Notes

1. *Harper's Weekly,* November 5, 1859, 707.
2. "Muscle Looking Up," *The Letter-Box,* 99.
3. "Commencement Exercises," *Sacramento Daily Union,* June 12, 1862.
4. "Harrisettes," *Philadelphia Daily Evening Bulletin,* November 25, 1865, 4.

5. Team rosters and firsthand accounts of the teams are available in the Vassar College archives.

6. Ibid.

7. Reminiscence of Kate Stevens. Miss Porter's School Archives.

8. "Miscellaneous Items," *Detroit Advertiser and Tribune,* July 23, 1867.

9. "Local and Incidental," *Constantine Weekly Mercury and St. Joseph County Advertiser,* August 8, 1867, 3.

10. "Sporting," *Albany Evening Journal,* July 12, 1867, 2.

11. Chadwick, *Ball Players' Chronicle,* July 25, 1867.

12. *Wellsville Free Press,* September 4, 1867, 3.

13. *Highland Weekly News* (Hillsborough, Ohio), September 5, 1867.

14. "Out Door Sports," *Newark Daily Advertiser,* September 16, 1867, 2.

15. "The Daily Avalanche," *Memphis Daily Avalanche,* November 11, 1867, 1.

16. "Girl Base Ball Clubs," *Utica Morning Herald,* October 17, 1867.

17. Quoted in Morris, *Baseball Fever,* 196.

18. "Boys and Girls . . .," *Mexico Independent,* March 18, 1868, 1.

19. *The Revolution,* August 6, 1868, 65–66.

20. "Female Club in Brooklyn," *Brooklyn Daily Eagle,* September 10, 1868, 2. This team does not seem to have been organized. Reporters may have confused advertisements for a female baseball performance at Tony Pastor's Opera House in late August and early September with an actual female team.

21. "Indiana News," *Indianapolis Journal,* November 2, 1868, 3.

22. Charles W. Hurd letter to his uncle, Charles H. Berry, April 8, 1869.

23. "Base-Ball," *Cincinnati Enquirer,* September 28, 1869. There is no definitive proof that these were teams of women. They may have been men's teams taking a dig at women who had just staged a major Woman's Suffrage Convention in Cincinnati earlier that month. A roster gives only last names and some initials.

24. "All Shapes and Sizes," *Bangor Daily Whig and Courier,* November 8, 1869.

25. *Cleveland Plain Dealer,* November 3, 1869, 2.

Female Baseball in the 1870s

Date	Place	State/ Terr.*	Type of Team	Comments
Aug. 1870	Jackson County	IN	Civic	"We learn that there are several female Base Ball Clubs in this State. . . ." "Two female base ball clubs are reported in Jackson County."[1]
	Detroit	MI	Civic	"Detroit has a female base ball club." "The women of Detroit are learning to play base ball."[2]
	Rockford	IL	Pick-up	"Word from Rockford that a base ball club, composed of married ladies . . . played a game yesterday with a picked nine of single ladies, on the grounds of the Forest City Club."[3]

Date	Place	State/ Terr.*	Type of Team	Comments
	New Lisbon	OH	—	Quip about a female baseball club. "One of the girls recently made a 'home run.' She saw her father [mother] coming with a big switch."[4]
Fall 1870	Cincinnati	OH	Grammar School	Girls at a grammar school in Cincinnati organized two baseball teams, the Favorites and Mountain Maids.[5]
	Lancaster	OH	Grammar Schools	Girls at the South Senior and South Junior grammar schools in Lancaster organized teams and scrimmaged each other.[6]
Jan. 1871	Cincinnati	OH	Civic	"Cincinnati has two female base burning [sic] clubs."[7]
July 1871	Crawfordsville	IN	Civic	"Crawfordsville has a female base ball club, and the Louisville *Commercial* proposes to match its printing office nine against the Amazonians."[8]
July 1871	Evanston	IL	Women's College	A team from the Evanston College for Women played a team from Northwestern University as part of a Fourth of July fund raising event organized by College president, Frances Willard.[9]
Aug. 1871	Evansville	IN	Civic	"A female base ball club has been organized in Evansville."[10]
Sept. 1871	Elgin	IL	Civic	"Elgin now boasts two base ball clubs, composed entirely of ladies. They are known respectively as the Originals and the Independents. . . ."[11]
Sept. 1871	Pittsburgh	PA	Civic	"Pittsburgh boasts of several female base-ball clubs."[12]
1872	Boston	MA	Grammar School	Alice Stone Blackwell, daughter of Lucy Stone and Henry Blackwell, played baseball with peers at the Harris Grammar school during recess.[13]
June 1872	—	MN	—	"The swiftest 'pitch' in the country is a young woman, aged 23, belonging to a Minnesota female base ball club."[14]

Date	Place	State/Terr.*	Type of Team	Comments
Fall 1872	Oakland	CA	Private Female Seminary	Baseball was the "first outdoor sport" at Mills Seminary when it opened in 1872.[15]
1873	Wichita	KS	Civic	Secondary source reports there was a ladies baseball club organized in Wichita in 1873.[16]
	—	OH	Schools	"Ohio girl students play base ball, and the newspapers talk of it. Well?"[17]
May 1873	Iowa City	IA	Civic	"Iowa City's female base ball club is ready to receive proposals— we should say challenges."[18]
Fall 1873	Boston	MA	Private School	Alice Stone Blackwell continued to play baseball with classmates after her parents moved her to Chauncy Hall School in the fall of 1873.[19]
	Salem	IA	Coed College	Whittier College, a coeducational Quaker institution had two baseball teams, one all-male and one, all-female.[20]
Apr. 1874	Rhinebeck	NY	Civic	"South street boasts of a female base ball club. They challenge the world."[21]
May 1874	Greenfield	MA	Female Boarding School	"A female boarding school in Greenfield has produced a base ball club. . . ."[22]
July 1874	Pittsfield	NH	Civic	"Pittsfield has a female base ball club."[23]
c. Aug. 1874	East Tawas and vicinity	MI	Civic	"The young ladies of East Tawas have organized an Amateur Base Ball Club that bids fair to eclipse all other organizations of the kind in this vicinity."[24]
Aug. 1874	Tarboro	NC	Civic	"A female base ball club has been organized in Tarboro."[25]
Sept. 1874	Harmonsburg	PA	Civic	"Happy Harmonsburg—they have the velocipede fever now for the first time; they are looking for the potato bug; and boast of a female base [ball?] club."[26]
1875	Honolulu	HI**	Coed Private School	Four teams comprised of 21 students, aged 15–19, and two teachers played at least two baseball matches at the Punahou School in 1875.[27]

Date	Place	State/Terr.*	Type of Team	Comments
June 1875	Reading	PA	Civic	"Reading has a beautiful female base ballist, who challenges 'Jhonny' Briton of Lewistown."[28]
July 1875	Laporte	PA	Civic	"Laporte has a female base ball club named Longstockings."[29]
Aug.–Sept. 1875	Springfield	IL	Professional/Theatrical	"The Female Base Ball Club, which was recently organized in Springfield and has been playing in the interior of Illinois, is composed of eighteen players, a blonde nine and a brunette nine."[31]
Fall 1875	Poughkeepsie	NY	Women's College	Students at Vassar College organized seven or eight teams.[30]
Late 1875	—	KY	Schools	"The baseball mania is prevalent in Kentucky, and even the girls at school join in to make up nines."[32]
Feb. 1876	Philadelphia	PA	Civic	"The ladies' base ball club has been organized in Philadelphia and will play during the Centennial year."[33]
Mar. 1876	St. Louis	MO	Professional/Theatrical	"Look out for the Female Base Ball Club, for it will soon make its appearance."[34]
Apr. 1876	Virginia	IL	Civic	". . . Virginia, Cass County, has a female base ball club, and it is named 'The Leap Year Winners.' This club has vanquished a male club of that place in a match game the other day."[35]
	Lafayette	IN	Civic	"Lafayette has parlor concerts. Also, a female base ball club."[36]
May 1876	Manitowoc	WI	Civic	"Manitowoc, Wis., has a female base ball club known as the Striped Stockings. But the girls will stop when running the bases to fix their bustles."[37]
Spring–Fall 1876	Poughkeepsie	NY	Women's College	Baseball was one of the sports physical educators taught students during the spring term and summer gym program. The clubs were reorganized in the fall of 1876.[38]

Date	Place	State/ Terr.*	Type of Team	Comments
June 1876	Brooklyn	NY	Civic	"The suggestion has been made that a female base ball club be originated and that ladies who wish to distinguish themselves this Centennial year be permitted the opportunity."[39]
	Providence	**RI**	—	"It is the fashion now for girls to play baseball & I think it is the best fun ever invented."[40]
July 1876	Paris	KY	Civic	"Now they are happy at Paris, Ky. They have a female base ball club."[41]
Aug. 1876	Erie	NY	Civic	"The little city of Erie has only thirty-three base ball clubs, but it has taken all the available men of the community and now the matrons are seriously considering the question of organizing themselves into the thirty-fourth nine."[42]
Sept. 1876	Gilead	CT	Civic	"Gilead, Conn., boasts a female base ball nine. It doesn't make it a femi-nine game, for all that. Gilead can't bamboozle the public mind that way."[43]
c. May 1877	Kingston	NY	Civic	"Nine young ladies in Kingston, N.Y. have organized a baseball club."[44]
Spring 1877	Poughkeepsie	NY	Women's College	Twenty-five of 338 students selected baseball as their optional form of exercise during the spring term.[45]
c. June 1877	Neodesha	KS	Civic	"There is a project on foot to arrange a match game of base ball between nine ladies of Neodesha and nine of Fredonia."[46]
June 1877	Kinsley	KS	Civic	"Our enterprising lady bucks, of Kinsley, have organized a Base Ball Club. . . . We understand they will practice daily until the 4th of July and then will be ready to give or take challenges from any quarter."[47]

Date	Place	State/Terr.*	Type of Team	Comments
c. July 1877	Fredonia	KS	Civic	"From the scoring around Fredonia about that match game of base ball between the 9 young ladies and as many young men, one's curiosity is aroused to know how many innings were made and who furnished the bat and ball."[48]
Aug. 1877	Williamsport	PA	Civic	". . . Williamsport is credited with a female base ball club."[49]
Sept. 1877	Neodesha	KS	School	"Since school has commenced the female ballist [sic] are up and doing."[50]
Jan. 1878	Auburn	NY	Civic	". . . . Our citizens need not be at all surprised this year if they see a lady base ball club on the diamond. . . ." "Auburn is anxious for a female base ball club." [51]
	Rochester	NY	Civic	"A female base ball club is to be organized in Rochester."[52]
Apr. 1878	Phoenix (Oswego County)	NY	School	Articles across the country carried articles about a team of school girls known as the Amazons.[53]
c. May 1878	Poughkeepsie	NY	Women's College	Poem in Vassar College Class Book for 1878 reported the difficulty one of the baseball team captains had finding enough players for her team.[54]
June 1878	Mercersburg	PA	Civic	"Mercersburg has a female base ball club. They want a young man for catch 'er."[55]
	Bayfield	MI	Civic	The *Marquette Mining Journal* reported that "none but married men are allowed to umpire and watch the girls slide in on the home base."[56]
	Danbury	CT	Fictional	"The only attempt on record of Danbury trying to organize a female base ball club occurred last week. . . . The idea was cogitated and carried out by six young ladies."[57]

Date	Place	State/Terr.*	Type of Team	Comments
	Syracuse	NY	Civic	"Syracuse is happy because she has a genuine female base ball club, under the name of 'Young Independents,' and an investigating exchange says its members wear red and white striped stockings."[58]
Aug. 1878	Jefferson	WI	Civic	"Jefferson has two female base ball clubs—the Calicos and Striped Stockings."[59]
	Manayunk	PA	Factory	"There was recently played at Manayunk a singular base ball match. The females in one of the mills challenged the young men working in the same establishment to play a game of base ball."[60]
Nov. 1878	—	—	—	"There are ten female base ball clubs batting their way through the world."[61]
Mar. 1879	New York City	NY	Professional/Theatrical	"A female base ball club, including two nines—handsomely costumed in silk and woolen—of 'American brunettes' and 'English blondes,' under the management of Sylvester F. Wilson of Camden, N. J., has lately been organized, . . ."[62]
c. May 1879	Philadelphia	PA	Professional/Theatrical	A group of men organized the Female Base Ball Club of New York and Female Base Ball Club of Philadelphia using some of the players from Wilson's defunct teams.[63]
May 1879	New Orleans	LA	Pick-up/Theatrical	Businessman H. E. Hezekiah organized the Lady Nine of Baltimore and the Lady Nine of Boston and promoted a "Grand Female Base Ball Festival" in the city on Sunday, June 15, 1879.[64]

Date	Place	State/ Terr.*	Type of Team	Comments
June 1879	Belfast	ME	—	"Two Belfast girls play ball with as much grace and energy as the sterner sex. One is pitcher and the other catcher.—[*Bangor Commercial.*] That takes the cake. Even Chicago doesn't boast a belle fast enough to do that."[65]
July 1879	Iowa City	IA	Civic	"Iowa City has a female base ball nine. We are not informed as to their 'rig,' and have a curiosity to know if they play in the regulation dress skirt. If they do, we have still a greater curiosity to see them run."[66]

* **Bold font** indicates first year state/territory is known to have had a female baseball team or player.
** Kingdom of Hawaii

Notes

1. "Items of Interest," *Kokomo Tribune,* September 8, 1870, 3.
2. "Afternoon Topics," *Critic Record* (Washington, D.C.), August 1, 1870, 4.
3. "Ladies at the Bat," *Chicago Tribune,* August 17, 1870, 4.
4. Printed in dozens of newspapers across the country. Examples: *Waterloo Courier,* September 15, 1870; *Plattsburg Sentinel,* November 25, 1870.
5. "Girls as Ballists," *New York Clipper,* November 26, 1870, 266.
6. Ibid.
7. "News Items," *Schoharie Union,* January 20, 1871. This quip may be a reference to teams of school girls mentioned by the *New York Clipper* in November 1870.
8. "Papers, Men and Things," *Cambridge City Tribune,* July 27, 1871, 1.
9. "Fourth of July: Under the Auspices of the Evanston Ladies' College Association," *The Tripod* (1871), 79. Reprinted in: "Chapter 3: Willard and Northwestern: The Evanston College for Ladies," *Radical Woman in a Classic Town Frances Willard of Evanston.* Northwestern University Archives. http://exhibits.library.northwestern .edu/archives/exhibits/willard/chapter_3 .pdf. It is not known whether the team from Northwestern was composed of men or women; there were very few women enrolled at Northwestern at the time.
10. *Indianapolis Journal,* August 23, 1871, 3
11. *Daily Illinois State Journal,* September 7, 1871.
12. *Reading Times,* September 30, 1871, 2.
13. Alice Stone Blackwell made numerous references to playing baseball with school friends in her journal. Journal reprinted in Merrill, *Growing Up in Boston's Gilded Age.*
14. "Gleanings," *Buffalo Evening Courier and Republic,* June 18, 1872. Reprinted across the country.
15. Information reported in: "History of the Mills College Athletic Association, 1899–1927." Cited by Gai Berlage, "Sociocultural History of the Origin of Women's Baseball at the Eastern Women's Colleges During the Victorian Period," *Cooperstown Symposium on Baseball and the*

American Culture (1989), Alvin L. Hall, ed. (Oneonta, N.Y.: Meckler, 1989): 105. Mills Seminary did not become Mills College until 1885.

16. Riske, "Ladies and Diamonds," (August 1978). NBHoF archives.

17. "Facts and Figures," *Woman's Exponent* 1, no. 23 (1873): 184.

18. "Miscellaneous Items," *Essex County Republican*, May 22, 1873.

19. Blackwell journal. Chauncy Hall was a prestigious school that trained the children of Boston's elite.

20. "Whittier College, Iowa," *Woman's Journal*, November 22, 1873, 370.

21. "The Local Switch," *Rhinebeck Gazette*, April 16, 1874.

22. *Iasco County Gazette*, May 28, 1874.

23. "New Hampshire," *Lowell Daily Courier*, July 11, 1874, 1.

24. "White Stockings," *Iosco County Gazette*, August 20 1874, 3.

25. "State New," *State Agricultural Journal* (Raleigh, N.C.), August 27, 1874, 7.

26. "Local Brevities," *Greenville Record-Argus*, September 26, 1874, 5.

27. *Tally-Book of the Punahou Base-Ball Club*, October 1869–February 1875. Punahou School Archives.

28. "State Notes," *Elk County Advocate*, June 17, 1875, 3.

29. "State News," *Reading Times*, July 9, 1875, 2.

30. Richardson, "Tendencies in Athletics," 526.

31. "Female Base Ball Club," *Inter-Ocean*, September 18, 1875, 5.

32. *New York Sunday Mercury*, January 9, 1876.

33. *Bucks County Gazette*, February 24, 1876, 2.

34. "Base Hits," *St. Louis Globe-Democrat*, March 12, 1876, 6.

35. "Suburban: Jacksonville," *St. Louis Globe-Democrat*, April 29, 1876, 3.

36. "Journal State Jottings," *Logansport Journal*, April 18, 1876, 2.

37. "General News," *Jackson Citizen Patriot*, May 25, 1876, 3.

38. "Annual Report of the Department of Physical Training 1875–1876," Lilian Tappan to President John H. Raymond, June 1876, VCSC; see also "Home Matters," *Vassar Miscellany* 5 (July 1876): 769, 773–75 and "College Notes," *Vassar Miscellany* 6, no. 1 (October 1876): 56.

39. *Brooklyn Daily Eagle*, June 21, 1876, 2.

40. Isabel Hill letter to mother Alice Hill and father Nathaniel Hill, from Providence, Rhode Island, June 4, 1876. Zaret database. WLCL, UM.

41. "Miscellaneous Items," *Brooklyn Daily Eagle*, July 20, 1876, 1.

42. "Town News," *Rochester Democrat and Chronicle*, August 4, 1876, 4.

43. "Lightning Flashes," *New York City Evening Telegram*, September 23, 1876, 2.

44. Unidentified clipping. Likely from a New York City paper dating from May 1877 based on other items on the page.

45. "Annual Report of the Department of Physical Training 1876–1877," Lilian Tappan to President John H. Raymond, June 1877, Vassar College Special Collections.

46. "Local News," *Neodesha Free Press*, July 13, 1877, 2. [KSHS].

47. "Local News," *Edwards County Leader*, June 21, 1877, 3. [KSHS].

48. "Fredonia Items," *Neodesha Free Press*, July 6, 1877, 3. [KSHS].

49. "State Items," *The North American* (Philadelphia), July 28, 1877. See also "Female Base Ball Club: Who Wants to Umpire It?" *Harrisburg Daily Independent*, July 16, 1877, 1.

50. "Local News," *Neodesha Free Press*, September 14, 1877, 2. Neodesha and nearby Fredonia, had female baseball nines during the summer too. See "Local News," *Neodesha Free Press*, July 13, 1877, 2. It is uncertain whether these teams were related to those that played over the summer in Neodesha.

51. "Some Base Ball Notes," *Auburn Daily Advertiser,* January 17, 1878, 4; "City News and Gossip," *Syracuse Sunday Times,* January 27, 1878,

52. "The News," *Plattsburgh Daily Republican,* January 26, 1878, 2. News appeared in many other papers as well.

53. The first report appeared as "Phoenix," *Oswego Daily Times,* April 26, 1878. As other newspapers reprinted the story they omitted the word "county" after Oswego, leading to the error that the team was in Oswego instead of Phoenix, New York. A report that the girls would play a men's nine appeared in "The Country 'Round: News About the State," *Evening Auburnian,* April 30, 1878, 1. It may be that two different teams, one composed of school girls and one composed of adult women, were playing in the county at this time.

54. "Poem, Prophecy and History," *1878 Class Book* (Vassar College), 23. VCSC.

55. "Jottings," *Harrisburg Daily Telegraph,* June 18, 1878, 4.

56. *Marquette Mining Journal,* June 29, 1878, cited in Morris, *Baseball Fever,* 196.

57. "The Female Base Ball Nine," *Mark Twain's Library of Humor* (New York, 1888), 126–29.

58. "County News," *Skaneateles Free Press,* June 29, 1878.

59. "State News," *Milwaukee Daily News,* August 8, 1878, 2.

60. "Petticoats in the Ball Field: Female Base Ballists at Play—The Fat Blonde Who Batted the Pitcher—A Ball Breaks Up the Game," *Inter Ocean,* August 14, 1878, 3.

61. "Wit and Humor," *Waukesha Freeman,* November 21, 1878, 1.

62. "Sporting Matters," *Lowell Daily Citizen,* March 27, 1879.

63. "Female Base Ball," *Cleveland Plain-Dealer,* June 25, 1879, 1.

64. *New Orleans Times,* May 27 and June 1, 1879.

65. *Boston Post,* June 9, 1879.

66. "Mere Mention," *Cedar Rapids Times,* July 31, 1879, 3.

Female Baseball in the 1880s

Date	Place	State/Terr.*	Type of Team	Comments
early 1880s	Honolulu	HI	Coed Private School	Alice Love (b. 1865) and Cara Isabel Carter (b. 1869) played baseball at Punahou in the early 1880s. Carter sometimes played on boys' teams.[1]
c. 1880s	—	OH	Civic/School	"In an Ohio village near my old home, there was a very flourishing Girls' Nine, some years ago. I well remember seeing part of a match game between the Girls' and Boys' Nines. . . ."[2]
Jan. 1880	—	—	—	"There are ten female base ball clubs batting their way through the world."[3]
Apr. 1880	Northampton	MA	Women's College	Residents of Hubbard House at Smith College organized two teams in April 1880.[4]

Date	Place	State/Terr.*	Type of Team	Comments
May 1881	Clayton	MI	Civic	"Clayton girls will have a base ball club. Two dozen pairs false calves and a car load of hickory clubs have been ordered."[5]
	Richmond	IN	Coed College	"The base ball fever is coming on both sides of the house. The ladies have organized a club and are practicing daily."[6]
Nov. 1881	North Edmeston	NY	Civic	"The female base ball club of this vicinity met for practice on Wednesday afternoon at the premises of Delos Giles."[7]
Apr./May 1882	Silver Creek	NY	Civic	"Silver Creek has a female base ball club."[8]
May/June 1882	Quincy	IL	Civic	"Several society girls residing south of Maine street have organized a base ball club and will begin practicing the festive game at once."[9]
1883	Philadelphia	PA	Factory	"The young women employed in a shoe factory in Philadelphia organized a club. . . ."[10]
	Philadelphia	PA	Civic	". . . and an amateur team in that city gloried in the appellation of the 'Mrs. Jane Duffy Club,' that lady being the manager and secretary."[11]
1883	Scranton	PA	—	"Three comely young women who could 'sting the first-baseman's hands from the home-plate, knock a ball beyond the diamond or throw it through a six-inch hole at a distance of 30 feet' tested the descriptive powers of gallant Scranton reporters."[12]
	Pottsville	PA	—	"In Pottsville, Pa. they had a girl twelve years old who could pitch a baseball with as much skill, dexterity and accuracy as the average amateur pitcher."[13]
Apr. 1883	—	—	—	"Female base ball clubs without number have been inflicted upon a long-suffering public."[14]

Date	Place	State/ Terr.*	Type of Team	Comments
May 1883	Rockport	IN	High School	"Rockport has a female base ball club. The first game was played last week on the college grounds."[15]
May 1883	South Chester and Philadelphia	PA	Theatrical	White barber, John Lang, organized Dolly Vardens 1 and Dolly Vardens 2 (teams of black women) for barnstorming games.[16]
	South Chester	PA	Theatrical	Lang reorganized his teams as Dolly Vardens and Captain Jinks. The barnstorming tour never took place.[17]
June 1883	Erie	PA	Civic	"Nine young women in Erie have formed a base ball club, and have offered to play with any female base ball club in the State." A subsequent article expanded the challenge to teams in New York as well.[18]
July 1883	Huntsboro	**AL**	Civic	"Miss Walker and eight other young ladies of Huntsboro, Ala. defeated a male nine there July 25 by a score of 20 to 11."[19]
	Olean	NY	—	Discussions in paper about whether to organize a team.[20]
Aug.-Dec. 1883	Philadelphia	PA	Professional/Theatrical	Sylvester Wilson (as H. H. Freeman) organized two barnstorming teams called variously: Young Ladies' Base Ball Club of Philadelphia, the Blondes and Brunettes, and the Belles of the Bat and Queens of the Emerald Diamond. They played at least 34 games in 20 cities in 9 states, drawing more than 20,000 spectators.[21]
Aug. 1883	Quincy	IL	Civic	Two women's teams organized; one on August 5 and a second circa August 23.[22]
	Almond	NY	Civic	"The Blondes and Brunettes, two female base-ball clubs of Almond, played a match game of ball at that place one day last week."[23]

Date	Place	State/Terr.*	Type of Team	Comments
	Fort Wayne	IN	Civic	" . . . Daisy Slack, a pert young lady living in Lagro, recently applied for a position in the female base ball nine now being organized in Fort Wayne."[24]
Dec. 1883– Dec. 1884	Brooklyn and Philadelphia	NY and PA	Professional/Theatrical	Wilson and a core group of players from his 1883 troupe traveled to New Orleans, where they reorganized for another tour.[25]
1884	North Bridgton	ME	Coed Academy	The school paper reported, "The boys had five baseball nines, the girls two."[26]
Jan. 1884	Honolulu	HI	Private School	The "Good Girls' Base Ball Club" of Punahou School played the "Good Boys' Base Ball Club" on January 8, 1884.[27]
Spring 1884	South Hadley	MA	Women's College	Players from the classes of 1885, 1886, and 1887 posed for a baseball team photo.[28]
May 1884	Glendive	**MT**	Civic	"The young ladies of Glendive have bought a ball and bat, and intend organizing immediately. If there are any other female base ball clubs in the Territory we should like to hear from them with a view to getting up a match."[29]
June 1884	Denver	**CO**	Civic	"The North Side is ahead again! This time it's the champion female base ball player. It is understood that the 'giddy girls' will form a club in the near future, in which case some boys will have to look to their laurels."[30]
Oct. 1884	Blunt	**SD**	Civic	"A female base ball club flourishes at Blunt, Dakota."[31]
1885	Ayer	MA	Civic	". . . last summer the girls of my age who lived here got up a base-ball nine."[32]
	Wellesley	MA	Women's College	*The Police Gazette* published a racy illustration purportedly depicting Wellesley freshmen playing baseball "like real little men."[33]

Date	Place	State/ Terr.*	Type of Team	Comments
Jan.–??? 1885	New Orleans	LA	Professional/Theatrical	P.S. Tunnison (or Tunison) recruited five of Wilson's players to organize Tunnison's Texas tour team. The team played one game on January 11 before departing for Texas.[34]
Apr.–May 1885	New Orleans	LA	Young Ladies' Base Ball Club	Wilson's 1885 troupe played its first game in mid-April but collapsed within a month. He had his pitcher and catcher play for amateur men's teams until he could reorganize the troupe in July.[35]
May 1885	Alton	IL	Civic	"The young lady base ballists are practicing and becoming very proficient, especially as pitchers and 'catchers.'"[36]
June 1885	Kirkwood	IL	Civic	"Kirkwood has a female base ball club."[37]
	Tallmadge	OH	High School/Pick-up	"There is to be a grand game of ball—the only female base ball club in the surrounding country. . . ."[38]
	Concord	NH	High School	The school paper reported that "some of the young ladies are quite expert in the national game."[39]
July–Dec. 1885	Cincinnati	OH	Professional/Theatrical	Wilson reorganized his 1885 troupe, adding a female military drill company to his entertainment troupe.[40]
Oct. 1885	Romney	WV	Civic/School	"Romney has a juvenile female base ball club."[41]
1886	—	—	Professional/Theatrical	Wilson took his combination female base ball club and military drill company on another barnstorming tour of the South. In July, his pitching battery played on a men's nine in Indiana, after which both were injured in a buggy accident.[42]
	South Hadley	MA	Women's College	Class Book of 1886 lists the "Senior representatives" of the base ball nine.[43]

Date	Place	State/ Terr.*	Type of Team	Comments
Feb. 1886	Tuskegee	AL	Women's College	Students at the Alabama Central Female College organized a baseball club that attracted notice in the local press.[44]
1886	San Francisco	CA	Professional/Theatrical	Victor E. M. Gutmann organized the Chicago Red Stockings and San Francisco Blue Stockings. The teams drew a few thousand fans to several exhibition games in San Francisco.[45]
May 1886	New Moorefield	OH	Civic	"[A]nother attractive feature that they are proud of is the charming female base ball club, recently organized. The young ladies are all expert players."[46]
June 1886	Ashton	IA	Civic	". . . Ashton, with a female base ball club, is bustling around for an opponent worthy of her willow."[47]
Aug. 1886	Norwich	CT	Civic	A group of society women organized a team. Kwai Pahn Lee, former secretary for the Chinese legation in Washington, D.C. and a skilled knuckleball pitcher, coached them. He later married one of the players.[48]
Sept. 1886	Gilmore	PA	Pick-up	Six hundred spectators attended the game organized and played by married and single women as a fund raiser for local churches.[49]
Nov. 1886	Bismarck	**ND**	Civic	"The last advertised game of ball by the Bismarck female base ball club was played last evening in Meadowland park, but owing to the beautiful weather the young ladies expect to continue the healthful and amusing sport for several weeks."[50]
Mar. 1887	Galt	CA	High School	"In Galt, Cal., all the high-school girls play ball with the young men."[51]
May 1887	Chicago	IL	Professional/Theatrical	"The formation of an unusual number of female base-ball clubs this season is noted by a Western contemporary."[52]

Date	Place	State/ Terr.*	Type of Team	Comments
July 1887	Chicago	IL	Queens of the Diamond	Professional mesmerist "Professor" E. G. Johnson organized the Queens of the Diamond to play an exhibition game against a team of boys aged 10–18 for July 4 festivities. About 5,000 spectators attended.[53]
Aug. 1887	Soquel	CA	Civic	"Soquel has a female base-ball nine."[54]
Sept. 1887	Asbury Beach	NJ	Civic	"Young ladies pitch base ball and occasionally catch at Asbury Beach."[55]
Apr. 1888	Nyack	NY	Civic	"It is said that a female base ball club is to be organized in Nyack this season."[56]
May 1888	Utica	NY	Civic	"Utica has a promising female base ball club. The girls practice in a ground so walled in that no one can see them, but they intend to cross bats with their brothers in a short time."[57]
July 1888	Hope	KS	Civic	An African American newspaper reported that a female team had been organized in Hope. It is uncertain whether members were black.[58]
	Elmira	NY	Civic	"Elmira has two female base ball clubs, and they recently played a game on Sunday. Naughty girls."[59]
Aug. 1888	Albuquerque	**NM**	Civic/Barnstorming	"Albuquerque, New Mexico, has organized a female base ball team. They are uniformed in a neat sailor waist and navy blue short skirts, and are now undergoing thorough practice before making a tour through Colorado, New Mexico and Texas."[60]

Date	Place	State/Terr.*	Type of Team	Comments
	Los Angeles	CA	Professional/Theatrical	Two men organized two teams of women and asked newspapers to promote their games. The *Los Angeles Times* reported that a number of the players had recently been employed as "beer-jerkers" at a local saloon until forced out of their jobs by the local police.[61]
c. 1889	Farmington	CT	Private Girls' School	Archives at Miss Porter's School has a photo of a school baseball team dated c. 1889.
Feb. 1889	Bangor	ME	School/Church	The President of the Children's Christian League urged girls at a church social to reconsider their plan to organize a female baseball team that season.[62]
	Meadville	PA	Coed College	A newspaper reported that Allegheny College would have a female baseball team that year.[63]
Apr. 1889	San Antonio	**TX**	Civic	"There is considerable talk of organizing a female base ball nine in the city."[64]
May 1889	Haddam	KS	Civic	"Haddam has a female base ball club."[65]
June 1889	Pocahontas	IA	Civic	"Pocahontas has a female base ball club and the *Record* says the bald heads watch them from a distance through spy-glasses. What's the matter with the front seats?"[66]
June–Nov. 1889	Chicago	IL	Professional/Theatrical	Sylvester Wilson (as W. S. Franklin) organized a new team known alternately as the Great and Only Young Ladies' Base Ball Club, Chicago Black Stockings, and Young Ladies Athletic Club of Philadelphia. This team played men's and boys' teams, including a colored men's nine in Williamsport, Pennsylvania.[67]

Date	Place	State/Terr.*	Type of Team	Comments
July 1889	Manistee	MI	Civic	"It is not generally known, but it is true all the same, that there is a growing tendency on the part of the ladies of Manistee to adopt base ball as a recreation."[68]
	Brooklyn	NY	Civic	"Two colored women, named Mary E. Thompson and Mary Jackson, who live in the classic precincts of Crow Hill, are members of a ladies' base ball club."[69]
July/Aug. 1889	McPherson	KS	Pick-up/Coed College	"Another amusing game of ball was played last evening between the female base ball club and the men." "Another ball club has been organized by the women, christened the Sun Flower Club."[70]
Aug. 1889	—	KS	Civic/Pick-up/School/College	"There are sixteen female base ball clubs in Kansas. Just imagine eighteen angry and excited females engaged in a discussion with one poor, unprotected umpire."[71]
	Near Colby	KS	Coed Normal School	"The matter of organizing a female base ball club among the teachers attending the institute has been spoken of. They will challenge a nine to be organized from among the male teachers."[72]
Aug. 1889	Pittsfield	MA	High School	"The female base-ball team of Pittsfield, Mass., high school will challenge a nine from the Fendle Mound Company of Poughkeepsie, some time."[73]
	Camp Shafter (Santa Cruz)	CA	Pick-up	"A baseball game was played here to-day between the ladies of the camp, assisted by Piccinnini, the colored mascot of Company B, and a nine under Lieutenant Ormsby."[74]

Date	Place	State/Terr.*	Type of Team	Comments
Sept. 1889	Unnamed Seaside Resorts	—	Pick-up	Upper-class women at summer resorts routinely played baseball in the nineteenth century. In 1889, writer Howard Fielding penned a humorous account of serving as umpire for a game between two women's teams.[75]
	Various	—	Schools	"Go to any country school, and at noon you will see the girls playing ball with great vim and relish."[76]
Oct. 1889	Mount Washington	**MD**	Civic	"There are nine young ladies, well known in the society of Mount Washington, in this county, who are so enthusiastically in love with base ball that they have formed themselves into a nine of their own. . . ."[77]

* **Bold font** indicates first year state/territory is known to have had a female baseball team or player.

Notes

1. Mary Charlotte Alexander and Charlotte Peabody Dodge, *Punahou, 1841–1891* (Berkeley: University of California Press, 1941), 344.

2. Susan Rhoda Cutler, Letter to the Editor, dated May 12, 1890 from Buffalo, New York. Published as: "Base-Ball For Girls," *Woman's Journal,* May 24, 1890, 162.

3. "Wit and Humor," *Daily Chronicle* (Marshall, Mich.), January 2, 1880, 1.

4. The Smith College archives includes a number of contemporary references to these teams in player journals and letters.

5. "Michigan," *Fort Wayne Daily Gazette,* May 19, 1881, 6.

6. The *Earlhamite* (school literary journal), (May 1881), 188. Thanks to Thomas Hamm, school archivist, for bringing this article to my attention. Word of the team at Earlham also appeared in: "Bat and Ball," *Syracuse Daily Courier,* June 13, 1881. This paper erroneously identified the location of Earlham as Ohio. It is actually in Richmond, Indiana, just across the Ohio border.

7. "North Edmeston," *Brookfield Courier,* November 9, 1881.

8. *Randolph Weekly Courant.* Date extrapolated from other articles on the page.

9. "Items in Brief," *Quincy Daily Herald,* May 7, 1882, 4. Teams were Striped Stockings and Fancy Stockings.

10. "Noteworthy Contests of 1883," 693.

11. Ibid.

12. Ibid.

13. Ibid.

14. "Strange Clubs," *Cleveland Herald,* April 7, 1883, 6.

15. "State News," *Indianapolis News,* May 21, 1883, 1. After the Rockport Collegiate Institute closed in 1873, the city of Rockport purchased the building and grounds and opened Rockport High School. E-mail from Erin Strobel, Spencer County Public Library, to author, May 25, 2011.

16. "Female Base Ballists: A Game That Did Not Come Off; Scenes at Lamokin Woods," *Chester Times*, May 18, 1883, 3; "Miss Harris's Base-Ball Nine: Dusky Dolly Vardens of Chester Give an Exhibition," *New York Times*, May 18, 1883, 1.

17. "A Novel Game of Base Ball Between Teams of Colored Girls," *Daily Times* (New Brunswick, N.J.), May 30, 1883, 1.

18. "Around the Circle," *Titusville Herald*, June 11, 1883, 4; "Neighboring News," *Niagara Falls Daily Gazette*, June 29, 1883, 1.

19. "Noteworthy Contests of 1883," 693.

20. "Emporium," *Olean Sunday Morning Herald*, July 29, 1883, 5.

21. The teams played in Pennsylvania, New Jersey, New York, Maryland, Massachusetts, Ohio, Kentucky, Missouri, and Illinois. The team was scheduled to play in Connecticut, but it is uncertain if it did. Spectator count is conservatively estimated based only on games in which newspapers commented on the size of the crowd. The largest audience was 4,000–5,000 in Cincinnati on Sunday, November 11.

22. "It Would Be Well," *Quincy Herald*, August 7, 1883, 3; "It May Be Remarked That," *Quincy Herald*, August 8, 1883, 3; "Items in Brief," *Quincy Herald*, August 23, 1883, 3.

23. *Watkins Express*, August 30, 1883). These are not Wilson's Blondes and Brunettes. They were in Philadelphia that week.

24. *Fort Wayne Daily Sentinel*, August 25, 1883, 3.

25. The new troupe played in at least six states and D.C.; Wilson sent teams on the road with William Phillips, Edward Everett, and Emile Gargh. "The Female Base Ball Club," *Poughkeepsie Daily Eagle*, May 18, 1884, 3; "Local Brevities," *Trenton Daily State Gazette*, June 30, 1884, 3; "Girls at the Bat," *Titusville Morning Herald*, August 1, 1884, 2; "The Female Nine at Jackson," *New Orleans Daily Picayune*, December 24, 1884, 8.

26. Cited in Hunter, *How Young Ladies Became Girls*, 237.

27. "Good Girls vs. Good Boys," *Honolulu Saturday Press*, January 12, 1884, 4.

28. Photo is in the Mount Holyoke College Library/Archives.

29. "Base Ball Notes," *Glendive Times*, May 10, 1884, 3.

30. "North Denver Notes," *Rocky Mountain News*, June 8, 1884, 4.

31. "Items of News," *Boston Investigator*, October 15, 1884, 6.

32. Ruth F, letter to the editor. "The Letter Box," *St. Nicholas* 13, no. 2 (May 1886): 556. Ruth was fourteen years old when she played on the team the previous year. She stated that she and her friends "played very nicely and enjoyed the fun."

33. *National Police Gazette*, July 18, 1885. No record of Wellesley students organizing baseball teams in 1885 has yet surfaced, but it is possible that the illustration was published in response to word that students *were* playing baseball.

34. It is uncertain whether the team ever played in Texas. *Galveston Daily News*, March 7, 1885, 3; "Base Ball: The Farewell of the Females," *New Orleans Daily Picayune*, January 11, 1885, 10; "The Female Nines," *Daily Picayune*, January 12, 1885, morning edition, 1.

35. *New Orleans Daily Picayune*, April 12 and 19, 1885; "Miscellaneous," *Louisiana Democrat*, April 29, 1885, 3; "Texarkana . . ." *Daily Arkansas Gazette*, May 6, 1885, 4; "Notes and Comments," *Sporting Life*, May 20, 1885, 7; *New York Clipper*, May 23, 1885, 147.

36. "City and County News," *Alton Evening Telegraph*, May 5, 1885, 3.

37. "Local Paragraphs," *Decatur Morning Review*, June 10, 1885, 3; "City News," *Quincy Daily Journal*, June 8, 1885, 4.

38. "'[Akron] Beacon' Letters: Tallmadge," *Summit County Beacon*, June 10, 1885, 3. Game was to be played at a school picnic.

39. *Concord Volunteer*. Cited in Hunter, *How Young Ladies Became Girls*, 237.

40. "Coming: The Young Ladies' Base Ball Club," *Kalamazoo Gazette*, July 26, 1885, 3; "Local Baseball Notes," *Milwaukee Sentinel*, August 16, 1885, 7; "Female Acrobats," *Omaha Daily Bee*, October 19, 1885, 8.

41. "Through the State: Items of Interest from Interior Exchanges," *Wheeling Register*, October 28, 1885, 1.

42. Pearl Emerson and May Hamilton played for a men's nine in a game at Evansville, Indiana, on July 28, 1886. Emerson survived but newspapers reported that Hamilton was fatally injured. "Accident to Female Base Ballists," *St. Louis Globe-Democrat*, July 29, 1886, 4.

43. Class Book of 1886, 25. Senior players were Louisa Cutler, Mary Goodenough, Orianna "Anna" Fitch, Harriet Prescott, and Marietta A. "Etta" Freeland. All but Freeland had played on the team depicted in an 1884 photo.

44. *Tuskegee Weekly Gazette*, February 20, 1886; quoted in Rhoda Coleman Ellison, *History of Huntingdon College, 1854–1954* (University of Alabama Press, 1954), 131–32.

45. See chapter 4 for details on the teams.

46. "Moorefield," *Springfield Globe-Republic*, May 5, 1886, 1.

47. "Iowa Items," *Omaha Daily Bee*, June 17, 1886, 4.

48. "Pahn Lee's Ball Nine: Young Ladies Play in It, and There is Nothing Nicer in Norwich," Boston Daily Globe, August 16 1886, 6.

49. "Married vs. Single Ladies at Base Ball," *Kalamazoo Gazette*, September 26, 1886, 3.

50. "Brief Mention," *Bismarck Daily Tribune*, November 17, 1886, 1.

51. *Wichita Globe*, March 18, 1887, 4.

52. *Chicago Daily Tribune*, May 30, 1887, 4.

53. "The Girls and Boys Play Ball: A Victory for the Former, Though the Score Doesn't Show It," *Chicago Tribune*, July 5, 1887, 1.

54. "Pacific Coast Items," *Daily Evening Bulletin* (San Francisco), August 13, 1887.

55. *Titusville Herald*, September 5, 1887, 3.

56. *Mount Kisco Recorder*, April 13, 1888, 2.

57. "News Summary," *Potsdam Courier and Freeman*, May 2, 1888.

58. "Kansas State News," *Nicodemus Cyclone*, July 13, 1888, 2.

59. "Vicinity," *Watkins Democrat*, July 19, 1888.

60. "Flashes From the Diamond," *Rochester Democrat and Chronicle*, August 12, 1888, 7. It is uncertain who organized this team and whether it ever made the planned barnstorming tour.

61. "Female Base-Ballists: The Latest 'Fake' Proposed for Los Angeles," *Los Angeles Times*, August 29, 1888, 1.

62. "Children's Christian League," *Bangor Daily Whig and Courier*, February 22, 1889, 3. The president's address to the girls was not a scheduled part of the formal program. He read a "short sketch" about an unnamed female base ball club before urging them to abandon their plans to organize a team.

63. "Short-Notes," *Canaseraga Times*, February 8, 1889.

64. "Base Ball Bites," *San Antonio Daily Light*, April 12, 1889, 1. It is uncertain whether this team ever played.

65. "North and Northwest," *Atchison Daily Champion*, May 28, 1889, 2.

66. *Emmet County Republican*, June 27, 1889.

67. "Amateur Base-Ball," *Inter Ocean*, June 9, 1889, 11; "A Female Baseball Club Disbands," *New Orleans Daily Picayune*, December 8, 1889, 14. Game against Colored men's nine reported in "Little Locals," *Lock Haven Evening Express*, September 28, 1889, 1.

68. "Base Ball Matters," *Manistee Democrat,* July 19, 1889, 1.

69. "Female Ball Players: How They Knocked Luke Kenney All Over the Diamond," *Brooklyn Daily Eagle,* July 23, 1889, 6.

70. *McPherson Daily Republican,* July 30 and 31, August 1 and 6, 1889, 3; *Wichita Daily Journal,* August 1, 1889, 1.

71. *Fort Worth Daily Gazette,* August 10, 1889, 4. The reporter may have exaggerated to make a joke. Given the history of women's baseball teams in Kansas, it is also possible there really were sixteen teams in the state.

72. *Thomas County Cat* (Colby, Kans.), August 15, 1889, 5. The article refers to a campus and a school building but does not specify which one. The fact that teachers are "attending" rather than just teaching at the institution leads to the assumption that it is a Normal School or college rather than a high school or grammar school.

73. "Our Girls Are Just Great," *Alton Daily Telegraph,* August 13, 1889, 4.

74. "Camp Shafter: Lady Visitors Distinguish Themselves at Baseball...." *Sacramento Daily Record-Union,* August 23, 1889, 2.

75. Howard Fielding, "The Girls Play Ball. A Woeful Story of an Unfortunate Man Who Umpired for Them: The National Game in Feminine Hands; It is Much More Dangerous Than a Sewing Circle But Not Quite so Scientific. Copyright 1889," *Kalamazoo Gazette,* September 15, 1889, 7. This may have been a fictional account but nonetheless reflected the popularity of baseball among female visitors to upper-class resorts.

76. "It is a Woman's Game," *Pittsburg Dispatch,* September 23, 1889, 5. Quoting Sylvester Wilson.

77. "Baltimore Girls Play Ball," *Kansas City Star,* October 3, 1889, 4.

Female Baseball in the 1890s

Date	Place	State/ Terr.*	Type of Team	Comments
c. 1890	Haverhill	MA	College Prep	Photograph taken c. 1890s shows students playing baseball on the lawn in front of Academy Hall.[1]
1890	Abington	PA	Private Girls' School	Photograph shows students at the Ogontz School playing baseball on a large, grassy field in 1890.[2]
Apr. 1890	Nevadaville	CO	Civic	"Mr. Mark G. Kobey ... will secure suits for the recently organized female base ball club of Nevadaville."[3]
—	—	—	Pick-up/Civic	*The Woman's Journal* prints a fictional account of a girls' baseball club organized at the suggestion of a mother.[4]
May 1890	Central [City]	CO	Civic	The members of a newly organized young ladies athletic club were preparing to form a base ball club.[5]

Date	Place	State/Terr.*	Type of Team	Comments
May–Oct. 1890	—	—	Professional/Barnstorming	Sylvester Wilson organized the Young Ladies Base Ball Club No. 1 (a.k.a. Chicago Blackstockings) with players from Cincinnati and Chicago in early May.[6]
June 1890	Chicago	IL	Professional/Theatrical	"Manager Elliott" organized two baseball clubs for public games during the first week of June. Though Elliott had promised the players $10 a week for the entire summer, he stole the gate money and disappeared after the teams' first game on June 7.[7]
	Utica	NY	Civic	The local newspaper reported that townswomen were in the process of organizing a team.[8]
July 1890	Beatrice	SD	Civic	"A female base ball club has been organized at Beatrice, Beadle county."[9]
	South Atchison	KS	Civic	"There is a young ladies' base ball nine in South Atchison that plays nearly every evening. The boys are trying to find out where they play."[10]
Aug. 1890	Norwich	CT	Civic	A group of sixteen-year-old girls from the same neighborhood organized the Polka Dots and Merry Maids.[11]
	Staten Island	NY	Civic	Female members of Huguenot's Harvard Social Association organized the Whites and Reds baseball teams.[12]
Early 1890s	Northampton	MA	Women's College	Students in the Class of 1895 at Smith College posed for a team photo.[13]
Apr.–Sept. 1891	—	—	Professional/Theatrical	Wilson organized up to four female baseball teams, including the Female Champions of the World, the Chicago Black Stocking Nine, and the Young Ladies Base Ball Club.[14]
Spring 1891	South Hadley	MA	Women's College	Students at Mount Holyoke reported that they had organized another base ball club.[15]

Date	Place	State/Terr.*	Type of Team	Comments
c. June–Sept. 1891	—	NY	Professional/Theatrical	Mark Lally, one of Wilson's former advance men, organized the Cincinnati Reds. A "female baseball war" ensued as Lally's and Wilson's teams competed for customers in the same area of New York.[16]
June 1891	Emporia	KS	Civic	"There are some parties in town who are agitating the organization of a female Base Ball Club. They have struck the wrong town."[17]
	Caledonia	NY	Civic	"The girls of Caledonia have organized a base ball nine, and they term themselves 'Belles of the Bat.'"[18]
	Blair	NE	Civic	"Pitcher Brott has organized a female nine. . . . They were out practicing twice this week and before long they expect to cross bats with the Tekamah nine, which is also composed of girls."[19]
	Tekamah	NE	Civic	"Tekamah's female base ball club says it can 'just beat the Blair girls too awfully quick.' If the ladies will come to Omaha and play a game the *World-Herald* will guarantee a 10,000 crowd."[20]
July 1891	Washington Court House	OH	Civic	"The society girls near Washington [Court House] . . . have dropped the tennis racquet and taken up the base-ball bat. An exciting and amusing game was played to-day between a nine they have just organized and a picked nine of the society young men."[21]
July/Aug. 1891	Stowe	PA	Civic	Mary Gemperling organized a female team and was trying to arrange games with other women's teams.[22]

Date	Place	State/ Terr.*	Type of Team	Comments
Aug. 1891	—	MN	Barnstorming	"A man named Armstrong, who says he lives in Cleveland, is in Minneapolis with the view of getting up two base ball teams composed of female players. If he succeeds in securing the services of eighteen foolish women he will have them play exhibition games in Minneapolis and St. Paul. He also intends taking them on a tour through the West."[23]
	Glasgow	PA	Civic	Pottstown, Pennsylvania, *Ledger* carried an article about this team and gave the players' names.[24]
	Mt. Morris	NY	Civic	"Mt. Morris has a female base ball club. When the giddy girls assemble for practice all the storekeepers take a holiday."[25]
	Rockford	IL	Factory	"It is reported that the girls on the second floor of the factory will organize a base ball club."[26]
	Johnson (City)	NY	Civic/Barnstorming	"The Johnson female base ball club will play a picked nine in this city, on Monday, Aug. 24."[27]
Sept. 1891	Philadelphia	PA	Barnstorming	"Help Wanted: Female. Young Ladies to join a female base ball club; correspondence strictly confidential. Address by letter, stating age, to Mr. P. Callahan, 1829 Lambert street."[28]
	Westwood	NJ	Grammar School	"James E. Demarest is the principal of the school with its more than one hundred scholars. . . . Miss Claude Ottignon interested the girls in baseball, which the boys played vigorously at noon and recess."[29]
1892	—	—	Barnstorming	The Young Ladies Base Ball Club of N.Y. (future New England Bloomer Girls) began its first season, playing 154 games with a record of 56–98.[30]

Date	Place	State/Terr.*	Type of Team	Comments
Mar. 1892	Los Angeles	CA	Barnstorming	Police and Humane Society officials intervene to stop John Doyle from completing his plot to exploit fourteen- to sixteen-year old girls by promising them $30-$90/month to travel with a baseball team.[31]
	Blair and Tekamah	NE	Civic	The *Omaha World Herald* announced in March that the teams would reorganize again. By June it reported that the Tekamah team had "resolved itself into a tennis club." In August it noted that the team in Blair had not yet reappeared on the scene.[32]
Spring 1892	Northampton	MA	Women's College	Students in at least two of the Smith College Houses (cottages) had baseball teams. The freshman and sophomore classes also had teams.[35]
Apr. 1892	Lodi	WI	High School	"Lodi has a female base ball team under the title of the 'Lodi High School Unrivalled Female Base Ball Club.'"[33]
	Ovid	NY	Civic	"Ovid has a female base ball club."[34]
	Denver	CO	Barnstorming	Clara Wilson organized the Chicago Reds (Colts) and Denver Blues to play exhibition games in Colorado. By June, eight of the players appeared on a new team (The Denver Female BBC) that began playing men's teams.[37]
Apr ?, 1892	New York City	NY	Barnstorming	The Cincinnati Reds opened the season on April 23. Soon thereafter, papers began calling it "Miss Lillie [sic] Arlington's Cincinnati Reds" in honor of its star pitcher, Lizzie Arlington. Maud Nelson played too.[36]

Date	Place	State/ Terr.*	Type of Team	Comments
May–Sept. 1892	New York City	NY	Barnstorming	The New York Champion Young Ladies BBC (a.k.a. Young Ladies BBC of New York) had multiple managers, including three men who were arrested in Missouri for attempting to defraud their players out of their earnings.[38]
June 1892	Alton	IL	Civic	"A female baseball nine is being organized in the eastern part of the city and the battery practices every day. Their grounds are near the foot of Henry street, opposite the Big Four freight house. A challenge is open to any other female nine in the city."[39]
	Andover	SD	Civic	"Andover [SD] has a ladies base ball club. Constant practice with the rolling pin make them experts with the 'stick.'"[40]
June– Sept. 1892	—	—	Barnstorming	New York Giants (a.k.a. "Champion Female Base Ball Club") play games against men's teams throughout New York.[41]
July 1892	—	—	Barnstorming	"The manager of the . . . [American Stars] club has gone to considerable expense to get a good club of lady ball players together for a tour of the states, and good ball playing is assured."[42]
Aug. 1892	Evanston	**WY**	Civic	"A female base ball club has been organized at Evanston."[43]
Sept. 1892	Sconset (Siasconset)	MA	Coed Pick-up	Teams of wealthy men and women played a pick-up game against each other using a tennis ball instead of a baseball, and parasols and a chair for the bases.[44]
Fall 1892	Bryn Mawr	PA	Women's College	Students played at least one game during fall term.[45]

Date	Place	State/Terr.*	Type of Team	Comments
1893	Thief River Falls	MN	Coed Civic	The Pennington County Historical Society of Thief River Falls has a studio portrait of a women's baseball team taken in 1893.[46] The photo depicts ten young women dressed in uniforms and posing with bats, a catcher's mask, and two men.
	Abington	PA	Private Girls' School	Students at the Ogontz School posed for a team picture. Some of the players wore the military rank of their military drill team.[47]
	Alinda	PA	Civic	Players posed for a team photograph sometime in 1893.[48]
	—	—	Barnstorming	Second season for the YLBBC of NY (future New England Bloomer Girls); team played 125 games with a record of 49–76.[49]
	Chicago	IL	Barnstorming	W. P. Needham's Boston Bloomer Girls tour as far west as Deadwood, South Dakota, during their inaugural season.[50]
Feb.–Mar. 1893	New York City	NY	Barnstorming	American Female Base Ball Club (former American Stars) kicks off its second season by embarking on a tour of Cuba. The tour ends after only one game when unruly spectators attack the players and destroy the playing venue in Almendares, Cuba.[51]
May 1893	Ann Arbor	MI	Coed College	Coed baseball team hosted a Grand Ballet at the University of Michigan.[52]
	Grand Forks	ND	Coed College	Women's teams played baseball every evening after supper at the University of North Dakota.[53]
May–??? 1893	—	—	Barnstorming	Third season of the Cincinnati Reds. Earliest known game of 1893 was May 6 in Bloomfield, New Jersey.[54]
July 1893	Greenwich	NY	Civic	"I hear that some of the ambitious society 'buds' are organizing a female base ball club."[55]

Date	Place	State/Terr.*	Type of Team	Comments
Aug. 1893	Milwaukee	WI	Barnstorming	Rose Royal's Female Base Ball Club played to general praise in Milwaukee on August 13 but had only four players available to travel to Waukesha for a game on August 26.[56]
	—	GA	Barnstorming	An unidentified female team played games in Georgia in late August.[57]
	Lenox	MA	Pick-up	Wealthy young men and women summering at the Lenox cottages organized two teams and played each other in front of a large crowd.[58]
1894	Oakland	CA	Women's College	The Mills College yearbook states that baseball was first introduced at Mills in 1894.[59]
	—	—	Barnstorming	Third season for the YLBBC of NY (future New England Bloomer Girls); team played 167 games with a record of 86–81.[60]
1894	New York City	NY	Barnstorming	Young Ladies Champions of the World Base Ball Club (newly renamed) began its third season in Brooklyn in early May. Maud Nelson was on the team, as were several of Wilson's former players and several members of the team that caused a riot in Cuba in 1893.[61]
	St. Louis	MO	Barnstorming	Wilson's former players, May Howard and Kittie Grant, played for the St. Louis–based New York Champion Young Ladies Ball Club. It toured Illinois, Kansas, and Iowa in May and June until the manager abandoned the team after a game in Dubuque.[62]
	Chicago	IL	Barnstorming	W. P. Needham's Chicago-based Boston Bloomer Girls play their second season.[63]
	New York City	NY	Barnstorming	Bertha Gordon, a member of the team that traveled to Cuba, pitched and caught for the newly organized New York Brunettes.[64]

Date	Place	State/Terr.*	Type of Team	Comments
May 1894	Ames	IA	Coed College	The junior class at the Iowa State Agricultural College included team rosters and a humorous illustration of a baseball game in its school yearbook.[65]
	Ottawa	KS	Coed College	A local newspaper reported that female students at Ottawa University had organized a baseball team.[66]
June 1894	New York City	NY	Pick-up	Newspaper article described the activities of the estimated 200,000 persons who visited Central Park one Sunday in June, noting that "half grown girls played baseball with their full grown brothers."[67]
	Natick	MA	Pick-up/Fund Raiser	"About 1000 people went to Outing Park yesterday afternoon to see a female base ball club from New York contest with a scrub team representing the clerks on Main Street. The proceeds were given to the striking lasters at J W Walcott & Co.'s factory. The female players won by a score of 20 to 18. . . ."[68]
July 1894	Fort Valley and Atlanta	GA	Pick-up	Atlanta, July 4, 1894: "A big affair is on at Brisbane Park, and the feature of the day was a game of base ball between negro girls from Fort Valley, Ga., and several negro women from this city."[69]
	Rhinebeck	NY	Civic	"A female base ball club is being organized. It will be called the 'Ostrich Feathers' and play its first game with the Pond Lillies on the home grounds on the 28th at 3 P.M."[70]
Aug. 1894	Brooklyn	NY	Civic	"[N]ine enterprising and sport-loving girls of Brooklyn have organized a club with the intent of knocking a leather-covered sphere about a field diamond."[71]

Date	Place	State/Terr.*	Type of Team	Comments
Oct. 1894	—	—	Women's College	Mills College student: "The idea of a baseball nine in a girl's college may shock the fastidious taste of some, but a sister college has proved that such a team can be supported and a young woman's dignity not suffer."[72]
1894 or 1895	Northampton	MA	Girls' Boarding School	Edith Hill's photo album (1894–95) contains photos of girls playing baseball at Mary A. Burnham School.[73]
1895	Chicago	IL	High School	The *National Police Gazette* published a risqué illustration of high school girls playing indoor baseball in Chicago.[74]
	—	—	Barnstorming	Fourth season of the YLBBC of NY (future New England Bloomer Girls); played 154 games with a record of 72–82.[75]
	—	—	Barnstorming	Maud Nelson joined W. P. Needham's Boston Bloomer Girls for its third season. The team played in Minnesota, Illinois, Iowa, South Dakota, Indiana, and Ohio.[76]
	—	—	Barnstorming	A team billed as the Trilby Bloomer Girls played games in Minnesota and Iowa.[77]
Apr. 1895	Lawrence	KS	Civic	"*The Lawrence Gazette* is responsible for the statement that a home talent girls' baseball club is to be organized in that city this summer."[78]
May 1895	Rockford	IL	Civic	"A great game of ball was played in the South Side park yesterday. A team of young ladies who call themselves the South Side Stars defeated a team of boys by a score of 12 to 1.[79]
June 1895	Philadelphia	PA	Barnstorming	Advertisement: "Two young ladies to join traveling ladies' base ball club. Call Greiner's Hotel, sixth above arch, to-day, between 2 and 5 P.M. R.C. Johnson."[80]

Date	Place	State/Terr.*	Type of Team	Comments
Aug. 1895	Chicago	IL	Pick-up	"At the Lakeside Hotel a female baseball nine is the latest thing the young women have got up. May Bourcaren is pitcher and Mrs. F. Murphy is catcher."[81]
	Cherokee	IA	Civic	"We understand that a number of Cherokee young ladies have organized a female base ball club...."[82]
Sept. 1895	Hooper	NE	Civic	"Hooper has a female base ball club and the girls have a record of beating a team made up of boys by a score of 9 to 3."[83]
1895–96	Various	ME and MA	Grammar	Eighteen young adult women replied to a survey that they had played baseball as schoolgirls.[84]
	South Hadley	MA	Women's College	Students at Mount Holyoke organized an Athletic Association and offered baseball as a sport.[85]
c. 1896	Pelham Manor	NY	Private School	Students at Mrs. Hazen's School posed for a team picture.[86]
1896	—	—	Barnstorming	Fifth season of the YLBBC of NY (future New England Bloomer Girls); played 136 games with a record of 64–72.[87]
	—	—	Barnstorming	Maud Nelson continued to play with W. P. Needham's Boston Bloomer Girls for the team's fourth season.[88]
Spring 1896	Cleveland	OH	Coordinate College	Students at the Women's College of Western Reserve University played their inaugural baseball season.[89]
	Poughkeepsie	NY	Women's College	From article about Vassar College in *Harper's Bazaar*: "In athletics, football, baseball, and basket-ball divide popular attention."[90]
July 1896	Galveston and Houston	TX	Civic	"Yes; I will bring Galveston's and also Houston's base ball clubs up [to Fort Worth]."[91]
1897	—	—	Barnstorming	Sixth season of the YLBBC of NY (future New England Bloomer Girls); played 198 games with a record of 109–89.[92]

Date	Place	State/ Terr.*	Type of Team	Comments
—	—	—	Barnstorming	Maud Nelson continued to play with W. P. Needham's Boston Bloomer Girls for the team's fifth season.[93]
	Spartanburg	SC	Women's College	Baseball was one of the most popular sports at Converse College.[94]
Feb. 1897	Oakland	CA	Women's College	Two Mills College teams played each other.[95]
Mar. 1897	Williamsburg	KY	Civic	"Williamsburg has a female base ball club."[96]
Apr. 1897	Argentine	KS	School/Civic	"Argentine, a town of many base ball 'fans,' has forged to the front this year, at the advent of the season, with a novelty. It will have several base ball clubs composed entirely of school girls who expect to play regular games every Saturday. Three 'nines' have already been organized and enough may be formed to arrange a Girls' City League."[97]
Apr./May 1897	Olivet	MI	Coed College	Coed and all-female House teams played baseball at Olivet College.[98]
May 1897	Springport	MI	Grammar School	"Some of the grammar room girls at Springport have organized a base ball club and will soon be open for a challenge."[99]
June 1897	Lowville	NY	Grammar School	"Two base ball teams have been organized at the State street school, to be known as the Miss Allen and Mrs. Jones teams."[100]
	Germantown	PA	Private Boarding School and Quaker School	"A novel and exciting game of base ball took place a few days ago at the Germantown Academy grounds between two teams composed of young ladies connected with the Walnut Lane Boarding School and the Friends' School, on Coulter street."[101]
July 1897	—	TX	Female player on men's team	"A Texas baseball club has a pretty young female pitcher. . ."[102]
	Meade	KS	Civic	"Meade has two base ball nines, composed of young ladies. . ."[103]

Date	Place	State/Terr.*	Type of Team	Comments
July 1897	Springfield	KY	Springfield Female Baseball Club	"The girls have 'got it.' Not sanctification, but baseball fever, and have donned their bloomers. . . . We now have everything necessary to a well regulated ball team. . . ."[104]
	Bardstown	KY	Civic	"We have had a communication from Bardstown to the effect that they are organizing a girl team, and will soon be ready to play us."[105]
1897 or 98	Salamanca	NY	Pick-up/Civic	Caption on photograph of women baseball players stated, "Ladies playing base ball at Island Park, Sala. 1897 or 1898."[106]
1898	—	—	Female Player on Men's Teams	Lizzie Arlington signed a contract to pitch in exhibition games for numerous teams in the Atlantic League. She also pitched for nonaffiliated men's teams in Philadelphia.[107]
	—	—	Barnstorming	Seventh season of the YLBBC of NY (future New England Bloomer Girls); played 177 games this season with a record of 116–61.[108]
	—	—	Boston Bloomer Girls	Maud Nelson continued to play with W. P. Needham's Boston Bloomer Girls for the team's sixth season.[109]
	Abington	PA	Private Girls' School	Students at Ogontz School continued to play baseball.[110]
	Oakland	CA	Women's College	Students at Mills College posed for a team photo. One is holding a bat and several have gloves. All are wearing bloomers.[111]
Jan. 1898	Safford	AZ	Civic	"Mr. Wm. Kirtland and Henry Nash of Safford have left for the Klindyke country. They are old time Arizonans. There is not much wonder at the movement as Safford has organized a female base ball club."[112]

Date	Place	State/Terr.*	Type of Team	Comments
Mar. 1898	Tucson	AZ	Coed College	"A game of base ball between the Tucson University girls and the University dormitory girls is announced for the first Sunday in April."[113]
Spring 1898	Germantown	PA	Quaker School	The 1898 yearbook of the Germantown Friends School reported: "The girls base-ball team died an easy death early in the season. The cricket team is the latest. Miss Pearson, captain of the deceased base-ball team, had quite a dispute with Mr. Walker, former captain of '98 cricket team, as to who was to have use of the grounds in the afternoons. This was finally satisfactorily settled, but for some reason or other the ball team died soon after."[114]
	Northampton	MA	Women's College	Students at Smith College continued to organize house teams for intramural games.[115]
	Spartanburg	SC	Women's College	Students continued to play baseball at Converse College.[116]
Apr./May 1898	Morris	NY	Civic/Barnstorming	"A female base ball nine has been organized in Morris. The members are practicing daily, weather permitting, and expect, during the season, to rival the record of the famous Cincinnati Reds of several years ago."[117]
Summer 1898	Westport Point	MA	Coed Pick-up	Ethel Fish, Smith College, Class of 1900, pasted a photo in her album of a coed baseball game played at Westport Point. It depicts a boy pitching overhand to a girl batter while other boys and girls look on.[118]

Date	Place	State/ Terr.*	Type of Team	Comments
June 1898	Rockford	IL	Pick-up/Fund Raiser	Upper class women of the city's Ladies' Union Aid Society organized and played in a baseball game as part of its third annual Woodmen Day fundraiser. The "Stars" and "Stripes" played five innings before "a large and enthusiastic audience" on June 4.[119]
1899	Abington	PA	Private Girls' School	Students at Ogontz School continued to play baseball.[120]
	—	—	Barnstorming	Eighth season of the YLBBC of NY (future New England Bloomer Girls); played 112 games this season with a record of 76–36.[121]
	—	—	Barnstorming	Seventh season of W. P. Needham's Boston Bloomer Girls. Maud Nelson was still with the team. Team played dozens of games in Canada, Minnesota, Michigan, Indiana, Kentucky, Virginia, North Carolina, Louisiana, and Arkansas.[122]
	—	—	Barnstorming	The Chicago Bloomer Girls, featuring a Maud "Nielsen" at shortstop, begin their inaugural season. They played games in Louisiana, Arkansas, and Kentucky.
	—	—	Barnstorming	The Sunday Telegraph Bloomer Girls kicked off their inaugural season.[123]
	Spartanburg	SC	Women's College	Team photo taken in 1899 depicts the Class of 1891 baseball team at Converse College.[124]
Spring 1899	South Hadley	MA	Women's College	Students at Mount Holyoke took up baseball again, organizing house teams to play against each other.[125]
	Northampton	MA	Women's College	Students at Smith College continued to organize house teams for intramural games.[126]

Date	Place	State/Terr.*	Type of Team	Comments
May 1899	Plainfield	IA	Civic	"Plainfield has a young ladies base ball club in training. The *Bell* of that city says of it: 'Some of the young ladies can twirl the pigskin with not a little skill, and can pound the sphere over the fence now and then.'"[127]
	New York City	NY	Theatrical	H. A. Adams and "William S. Franklin" (a.k.a. Sylvester Wilson) organized a short-lived baseball operation.[128]
June 1899	Kalamazoo	MI	School girls/Civic	"Since the Boston Bloomer girls played the Hubs there have been two baseball teams organized by the little girls of Kalamazoo. Harriet Kinney is captain of one of these teams and Fawn and Pauline White are organizing the other."[129]

* **Bold font** indicates first year state/territory is known to have had a female baseball team or player.

Notes

1. Photo is dated between 1880s and 1910s, but based on the clothing worn, I estimate it was taken in the 1890s. Available online through Historical New England. http://www.historicnewengland.org/collections-archives-exhibitions/collections-access/collection-object/capobject?gusn=GUSN-194813&searchterm=baseball.

2. Photo is in the collection of the Penn State Abington Archives.

3. "Personal," *Central City Weekly Register-Call,* April 25, 1890.

4. S.E.R., "The Girls' Nine," *Woman's Journal* 21, no. 17 (April 26, 1890): 134.

5. "The Ladies to the Front," *Weekly Register-Call,* May 9, 1890.

6. *Sandusky Daily Register,* May 9, 1890, 4; "City and Vicinity," *Watertown Daily Times,* August 2, 1890; "A Disgraceful Move . . ." *Sporting Life,* August 30, 1890, 8.

7. "Female Base Ballists Are Angry: Their Manager Skips Out and Leaves Them Forty Cents," *Chicago Tribune,* June 9, 1890, 3.

8. "Tom's Chat: Female Base Ballists," *Utica Sunday Tribune,* June 8, 1890.

9. "The Two Dakotas," *Omaha Daily Bee,* July 8, 1890, 4.

10. *Atchison Daily Globe,* July 25, 1890.

11. "For Women's Eyes: Things That Will Interest the Feminine Mind," *Albany Evening Journal,* August 16, 1890, 6.

12. "'Lady Champions' at Ball: Disgraceful Sunday Exhibition With the Allertons at Monitor Park, Weehawken," *New York Herald,* September 1, 1890, 6.

13. Photo depicts nine young women wearing long dresses, holding a bat, ball, and catcher's mask. It appears to be a House team. The photo could have been taken anytime between the fall of 1891 and the spring of 1895. SCA.

14. "Sporting Odds and Ends," *Yenowine's Illustrated News,* September 6, 1891, 7. The reporter may have mistakenly assumed that the Cincinnati Reds was Wilson's team.

15. *The Mount Holyoke,* Commencement Issue, June 1891. MHCLA. Students referred to their team as "our first base ball club." They hoped to compete with "nines of other colleges" the following year. This did not happen.

16. *Bloomsburg Columbian,* June 5, 1891, 1; "Diamond Dust," *Wheeling Register,* July 28, 1891, 3.

17. *Emporia Daily Gazette,* June 13, 1891. It is not known if this team was organized.

18. "Vicinity Notes," *Caledonia Advertiser,* June 18, 1891. This was not one of Wilson's teams and does not seem to have been a barnstorming team. The article went on to say that the girls kept the dates of their games secret from the press.

19. "Female Base Ball Clubs," *Omaha World Herald,* June 28, 1891, 10. The article lists the players' names.

20. "Nebraska Sporting Notes," *Omaha World Herald,* August 9, 1891, 7.

21. "Belles at the Bat: Society Girls Play Base-ball, with a Preacher Acting as Umpire," *Daily Inter Ocean,* July 13, 1891.

22. Reported in: Michael T. Snyder, "Ladies' Team Drew Large Crowd to Special Game," *The Mercury,* June 5, 2005, E-1 and E-3.

23. "Catch-Penny Affairs: The Effort to Make a Little Money Out of Base Ball Side Shows," *Sporting Life,* August 1, 1891, 12. It is uncertain whether these teams were ever organized.

24. Snyder, "Ladies' Team," E-3.

25. "State News," *Oswego Daily Times,* August 10, 1891, 1.

26. "Time Tower Talk: About What the Watch Makers are Doing in the Mill," *Rockford Morning Star,* August 16, 1891, 1.

27. "Brief Mention," *Oswego Daily Times,* c. August 21, 1891. Johnson is 134 miles west of Oswego; the team may have barnstormed.

28. *Philadelphia Inquirer,* September 30, 1891, 6. It is uncertain whether this team was ever organized, although an article in September mentioned a female baseball club from Philadelphia. "The Colored People's Fair: An Outline of the Programme That Has Been Arranged," *Richmond Dispatch,* September 20, 1891, 8.

29. "'Come In On The Hit': Pretty Girls in Westwood, N. J., Have Great Sport at Baseball," *State* (S.C.), October 6, 1891, 3. From the *New York World.*

30. An article for the "Ladies Base Ball Club" published in March 1901 states that the club was preparing for its tenth season. By this time, the team is being called the New England Bloomer Girls. Advertisement, *St. Louis Republic,* March 27, 1901. Includes record for each season between 1892 and 1900.

31. "Female Baseball Nine: A Scheme Knocked in the Head by the Authorities; Only Girls Between the Ages of Fourteen and Sixteen Years Wanted by the Management—A Queer Outfit," *Los Angeles Times,* March 7, 1892, 8.

32. "Nebraska Sporting Notes," *Omaha World Herald,* March 13, 1892, 13; "Nebraska Sporting Notes," *Omaha World Herald,* March 27, 1892, 9; "Nebraska Notes," *Omaha World Herald,* June 12, 1892, 11; "Nebraska Sporting Notes," *Omaha World Herald,* August 21, 1892, 7.

33. "Local News Brieflets," *Wisconsin State Register,* April 30, 1892, 3; "Editorial Views, News, Comment," *Sporting Life,* May 7, 1892, 2.

34. *Union Springs Advertiser,* April 28, 1892.

35. On May 2, 1892, Anne Marie Paul (Class of 1894), Captain of the Wallace House Base Ball Nine, wrote a letter challenging the Hatfield House Base Ball Nine to a five-inning game on May 4. SCA. On May 9, 1892, teams comprised of freshmen and sophomores played against

each other. This game was covered in numerous newspapers as far away as Chicago. Edith Hill later wrote that "baseball of a sort was an after-supper fad" that year. Edith Naomi Hill, (editor of the *Smith College Alumnae Quarterly*), "Senda Berenson: Director of Physical Education at Smith College, 1892–1911," *Research Quarterly of the American Association for Health, Physical Education, and Recreation* 12, supplement (October 1941): 600. Cited in Verbrugge, *Able-Bodied Womanhood,* 182.

36. "Hard Lines for Female Baseball: The Girl Ball-Players Had to Stop Swing Bats," *New York World,* April 25, 1892, 1; "Sports and Sport: Wouldn't Allow the Girls to Play," *Wheeling Register,* April 26, 1892, 3.

37. "Denver's Feminine Ball Players," *Rocky Mountain News,* April 30, 1892, 2; "Chased the Flies: The Young Women Put in a Lively Afternoon at the Broadway Athletic Park . . .," *Rocky Mountain News,* May 23, 1892, 3; "Female Ball Game: The Denver Team Will Cross Bats With the Capitols Sunday," *Cheyenne Daily Sun,* June 25, 1892.

38. *Emporia Daily Gazette,* May 26, 1892; "Amusements," *Wichita Daily Eagle,* May 28, 1892, 5; "General Notes," *Buffalo Courier,* August 12, 1892, 8. R. C. Johnson, John E. Nolen, and James A. Arlington were arrested in Kansas City on August 29 after stealing the gate money from a game in Winston, Missouri. "Ran Away With the Cash," *Emporia Daily Gazette,* August 29, 1892; *Atchison Daily Globe,* September 2, 1892.

39. *Alton Evening Telegraph,* June 3, 1892, 3.

40. "South Dakota News," *Sun,* June 30, 1892, 3.

41. "Female Base Ballists," *Utica Sunday Tribune,* June 26, 1892; "Observations," *Utica Daily Observer,* June 27, 1892, 2; "'Twill be a Great Day': The Celebration To-Morrow Promises Great Things," *Utica Sunday Tribune,* July 3, 1892; "The Female Base Ball Players," *Utica Daily Press,* July 5, 1892, 1; "Sporting World: Summary of Interesting Events in the Fields of Sport," *Oswego Daily Times,* September 6, 1892, 2. Dateline: Warsaw, September 3.

42. Very little is known about this team apart from its appearance in Saginaw, Michigan, in early July 1892. "Carrollton," *Saginaw News,* June 28, 29, and 30 and July 1, 2, and 5, 1892.

43. "Short Stories: A Batch of Paragraphs Mostly on Town Happenings," *Cheyenne Daily Sun,* August 16, 1892, 3.

44. "Base Ball: Girls and Base Ball; A Girlish Description of a Game by Girls; An Umpire in White Lawn—A Home Plate Concealed by the Catcher's Petticoats, Etc.," *Sporting Life,* September 10, 1892, 11.

45. Annual Reports and Constitution of the Athletic Association of Bryn Mawr College. Report for the Year 1892–1893. BMCA. Calendar of Athletic Events lists one outdoor baseball game, played on October 12, 1892.

46. Photo available at: http://reflections.mndigital .org/cdm/singleitem/collection/penn/id/111/rec/186.

47. The photo resides in the collection of the Penn State Abington Archives.

48. Thanks to Bob Mayer for bringing this photograph to my attention. It is in his personal collection.

49. Advertisement, *St. Louis Republic,* March 27, 1901. Includes record for each season between 1892 and 1900.

50. It is difficult to determine the exact date when Needham founded his team. An article in the *Sioux City Journal,* on August 30, 1895 stated that the Boston Bloomer Girls were organized in "the Hub" in May 1894, but articles in the *Sheridan Post* and *Arizona Republican* in 1897 stated that the team was in its fifth season, while the *Utica Daily Press* stated in July 1902 said the team was on its tenth annual tour. These articles date the team to 1892. An article in the *Waterloo Daily Reporter* on September 10, 1902, and another in the *Kerkhoven Banner* on June 3, 1904, state

that the Boston Bloomer Girls team was organized by W. P. Needham in 1893; a photograph of the team in Deadwood, South Dakota, in 1893 proves that they were playing games at least by 1893.

51. "A Female Base Ball Club in Danger: Attacked by a Cuban Mob and One of the Players Hurt," *Brooklyn Daily Eagle,* March 6, 1893, 10. See details in chapter 5.

52. No additional information about this team has surfaced, apart from a single newspaper article: "Freshman Banquet," *Kalamazoo Gazette,* May 13, 1893, 1. Dateline: Ann Arbor.

53. "Field Day Sports: University Notes," *Grand Forks Herald,* May 7, 1893, 4; "Nubs of News," *Grand Forks Herald,* May 13, 1893, 8.

54. *Trenton Evening Times,* May 4, 1893, 4. Roster for the game included both Maude Nelson and Lizzie Arlington, along with Lottie Livingston, who had been on the team attacked in Cuba in March.

55. "Atlantic Breezes: Echoes From Greenwich," *New York Herald,* July 9, 1893, 14.

56. "Young Women Play Ball," *Milwaukee Sentinel,* August 14, 1893, 2; "Boys in Dresses: Female Base Ball Game a Great Big Fizzle," *Waukesha Freeman,* August 31, 1893, 4.

57. "The Girls Play Ball: And Entertained Quite a Crowd in Spite of the Rain," *Macon Telegraph,* August 22, 1893, 2.

58. "Girls Who Play Baseball: How Some Young Women at Lenox Amuse Themselves," *New York Times,* September 3, 1893, 12; "Lenox is Still Gay. Outdoor Sports Claim the Attention of the Younger Set: Events at Pittsfield," *New York Herald,* September 3, 1893, 26.

59. Mills College yearbook for 1914–1915 cited by Gai Berlage, "Sociocultural History," 105.

60. Advertisement, *St. Louis Republic,* March 27, 1901. Includes record for each season between 1892 and 1900.

61. "Girl Base Ball Players. . . ." *Brooklyn Daily Eagle,* May 6, 1894, 7.

62. "How One of the Female Ball Nine Deserted Husband and Babes—Stuck on Being an Actress—She Tagged the Runner and He Hurt Her Arm," *Quincy Daily Herald,* June 8, 1894, 8; "Female Ball Tossers: Game in Progress This Afternoon at the West Side Park," *Cedar Rapids Evening Gazette,* June 19, 1894, 5; "The City in Brief," *Cedar Rapids Evening Gazette,* June 30, 1894, 8.

63. "Bloomer Girls vs. Gulfs," *Denver Evening Post,* August 6, 1898, 5. This was the team's sixth season.

64. "Girls Played Ball. Two Thousand People Watched Them Do It," *Jersey Evening Journal,* July 3, 1894, 6. It is uncertain how long this team lasted. Gordon's real name was Mattie Myers.

65. *The Bomb,* 1895, (school yearbook), n.p. Until 1925, members of the junior class published the school yearbook the year before they graduated, but dated the cover with their class year. Thus, although the date on the cover of the yearbook describing the female baseball teams is 1895, the book was actually published in 1894. Thanks to Becky S. Jordan, reference specialist, Special Collections/University Archives, Iowa State University, for bringing this information to my attention.

66. "Miscellaneous," *Ottawa Evening News,* May 11, 1894, 2.

67. "Throngs in Central Park. . . ." *New York Herald Tribune,* June 11, 1894, 4.

68. "Girls Help Strikers," *Boston Journal,* June 4, 1894, 7.

69. "Celebrating the Fourth: Negro Women Play Base Ball at Brisbane Park," *Columbus Daily Enquirer,* July 5, 1894, 1.

70. "Notes," *Rhinebeck Gazette,* July 21, 1894.

71. "Girl Baseball Players: They are Fond of the Sport and Wear Nice Costumes," *Grand Rapids Press,* August 11, 1894, 7.

72. The "sister college" is unnamed. "Athletics," *The White and Gold* 1, no. 1 (October 1894), Special Collections, F. W. Olin Library, Mills College.

73. Edith Naomi Hill Papers, Box #867, Folder #2, "Capen School Album." SCA.

74. *National Police Gazette,* March 16, 1895.

75. Advertisement, *St. Louis Republic,* March 27, 1901. Includes record for each season between 1892 and 1900.

76. "Bloomer Girls vs. Gulfs," *Denver Evening Post,* August 6, 1898, 5. Article reports that the team had been together for six seasons.

77. Very little is known about these teams apart from articles about games in July. "Trilbies vs. Winonas: Two Games on the Fourth Result in a Tie," *Winona Daily Republican,* July 5, 1895, 3; "News of the States," *Cedar Rapids Evening Gazette,* July 31, 1895, 2. Given the route of travel of the Boston Bloomer Girls this season, it is possible these articles were about the Boston Bloomer Girls team that does not appear in articles until July—also playing in Minnesota.

78. "Kansas and Kansas," *Kansas City Times,* April 11, 1895, 4.

79. "Girls Played Ball," *Rockford Morning Star,* May 22, 1895, 6.

80. Advertisement, *Philadelphia Inquirer,* June 24, 1895, 8.

81. "Lively Times at Fox Lake," *Chicago Tribune,* August 18, 1895, 14. The Lakeside Hotel was a resort on the shores of Fox Lake, about fifty miles northwest of Chicago.

82. "Mere Mentions," *Cherokee Democrat,* August 21, 1895, 5.

83. "Nebraska," *Omaha Daily Bee,* September 23, 1895, 5.

84. J. R. Street, "A Study in Moral Education," *Pedagogical Seminary* 5, no. 1 (1897): 23.

85. Mildred S. Howard, "A Century of Physical Education," *Mount Holyoke Alumnae Quarterly* 19, no. 4 (February 1936): 214.

86. Photograph available at http://historicpelham.blogspot.com/2010/02/photograph-of-only-known-19th-century.html.

87. Advertisement, *St. Louis Republic,* March 27, 1901. Includes record for each season between 1892 and 1900.

88. "Bloomer Girls vs. Gulfs," *Denver Evening Post,* August 6, 1898, 5. Article reports that the team had been together for six seasons.

89. "How Women's College Girls Play Ball," *Cleveland Plain Dealer,* May 7, 1896, 5.

90. Annie E. P. Searing, "Vassar College," *Harper's Bazaar,* May 30, 1896, 469.

91. "Railway Interests," *Galveston Daily News,* July 22, 1896, 3.

92. Advertisement, *St. Louis Republic,* March 27, 1901. Includes record for each season between 1892 and 1900.

93. "Bloomer Girls vs. Gulfs," *Denver Evening Post,* August 6, 1898), 5. Article reports that the team had been together for six seasons.

94. Per Jeffrey R. Willis, director of Archives and Special Collections, Converse College.

95. "Athletic California College Girls in the Rain. A Sprightly Account of a Game Played on the Quiet—Bloomers and All the Paraphernalia—They Slide for Bases in the Mud," *Kansas City Star,* February 14, 1897, 7.

96. "News Briefly Told," *Semi-Weekly Interior Journal* (Stanford, Ky.), March 12, 1897, 2.

97. "Argentine Girls Play Ball. Several Clubs Already Organized and a Girls' League May Be Formed," *Kansas City Star,* April 18, 1897, 6.

98. "College Cullings," *The Echo* 9, no. 11 (April 20, 1897): 113–14. OCA; "Umpire Safe Here. Olivet College Girls Will Play Base Ball. And Falling Hairpins or Untied Shoe Laces Will Not Stop the Game," *Grand Rapids Press,* May 15, 1897, 7; "A Notable Game of Baseball," *New York Evening Sun,* May 22, 1897.

99. "Educational Column," *Springport Signal,* May 21, 1897, 4; "Jackson County News," *Jackson Citizen Patriot,* May 22, 1897, 9.

100. "Brief Mention," *Lowville Journal and Republican,* June 10, 1897, 5; "We and Our Neighbors: News and Notes From Nearby Towns," *Brookfield Courier,* June 23, 1897, 4.

101. "Girls On The Diamond. Germantown Maidens Who Can Give the Phillies Pointers." *Wilkes-Barre Times,* June 30, 1897, 3. Germantown Academy was a boys' school in Germantown, a suburb of Philadelphia. The Friends' School was a coeducational girls' prep school in the same area, and the Walnut Lane School was a girls' boarding school.

102. *Denver Evening Post,* July 20, 1897, 4.

103. "The Interviewed," *Dodge City Globe-Republican,* July 15, 1897, 4.

104. "Odds and Ends of Gossip," *Springfield News-Leader,* July 29, 1897, 1.

105. Ibid.

106. (Willard) Gibson Family Album, WLCL, UM. Call No. A.1.1897.2.

107. See chapter 5 for details.

108. Advertisement, *St. Louis Republic,* March 27, 1901. Includes record for each season between 1892 and 1900.

109. "Bloomer Girls vs. Gulfs," *Denver Evening Post,* August 6, 1898, 5. Article reports that the team had been together for six seasons.

110. Penn State Abington College Library, Ogontz School for Girls Archive Collection includes team member lists and results of games played between 1898 and 1933. Lil Hansberry, archivist, e-mail to author, August 29, 2008.

111. Special Collections, F. W. Olin Library, Mills College. Handwritten caption says, "Our baseball wonders '98."

112. *Phoenix Weekly Herald,* January 20, 1898.

113. Report from *Tucson Star* reprinted in: "Territorial News," *Weekly Phoenix Herald* (Ariz.), March 24, 1898, 4.

114. *The Pastorian* (Yearbook of the Germantown Friends School), 1898. E-mail from Carl Tannenbaum to Tim Wiles (Cooperstown Hall of Fame Library), January 12, 2015; forwarded to author.

115. On June 3, 1898, Fanny Garrison (Class of 1901) wrote to her family, "To-day, I indulged in a game of base-ball—playing on a freshman team under May Lewis, against the Dickinson House. We won 13 to 12." Ethel Fish (Class of 1900) played on the "White Squadron team at Smith College in the spring of 1898. SCA.

116. This is speculation on my part, based on the fact that the school's yearbooks for 1897 and 1899 both contain photos of female baseball teams. The yearbook for 1898 is missing from the archives, but it appears likely that students would have also played in 1898.

117. "In Central New York: All Around Us," *Ostego Farmer,* (Cooperstown, N.Y.), April 29, 1898), 1.

118. Ethel Fish photo album. SCA.

119. Rockford newspapers began publicizing the event as early as May 11. Articles included: "Fares Please: Trolley Day Set for Saturday, June 4, By the Ladies' Aid Society," *Daily Register Gazette,* May 11, 1898, 3; "Play Ball For Charity . . .," *Morning Star,* May 15, 1898, 9; "Fair Ones in Game . . .," *Morning Star,* May 24, 1898, 8; "Belles of the Ball . . .," *Daily Register Gazette,* June 4, 1898, 7.

120. Penn State Abington College Library, Ogontz School for Girls Archive Collection includes team member lists and results of games played between 1898 and 1933. Lil Hansberry, archivist, e-mail to author, August 29, 2008.

121. Advertisement, *St. Louis Republic,* March 27, 1901. Includes record for each season between 1892 and 1900.

122. "The Boston Bloomers: Ladies Champion Base Ball Club of the World," *New Ulm (Minn.) Review,* September 20, 1899, 7. Article reports that the team had been together for seven seasons.

123. "Oil Tankers Book Bloomer Girls." *Decatur Daily Review,* July 6, 1909, 5. Article stated

that the same Sunday Telegraph Bloomer Girls team that had been playing in Taylorville for the past ten years would be playing a game with the Oil Tank leaguers.

124. Photo appears in the 1899 school yearbook.

125. On May 20, the Rockefeller and Porter Hall teams faced off in a baseball game. "College Notes," *The Mount Holyoke,* June 1899, 19.

126. Rachel Studley to Smith College archivist, written sometime between 1916 and 1918. Studley names some of the players and describes the ball as being an official hard ball used in a game between the Amherst and Williams men's teams. SCA.

127. "Items From Exchanges From Neighboring Towns," *Nashua Reporter,* May 18, 1899, 5.

128. "A Missing Partner: Lady Baseball Players' Manager Left With Cash; Levied on Bloomers; Manager Smithson of the Cricket Grounds Determined to Have his Share of the Receipts—Manager Franklin Arrested—His Partner Adams Is Missing," *Jersey Journal,* May 31, 1899, 4.

129. "Girl Ball Club: Two Clubs Organized, Miss Harriet Kinney Being Captain of One," *Kalamazoo Gazette,* June 4, 1899, 1; "News and Notes," *Daily Telegram,* June 7, 1899, 8.

Notes

Preface

1. McDowell was named *Sporting News* "Pitcher of the Year" in 1970 for leading the league in strikeouts for a third straight season. Fosse had an excellent year in 1970, tallying hits in twenty-three consecutive games at one point and finishing with a Gold Glove Award.

Acknowledgments

1. "Miscellaneous Wit & Wisdom," National Churchill Museum, http://www.national churchill museum.org/wit-wisdom-quotes.html.

Introduction

1. Arthur T. Noren, *Softball* (New York: The Ronald Press, 1966), 44.

2. Emma Span, "Is Softball Sexist?" *New York Times,* June 6, 2014, http://www.nytimes .com/2014/06/07 /opinion/is-softball-sexist.html?_r=0.

3. Sarah Fields provides detailed information about a number of these lawsuits in *Female Gladiators: Gender, Law, and Contact Sport in America* (Urbana: University of Illinois Press, 2005), 16–33.

4. Johan Huizinga, *Homo Ludens* (London: Routledge and Kegan Paul, [1938] 1949), 1 and 4.

5. John Thorn, *Baseball in the Garden of Eden: The Secret History of the Early Game* (New York: Simon & Schuster, 2011), ix.

6. The term "gender neutral" as used in this study describes only how particular sports are generally perceived by the public. For a sport to be gendered as masculine does not mean that no women play it; conversely, for a sport to be perceived to be a women's sport does not mean that men do not play it. Gender-neutral sports are those played in relatively equal numbers by identical or similar rules.

7. Mary G. McDonald and Susan Birrell, "Reading Sport Critically: A Methodology for Interrogating Power," *Sociology of Sport Journal* 16 (1999): 283–300; Fields, *Female Gladiators*; Susan K. Cahn, *Coming on Strong: Gender and Sexuality in Twentieth-Century Women's Sports* (New York: Free Press, 1998); Eileen McDonagh and Laura Pappano, *Playing With the Boys: Why Separate Is Not Equal in Sports* (New York and Oxford: Oxford University Press, 2009);

Michael A. Messner, *Taking the Field: Women, Men, and Sports* (Minneapolis and London: University of Minnesota Press, 2002); Michael A. Messner, *Out of Play: Critical Essays on Gender and Sport* (Albany: State University of New York Press, 2007); J. A. Mangan, and Roberta J Park, *From "Fair Sex" to Feminism: Sport and the Socialization of Women in the Industrial and Post-Industrial Eras* (London: Frank Cass, 1987).

8. In *The Manly Art: Bare-Knuckle Prize Fighting in America* (Ithaca, N.Y.: Cornell University Press, [1986] 2010), Elliott Gorn used prizefighting to analyze the intersections of social class, ethnicity, and gender in nineteenth-century America. Riess applied a similar approach to the study of sport in "Sport and the Redefinition of American Middle-Class Masculinity," *International Journal of the History of Sport* 8, no. 1 (May 1991): 5–27. Kimmel focused on baseball and masculinity in "Baseball and the Reconstitution of American Masculinity, 1880–1920," in Michael Messner and Donald Sabo, eds., *Sport, Men and the Gender Order* (Champaign, Ill.: Human Kinetics, 1992), 55–66; Cahn, *Coming on Strong.*

9. Jules Tygiel, *Past Time: Baseball as History* (New York: Oxford University Press, 2000), 8–12.

10. John Thorn provides a detailed account of how the origins myth of baseball was planted in the early twentieth century in chapter 1, "Anointing Abner," and chapter 12, "The Religion of Baseball" of *Baseball in the Garden of Eden,* 1–23, 273–96.

11. Messner, *Taking the Field,* xviii–xxii.

12. Daniel Nathan, *Saying It's So: A Cultural History of the Black Sox Scandal* (Urbana: University of Illinois Press, 2005), 8–9.

13. E-mail from Susan Cahn to Anne Firor Scott, Sara Evans, and Elizabeth Faue, June 4, 1998, published in "Women's History in the New Millennium: A Conversation across Three 'Generations': Part 2," *Journal of Women's History* 11, no. 2 (1999): 203.

14. Quoted in Nathan, *Saying It's So,* 12.

15. Tygiel, *Past Time,* 15–16.

16. Steven Riess, *Touching Base: Professional Baseball and American Culture in the Progressive Era* (Westport, Conn.: Greenwood Press, 1980), 13–14.

17. Walter Hakanson is generally crediting with suggesting the term "softball" in 1926 at a meeting of the National Recreation Congress. The name slowly gained adherents. It was not until 1934 that the Joint Rules Committee on Softball published standardized rules for the sport. See "The History of Softball," International Softball Federation, http://www.isfsoftball.org/english/the_isf/history_of_softball.asp.

Chapter 1. Creating a National Pastime

1. "A Defense of Baseball as a 'Manly Exercise,'" *New York Times,* September 27, 1856. Quoted in Dean Sullivan, ed., *Early Innings: A Documentary History of Baseball, 1825–1908* (Lincoln: University of Nebraska Press, 1995), 21.

2. "Out-Door Sports: Base-Ball, Croquet, Quoits and Lacrosse," *Quincy (Ill.) Whig,* July 13, 1868, 4.

3. Huizinga, *Homo Ludens,* foreword and 1.

4. Homer, *The Odyssey,* Samuel Butler, trans., Book VI, 53 and Book VIII, 69.

5. The College Customs of Harvard College, Anno 1734–35, as transcribed by Richard Waldron, Class of 1738, which appears at "A Collection of College Words and Customs by Benjamin Homer Hall," http://www.fullbooks.com/A-Collection-of-College-Words-and-Customs5.html.

6. John Newbery, *A Little Pretty Pocket-Book, Intended for the Instruction and Amusement of Little Master Tommy and Pretty Miss Polly* (London: John Newbery). Quoted in David Block, *Baseball Before We Knew It: A Search for the Roots of the Game* (Lincoln: University of Nebraska Press, 2005), 178.

7. For details on regional variations of bat and ball games and the spread of the New York game, see Thorn, *Baseball in the Garden*, 26–104; Warren Goldstein, *Playing For Keeps: A History of Early Baseball* (Ithaca, N.Y.: Cornell University Press, [1989] 2009), 1–83; George B. Kirsch, *Baseball and Cricket: The Creation of American Team Sports, 1838–72* (Urbana and Chicago: University of Illinois Press, [1989] 2007), 41–77; Benjamin G. Rader, *Baseball: A History of America's Game,* 3rd ed. (Urbana and Chicago: University of Illinois Press, 2008), 1–18.

8. Howard P. Chudacoff, *Children at Play: An American History* (New York: New York University Press, 2007), 61.

9. *National Advocate,* April 25, 1823, quoted in Peter Morris, *Baseball Fever: Early Baseball in Michigan* (Ann Arbor: University of Michigan Press, 2003), 8.

10. Reprinted in Sullivan, ed., *Early Innings,* 5.

11. The Origins Committee of the Society for American Baseball Research (SABR) maintains a superb collaborative resource for scholars of early baseball at http://protoball.org. The site includes numerous articles and primary resources related to early bat and ball games in the United States.

12. Michael S. Kimmel, *Manhood in America: A Cultural History* (New York: Oxford University Press, 2006), 3; Gail Bederman, *Manliness and Civilization: A Cultural History of Gender and Race in the United States, 1880–1917* (Chicago: University of Chicago Press, 1995), 6–7.

13. E. Anthony Rotundo, *American Manhood: Transformations in Masculinity from the Revolution to the Modern Era* (New York: Basic Books, 1993), 3–4; Kimmel, *Manhood in America,* 6. Elliott Gorn has confirmed that men in antebellum America were already using prizefighting, baseball, cricket, and other sports to reinforce gender ideals.

14. Gorn, *Manly Art.*

15. Thorn, *Baseball in the Garden,* 86 and 89–99.

16. For details, see Kirsch, *Baseball and Cricket,* 1989), 50–77; Rader, *Baseball: A History,* 5–18; Thorn, *Baseball in the Garden,* 64–84.

17. See Protoball site in Goldstein, *Playing for Keeps,* 27–31 and Thorn, *Baseball in the Garden,* 85–104.

18. Morris, *Baseball Fever,* 10–13.

19. Cited in Rader, *Baseball: A History,* 9.

20. Fifty-eight clubs, including twenty new clubs from around the country, sent delegates to the Sixth Annual Convention of the NABBP in December 1860. "Patrick Mondout, "1861 Baseball Convention," Baseball Chronology: The Game Since 1845, http://www.baseball chronology.com/baseball/Years/1861/Convention.asp.

21. The players and media moguls who ultimately created baseball's "center" would not have recognized the concept as Messner uses it, but there is no question that the organizations they created to manage the rules and reputation of their sport, and the narratives they spun in local and national publications to shape the culture of the game, created the foundation on which subsequent men solidified control of what became Major League, NCAA, and Little League baseball.

22. Quoted in Goldstein, *Playing for Keeps,* 49.

23. Messner, *Taking the Field,* xxi.

24. For details on the rise of sporting periodicals, see John Thorn, "The New York Clipper and Sporting Weeklies of Its Time," *Base Ball: A Journal of the Early Game* 3, no. 1 (Spring 2009): 107–13.

25. For insights on how Chadwick and journalists shaped the structure and culture of baseball, see Tygiel, "The Mortar of Which Baseball is Held Together: Henry Chadwick and the Invention of Baseball Statistics," in *Past Time,* 15–34; Peter Morris, *But Didn't We Have Fun? An Informal History of Baseball's Pioneer Era, 1843–1870* (Chicago: Ivan R. Dee, 2008), 62–67;

Kirsch, *Baseball and Cricket,* 61–63; R. Terry Furst, *Shaping the Image of the Game: Early Professional Baseball and the Sporting Press* (Jefferson, N.C.: McFarland Press, 2014); Mitchell Nathanson, "Gatekeepers of Americana: Ownership's Never-ending Quest for Control of the Baseball Creed," *Nine: A Journal of Baseball History and Culture* 15, no. 1 (Fall 2006): 68–87.

26. For insights on attitudes toward physical fitness in antebellum United States, see Jan Todd, *Physical Culture and the Body Beautiful: 'Purposive' Exercise in the Lives of American Women, 1800–1870* (Macon, Ga.: Mercer University Press, 1998), 33–86.

27. "Men and Boys Sports," *Daily National Intelligencer,* March 22, 1822.

28. Quoted in Edward M. Hartwell, "Physical Training in American Colleges and Universities," *Circulars of Information of the Bureau of Education, No. 5—1885* (Washington, D.C.: Government Printing Office, 1886), 553. Warren was a prominent surgeon and professor of anatomy and surgery at the Harvard Medical School. *Harper's Weekly* reached a similar conclusion in 1859: "The Cricket Mania," *Harper's Weekly,* October 10, 1859, 658.

29. John Thorn, *The Game for All America* (St. Louis: Sporting News, 1988), 13, quoted in Morris, *Baseball Fever,* 8. Thorn was commenting on the difficulty adult town ball players in Philadelphia had trying to field teams in the 1830s, but his comments apply more broadly to any adult men playing what contemporaries perceived as children's games.

30. *Spirit of the Times,* March 1860, in Morris, *But Didn't We Have Fun?* 49.

31. *Harper's Monthly* 13 (1856): 642; *Atlantic Monthly* 1 (1858): 881.

32. *Rochester Union and Advertiser,* August 12, 1858, 3.

33. For insights on the Muscular Christianity movement, see Steven A. Riess, "Sport and the Redefinition Middle-Class Masculinity in Victorian America," in S. W. Pope, ed., *The New American Sport History: Recent Approaches and Perspectives* (Urbana: University of Illinois Press, 1997), 173–84, and Elliott J. Gorn, "Sports Through the Nineteenth Century," in Pope, *New American Sport History,* 49–51.

34. Quoted in Riess, "Sport and the Redefinition," 180.

35. Cited in Goldstein, *Playing for Keeps,* 31.

36. *New York Sunday Mercury,* October 21, 1853.

37. *Spirit of the Times,* January 31, 1857, reprinted in Sullivan, ed., *Early Innings,* 24.

38. For insights on antebellum women's activism in moral reform societies, see Nancy A. Hewitt, *Women's Activism and Social Change: Rochester, New York, 1822–1872* (Ithaca, N.Y.: Cornell University Press, 1984); Carroll Smith-Rosenberg, "Beauty, the Beast, and the Militant Woman: Sex Roles and Sexual Standards in Jacksonian America," in *Women, Families, and Communities: Readings in American History, Vol. One: to 1877,* ed. Nancy A. Hewitt (Glenview, Ill.: Scott, Foresman/Little, Brown Higher Education, 1990), 124–38; Sara M. Evans, "The Age of Association, 1820–1845," in *Born for Liberty: A History of Women in America* (New York: Free Press [1989] 1997), 67–81.

39. The late Craig B. Waff compiled a database of more than 1,680 ballgames played in the United States and Canada between 1845 and 1860. He found an additional eight hundred or so games for the same era that he had not entered into his database prior to his death. Waff's database is available at "The Craig B. Waff Games Tabulation," Protoball Web site. http://protoball.org/The_Craig_B._Waff_Games_Tabulation.

40. Tygiel, *Past Time,* 15–16. Chadwick's comments appeared in his publication *Beadle's Dime Base-Ball Player* in 1860; quoted in Riess, "Sport and the Redefinition," 183.

41. David Block, *Baseball Before We Knew It,* 139–42, 154–56.

42. Catriona Parratt, *'More Than Mere Amusement:' Working-Class Women's Leisure in England, 1750–1914* (Boston: Northeastern University Press, 2001), 31.

43. See the next section for details on Austen's, Mitford's, and Marcet's references to female baseball players.

44. Joseph Strutt, *The Sports and Pastimes of the People of England; Including the Rural and Domestic Recreations, May Games, Mummeries, Shows, Processions, Pageants, & Pompous Spectacles From the Earliest Period to the Present Time,* 3rd ed. (London: Thomas Tegg, [1801] 1845). Google Books.

45. Strutt, *Sports and Pastimes,* 106.

46. Parratt asserts that while Victorians would eventually stamp cricket "the manliest of English sports," it was, "in the eighteenth and early nineteenth centuries also a game for women." She documents the existence of female cricket players as early as 1745 and notes that women's matches were well attended by paying spectators. Parratt, *More Than Mere Amusement,* 32.

47. Anne Firor Scott, "The Ever Widening Circle: The Diffusion of Feminist Values from the Troy Female Seminary 1822–1872," *History of Education Quarterly* 19, no. 1 (Spring 1979): 3–5.

48. "City Items . . . Base Ball," *Portland (Me.) Transcript,* June 18, 1859. The "Bloomer costume" would remain a socially divisive clothing option for women throughout the nineteenth century. Elizabeth Smith Miller designed the "short dress" (Turkish pants with a short skirt) in early 1851. She introduced the comfortable, though radical, garment to Elizabeth Cady Stanton shortly thereafter, and she and Stanton began wearing it in public. Amelia Bloomer advocated the outfit in her women's rights publication, *The Lily.* Women who wore bloomers faced verbal and sometimes physical opposition. "Elizabeth Smith Miller on Dress Reform." Elizabeth Smith Miller Collection, New York Public Library, available at http://www.assumption.edu/whw/Smith_Miller_on_dress.html, and in Theodore Stanton and Harriot Stanton Blatch, eds., *Elizabeth Cady Stanton: As Revealed in Her Letters, Diary and Reminiscences,* Vol. 2 (New York: Harper & Bros., 1922), 27.

49. *Albany Morning Times,* May 16, 1859, 2.

50. *Troy (N.Y.) Daily Times,* May 17, 1859, 2.

51. "Crinoline and Ball-Playing," *Genesee County (N.Y.) Herald,* May 28, 1859, and "City Items . . . Base Ball," *Portland Transcript,* June 18, 1859.

52. William S. Brand and Robert Rose, *A History of the Pioneer Families of Missouri* (St. Louis, 1876), 223. Thanks to Jeff Kittel.

53. "Sports in Honolulu," *Polynesian,* December 26, 1840. "Boston-Style 'Bat and Ball' Seen in Honolulu, HI," Entry 1840.38, SABR Protoball. Posted by George Thompson on January 3, 2010. Thompson believes the author of the article was James Jarves, who had been born in Boston in 1818 and served as editor of the *Polynesian* after moving to Hawaii. The baseball game he described was the Massachusetts form then popular in New England.

54. *Macon Daily Telegraph,* March 2, 1860. "Old-Fashioned Ballgame Noted in Antebellum GA" Entry 1840C.23, SABR Protoball. Posted by John Thorn on September 11, 2007. The article reported that a group of gentlemen were preparing to form another baseball club and that the game would be played "after the fashion in the South *twenty years ago,* when old field schools were the scenes of trial of activity, and *rosy cheeked girls were the umpires"* (emphasis added).

55. Elias Molee, *Molee's Wanderings, An Autobiography* (private printing, 1919), 34. Cited by Tom Altherr, "Coed Cat Games in Wisconsin in the Early 1850s," *Originals* 4, no. 1 (January 2011): 2. Entry 1850S.47, SABR Protoball.

56. Undated letter from Frances Dana Barker Gage to the *Tribune,* reprinted in "Muscle Looking Up," Harriett N. Austin and James C. Jackson, eds., *The Letter-Box,* Vols. 1 and 2, 1858–59 (Dansville, N.Y., 1859): 99.

57. Catharine E. Beecher, *A Treatise on the Domestic Economy, for the use of Young Ladies at Home and at School* (New York, 1848), 48.

58. Catharine E. Beecher, *Physiology and Calisthenics: For Schools and Families* (New York, 1856), iv.

59. Jane Austen, *Northanger Abbey* (Arc Manor ed. [1818], 2007), 9. Google Books. Austen's reference to a young girl enjoying baseball also appeared in Sarah Josepha Hale's *Woman's Record; or Sketches of all Distinguished Women From "The Beginning" Till A.D. 1850 Arranged in Four Eras With Selections From Female Writers of Every Age* (New York, 1853).

60. Louisa C. Tuthill, *The Young Lady's Home* (New Haven, Conn., 1839), 247.

61. Jane Marcet, *Conversations on Natural Philosophy; In Which The Elements of That Science Are Familiarly Explained, and Adapted To The Comprehension of Young Pupils* (London, 1822), 13. Thanks to David Block for bringing this to my attention. Christie Anne Farnham notes that Marcet's *Conversations on Chemistry* (1806) went through twenty-three U.S. editions, plus twelve editions of imitations. See *The Education of the Southern Belle: Higher Education and Student Socialization in the Antebellum South* (New York: New York University Press, 1994), 83.

62. Mitford mentions baseball-playing girls in four of her stories. In "The Tenants of Beechgrove," Mitford describes Mary North as a young girl who not only played with dolls, but enjoyed playing baseball, sliding, and "romping." In "Jack Hatch," Mitford describes the butterfly-like metamorphosis of carefree, frolicking girls into subdued "village belles." The sketch's female narrator describes girls at various stages of maturity, including the "sunburnt gipsy of six" who unhappily finds herself holding a mop in one hand and a pitcher in another while "her longing eyes [are] fixed on a game of base-ball at the corner of the green." By age ten, the young girl is eschewing "dirt and base-ball, and all their joys," in order to devout more time to schoolwork and feminine fashions. In her third collection of sketches, Mitford describes four girls "scrambling and squalling at baseball" on one side of a road while a group of boys plays marbles on the other. Mary Russell Mitford, *Our Village* sketches, reprinted in *The Works of Mary Russell Mitford* (Philadelphia, 1841), 83, 93, 151. Google Books. Mitford also mentions baseball in a collection of essays entitled *Belford Regis* (1835).

63. See, for example, *Charleston Courier,* August 21, 1828, 2 and *New York Commercial Advertiser,* August 1, 1835, 2. Publishers in Britain and the United States reissued the volumes in multiple editions throughout the nineteenth century.

64. "Correspondence," *Harper's Weekly,* November 5, 1859, 707. Guiwits's full name, age, and occupation were determined from censuses.

65. Gage, "Muscle Looking Up," 99.

66. "Provisional Prospectus of the Raritan Bay Union," Broadside. c. 1853. William L. Clements Library, University of Michigan (WLCL, UM).

67. Gage, "Muscle Looking Up," 99. See also "New York Correspondence," *Charleston Courier,* June 26, 1855, 2; *New York Herald,* September 16, 1856, 9; "Eagleswood School," *Christian Inquirer,* June 28, 1856, 10 and 39.

68. Gage, "Muscle Looking Up," 99.

69. Ibid. Dansville Seminary was incorporated in January 1858 in Dansville, Livingston County, New York.

70. *Sacramento Daily Union,* June 12, 1862. Note: A number of previous histories of women's baseball (including my own) have associated "games of ball" in the mid-1860s with Mills College in Oakland. This is incorrect and is based on secondary sources that confuse Mills College with the Benicia Seminary. The confusion stems from the fact that Mills Seminary (later, Mills College) founders, Cyrus and Susan Mills, purchased and ran the Benicia Seminary between 1866 and 1871 before moving to Oakland with some of Benicia's teachers and students to open the Mills Seminary. The Benicia Seminary continued to operate as a separate institution for more than a decade after the Mills left. See Elias Olan James, "Some Notes on the History of the Benicia Seminary," unpublished manuscript for further details. Bancroft Library, University of California at Berkeley.

71. The New York form of baseball had arrived in California as early as 1847 during the Mexican-American War when soldiers from the New York Volunteer Regiment introduced the game to the Spanish-speaking inhabitants of Santa Barbara. Newspapers in Sacramento and surrounding towns regularly reported on baseball clubs and matches throughout the 1850s, and reports of baseball matches and tournaments in San Francisco and Sacramento began appearing in eastern publications like *Porter's Spirit of the Times* and the *New York Clipper* by 1860. For details, see "Chronology: California" and "Games Tab: California," SABR Protoball. www.protoball.org.

72. Benicia was the state capital of California for thirteen months in 1853 and 1854.

73. The Benicia Young Ladies Seminary was operated between 1854 and 1871 by Mary Atkins (1854–1863; 1865) and Cyrus and Susan Mills (1866–1871).

74. See "Benicia Young Ladies Seminary: Seventh Annual Examination," *Sacramento Daily Union,* September 1,1859, 1 and *Sacramento Daily Union,* September 2, 1859, 3 The former article describes the playground as being "an even slope, warmed by the morning and midday sun, which is used as the recreation ground. It is one hundred by one hundred and twenty-five feet in size, and well protected by the high fence." Though quite small for baseball, it would have been suitable for baseball as played by young girls. Students could enroll in the preparatory course at Benicia as young as age seven. From 1857 through 1865, preparatory students always outnumbered seminary students by a fairly wide margin. Any "games at ball" at Benicia were played by young girls, not college-age women. Graces was a popular game for girls in which two players tossed and caught a hoop using rods held in their hands.

75. The Mills came to Benicia from Punahou School, where male and female students played baseball regularly. See next chapter for details.

Chapter 2. *Contesting a National Pastime*

1. For details, see chapter 4, "Civil War Interlude" of Kirsch, *Baseball and Cricket*, chapter 6, "Their Ranks Became So Thinned That Disruption Followed: Baseball During the Civil War," of Peter Morris, *Baseball Fever: Early Baseball in Michigan* (Ann Arbor: University of Michigan Press, 2003). Larry McCray, "Ballplaying in Civil War Camps: An Overview of an Enriched Data Base," (2009), SABR Protoball.

2. Tygiel, *Past Time*, 13.

3. "The Playground: Base Ball," *Oliver Optic's Magazine; Our Boys and Girls,* June 15, 1867, 287.

4. Goldstein, *Playing for Keeps*, 38–39.

5. "The Professional Player," *New York Times*, March 8, 1872, 4. This lengthy editorial against professionalism appeared just one year after professional clubs banded together to form the National Association of Professional Base Ball Players and began to assert their control over the "national" pastime.

6. The resolution was offered by Thomas W. Cantwell, captain of the First Nine of the National Club of Albany, New York. Reprinted in: Dean A. Sullivan, ed., *Early Innings: A Documentary History of Baseball, 1825–1908* (Lincoln: University of Nebraska Press, 1995), 39. After the demise of the amateur association they had helped create, the New York Knickerbockers tried to form another association to continue fighting for amateurism. The new association lasted only from 1871 to 1874. Rader, *Baseball: A History*, 28.

7. The term "semi-professional"—someone who earns money doing something but does not rely on it as their sole livelihood—did not exist at the time. It was first used c. 1890 and came into the popular vernacular in the early 1900s.

8. Sullivan, *Early Innings*, 83–88.

9. For details, see John Thorn, "The *New York Clipper* and Sporting Weeklies of Its Time,"

Base Ball: A Journal of the Early Game 3, no. 1 (Spring 2009): 107–13 and Goldstein, *Playing for Keeps,* 7–10.

10. By 1890, there were seventeen other professional baseball leagues besides the National League—the only one of the nineteenth-century professional leagues still in existence today. The American League was not organized until 1903. For details on some of the short-lived professional leagues of the 1870s and 1880s, see Rader, *Baseball: A History,* 42–59.

11. "Girl Base Ball Clubs," *Utica (N.Y.) Morning Herald and Daily Gazette,* October 17, 1867.

12. "Muffin" games were staged for frivolous fun, not serious competition. For details, see Morris, "Moving Forward: 'Muffin' Ballplayers Start a New Tradition," in *But Didn't We Have Fun?* 213–26.

13. *New York Sunday Mercury,* August 5, 1866.

14. Bruce Allardice, "The Spread of Base Ball, 1859–1870: Some New Data on the Early Diffusion of Base Ball in the United States," SABR Protoball, September 2013. Using online search engines to determine the number of references to "base ball" in newspapers and publications between 1859 and 1870, Allardice demonstrates that the popularity of baseball skyrocketed after the war. Allardice's timeframe ends at 1870 and he does not break out the types of teams. My research indicates that baseball continued to grow in popularity and that players organized many different types of teams.

15. William R. Hooper, "Our National Game," *Appleton's Journal: A Magazine of General Literature* 5, no. 100 (February 25, 1871): 225.

16. See appendices for information on individual teams. The twenty-one states with female teams and players between 1865 and 1879 were: Pennsylvania, Michigan, Florida, Ohio, Massachusetts, Indiana, Minnesota, Kansas, Iowa, New Hampshire, North Carolina, Rhode Island, Kentucky, Illinois, Connecticut, Maine, New Jersey, New York, and Wisconsin. The latter three states and the Kingdom of Hawaii had had female teams or players prior to 1860. These facts were compiled from my own research in nineteenth-century newspapers and periodicals.

17. Because of the dearth of primary sources relating to black female baseball players, it is difficult to draw analytical conclusions about the subject. The lack of sources could indicate either that black girls and women rarely played baseball (despite the fact that black boys and men did) or it could simply indicate that evidence of their playing has not yet come to light or was not documented. The earliest known black women's baseball teams originated in Philadelphia in the summer of 1883. These are described in chapter 4. Other black players and teams are mentioned in the appendices. I found no evidence in primary sources that there was a Dolly Varden team in Philadelphia in 1867. This seems to be an error that has crept into secondary sources.

18. Morris, "Moving Forward," 213–26; "Catch-Penny Affairs: The Effort to Make a Little Money Out of Base Ball Side Shows," *Sporting Life,* August 1, 1891, 12.

19. Professional women's teams are described in chapters 3, 4, and 5.

20. Morris, *But Didn't We Have Fun?* 3–6.

21. Ibid., 213–16.

22. For background on the popularity of other recreational activities, see Matthew Alegro, *Pedestrianism: When Watching People Walk Was America's Favorite Spectator Sport* (Chicago: Chicago Review Press, 2014); Elliott J. Gorn and Warren Goldstein, *A Brief History of American Sports* (New York: Hill & Wang, 1993); Gorn, *The Manly Art;* Robert C. Allen, *Horrible Prettiness: Burlesque and American Culture* (Chapel Hill: University of North Carolina Press, 1991); James W. Cook, ed., *The Colossal P. T. Barnum Reader* (Urbana: University of Illinois Press, 2005).

23. Michael Oriard, *Reading Football: How the Popular Press Created an American Spectacle* (Chapel Hill: University of North Carolina Press, 1993).

24. The first issue of *Beadle's Dime Base Ball Player* included the rules of the Massachusetts game and a report on the rules convention of the New York–based NABBP. Patrick Mondout, "Beadle's Dime Base-Ball Player," Baseball Chronology. http://www.baseballchronology.com/ baseball/Books/Classic /Beadles-Dime-Baseball-Player/. SABR's Protoball site includes a chronology of early baseball newspaper coverage. See http://protoball.org /Chronology:Newspaper _Coverage.

25. Tygiel, *Past Time*, 11–12. Tygiel cites Melvin L. Adelman, *A Sporting Time: New York City and the Rise of Modern Athletics, 1820–1870* (Urbana: University of Illinois Press, 1986).

26. The Washington Nationals played in Columbus, Cincinnati, Louisville, Indianapolis, St. Louis, and Chicago between July 13 and 29, 1867. Large crowds turned out to watch the contests, and a number of baseball historians believe the tour helped spread the New York style of play to the Midwest. Eric Miklich, "1867 Washington Nationals Tour," 19c Base Ball, http:// www.19cbaseball.com/tours-1867-washington-nationals-tour.html. Tour schedule: http://www .19cbaseball.com/tours-1867-1870-cincinnati-red-stockings-tour-2.html.

27. "Base-Ball," *Harper's Weekly,* June 17, 1865, 371.

28. "Out-Door Sports: Base-Ball, Croquet, Quoits and Lacrosse," *Quincy (Ill.) Whig,* July 13, 1868.

29. Chermany was a bat and ball game played in the South (particularly in Virginia) as early as the 1840s. See Protoball.org/Chermany. For information on southern bat and ball games, see Tom Altherr, "1850.38, Southern-Ball-Games," *Base Ball: A Journal of the Early Game* 5, no. 1 (Spring 2011): 103–5.

30. George William Bagby, *What I Did With My Fifty Millions*. By Moses Adams. In *Edited From the Posthumous Ms. by Caesar Maurice, Esq., of the Richmond (VA.) Whig* (Philadelphia, 1874), 43. Google Books.

31. Cited in Kirsch, *Baseball and Cricket,* 202.

32. "Earliest Baseball Clubs," Baseball Memory Lab. See http://mlb.mlb.com/memorylab /spread_of_baseball /earliest_clubs.jsp. Bill O'Neal notes that a game between the Houston Stonewalls and the Galveston Robert E. Lees on April 21, 1867, was one of the first to be reported in detail in local papers. In 1872, an amateur team from New Orleans traveled to Texas via stagecoach and played teams in Dallas, Waco, and Austin. See *The Texas League: A Century of Baseball* (Austin: Easkin Press, 1987), cited at "Early Texas Baseball," http://www .lsjunction.com/facts /tx _bball.htm.

33. "Base Ball: Gossip About the Patrons of the Bat and Ball," *New Orleans Times,* May 1, 1879.

34. Rev. J. T. Crane, "Popular Amusements, Part II," *The Ladies' Repository: A Monthly Periodical, Devoted to Literature, Arts, and Religion* 27 no. 8 (August 1867): 478–79.

35. Ibid.

36. See, for example, "Local and Incidental," *Constantine Weekly Mercury and St. Joseph County (Mich.) Advertiser,* August 8, 1867, 3; "Miscellaneous Items," *Detroit Advertiser and Tribune,* July 23, 1867; *Highland (Ohio) Weekly News,* September 5, 1867, quotes the *McConnelsville (Ohio) Herald*. "At Home and Abroad," *Jersey Journal,* July 29, 1867, 2; *Wellsville (N.Y.) Free Press,* September 4, 1867, 3; "Out Door Sports," *Newark Daily Advertiser,* September 16, 1867, 2. The team in Florida was mentioned in numerous newspapers, including "Sporting," *Albany Evening Journal,* July 12, 1867, 2 and "Miscellaneous Items," *Brooklyn Daily Eagle,* July 20, 1867, 1.

37. Thorn, *Baseball in the Garden,* 69. Chadwick's *Ball Players' Chronicle* was first published on June 6, 1867.

38. Henry Chadwick, *Ball Players' Chronicle,* July 25, 1867, in Federal Writer's Project, Il-

linois: Work Project Administration, *Baseball in Old Chicago* (Chicago: A.C. McClurg, 1939), 8–9.

39. See, for example, "Miscellaneous Items," *Detroit Advertiser and Tribune,* July 23, 1867; "News Paragraphs," *Eau Claire (Wisc.) Daily Free Press,* August 8, 1867, 1; *Indiana Herald,* November 27, 1867, 2; "The Daily Avalanche," *Memphis Daily Avalanche,* November 11, 1867, 1; *Gettysburg Star,* November 20, 1867, 1; "Things in General," *Lowville (N.Y.) Democrat,* September 4, 1867; "At Home and Abroad," *Jersey Journal,* July 29, 1867, 2; *Daily National Intelligencer,* November 22, 1867, 2; *Leavenworth (Kans.) Weekly Conservative,* October 3, 1867; *St. Joseph Advertiser* cited in *Niles (Mich.) Weekly Times,* September 12, 1867, 3.

40. *Niles Weekly Times,* September 12, 1867, 3. Dan, Beersheba, and Ashkelon were ancient cities of Israel. Gath was a Philistine city-state of the same period. Thanks to John Kovach for bringing this article to my attention.

41. *Wellsville Free Press,* September 4, 1867, 3. Thanks to Priscilla Astifan for bringing this article to my attention.

42. *Niles Weekly Times,* September 12, 1867, 3.

43. "The Daily Avalanche," *Memphis Daily Avalanche,* November 11, 1867, 1; *Indiana Herald,* November 27, 1867, 2.

44. Newspapers had carried occasional reports of men dying during or immediately after bat and ball games; many reporters who mentioned Amaret Howard's death would have remembered the untimely baseball-related death of twenty-one-year-old Brooklyn Excelsior star Jim Creighton, just five years earlier. See details on Creighton's death and other baseball-related deaths at http://www.protoball.org.

45. "Local," *Coldwater (Mich.) Sentinel,* November 22, 1867, 3. Howard shows up in the 1850 census as "Amorette" and in the 1860 census as "Amaret." In 1860 she was fourteen years old; her household consisted of her father, Goodwin (age thirty-six), her mother, Betsey (age thirty-seven), several siblings, (one older and three younger), plus two farm hands and a domestic servant.

46. For insights on the women's rights movement of the time, see Mari Jo Buhle and Paul Buhle, eds., *The Concise History of Woman Suffrage: Selections from the Classic Work of Stanton, Anthony, Gage, and Harper* (Urbana: University of Illinois Press, 1979), esp. 89–158; Alice S. Rossi, "Social Roots of the Woman's Movement in America," in *The Feminist Papers: From Adams to de Beauvoir* (Boston: Northeastern University Press, 1973), 241–81.

47. Examples of papers that reprinted the article include: *Daily Iowa State Register,* September 27, 1867, 2; *Flake's Bulletin* (Galveston, Tex.), October 6, 1867, 2; *Defiance (Ohio) Democrat,* October 26, 1867, 4; *Salt Lake Daily Telegraph,* October 30, 1867.

48. "Sexual Assimilation," *Daily Iowa State Register,* September 27, 1867, 2.

49. Ibid.

50. "Base Ball on the Brain," *Easton (Md.) Gazette,* September 27, 1867. Thanks to Robert Tholkes for bringing this to my attention.

51. From the 1840s onward, the popular press in the United States frequently published unflattering accounts and cartoons about women's rights activists. Rather than address women's objectives with well-reasoned discourse, some critics attempted to debase and sexualize them. For examples of caricatures of women's rights activists in general, see the images from *Harper's Weekly* (1859) and Currier and Ives (1869) at: Michael O'Malley, Women and Equality," Exploring U.S. History Web site, http://chnm.gmu.edu/exploring/19thcentury/womenandequality/.

52. In 1868, Peterboro boasted a robust manufacturing base anchored by a cheese factory that turned out 220,000 pounds of cheese annually, and a cheese box factory that made 20,000 boxes a year. Mechanical shops, a flouring mill, carriage shop, sawmill, and planing mill, provided ample employment opportunities and services to residents of Peterboro and the nearby

towns of Canastota, Cazenovia, and Oneida. Hamilton Child, *Gazetteer and Business Directory of Madison County, NY for 1868–9* (Syracuse, N.Y.: Journal Office, 1868).

53. Winthrop S. Scudder, *Gerrit Smith Miller: An Appreciation* (Dedham, Mass.: Noble and Greenough School, 1924), 17.

54. "The Last Sporting Sensation: A Female Base Ball Club at Peterboro," *New York Clipper,* August 29, 1868: 163; "Sporting: . . . Remarkable Female Base Ball Match—Something New," *Chicago Daily Tribune,* August 29, 1868, 4. It was common practice in the nineteenth century for baseball clubs to select a "playing nine" or "senior nine" composed of its most skilled players, and one or more "junior nines" composed of younger and/or less skilled players. My research indicates that it is unlikely the Peterboro club really had fifty members.

55. "The Last Sporting Sensation," 163; "Remarkable Female Base Ball Match," 4. Note: None of the contemporary reports states exactly when the public exhibition game took place, and considerable confusion ensued for historians because articles about the game reprinted as late as two months after the fact still reported the date of the game as "last Saturday." I determined the actual date of the game (Saturday, July 25) by locating the earliest reference to the game—the letter penned by Elizabeth Cady Stanton on August 1, 1868, from Peterboro and published in *The Revolution* on August 6, 1868.

56. Gerrit Smith to Elizabeth Cady Stanton, 1869. Reprinted in Octavius Brooks Frothingham, *Gerrit Smith: A Biography* (New York, 1878), 124. Gerrit Smith's sprawling estate in Peterboro was an active station on the Underground Railroad, and he frequently hosted prominent political and social activists in his home, including Frederick Douglass and John Brown. Smith did not limit his activities to private philanthropy; he ran for numerous political offices, including governor of New York (in 1840 and 1858) and president of the United States (in 1848, 1852, and 1856). Smith was elected to the U.S. House of Representatives in 1853.

57. "Woman's Rights Convention," *Brooklyn Eagle,* September 10, 1852, notes that "Mrs. Gerrit Smith, of N.Y." was one of the officers present at the Woman's Rights Convention that assembled at Syracuse on Sept 8, 1852.

58. See chapter 1, note 48.

59. "Editors' Table: Waifs," *Hamilton Literary Monthly* 3, no. 2 (September 1868): 69. Hamilton College Archives. The Grecian Bend was the name given to a specific posture that some upper-class women attempted to model in the mid-nineteenth century. The unnatural position was achieved by wearing clothing that bent their bodies into a pose mimicking a Greek statue.

60. Susan B. Anthony and Elizabeth Cady Stanton cofounded *The Revolution* in early 1868; they promoted social causes, particularly women's rights, in its pages.

61. "Editorial Correspondence," *The Revolution* 2.5, August 6, 1868, 66.

62. *Cleveland Plain Dealer,* August 11, 1868, 2.

63. "Central New York News: Madison County," *Syracuse Daily Journal,* August 12, 1868, 6; "Female Base 'Ballists,'" *The Sun* (New York City), August 13, 1868, 1; "Gleanings," *Buffalo Evening Courier and Republic,* August 13, 1868; *Cincinnati Daily Gazette,* August 14, 1868, 2; "Feminine Base Ballists," *New York Clipper,* August 15, 1868, 149; "Base Ball Notes," *New York Herald,* August 16, 1868, 7, and "Local and County Matters: Feminine Base Ball Players," *Madison (N.Y.) Observer,* August 16, 1868. "Mail Gleanings," *Philadelphia Inquirer,* August 17, 1868, 2.

64. "Mail Gleanings," *Philadelphia Inquirer,* August 17, 1868, 2.

65. *Cazenovia (N.Y.) Republican,* August 19, 1868, 3; *Madison (Ind.) Observer,* August 16, 1868, 2; "Feminine Base Ball Players," *Oneida (N.Y.) Dispatch,* August 21, 1868, 2; "Clippings and Drippings: Miscellaneous," *St. Joseph Herald,* August 22, 1868, 2; untitled, *New Bedford (Mass.) Republican Standard,* August 27, 1868, 3; "Miscellaneous Items," *Blairsville (Pa.) Press,* September 11, 1868, 1; "Hon. Gerrit Smith at Home," *Boston Investigator,* March 3, 1869, 5.

66. E. L. Taylor to Gerrit Smith, Columbus, Ohio, August 17, 1868. Gerrit Smith Papers, Special Collections Research Center, Syracuse University Library.

67. "The Last Sporting Sensation, 163; "Remarkable Female Base Ball Match, 4; "The Last Sporting Sensation," *Syracuse Courier and Union,* August 31, 1868. The quotations in the text are from the anonymous source.

68. Only the Chicago article did not include the comment that they expected to see Mary Sterns playing next year.

69. "Base Ball," *Buffalo Evening Courier and Republic,* September 7, 1868; "Ladies Playing Ball," *Rochester (N.Y.) Evening Express,* September 8, 1868; "Lady Base Ball Players," *Schenectady (N.Y.) Daily Evening Post,* September 8, 1868); "Ladies Playing Base Ball," *Madison Observer* (16 Sep 1868), 2; "The Last Illustration of Woman's Rights—A Female Base-Ball Club at Peterboro, N. Y.," *The Day's Doings,* October 3, 1868, 275 and 280.

70. Emily Howland scrapbook. NAWSA Collection, Sec XVI, No. 2, Library of Congress Rare Book and Special Collections Division. The date of the clipping can be roughly approximated because it is pasted alongside other clippings from 1868 reporting on the activities of the women's rights movement and the successes of individual women making inroads into previously all-male professions. The fact it was cited in later articles indicates it predated at least September 7.

71. For an overview of tensions within the women's rights movement of the mid-nineteenth century, see Buhle and Buhle, *Concise History,* 12–22.

72. "Base Ball Notes," *New York Herald,* August 16, 1868, 7.

73. "The National Game," *New York Herald,* October 11, 1868, 6.

74. *Sporting Times,* August 29, 1868, 1. Thanks to John Thorn for bringing this illustration to my attention.

75. "The Last Illustration of Woman's Rights—A Female Base-Ball Club at Peterboro, N. Y.," *The Days' Doings,* October 3, 1868, 280.

76. A search of the scrapbooks of several prominent women's rights activists, including Susan B. Anthony and Matilda Joslyn Gage, yielded only the undated clipping about the Peterboro game in Emily Howland's scrapbook mentioned earlier. NAWSA Collection, Library of Congress. Neither Susan B. Anthony, Elizabeth Cady Stanton, Ann Smith (Nannie's grandmother), nor Elizabeth Smith Miller mentioned the baseball club in private correspondence written immediately before or after the public game. Not even Elizabeth Smith Miller's diary, which she kept sporadically between Nannie's birth in 1856 and 1869, mentions the game. Madison County Historical Society. Ann Gordon, editor of a multivolume compilation of Stanton's correspondence, has not found a single additional reference to girls playing baseball in any of Stanton's voluminous correspondence. E-mails from Ann Gordon to author, summer 2008.

77. *American Annals of Education* (1835), cited in Thomas Woody, *A History of Women's Education in the United States* (2 vols.) (New York: The Science Press, 1929), vol. 2, p. 101. See, for example, *The Dangers of Crinoline, Steel Hoops, &c.* . . . (London, 1858). Google Books. "The Abatement of Crinoline," *New York Evening Post,* July 23, 1859, 1; *Albany Morning Times,* May 16 and 21, 1859, 2; "Evil Influence of Crinoline on Wedlock," *San Francisco Bulletin,* July 26, 1859, 1.

78. Gerrit Smith, letter to Elizabeth Cady Stanton, 1869. Reprinted in Frothingham, *Gerrit Smith,* 125. Smith was criticized by some for his public stand on dress reform. See, for example, "The Last Ism—Dress Reform," *Brooklyn Eagle,* January 14, 1857, 2.

79. "Editorial Correspondence," *The Revolution* 2.6, August 13, 1868, 81–82.

80. "Editorial Correspondence," *The Revolution* 2.5, August 6, 1868, 66.

81. Ibid., 275.

82. Morris, *Baseball Fever,* 196.

83. For insights on attitudes toward women's bodies, see Martha H. Verbrugge, *Able-Bodied Womanhood* (New York: Oxford University Press, 1988) and Patricia A. Vertinsky, *Eternally Wounded Women: Women, Doctors and Exercise in the Late Nineteenth Century* (Urbana: University of Illinois Press, 1994).

84. The vast majority of female baseball players of the nineteenth century fell into the former group. It was not until the late nineteenth century that more players began wearing bloomers and trying to play regulation baseball. Some of the players on professional barnstorming teams wore pantaloons or slacks.

85. Jeannette L. Gilder, *The Autobiography of a Tomboy* (New York: Doubleday, Page, 1900), 287. Thanks to Tom Altherr for bringing this account to my attention.

86. A contemporary newspaper source validates Gilder's memory. In September 1867 the *Newark Daily Advertiser* informed its readers that baseball was "rampant" in Bordentown and that the "enthusiasm on this subject has reached the female persuasion." The paper went on to report that young ladies in town had organized two teams called the Belle Vue and the Galaxy. "Out Door Sports," *Newark Daily Advertiser,* September 16, 1867, 2.

87. Gilder, *Autobiography of a Tomboy,* 288–89.

88. "Sporting: Goose Race and Base Ball," *New Orleans Daily Picayune,* (October 3, 1869, 16.

89. Ibid.

90. See appendices.

91. Most of the surviving historical artifacts relating to nineteenth-century female baseball players came from middle- and upper-class players because they were the ones who had the leisure time and money to write letters, maintain scrapbooks, and hire photographers. We have only sporadic and indirect evidence of working-class girls and women playing baseball.

92. Reminiscence of Grace Aspinwall. Miss Porter's School archives. Gloria Gavert, school archivist, letter to author, November 19, 1990.

93. Ibid.

94. Charles W. Hurd to Charles H. Berry, April 8, 1869. http://cgi.ebay.com/EARLY -ANTIQUE-HISTORIC-LETTER-1869-T206-OLD-JUDGE-/140434365961?pt=Vintage _Sports_Memorabilia#ht_1754wt_1139. Thanks to David Block for bringing this letter to my attention.

95. Annie G. (Howes) Barus, Vassar Class of 1874. Quoted in: "Hannah Lyman," *Vassar Encyclopedia,* http://vcencyclopedia.vassar.edu/matthew-vassar/hannah-lyman/index.html. Barus most likely played the Massachusetts form of baseball during the 1860s.

96. For insights on early childhood education, see Nancy Beadie and Kim Tolley, *Chartered Schools: Two Hundred Years of Independent Academies in the United States, 1727–1925* (New York: Routledge, 2002); Jane H. Hunter, *How Young Ladies Became Girls: The Victorian Origins of American Girlhood* (New Haven, Conn.: Yale University Press, 2003); David Tyack and Elisabeth Hansot, *Learning Together: A History of Coeducation in American Public Schools* (New York: Russell Sage Foundation, 1992); Mary Kelley, *Learning to Stand and Speak: Women, Education, and Public Life in America's Republic* (Chapel Hill: University of North Carolina Press, 2008); Margaret A. Nash, *Women's Education in the United States, 1780–1840* (New York: Palgrave Macmillan, 2005).

97. For insights into Sarah Porter's life, see Louise L. Stevenson, "Sarah Porter Educates Useful Ladies, 1847–1900," *Winterthur Portfolio* 18, no. 1 (1983): 39–60.

98. Ibid.

99. Reminiscence of Kate Stevens. Miss Porter's School archives. Gloria Gavert, school archivist, letter to author, November 19, 1990.

100. See Verbrugge and Vertinsky, *Able-Bodied Womanhood*, for insights on attitudes regarding the limitations of the female body.

101. *Lancaster (Ohio) Gazette* article reprinted in: "Girls as Ballists," *New York Clipper*, November 26, 1870, 266.

102. Ibid.

103. Cartwright's three sons, DeWitt, Bruce, and Alexander Jr. attended Punahou School—DeWitt from 1858 to 1860, Bruce from 1864 to 1869, and Alexander Jr. from 1866 to 1869. It is conceivable that one or all of Cartwright's sons were members of the baseball teams organized by students at Punahou. William De Witt Alexander, *Oahu College: List of Trustees, Presidents, Instructors, Matrons, Librarians, Superintendents of Grounds, and Students, 1841–1906*, (Honolulu: Hawaiian Gazette, 1907).

104. *Punahou Mirror* 1, no. 2, May 13, 1875. Cooke Library, Punahou School. This is the earliest documented female baseball team at Punahou, although they may well have played earlier. In his book, *Hawaii Sports: History, Facts, and Statistics* (Honolulu: University of Hawaii, 1999), 2, Dan Cisco states that girls organized a team at Punahou in 1874 but he does not provide a source for his information. It is possible he inferred the information from the Tally Book. On the page facing the roster for the girls' team of 1875–1876, there is a page that is blank except for the words, "Base Ball" and "Punahou, Nov 13, 74." This page is numbered 204. The facing page is numbered 207. The date on page 204 may be referring to the roster, but this is not certain, particularly because there are two pages missing and because page 207 has its own title and date: "Punahou Base Ball Club, 1875–76."

105. Alice Stone Blackwell, journal entry, Wednesday, April 10, 1872. Reprinted in: Marlene Deahl Merrill, ed., *Growing Up in Boston's Gilded Age: The Journal of Alice Stone Blackwell, 1872–1874* (New Haven, Conn. and London: Yale University Press, 1990), 60. Blackwell was attending Harris Grammar School in the Dorchester neighborhood of Boston at the time she and friends played baseball together. Merrill identifies "Sadie" as Sadie Wilson, a friend of Blackwell's who was one year ahead of her in school. Thanks to Dorothy Jane Mills for bringing Blackwell's journal entries about baseball to my attention.

106. Ibid., 60–61.

107. Blackwell's references to baseball appear in the following entries for 1872: April 27 and 30, May 4, 8, 15, 18, 20, 22, and 23, and June 4 and 13.

108. In her journal entry for June 27, 1873, Alice Blackwell mentions being embarrassed when her mother made "a tremendous mistake" during her remarks by commenting that the best scholar [Alice] was also the "best base ball player." The truth was "exactly the reverse," in Blackwell's words. Merrill, 181. There is no evidence that Blackwell played baseball after she left school.

109. "Facts and Figures," *Woman's Exponent* 1, no. 23 (1873): 184. Published primarily for Mormon women, the *Women's Exponent* was a strong advocate for women's suffrage.

110. There were many different types of colleges in the United States in the nineteenth century. The type of college women attended, its geographic location, and the era in which they attended, shaped their experiences. For insights on college life for female students at different types of nineteenth-century institutions, see Helen Lefkowitz Horowitz, *Alma Mater* (Amherst: University of Massachusetts Press, 1993) and *Campus Life: Undergraduate Cultures from the End of the Eighteenth Century to the Present* (Chicago: University of Chicago Press, 1987); Andrea G. Radke-Moss, *Bright Epoch: Women and Coeducation in the American West* (Lincoln: University of Nebraska Press, 2008); Patricia A. Palmieri, *Educating Men and Women Together: Coeducation in a Changing World* (Urbana: University of Illinois Press, 1987); Barbara Miller Solomon, *In the Company of Educated Women: A History of Women and Higher Education in America*

(New Haven, Conn.: Yale University Press, 1985); Geraldine Joncich Clifford, *Lone Voyagers: Academic Women in Coeducational Institutions, 1870–1937* (New York: The Feminist Press at CUNY, 1993); Christine A. Ogren, *The American State Normal School: "An Instrument of Great Good"* (New York: Palgrave Macmillan, 2005); Farnham, *The Education of the Southern Belle.*

111. In 1870, only 21 percent of the 1 percent of eighteen to twenty-four-year-olds who attended college in the United States were women; by 1900 that number had grown to just 36 percent despite the founding of more than a dozen women's colleges and the proliferation of scores of coeducational normal schools, land-grant colleges, and universities during the intervening time period. David O. Levine, *The American College and the Culture of Aspiration, 1915–1940* (Ithaca, N.Y.: Cornell University Press, 1986), 64.

112. E. M. (Elizabeth) Powell, "Physical Culture at Vassar College," *Herald of Health and Journal of Physical Culture* 13 (New York: Miller, Wood) (March 1869): 133. Powell was the physical training instructor at Vassar from 1866 to 1870.

113. Francis A. Wood, *Earliest Years at Vassar—Personal Recollections* (Poughkeepsie, N.Y.: Vassar College Press, 1909), 22.

114. Information on students compiled from: *Alumnae Register*, Vassar College Special Collections (VCSC); demographic information is from Wood, *Earliest Years at Vassar*, 8 and James Monroe Taylor and Elizabeth Hazelton Haight, *Vassar* (New York: Oxford University Press, 1915), 55–56. Special students were those pursuing studies in music or art primarily. They were not required to follow the same curriculum designed for students in the regular academic program. Preparatory students were studying to qualify for enrollment in the regular program. For a fuller treatment of player demographics, see Shattuck, "Bats, Balls and Books," 99–109. http://www.la84 foundation.org/SportsLibrary/JSH/JSH1992/JSH1902/jsh1902b.pdf.

115. "Annual Report of the Department of Physical Training 1876–1877," Lilian Tappan to President John H. Raymond, June 1877, Vassar College. VCSC.

116. Examples are cited throughout the book (e.g., reminiscences and letters from Minnie Stephens, Sophia Foster Richardson, Rachel Studley, etc.).

117. Pamela Dean, "'Dear Sisters' and 'Hated Rivals': Athletics and Gender at Two New South Women's Colleges, 1893–1920," *Journal of Sport History* 24, no. 3 (Fall 1997): 352.

118. "The train" was a reference to the long back portion of a dress or skirt. They were a popular women's clothing style throughout the nineteenth century and can still be seen on wedding dresses and formal gowns. In "A Girls' College Life," *The Cosmopolitan* 32, no. 2 (June 1901): 188–95.

119. Minnie Stephens [Allen], undated letter to her former classmates. Minnie Stephens 1883 papers, Smith College Archives (SCA). In the document Stephens mistakenly recalled that the teams were organized "Way back in '79." Other student accounts indicate that the teams were actually organized in the spring of 1880 during Stephens's first year at the school.

120. "Poem, Prophecy and History," *1878 Class Book*, 23. VCSC.

121. "Vassar Athletic Association," *Vassar Miscellany* 26, no. 3 (December 1896): 138.

122. *Chicago Times,* October 22, 1869, quoted in Robert Pruter, "Youth Baseball in Chicago, 1868–1890: Not Always Sandlot Ball," *Journal of Sport History* 26, no. 1 (Spring 1999): 6.

123. For background information on the Northwestern Female College at Evanston, see Dwight F. Clark, "A Forgotten Evanston Institution: The Northwestern Female College," *Journal of the Illinois State Historical Society* 35, no. 2 (June 1942): 115–32 and Patrick M. Quinn, "Coeducation at Northwestern," *Northwestern Perspective* 1, no. 1 (Winter 1988): 42–45. For almost fifteen years, the women's college had steadily outdrawn the all-male Northwestern University. The latter graduated forty-one students, while the former graduated seventy-two. Once Northwestern University agreed to admit female students, the women's college lost its constituency.

124. "Home Matters," *The Vassar Miscellany* 5, no.1 (October 1875): 593.

125. Sophia Foster Richardson, "Tendencies in Athletics for Women in Colleges & Universities," A Paper Presented to the Association of Collegiate Alumnae, October 31, 1896, *Appleton's Popular Science Monthly* 50 (February 1897): 526. Richardson included an account of how she and fellow students organized seven or eight baseball teams during her freshman year in the fall of 1875. She attributed the rise of the teams to "a few quiet suggestions from a resident physician wise beyond her generation." The physician was Dr. Helen Webster, who assumed her new duties at Vassar in the spring of 1874. According to Richardson, Webster continued to encourage the girls to play even after one of them was injured during a game. Team names are from Harold Seymour and Dorothy Mills Seymour, *Baseball: The People's Game* (New York: Oxford University Press, 1990), 447.

126. Letter from Katharine Griffis to Mary Grace Toll Hill, November 9, 1875. Available digitally at http://digitallibrary.vassar.edu/fedora/repository /vassar%3A24317.

127. Ibid.

128. "College Notes," *The Vassar Miscellany* 6, no.1 (October 1876): 56.

129. Richardson, "Tendencies in Athletics," 526.

130. "Home Matters," *The Vassar Miscellany* 5, no. 2 (January 1876): 647.

131. "Home Matters," *The Vassar Miscellany* (July 1876): 769 and 774.

132. "After the Game," reprinted from *The Princetonian* in *Syracuse Journal*, February 11, 1880.

133. The only known existing reference to baseball at Whittier College comes from a letter to the editor sent from Whittier by "Ace" on October 27, 1873. "Whittier College, Iowa," *Woman's Journal*, November 22, 1873, 370.

134. Packer had graduated in Whittier's inaugural class of 1871.

135. School history is from Louis Thomas Jones, *The Quakers of Iowa*, Part 4, "Benevolent and Educational Enterprises." Available at: http://iagenweb.org/history/qoi/QOIPt4Chp5.htm.

136. See Appendices A and B for details.

137. *National Chronicle* (Boston), October 30, 1869, 259; *Cleveland Plain Dealer*, November 3, 1869, 2; "Female Club in Brooklyn," *Brooklyn Daily Eagle*, September 1868, 2; "Base-Ball," *Cincinnati Enquirer*, September 28, 1869.

138. Examples of coverage of women's teams: "Afternoon Topics," *Critic Record* (Washington, D.C.), August 1, 1870, 4; "Miscellaneous Items," *Sacramento Daily Union*, September 23, 1870, 4; "Current Notes," *Morning Oregonian*, August 15, 1870, 2; *Houston Daily Union*, August 18, 1870; "News Paragraphs," *Wisconsin State Journal*, September 16, 1870, 2; "Items of Interest," *Kokomo (Ind.) Tribune*, September 8, 1870, 3; "Girls as Ball Players," *New York Clipper*, November 26, 1870, 266.

139. Wichita, Kansas team: Milt Riske, "Ladies and Diamonds—Out West—And They Weren't Always 'Ladies' on the Old Barnstorming Tours," (August 1978). Miscellaneous clipping file, NBHoF archives. Source of article is unknown; Iowa City team: "Miscellaneous Items," *Essex County (N.Y.) Republican*, May 22, 1873; Paris, Kentucky team: "Current Notes," *Boston Journal*, July 15, 1876, 2; Tarboro, North Carolina team: "State New," *State Agricultural Journal*, August 27, 1874), 7, and "Wayside Notes," *Daily Charlotte Observer*, September 18, 1874, 1.

140. "Ladies at the Bat," *Chicago Tribune*, August 17, 1870, 4. An article penned by Matilda Fletcher, a special correspondent for the *Iowa State Register*, after a visit to Rockford gave the score as 30–6. Reprinted in: "Illinois From the Cars," *Rockford Weekly Register-Gazette*, September 17, 1870, 7. *New York Clipper*, September 3, 1870, 173.

141. "Papers, Men and Things," *Cambridge City (Ind.) Tribune*, July 27, 1871, 1.

142. "Suburban: Jacksonville," *St. Louis Globe-Democrat*, April 29, 1876, 3.

143. "Local News," *Neodesha (Kans.) Free Press* (13 Jul 1877), 2.

144. "State Notes," *Elk County (Pa.) Advocate,* June 17, 1875, 3.

145. Though the social class of female baseball players is rarely mentioned in newspaper articles, it is probable that most players on civic, pick-up, and college baseball teams were from middle and upper classes. They were treated differently by the press. There is a stark contrast between the often hostile reporting on working-class barnstorming women's baseball teams in the 1870s and 1880s and the benign or positive coverage of coed civic, pick-up, and college teams. See following chapters for details on barnstorming teams.

146. "Boating and the Ballet," *New York Times,* July 24, 1870, 4.

147. "Current Notes," *Morning Oregonian,* August 15, 1870, 2.

148. William R. Hooper, "Our National Game," *Appleton's Journal: A Magazine of General Literature* 5, no. 100 (February 25, 1871): 226.

149. Ibid.

150. "White Stockings," *Iosco County (Mich.) Gazette,* August 20, 1874, 3. See also an account of a game in Williamsport reprinted in *Harrisburg Daily Independent,* July 16, 1877, 1 and July 20, 1877, 3.

151. Bailey's story appeared in newspapers as early as June 1878. "A Female Base-Ball Club," *Buffalo Morning Express,* June 26, 1878, 1. Bailey included the story in: "A Female Base-Ball Club," in *The Danbury Boom! With a Full Account of Mrs. Cobleigh's Action Therein! Together With Many Other Interesting Phases in the Social and Domestic History of That Remarkable Village* (Boston, 1880), 75–79. Twain published it as "The Female Base Ball Nine" in *Mark Twain's Library of Humor* (New York, 1888), 126–29.

152. See, for example, Therese Oneill, "12 Cruel Anti-Suffrage Cartoons," *The Week* Web site, http://theweek .com /articles/461455/12-cruel-antisuffragette-cartoons.

153. "General News," *Jackson Citizen Patriot,* May 25, 1876, 3; "Notes About Women," *Kalamazoo Gazette,* June 4, 1876, 2. "Lightning Flashes," *New York Evening Telegram,* September 23, 1876, 2.

Chapter 3. Commodifying a National Pastime

1. Cited in Thorn, *Baseball in the Garden,* xiv.

2. "Major League Baseball" is a professional organization created in 2000 by the National and American leagues. It is led by a commissioner of baseball. Through this formal business structure, MLB officials promote the sport. They oversee thirty major league teams in the NL and AL and the over two hundred teams in the minor leagues. They also help manage international baseball tournaments. The term "Organized Baseball" often denotes the totality of professional leagues and teams overseen by the MLB; I use the terms interchangeably in this book.

3. Fully half of MLB's thirty teams were worth at least $1 billion each in 2015; none of the thirty was worth less than $600 million. Mike Ozanian, "MLB Worth $36 Billion As Team Values Hit Record $1.2 Billion Average," Forbes, http://www.forbes.com/sites/mikeozanian/2015/03/25/mlb-worth-36-billion-as-team-values-hit-record-1-2-billion-average/.

4. See, for example, definitions of "profession" and "professional" in Thomas Sheridan, *A Complete Dictionary of the English Language* (1797) and Noah Webster, *Improved Pronouncing Dictionary of the English Language* (1870), Google Books.

5. Male professionals earned approximately $1,200–1,300 for an eighty-game season while managers generally promised female player-performers $5–10 per week plus expenses but often paid them far less. Insights on the pay scales appeared in "Feminine Field Fun: Female Base Ballists on the Diamond—Score 23 to 10, in Seven Innings," *Rochester Democrat and Chronicle,*

August 13, 1879, 4. Kathy Peiss writes that 56 percent of female factory workers in turn-of-the-century New York City earned less than $8.00 per week; those working in retail stores earned even less. This was at a time when the living wage was estimated by economists to be $9–10 per week. *Cheap Amusements: Working Women and Leisure in Turn-of-the-Century New York* (Philadelphia: Temple University Press, 1986), 52,

6. "Belles of the Bat: At Bates' Park Tomorrow—Revival of Ancient Open-air Pastimes for Women," *Saginaw Evening News,* August 3, 1889, 7. Quoting the *New York Herald.*

7. *Cincinnati Commercial,* April 1, 1882.

8. Attendance figures for the women's games are extrapolated by averaging the high and low figures from newspaper accounts. Some reports provided only a description ("a large crowd") rather than a numerical figure. These games are not included in the average attendance figures.

9. Letter from Harry Wright to Frederick Long, April 28, 1875, Washington, D.C. Richard Hershberger, e-mail to 19cBB Group, April 23, 2015. Archived at: https://groups.yahoo.com/neo/groups/19CBB/conversations/messages /15649.

10. See account of the Red Stockings and Blue Stockings later in this chapter and details on Sylvester Wilson's teams in chapter 4.

11. Janet Davis, *The Circus Age Culture and Society under the American Big Top* (Chapel Hill: University of North Carolina Press, 2002); M. Alison Kibler, introduction to *Rank Ladies: Gender and Cultural Hierarchy in American Vaudeville* (Chapel Hill: University of North Carolina Press, 1999), 1–21; Rachel Adams, *Sideshow U.S.A.: Freaks and the American Cultural Imagination* (Chicago: University of Chicago Press, 2001), 1–59; P. T. Barnum, *The Colossal P. T. Barnum Reader: Nothing Else Like It in the Universe,* ed. James W. Cook (Urbana: University of Illinois Press, 2005); Karen Halttunen, *Confidence Men and Painted Women: Study of Middle Class Culture in America, 1830–70.* (New Haven, Conn.: Yale University Press, 1986).

12. *Boston Post,* January 21 and 22, 1877, cited in: Dahn Shaulis, "Pedestriennes: Newsworthy but Controversial Women in Sporting Entertainment," *Journal of Sport History* 26, no. 1 (Spring 1999): 34.

13. James E. Brunson III, "'A Mirthful Spectacle': Race, Blackface Minstrelsy, and Base Ball, 1874–1888," *NINE: A Journal of Baseball History and Culture* 17, no. 2 (Spring 2009): 16. Brunson writes that a minstrel show promoter organized and funded Cleveland's Forest Citys of the National Association in 1869 and that Lew Simmons, a minstrel entertainer, secured a $16,000 loan from circus promoter Adam Forepaugh in 1883 to purchase a part interest in the American Association's Philadelphia Athletics.

14. Rader, *Baseball: A History,* 39.

15. Quoted in Thorn, *Baseball in the Garden,* 178. "Kicking" was the practice of complaining loudly at the umpire. This complaining frequently included copious amounts of cursing and could involve kicking dust on the umpire's shoes.

16. Rader, *Baseball: A History,* 29.

17. Morris, *But Didn't We Have Fun?* 160–83.

18. Kirsch, *Baseball and Cricket,* 240–44, 250.

19. Rader writes, "The gross receipts of a typical nineteenth-century pro baseball team were closer to those of a corner saloon than to those of Andrew Carnegie's steel works or John D. Rockefeller's oil empire." *Baseball: A History,* 36.

20. Kirsch, *Baseball and Cricket,* 254.

21. Information on the development of nineteenth-century baseball leagues is from Rader, "The First Professional Leagues," chapter 4, *Baseball: A History,* 42–77. For details on Hulbert's role in creation of the National League, see Thorn, *Baseball in the Garden,* 154–64.

22. Other nineteenth-century professional baseball leagues included the American Associa-

tion (1882–1891), the Union Association of Professional Base-Ball Clubs (1884–1885), and the Players' League (1889–1890). The IAPBBP lasted from 1877 through 1880. It reformed briefly from 1888 to 1890.

23. Major League team owners created the position of commissioner of baseball in late 1920 to restore baseball's reputation in the wake of the Chicago Black Sox scandal of 1919. See Nathan, *Saying It's So* for details on the scandal.

24. "Female Ball-Players: Two Female Teams Make Sport for the Boys Yesterday," *Cincinnati Daily Enquirer,* August 27, 1879, 8.

25. Robert C. Allen, *Horrible Prettiness: Burlesque and American Culture* (Chapel Hill: University of North Carolina Press, 1991), xii.

26. Ibid., 179.

27. Advertisement, *Brooklyn Daily Eagle,* August 31 and September 3 and 5, 1868, 1.

28. Advertisement, *Cleveland Plain Dealer,* February 15, 1872, 3; "Amusements," *Cleveland Plain Dealer,* May 17, 1878, 4.

29. Advertisement, *New York Clipper,* August 14, 1875, 160.

30. "Local Brevities," *Los Angeles Daily Herald,* April 6, 1876, 3; "City and Vicinity," *Daily Rocky Mountain News,* January 17, 1879); "Puts and Calls," *Central City (Colo.) Daily Register-Call,* January 20, 1879; "Amusements," *Salt Lake Daily Tribune,* January 25, 28, and 29, 1879), 1; *Reno Evening Gazette,* February 3–6, 1879, 3.

31. "Local Matters: Women at the Bat—A Base Ball Burlesque in Baltimore," *Baltimore Sun,* July 8, 1879, 1; "Letter From Washington: The Female Base-Ballists . . ." *Baltimore Sun,* July 10, 1879, 4.

32. "Sporting Notes: Baseball," *Detroit Post and Tribune,* August 18, 1879, 4; "Reds and Blues: The Way the Women With the Stockings Burlesqued Base Ball," *Buffalo Morning Express,* August 15, 1879, 2.

33. "Sporting News . . ." *Daily Inter-Ocean,* July 31, 1875, 12.

34. "St. Louis in Splinters," *St. Louis Globe-Democrat,* September 20, 1875, 4. The article notes that after police prevented the troupe from giving a second exhibition in St. Louis on September 19, the "Chicago portion of the Female Base Ball Combination" headed back to Chicago.

35. Information on the managers is from the U.S. Census (1860 and 1880), Springfield City Directories, and various newspaper articles, including: "The Female Baseball Club," *New York Clipper,* September 18, 1875, 194; "The Diamond Field: The Girls on the Turf—The Blondes Walk Away with the Brunettes," *Illinois State Register,* September 13, 1875, 2; "Notes on the Fly," *Syracuse Daily Courier,* September 13, 1875; *Daily State Journal,* September 14, 1875.

36. "In Brief" column, *Illinois State Register,* September 2 and 3, 1875, 4.

37. *Augusta (Ga.) Chronicle,* September 9, 1875; *St. Louis Republican,* September 10, 1875; "Notes on the Fly," *Syracuse Daily Courier,* September 13, 1875; "Base Ball," *Brooklyn Daily Eagle,* September 14, 1875, 2; *Elkhart Evening Review,* September 15, 1875, 2; "A Base Hit," *Cincinnati Daily Enquirer,* September 15, 1875, 8; *Utica Morning Herald,* September 17, 1875; "Sporting," *Oswego Daily Times,* September 17, 1875.

38. Advertisement, *Illinois State Register,* September 9–11 and 13, 1875, 1.

39. One paper called the enclosure a "calico wall about 10 feet in height." "Female Ball Catchers: The Divine Right of Woman's Suffrage Extended to the Green Diamond," *Bloomington Pantagraph,* September 15, 1875, 5.

40. Ibid.

41. "Female Ball Tossers: An Unseemly Exhibition at the Red Stocking Park Yesterday—Championship Record," *St. Louis Republican,* September 19, 1875. "The Female Muffers in St. Louis," *St Louis Globe-Democrat,* September 19, 1875, 6.

42. "The Female Ball Tossers," *Daily State Journal,* September 20, 1875. "Services of the Female Frauds Dispensed With," *St. Louis Globe-Democrat,* September 20, 1875.

43. "Female Base Ball Club," *Inter-Ocean,* September 18, 1875, 5.

44. "Female Ball Catchers," 5. I determined player attrition by comparing published team rosters when available.

45. "A Base Hit," *Cincinnati Daily Enquirer,* September 15, 1875, 8. Quotes *St. Louis Globe-Democrat* report that "nearly all" of the players had been hired in St. Louis and were "formerly connected with variety shows."

46. "Base Ball," *Boston Daily Advertiser,* September 29, 1875; "St. Louis in Splinters," *St. Louis Globe-Democrat,* September 20, 1875, 4.

47. "Sunday Gossip," *Syracuse Sunday Courier,* September 20, 1875; "Base-ball," *New York Times,* September 21, 1875, 5.

48. "The Red Stockings and White Stockings Must Yield the Palm to the Striped Stockings— The 'Blondes and Brunettes' Take to the Field—A Friendly Contest with a 'Picked Nine' of the Male Persuasion," *New York Varieties,* September 30, 1875, 4 and 16. The fact that the women "beat" the men should not be construed to mean that the women won a head-to-head athletic contest. It is clear from other reporting on female baseball teams in the nineteenth century that arranging a particular outcome was part of the entertainment fun.

49. "Female Ball Catchers," 5; "Female Base Ball Club," 5; "The Female Ball Tossers"; "Items of News," *Boston Investigator,* September 29, 1875, 7.

50. "Miscellaneous: A New Sensation in the Sporting World," *The Days' Doings,* October 2, 1875, 7; *Palmyra (Mo.) Spectator,* October 15, 1875; "All Sorts," *Illinois Monitor,* October 30, 1875, 4; "A Female Base-Ball Club," *Jackson Citizen Patriot,* November 20, 1875, 3.

51. "The History of Baseball in an In-And-Out Town," *Illinois Times,* April 14–20, 1978.

52. Cited in: "A Base Hit," *Cincinnati Daily Enquirer,* September 15, 1875, 8.

53. "The Female Base Tossers," *Daily State Journal,* September 13, 1875.

54. "The Diamond Field: The Girls on the Turf—The Blondes Walk Away with the Brunettes," *Illinois State Register,* September 13, 1875, 2.

55. "Female Ball Catchers," 5.

56. Untitled, *Harrisburg Telegraph,* September 23, 1875, 1.

57. "Notes from Bloomington," *Inter Ocean,* September 16, 1875, 5. Special Telegram to the *Inter-Ocean,* September 14, 1875.

58. "The Female Muffers in St. Louis," *St Louis Globe-Democrat,* September 19, 1875, 6.

59. "Female Ball Tossers: An Unseemly Exhibition at the Red Stocking Park Yesterday— Championship Record," *St. Louis Republican,* September 19, 1875.

60. *Bucks County (Pa.) Gazette,* February 24, 1876, 2; *St. Louis Republican,* February 27, 1876.

61. "Base Hits," *St. Louis Globe-Democrat,* March 12, 1876, 6.

62. *St. Louis Globe-Democrat,* April 6, 1879, 13.

63. Details on Wilson's numerous arrests and trials in Nebraska and Ohio between 1872 and 1875 are gleaned primarily from newspapers and from a report written about Wilson by the New York Society for the Prevention of Cruelty to Children for prosecutors at his 1903 trial. The unpublished "Brief for the People" is part of the files of the N.Y. Court of General Sessions for *People Against Sylvester F. Wilson,* New York City Municipal Archives (NYCMA). Hereafter cited as "NYSPCC People's Brief."

64. "Over the River: The Wilson Case," *Philadelphia Inquirer,* November 13 1877, 3; NYSPCC People's Brief.

65. "Minor Notes," *Nemaha Valley (Nebr.) Journal,* April 18, 1872, 2; "A New Paper," *Nemaha Valley Journal,* October 9, 1872; *Nemaha Valley Journal,* May 15, 1873. Thanks to Bill Rowan (Tri-State Corners Genealogical Society) for finding the Wilson-Train-Nemaha connection.

66. "Stanton, Elizabeth Cady," *American National Biography Online*, http://www.anb.org /articles/15/15-00640.html. Willis Thornton, *The Nine Lives of Citizen Train* (New York: Greenberg Press, 1948) and "Notes From Omaha: Growth of George Francis Train's City . . ." *Philadelphia Inquirer*, February 5, 1877, 2.

67. "NYSPCC People's Brief."

68. "Over the River, 3; "The Reading Engineers: Progress of the Strike . . . Train's Championship Discountenanced and Countenanced . . .," *Philadelphia Inquirer*, April 18, 1877, 2; "Wilson, the Ticket Scalper: His Bail Fixed at $5000—A Telegram From George Francis Train," *Philadelphia Inquirer*, June 14, 1877, 3; "Train Still Talking," *Philadelphia Inquirer*, November 20, 1877, 3.

69. *Chicago Tribune*, March 30, 1879.

70. "Sporting Matters," *Lowell (Mass.) Daily Citizen*, March 27, 1879; "Amusement Notes," *Harrisburg Daily Independent*, March 28, 1879, 1.

71. "Room For The Women," *Syracuse Daily Courier*, May 13, 1879; "Women at the Bat," *New Brunswick (N.J.) Daily Times*, July 11, 1879, 3.

72. "Red and Blue Legs: A High Old Game of Base Ball By Eighteen Women," *Washington Post*, May 12, 1879, 1.

73. *Chicago Tribune*, March 30, 1879, 10.

74. James William Beul, *Mysteries and Miseries of America's Great Cities: Embracing New York, Washington City, San Francisco, Salt Lake City, and New Orleans* (St. Louis and Philadelphia, 1883). Google Books.

75. "NYSPCC People's Brief." The *Sporting Life* reported on April 22, 1891 that Wilson had lived with some of his underage team members during this period.

76. "Red and Blue Legs," 1; "Gotham Gossip: . . ." *New Orleans Times Picayune*, May 27, 1879, 2; Mary Callahan and "Theresa" were runaways. "Deluded Female Ball-Players," *Chicago Tribune*, May 27, 1879. Encouraging runaways was a lifelong pattern for Wilson, who was eventually imprisoned in Sing Sing, in Ossining, New York, for "abducting" a fifteen-year-old. See chapter 5.

77. "Baseball by Ladies," *New York Herald*, May 13, 1879, 10.

78. Uniforms described in "Electric Sparks," *Syracuse Daily Courier*, April 2, 1879. Wilson's claims are from an interview with the *San Antonio Daily Light*, January 29, 1886.

79. "Red and Blue Legs," 1.

80. Ibid.

81. Ibid.

82. Ibid.; "Baseball by Ladies," *New York Herald*, May 13, 1879, 10, and "Female Base Ball: The Latest Athletic Speculation . . ." *Buffalo Daily Courier*, May 15, 1879, 1.

83. "Red and Blue Legs," 1; "Room For The Women."

84. "The Ladies' Athletic Association: Why the Manager and Treasurer Were Put in Jail Yesterday," *New York Herald*, May 25, 1879, 8; "Christian Wilson, Abductor: Some Account of His Career—Near the End of His Rope," *New York Times*, August 16, 1891, 14.

85. Newspapers reported that players Kitty Byrnes (real name, Gracie Clinton) and Mary Callahan had gone to Wilson's lodging at the Hamilton House on May 19 to demand their wages. The pair had spent the previous night on the streets. Wilson offered them lodging for the night and promised their pay would be forthcoming. Instead, he and Powell seduced the young girls, who reported the incident to law enforcement. Two days after the arrest, Mary Callahan's aunt, and the mother of the right-fielder, identified only as "Theresa," appeared at the 57th Police Court to address truancy charges against the underage girls and to ask the court how they could prevent the young women from running away from home to play on Wilson's baseball teams. Callahan lived at 219 East 21st St., in the heart of New York City's "Tenderloin

District." "Theresa" ran away from an ostensibly respectable family on West 32nd St. Neither of the girls' ages are known, but the *New York Times* reported at Wilson's 1891 trial that some of the players on his 1879 team were fourteen and fifteen years old. "The Ladies' Athletic Association," 8; "Deluded Female Ball-Players," *New York Times*, June 10, 1879.

86. "NYSPCC People's Brief." Court of General Sessions appearance confirmed in Roll #41, Court of General Sessions Minutes, June 1879, p. 36. NYCMA. In a letter to Judge Cowing of the New York Court of General Sessions, written c. August 14, 1903, Wilson claimed that District Attorney Phelps had dropped these charges when he became convinced that the charges stemmed from a case of blackmail by one of the player's aunts. See Wilson court records for August 1903, NYCMA.

87. "Women Base Ballists: Abandoned by Their Manager. A Midnight Concert in Philadelphia—Story of their Wrongs—Working Their Way Homeward by Playing on the Route," *Cleveland Plain-Dealer*, August 19, 1879, 1. Though the young woman never directly names Wilson or Powell as team managers, it is unlikely that there were any other female baseball teams in New York City in May 1879 beside their teams. The young woman may have joined the troupe later and played in only one of its six games.

88. For details on the NL reserve rule, see Morris, Section 18.2.1, "Reserve Rule/Clause" in *A Game of Inches: The Story Behind the Innovations That Shaped Baseball* (Chicago: Ivan R. Dee, 2010), 465–67.

89. "The World of Sports," *Daily Alta California*, October 7, 1879, 8.

90. Advertisement, *New Orleans Times*, May 27 and June 1, 1879.

91. "Base Ball: Gossip About the Patrons of the Bat and Ball," *New Orleans Times*, May 1, 1879; "Base Ball," *New Orleans Times*, May 28, 1879.

92. Concerned by the frequent epidemics caused by New Orleans's notoriously poor sanitation system, physicians and local businessmen formed the New Orleans Auxiliary Sanitary Association in 1879 to promote private funding of public sanitation projects. Craig E. Colten, *An Unnatural Metropolis: Wresting New Orleans from Nature* (Baton Rouge: Louisiana State University Press, 2006), 47–54.

93. "Base-Ball: Items of Interest About the National Game," *New Orleans Times*, June 8, 1879.

94. "The Lady Players: Public Appearance of the Female Base Ball Parties," *New Orleans Times*, June 14, 1879; "A Way to Spend the Sabbath," *New Orleans Daily Picayune*, June 16, 1879; "Local news: . . . The Lady Nines: A Day of Novel Sport at the Fair Grounds—a Mule Race with Female Riders—Women of the Bat and Ball," *New Orleans Times*, June 16, 1879.

95. "The Marvelous Lady Nine: The Attraction at the Fair Grounds Next Sunday, and the Street Parade Today," *New Orleans Times*, June 13, 1879; "Licensed or Unlicensed?" *New Orleans Daily Picayune*, June 15, 1879. The papers that endorsed the event were the *Times*, the *Democrat*, the *City Item*, and the *German Gazette*. The *Daily Picayune* refused.

96. *New Orleans Times*, June 16, 1879.

97. "The Sequel: The Incidents that Followed the Festivities at the Fair Grounds—Demands for Payments That Could Not be Met—Ruffianism, Rowdyism and Robbery Wind Up the Night, 'Till the Grounds are Cleared by the Police," *New Orleans Times*, June 17, 1879.

98. *Daily Picayune*, June 17 and 20, 1879.

99. "Base Ball," *Philadelphia Inquirer*, June 24, 1879, 2.

100. The associates were: W. S. Moore, advance agent; Harry Morris, manager; John Walsh, contracting agent; Chas. Dooley, umpire; W. S. Fox, treasurer. Nothing further is known about the men; the names may be aliases. "Something About the Red Stockings and Blue Stockings: A Novel Amusement—Organization of the Nines; etc.," *Fort Wayne Sentinel*, August 19, 1879, 4.

101. "Crowd at Oakdale: A Game of Base Ball Between Female Clubs," *Philadelphia Inquirer*,

July 5, 1879, 2. "Remarkable Scene at a Game of Base-ball Played by Variety Actresses," *Chicago Tribune*, July 5, 1879, 5B.

102. "Local Matters: Women at the Bat—A Base Ball Burlesque in Baltimore," *Baltimore Sun*, July 8, 1879, 1. Only 250 individuals attended the follow-on game. "Local Matters: More Female Base Ball," *Baltimore Sun*, July 9, 1879, 4; "Washington: Beats Congress," *Cincinnati Enquirer*, July 10, 1879, 1; "Letter From Washington: The Female Base-Ballists . . ." *Baltimore Sun*, July 10, 1879, 4.

103. "Women Base Ballists: Abandoned by Their Manager. A Midnight Concert in Philadelphia—Story of their Wrongs—Working Their Way Homeward by Playing on the Route," *Cleveland Plain-Dealer*, August 19, 1879, 1.

104. Ibid.

105. Schedule based on contemporary newspaper articles including: "Women at the Bat," *New Brunswick Daily Times*, July 11, 1879, 3; "Sporting Notes: The Female Base Ballists," *Jersey City Evening Journal*, July 14, 1879, 4; "Female Ball Players: Novel Methods They Employ in Interpreting the National Game," *New Haven (Conn.) Register*, July 16, 1879, 1; "Female Base Ball: Some Runs in the Rain," *Providence Journal*, July 17, 1879.

106. "Crowd at Oakdale," *Philadelphia Inquirer*, July 5, 1879, 2.

107. "Female Base Ballists: Game at New Haven Breaks Up in a Row," *Boston Daily Globe*, July 15, 1879, 2; "Female Base Ball Players: A Disgraceful Scene in New Haven," *New York Herald*, July 15, 1879, 8. "Female Base Ball Players," *Hartford Daily Courant*, July 16, 1879, 4.

108. "The Ball Field," *Worcester (Mass.) Daily Spy*, August 6, 1879, 4.

109. *Hagerstown (Md.) Herald and Torch*, July 16, 1879, 2.

110. "Letter From Washington: The Female Base-Ballists . . ." *Baltimore Sun*, July 10, 1879, 4; "Editorial," *Washington Post*, July 10, 1879, 2.

111. Schedule created from contemporary newspaper reports.

112. "Sporting Matters: Base Ball," *Springfield (Mass.) Republican*, August 6, 1879, 4; "Base Ball: The Female Players Come to Grief Again," *New Haven Evening Register*, August 6, 1879, 1.

113. "The Female Players and Their Troubles—Notes of the Game," *New Haven Register*, August 7, 1879, 4. There is evidence that Sylvester Wilson was associated with the teams. Though Gilmore claimed the teams were distinct from Wilson's, the *Chicago Tribune* of July 5, 1879, named him as manager. Subsequent articles in September and October mentioned a manager "Frankhouse" (a possible Wilson alias) and manager "U.S. Franklin" (a known Wilson alias). "Ohio News," *Decatur Daily Review*, September 22, 1879, 2; "The World of Sports," *Daily Alta California*, October 7, 1879, 8.

114. "Reds and Blues: The Way the Women With the Stockings Burlesqued Base Ball," *Buffalo Morning Express*, August 15, 1879, 2.

115. "Berkshire County: Pittsfield," *Springfield Republican*, August 8, 1879, 2.

116. The account of the men's deaths was reported across the country as far west as California. The Cleveland paper that broke the story recanted the next day, reporting that all five had made it to shore after their sailboat capsized. "Five Men Meet Death: A Boat Capsizes in the Neighborhood of the Water Works Crib and Five Souls are Lost," *Cleveland Plain-Dealer*, August 15, 1879, 1; "Still in the Land of the Living," *Cleveland Plain Dealer* (Evening), August 16, 1879, 1. The *Jackson Citizen Patriot* of August 16, 1879, asserted that the men's ordeal proved that people should not attend female baseball games.

117. "Louisville," *Cincinnati Enquirer*, August 26, 1879, 2.

118. "Springfield . . . Fatal Row at a Base-Ball Game . . .," *Cincinnati Daily Enquirer*, September 2, 1879; "Baseball Notes," *New York Clipper*, September 13, 1879; "Ohio News," *Decatur Daily Review*, September 22, 1879, 2.

119. "A Different Story About the Female Base Bawlers," *Wheeling (W. Va.) Register* (September 5, 1879), 4; "'Busted' Female Ball Players: Three Girls Who Have Doubtless Had Enough of the 'National Game,'" *Harrisburg Daily Independent,* September 6, 1879, 4; "The National Girls: Remnants of Broken Female Base Ball Clubs," *Rocky Mountain News,* September 28, 1879, 12.

120. See, for example, "New York Female Base Ball Enthusiasts," *Sporting Life,* August 12, 1885, 2.

121. "The Female Muffers in St. Louis," *St Louis Globe-Democrat,* September 19, 1875, 6.

122. "Sporting Notes: Baseball," *Detroit Post and Tribune,* August 18, 1879, 4.

123. *St. Louis Globe-Democrat,* April 6, 1879, 13.

124. "Local Matters: Women at the Bat—A Base Ball Burlesque in Baltimore," *Baltimore Sun,* July 8, 1879, 4.

Chapter 4. Molding Manly Men and Disappearing Women

1. *Appletons' Annual Cyclopaedia and Register of Important Events of the Year 1885,* Vol. 10 (New York, 1886): 77.

2. "It is a Woman's Game," *Pittsburg Dispatch* September 23, 1889, 5. The article is quoting Sylvester F. Wilson as he seeks to convince the public that his female baseball troupe is a respectable operation.

3. Rader describes the state of the professional game in his introduction to Sullivan, *Early Innings,* xvii.

4. Quoted in Thorn, *Baseball in the Garden,* 231.

5. Robert Elias, *The Empire Strikes Out: How Baseball Sold U.S. Foreign Policy and Promoted the American Way Abroad* (New York: New Press, 2010), 21–26. Elias highlights the racism and jingoism of participants and the media.

6. *Sporting Life,* February 6, 1889, 3.

7. Elias, *Empire Strikes Out,* 25.

8. Alan H. Levy, "Jim Crows of a Feather: A Comparison of the Segregation and Desegregation Eras in Professional Baseball and Football," in William M. Simons, ed., *The Cooperstown Symposium on Baseball and American Culture* (Jefferson, N.C.: McFarland, 2002), 156–57.

9. Ibid., 155–56.

10. Beginning in the 1890s with Lizzie Arlington and continuing well into the twentieth century, talented female athletes like Alta Weiss, Jackie Mitchell, and Elizabeth Murphy were sometimes hired to play for men's minor league or semiprofessional teams.

11. The term "disappeared" when used of female baseball players evokes a magician's slight-of-hand trickery when objects are made to seem as if they are no longer present. Jean Allman applies this concept to gender history in "The Disappearing of Hannah Kudjoe: Nationalism, Feminism, and the Tyrannies of History," *Journal of Women's History* 21, no. 3, (2009): 13–35. Allman describes how Ghanaian officials removed all trace of Hannah Kudjoe's active role in founding the nation from public records and archives. As my research demonstrates, female baseball players were always right in front of the collective "us" in each generation, yet somehow their story was simultaneously "disappeared" as "we" watched.

12. This chapter describes some of the professional women's teams that competed with men's teams for spectators' leisure dollars, but women were not the only ones peddling novel baseball games. See, for example, "Chinese Ball Players," *Watertown (N.Y.) Daily Times,* April 21, 1883, 1; *New York Clipper,* December 29, 1883, 693; *Marquette (Mich.) Daily Mining Journal,* August 22, 1889, 8; *Sporting Life,* August 1, 1891, 12. Black minstrel troupes routinely challenged locals to baseball matches as a way to attract spectators to their shows. Lynn Abbott and Doug Seroff,

Out of Sight: The Rise of African American Popular Music, 1889–1895 (Jackson: University Press of Mississippi, 2009), 65. Thanks to Heather Cooper for this reference.

13. Each issue included circulation numbers.

14. "Notes and Comments," *Sporting Life,* August 20, 1883, 7.

15. Details on Wilson's teams and Richter's response to them appear later in the chapter.

16. Two clubs dropped out of the NL after the first year, and the league fielded only six clubs in 1877 and 1878. (Three of the six teams in the NL in 1878 had not been members in 1877). It was not until the 1882 season that the league fielded the same eight teams it had fielded the previous year. In 1883, two of those eight teams dropped out and were replaced with two new teams. http://www.baseball-reference.com/.

17. Names of clubs in the American Association (1882–1891) and Union Association are available at Baseball-Reference.com. The AA expanded to eight teams in 1883 and thirteen teams in 1884; it generally had eight teams. The UA lasted only one season.

18. Mark Sheldon, "American Association Remembered," www.m.reds.mlb.com/news/article/1940267/. Cites research by David Nemec for "The Beer and Whiskey League: The Illustrated History of the American Association—Baseball's Renegade Major League."

19. From its inception, NL team owners had agreed to honor one another's blacklists. Team owners regularly colluded to set fees for uniforms and travel expenses and to regulate player wages. Morris, *A Game of Inches,* Section 18.2.2, "Blacklists;" Section 18.2.3, "National Agreement," 467–68.

20. Ibid., Section 18.3.1, "Unions," 468–69.

21. *Utica Morning Herald,* September 17, 1875.

22. *Chicago Tribune,* June 2, 1878. The paper quotes "a wandering newspaper from Oswego, New York."

23. John M. Ward, *Base-Ball: How To Become a Player; With the Origin, History and Explanation of the Game* (Philadelphia, 1888). The information cited here is from: "The Origin of Base-ball: From Advance Sheets of John M. Ward's 'Base-ball,' (Athletic Pub. Co.)," *Publishers' Weekly* 33, no. 852 (May 26, 1888): 812.

24. See citations for same sources in chapter 1.

25. Introduction to Ward, *Base-Ball,* Library of Alexandria Online Preview, Google Books.

26. *Freeborn County (Minn.) Standard,* September 15, 1870, 7. Quip also appeared in "Gleanings," *Waterloo (Iowa) Courier,* September 15, 1870, 3, although this version stated that the "mother" had the big switch.

27. "Jottings," *Harrisburg Daily Telegraph,* June 18, 1878, 4.

28. *New Orleans Daily Picayune,* June 16, 1879.

29. "Notes and News," *Cincinnati Enquirer,* August 4, 1879, 8.

30. *Fort Worth Weekly Gazette,* August 10, 1889, 4.

31. *Denver Evening Post,* July 20, 1897, 4.

32. See, for example: *Jamestown (N.Y.) Journal,* September 16, 1870, 7; "Personal," *Titusville (Pa.) Herald,* September 20, 1870, 4; "Items of Interest," *Glenwood (Iowa) Opinion,* September 24, 1870, 1; "Chit Chat," *Syracuse Daily Standard,* September 24, 1870, 1; "Tea Table Gossip," *Utica Daily Observer,* October 4, 1870; "Editorial Clips and Nips," *Minnesotan-Herald,* October 15, 1870, 4; "New Lisbon, Ohio," *Arkansas Morning Republican,* October 17, 1870, 3; *Lafayette Monthly* (Paper of Lafayette College in Easton, Pa.), July 1871, 412.

33. Gender marking is generally associated with how words in different languages have feminine and masculine connotations. Gender marking can also be visual. See Margaret Carlisle Duncan and Michael Messner, "The Media Image of Sport and Gender," in *Media Sport,* ed., Lawrence A. Wenner (London and New York: Routledge, 1998), 170–85.

34. "A Brief History of Baseball Cards," http://www.cycleback.com/1800s/briefhistory.htm.

35. For detailed information on American tobacco cards, see Robert Forbes and Terence Mitchell, *American Tobacco Cards: Price Guide and Checklist* (Richmond, Va.: Tuff Stuff Books, 1999).

36. "Female Baseballists: Their Pictures Cause a Small Sensation; How the Pictures Are Used to Advertise Cigarettes—What Mayor Hillyer Says—Stories About the Cigarette Makers—What the Pictures Cost—Immense Sales of The, Etc.," *Atlanta Constitution,* July 16, 1886, 7; "A Craze for Photographs: Pictures of Pretty Scenes and Prominent Places in Great Demand," *Logansport (Ind.) Pharos,* February 10, 1887, 2; Reprinted in: "A Craze for Photographs," *Fitchburg (Mass.) Sentinel,* April 16, 1887, 5.

37. A photograph of the complete set of the S.W. Venable cards plus background information on the cards appears on the Legendary Auctions Web site. See Lot #1256. http://www.legendary auctions.com/LotDetail.aspx ?inventoryid=122030&searchby=0&searchvalue=None&page= 0&sortby=0&displayby=2&lotsperpage=100&category=30&seo=1892–94-N360-Venable -Female-%22Baseball-Scenes%22-Tobacco-Cards-SGC-Graded-Collection-%2812-Different %29-Inc.

38. "The Modern Nude in Art: A Recent Craze in Boston for Posing Undraped Before the Camera of the Photographer," *St. Paul Daily Globe,* July 10, 1887, 20; "The Vanity of the Fair: Mania of Beautiful Boston Belles; They Pose Before the Camera in Art's Economy of Costume as Nymphs, Psyches and Venuses for Photographs," *Galveston (Tex.) Daily News,* July 10, 1887, 8.

39. Ibid.

40. "All Around Town," *Buffalo Daily Courier,* June 21, 1886; "War on the Obscene," *Auburn (N.Y.) Sunday Dispatch,* December 26, 1886, 1.

41. *National Police Gazette,* July 18, 1885.

42. Allegheny College Archives, Wayne and Sally Merrick Historic Archival Center, Pelletier Library, Allegheny College.

43. "A Last Resort," *Puck,* July 28, 1886, 343. The poet is likely Horace S. Keller.

44. *The Great Match, and Other Matches* was originally published anonymously in 1877 and has been incorrectly attributed to John Townsend Trowbridge according to sport historians Trey and Geri Strecker. They attribute it to Mary Prudence Wells Smith (1840–1930). See *The Great Match and Our Base Ball Club: Two Novels from the Early Days of Base Ball* (McFarland Historical Baseball Library). Google Books.

45. Smith, *Great Match,* 47–48.

46. Ibid., 41.

47. *Titusville Herald,* September 5, 1887, 3.

48. "The Maiden Base Ballist," *Saginaw (Mich.) Evening News,* August 5, 1889, 5.

49. "Notes and Gossip," *Sporting Life,* August 16, 1889, 4.

50. "Personal," *Ogdensburg (N.Y.) Daily Journal,* July 23, 1890.

51. *Chicago Tribune,* March 21, 1880. The existence of a female baseball club in Iowa City had been reported in the *Cedar Rapids Times* on July 31, 1879.

52. In October 1879, for example, the *Weekly Louisianian,* an African American paper, printed a letter from a D.C. correspondent who reported that he and a group of men (including Frederick Douglass Jr.) had thoroughly enjoyed playing in a game pitting married men against single men. The game had been publicized in advance and the grandstand was "gay with the Sisters, Cousins and Aunts of the combatants" who showered the victorious singles with flowers. "Washington. From an Occasional Correspondent," *Weekly Louisianian,* October 11, 1879, 1.

53. "New York Female Base Ball Enthusiasts," *Sporting Life,* August 12, 1885, 2.

54. Connie Mack, *My 66 Years in the Big Leagues: The Great Story of America's National Game* (Philadelphia: John C. Winston, 1950), 134. Mack began his career in 1886.

55. "New York Female Base Ball Enthusiasts." Richter obviously knew about female baseball players because he regularly reported on Wilson's professional teams and, as a newspaperman, he must have read others' accounts of female school, college, civic, and pick-up teams.

56. Hunter, *How Young Ladies Became Girls,* 237.

57. "[Akron] 'Beacon' Letters: Tallmadge," *Summit County (Ohio) Beacon,* June 10, 1885, 3; "Our Girls Are Just Great," *Alton (Ill.) Daily Telegraph,* August 13, 1889, 4. It is uncertain whether the players on the Fendle Mound Company team were men or women or whether the game took place.

58. "Noteworthy Contests of 1883," *New York Clipper,* December 29, 1883, 693; "Good Girls vs. Good Boys," *Honolulu Saturday Press,* January 12, 1884, 4; *Wichita Globe,* March 18, 1887, 4.

59. Journal of Evelyn Jean Forman, April 27, 1880, Evelyn Jean Forman 1883 papers, SCA.

60. "Our Nine," Mary H. A. Mather Memory Book, May 8, 1880 entry. Mary H. A. Mather 1883 papers, SCA.

61. Ibid.

62. Letter from Mabel Allen to her mother, May 6, 1880. SCA. On April 7, 1880, Allen had written to her mother that she was friends with "Max" Taylor, "Bobbie" Robbins, and "May" Rice and that she might room with Taylor and Rice the next year. All three women played on one of the two Hubbard House teams in the spring of 1880.

63. Mather Memory Book. SCA.

64. Stephens' account. SCA.

65. The *Class Book* of 1886 gives each player's name and a brief vignette about her. "Fourth Chronicle," *Class Book Containing Class Day and Woodbine Exercises, Mt. Holyoke, 86* (Springfield, Mass.: Cyrus W. Atwood, 1886), 23–25. Mount Holyoke College Library and Archives (MHCLA).

66. "Items in Brief," *Quincy (Ill.) Daily Herald,* May 7, 1882, 4.

67. "Noteworthy Contests of 1883"; "Female Ball Players: How They Knocked Luke Kenney All Over the Diamond," *Brooklyn Daily Eagle,* July 23, 1889, 6.

68. "North Denver Notes," *Rocky Mountain News,* June 8, 1884, 4; "Items of News," *Boston Investigator,* October 15, 1884, 6; *St. Paul Daily Globe,* September 2, 1885; David Nevar's research on townball includes information on Anne Marie Boren Bigelow (b. 1873, Utah) who recalled playing townball with childhood friends. "Town Ball," http://webpages.charter.net/joekuras/townball2.htm.

69. "Brief Mention," *Bismarck Daily Tribune,* November 17, 1886, 1; "Flashes From the Diamond," *Rochester Democrat and Chronicle,* August 12, 1888, 7; "Base Ball Bites," *San Antonio Daily Light,* April 12, 1889, 1. A number of barnstorming female baseball teams played games in Texas before 1889, but this is the first known example of female residents of Texas contemplating their own team. It is uncertain whether the team was formed.

70. *Emmet County (Iowa) Republican,* June 27, 1889. The back of the team photograph has the handwritten name of the team plus the dates September 14, 1886 and January 5, 1887, and the printed name and location of the photographer—J. R. McGarrity. Photo from the collection of Joann Kline.

71. *Fort Worth Daily Gazette,* August 10, 1889, 4. "North and Northwest," *Atchison Daily Champion,* May 28, 1889, 2; "Base Ball Extraordinary," *McPherson (Kans.) Daily Republican,* July 30, 1889, 3; *McPherson Daily Republican,* July 31, 1889, 2–3; *Wichita Daily Journal,* August 1, 1889, 1; *McPherson Daily Republican,* August 1, 1889, 3; *McPherson Daily Republican,* August 6, 1889, 3; *Thomas County Cat* (Colby, Kans.), August 15, 1889, 5.

72. "Kansas State News," *Nicodemus Cyclone*, July 13, 1888, 2.

73. "Married vs. Single Ladies at Base Ball," *Kalamazoo Gazette*, September 26, 1886, 3; *New York Clipper*, October 2, 1886, 457.

74. Untitled, *Titusville Herald*, September 5, 1887, 3; *Mount Kisco (N.Y.) Recorder*, April 13, 1888, 2; "Utica's Female Base Ball Club," *Utica Daily Observer*, May 4, 1888, 8; "Dew Drops and Rainbow Flies," *Boston Globe*, May 4, 1888, 5; "Base Hits," *Lowell (Mass.) Daily Courier*, May 5, 1888; *Utica Weekly Observer*, May 8, 1888; "Sweet Things in Base Ball Costume," *Omaha Daily Bee*, May 14, 1888, 4; "Local and Miscellaneous," *Sodus (N.Y.) Alliance*, May 16, 1888; "Village and Vicinity," *Clinton (N.Y.) Courier*, May 16, 1888, 1; *Atchison Daily Globe*, May 19, 1888, 2; "Vicinity," *Watkins (N.Y) Democrat*, July 19, 1888.

75. "Base Ball Matters," *Manistee (Mich.) Democrat*, July 19, 1889, 1.

76. "Baltimore Girls Play Ball," *Kansas City Star*, October 3, 1889, 4.

77. "Pahn Lee's Ball Nine: Young Ladies Play in It, and There is Nothing Nicer in Norwich," *Boston Daily Globe*, August 16, 1886, 6. The Norwich City Directory lists Rudd's occupation as "farmer."

78. "Pahn Lee's Ball Nine," 6; See also, *Sporting Life*, August 25, 1886, 5.

79. Dolly Varden was a character in Charles Dickens's novel, *Barnaby Rudge* (1835) and also referred to a type of brightly colored dress popular in the 1870s. John Thorn identifies Lang as the originator of the black women's teams in *Baseball in the Garden*, 193.

80. "Baseball: The Washington and Philadelphia Nines Defeated," *New York Times*, September 13, 1882.

81. "Female Base Ballists: A Game That Did Not Come Off; Scenes at Lamokin Woods," *Chester (Pa.) Times*, May 18, 1883, 3. "Miss Harris's Base-Ball Nine: Dusky Dolly Vardens of Chester Give an Exhibition," *New York Times*, May 18, 1883, 1; "A Novel Game of Base Ball Between Teams of Colored Girls," *New Brunswick (N.J.) Daily Times*, May 30, 1883, 1.

82. Wilson operated female baseball teams almost continuously between August 1883 and November 1886 and then again between 1889 and 1891. After his release from prison in August 1898 he organized another team in May 1899. Wilson was imprisoned again between August 1899 and 1900 for immoral behavior. In January 1903 he began advertising for investors in another female baseball (and basketball) troupe. He was arrested again in June and sentenced to nine years in Sing prison; he died in the state mental institution for prisoners. See chapter 5 for details.

83. "Notes and Comments," *Sporting Life*, May 20, 1885, 7.

84. This number was determined by scouring the rosters of hundreds of newspaper articles about Wilson's team. Note that this number represents the *minimum* number of girls Wilson hired. Most articles did not name players. Additionally, the number only represents baseball players—dozens of girls and young women traveled with Wilson's troupe as part of his "Female Cadets" and drill companies who are rarely identified in newspapers.

85. "Base Ball Belles," *Camden (N.J.) Post*, August 29, 1883, 1; "Victorious Blondes," *Auburn (N.Y.) News and Bulletin*, September 21, 1883, 1; "Angelic Batters," *Eau Claire (Wisc.) News*, October 6, 1883, 2.

86. The National League generally charged fifty cents for games, hoping that higher ticket prices would draw a more gentile audience. Wilson experimented with different pricing schemes throughout the season but generally kept prices low.

87. "Female Ball Tossers: Freeman & Howard, of Philadelphia, Will Play Two Female Base Ball Nines at League Park in October—A Novelty on the Diamond Which Will Attract a Big Crowd." *Fort Wayne (Ind.) Daily Gazette*, August 20, 1883, 7; "The City," *Fort Wayne Daily Sentinel*, September 15, 1883, 3; "Sporting Snaps," *South Bend (Ind.) Evening Register*, Sep-

tember 15, 1883, 5; "Notes and Comments," *Sporting Life,* September 24, 1883, 6; "On the Fly," *Sporting Life,* October 15, 1883, 6; "Notes and Comments," *Sporting Life,* November 14, 1883, 3; unnamed St. Louis paper, c. November 1883; "Local Miscellany: Brevities," *Quincy Daily Whig,* November 27, 1883, 8.

88. Text is from a large illustrated advertisement that appeared in the *Philadelphia Record* on September 10, 1883. The same ad, minus the illustration appeared in the *Philadelphia Ledger* on the same date. Similar ads were repeated in most cities that the troupe visited. See, for example, *Worcester (Mass.) Daily Spy,* September 28, 1883, 2.

89. "Blondes and Brunettes at Baseball," *New York Tribune,* September 23, 1883, 2.

90. *Philadelphia Record,* August 31, 1883; Philadelphia Press, August 31, 1883, 5.

91. *Philadelphia Record,* September 2, 1883, 4. "The Ladies Base Ball Club: They Play Another Exhibition Game at City Hall Park," *Camden Post,* September 4, 1883, 1.

92. "Feminine Ball Tossers: How the Quaker City Girls Handle the Bat on the Diamond Field," *Chester Times,* September 7, 1883, 3; "Won By the Blondes: How They Figured on the Diamond at the Oriole Festival," *St. Louis Globe-Democrat,* September 13, 1883, 4.

93. The 42,000 figure is determined by adding the average of 1,500 spectators for the twenty-three games with available statistics to the remaining five games for which no statistics are available.

94. "Notes and Comments," *Sporting Life,* September 10, 1883, 7; *Sporting Life,* September 24, 1883, 3; "Notes and Comments," *Sporting Life,* September 24, 1883, 6.

95. "Beauty at the Bat: Feminines on the Base Ball Field," *Cleveland Plain Dealer,* November 1, 1883, 1.

96. "On the Fly," *Sporting Life,* December 19, 1883, 3.

97. "Base Ball: Girls and Base Ball; A Girlish Description of a Game by Girls; An Umpire in White Lawn—A Home Plate Concealed by the Catcher's Petticoats, Etc.," *Sporting Life,* September 10, 1892, 11. Reprinted from the *Boston Globe,* the article was written by Dorothy Thurston, one of the players.

98. "Radiant Richmond: Satisfied That Lancaster is the Only Club to Be Feared," *Sporting Life,* July 23, 1898, 17. See chapter 5 for more about Arlington.

99. "Important," *Markdale (Ontario, Can.) Standard,* December 25, 1883, 2.

100. "Notes and Comments," *Sporting Life,* January 30, 1884, 3; *New York Clipper,* April 12, 1884, 63.

101. *New York Clipper,* April 12, 1884, 63.

102. "Base Ball Notes," *Cleveland Herald,* April 11, 1884, 3; "General Sporting Notes," *Quincy Daily Journal,* April 16, 1884, 3.

103. *Sporting Life,* May 28, 1884. Everett initially invested $8, adding $23 on May 28 despite claiming that he had not received one-fourth of the profits Wilson had promised for his services.

104. "Notes and Comments," *Sporting Life,* April 9, 1884, 5.

105. "Did Not Appear," *Chester Times,* May 6, 1884, 4; "In and About South Chester," *Chester Times,* May 7, 1884, 3; *Poughkeepsie Daily Eagle,* May 12, 1884, 2. The article refers to "Rondout" as game site. Rondout had been a port on the Hudson River that served Kingston; it merged with Kingston in 1872.

106. *Poughkeepsie Daily Eagle,* May 12, 1884, 2.

107. "The Female Base Ball Club," *Poughkeepsie Daily Eagle,* May 18, 1884, 3; *Jersey Journal,* May 21, 1884, 1.

108. "Notes and Comments," *Sporting Life,* May 28, 1884, 7.

109. "General News," *Syracuse Daily Journal,* May 20, 1884, 1; "Notes About Town," *The North American,* May 21, 1884; "Notes," *Cincinnati Commercial Tribune,* May 28, 1884, 3.

110. "Notes and Comments," *Sporting Life,* May 28, 1884, 7.

111. "Bulletined News," *Auburn (N.Y.) News and Bulletin*, June 6, 1884, 4; "Female Base Ballists," *Oswego (N.Y.) Palladium*, June 9, 1884; untitled, *Atchison Globe*, June 9, 1884.

112. *Atchison Globe*, June 9, 1884.

113. "Female Ball Players in a Plight," *New York Times*, July 8, 1884, 5; "Female Ball Players Stranded," *Chicago Daily Tribune*, July 8, 1884, 6; "Girl Baseball Players: Eighteen Philadelphia Blondes and Brunettes Starving in Baltimore," *Atlanta Constitution*, July 9, 1884, 3; "Notes and Comments," *Sporting Life*, July 16, 1884, 6.

114. *St. Paul Daily Globe*, September 7, 1884, 15.

115. "Female Base Ballists," *Lebanon (Pa.) Daily News*, October 6, 1884, 4; "Young Women at the Bat: They Play a Game of Ball with the Merritts—A Disappointed Crowd," *Lebanon Daily News*, October 10, 1884, 4.

116. "Female Ball Players in Trouble," *The North American*, October 16, 1884; "Base Ball Notes," *Lancaster (Pa.) Daily Intelligencer*, October 16, 1884, 2; *Sporting Life*, October 22, 1884; *New York Clipper*, October 25, 1884, 508.

117. It is uncertain whether the game in Maryland was ever played. Both D.C. games were played. "A Ladies' B. B. C. Desires to Play the Mountain City, *Frederick (Md.) Weekly News*, October 18, 1884, 5; *New York Clipper*, November 1, 1884, 524; *Sporting Life*, November 5, 1884; "Sports and Pastimes," *Salt Lake City Herald*, November 16, 1884, 11.

118. "The Weldon Fair," *Wilson (N.C.) Advance*, November 14, 1884, 3.

119. *New Orleans Daily Picayune*, December 20, 1884, 8; "The Female Nine at Jackson," *Daily Picayune*, December 24, 1884, 8; "The Female Nine in Town," *Daily Picayune*, December 26, 1884, 5 and 8; "The Female Nine," *Daily Picayune*, December 27, 1884, 8; *Times-Picayune*, December 28, 1884, 4.

120. *Sporting Life*, November 26, 1884.

121. "The Female Tramps: Disgraceful Conduct of the Girl Players in Georgia," *Sporting Life*, December 24, 1884, 5.

122. *New Orleans Daily Picayune*, January 3, 1885, 4; "Base Ball: At Sportsmen's Park," *Daily Picayune*, January 4, 1885, 14; "Base Ball: The League Clubs Keep Out of the Rain But the Females Play," *Daily Picayune*, January 5, 1885, morning edition, 8.

123. *Galveston Daily News*, March 7, 1885, 3.

124. "The Female Nines," *New Orleans Daily Picayune*, January 12, 1885), morning edition, 1; *New York Clipper*, January 24, 1885, 716.

125. Wilson-Giles Divorce Records. Sworn testimony of Kate F. (Giles) Wilson and Maria M. Giles (Kate's mother) to investigator Richard T. Miller, January 3, 1888. NYSA.

126. *New York Clipper*, March 21, 1885, 10.

127. "Palestine," *Galveston Daily News*, April 22, 1885, 4; "The State Capital . . .," *Galveston Daily News*, April 25, 1885, 5; Rays of Light: Gathered by Reporters on Their Tours Through Town," *San Antonio Light*, April 25, 1885, 4; *Galveston Daily News*, April 28, 1885, 8; "Bayou City Locals . . .," *Galveston Daily News*, May 1, 1885, 6. "Texarkana . . ." *Daily Arkansas Gazette*, May 6, 1885, 4; *New York Clipper*, May 23, 1885, 147.

128. Ibid; "Notes and Comments: Memphis Notes," *Sporting Life*, May 27, 1885, 7.

129. Details on the travels of the 1885 troupe were compiled from contemporary newspaper articles. Wilson claimed that his 1885 team had traveled six thousand miles and played three hundred games in 275 cities. *Kansas City Star*, November 7, 1885.

130. "Longs For the Field: An Indianapolis Maiden Leaves Her Home to Join the Female Base Ball Club," *Fort Wayne Sentinel*, July 2, 1885, 4; "The Darlings Done Up: The Nine Muses Suffer an Ignominious Defeat at the Driving Park," *Kalamazoo Gazette*, August 1, 1885, 3; "They Can't Throw," *Wisconsin State Journal*, August 28, 1885, 4; "Friday's Baseball Match," *Eau Claire Daily Free Press*, August 29, 1885, 3.

131. "The Female Combination," *Freeport (Ill.) Journal-Standard,* September 18, 1885, 4.

132. The few rosters available for the 1885 season indicate that both May Lawrence and Pearl Emerson played on the reorganized 1885 team. Players Florence Elliot and Viola Temple may have been the Polly Elliot and Nina Temple, who had played for Wilson in 1884.

133. "Female Acrobats," *Omaha Daily Bee,* October 19, 1885, 8. The reporter described separate eating, sleeping, and exercise areas in the railcar. The troupe carried dumbbells and Indian clubs for those who enjoyed gymnastic exercises.

134. "Longs For the Field: An Indianapolis Maiden Leaves Her Home to Join the Female Base Ball Club," *Fort Wayne Sentinel,* July 2, 1885, 4; "City News," *Fort Wayne Daily Gazette,* August 19, 1885, 6.

135. In late September 1885, one group of players stayed in Davenport, Iowa, while the rest headed for a game in Cedar Rapids. They reunited in Clinton. "Davenport Briefs," *Davenport Daily Gazette,* September 29, 1885, 2; Emile Gargh was managing one of Wilson's teams at this point. On October 30, the troupe's "first nine," augmented by some men, played a game in Atchison, Kansas, while the "second nine" played in Severance. "Female Ball Tossers," *Kansas City Times,* November 2, 1885, 2.

136. "Served Them Right," *Orangeburg (S.C) Times and Democrat,* July 15, 1886, 1; "Girls in the Game: Lithe-Limbed Lassies at the Bat and Ball," *St. Paul Daily Globe,* August 30, 1885, 3; *Janesville (Wisc.) Daily Gazette,* September 14, 1885, 4.

137. "Local Baseball Notes," *Milwaukee Sentinel,* August 16, 1885, 7.

138. "Oconto," *Oshkosh (Wisc.) Daily Northwestern,* August 21, 1885, 3.

139. *Milwaukee Sentinel,* August 16, 1885, 7; "Facing the Girls . . ." *Milwaukee Sentinel,* August 17, 1885, 5.

140. *Oshkosh Daily Northwestern,* August 24, 1885, 4; "Facing Powder and Ball: Waukesha Belles and Female Batters Meet the Militia," *Milwaukee Daily Journal,* August 26, 1885, 1; "First Regiment Encampment," *Milwaukee Sentinel,* August 27, 1885, 8; "Gov. Rusk Visits the Camp: Complimenting the First Regiment of National Guard," *Milwaukee Daily Journal,* August 27, 1885, 1; "They Can't Throw," *Wisconsin State Journal,* August 28, 1885, 4; "Madison: Social Enjoyments of the Week at the State Capital—Personal Mention," *Milwaukee Sentinel,* August 30, 1885, 11; "Friday's Baseball Match," *Eau Claire Daily Free Press,* August 29, 1885, 3.

141. "Girls in the Game: Lithe-Limbed Lassies at the Bat and Ball," *St. Paul Daily Globe,* August 30, 1885, 3; "Baseball Among Girls," *Washington Post,* September 13, 1885, 6; "Girls Playing Base Ball," *Kansas City Times,* September 14, 1885, 2; "Girls Playing Base-ball: The Dear Creatures Win the Game and Display Great Science," *Syracuse Herald,* September 20, 1885, 5.

142. "Stillwater News: The Last Day of the Washington County Fair . . . Girl Ball Tossers," *St. Paul Daily Globe,* August 30, 1885, 6; "Stillwater News: The Fairies of the Field Defeated by Stillwater Boys; Talk by a Street Gamin—Notes About Town, *St. Paul Daily Globe,* August 31 and September 1, 1885, 5.

143. "Burlesque Base Ball: Lady Players That Know Nothing About the Game," *St. Paul Daily Globe,* September 1, 1885, 2.

144. "Female Baseball Players: Whose Champion Play is Playing the Public for Suckers," *Daily Nebraska State Journal,* October 24, 1885, 7; "Female Base Ballers," *Omaha Daily Bee,* October 24, 1885, 5.

145. "In Financial Trouble," *Omaha Daily Bee,* October 24, 1885, 5.

146. "The Female Ball Tossers: *St. Joseph Gazette,*" *Kansas City Times,* November 2, 1885, 4; "Female Ball Tossers," *Kansas City Times,* November 2, 1885, 2; "Personal," *Atchison Daily Globe,* October 28, 30, and 31, 1885.

147. "Female Ball Tossers," *Kansas City Times,* November 2, 1885, 2; "An Advance Agent Arrested: An Attache of the Female Base Ball Organization in Trouble," *Kansas City Star,*

November 2, 1885, 2; "Female Baseball Club Stranded," *Kansas City Times,* November 3, 1885, 8. The assistant manager's name was spelled "Sporr" and "Spoor."

148. "Winsome Witnesses: The Female Base Ball Club in Court—Sporr Discharged," *Kansas City Star,* November 2, 1885, 5.

149. Advertisement, *Kansas City Star,* November 7, 1885, 3; "What '*The Times*' Would Like to Know," *Kansas City Times,* November 6, 1885, 4; "The Valley Cities: Summary of Yesterday's News from Neighboring Towns . . . Independence," *Kansas City Times,* November 13, 1885, 3.

150. "Notes and Comments," *Sporting Life,* November 11, 1885, 3.

151. "Base Ball," *Brenham (Tex.) Weekly Banner,* February 25, 1886, 3; "Sherman Siftings: . . . A Novel Game of Base Ball," *Galveston Daily News,* December 26, 1885; "Sporting Notes," *Daily Nebraska State Journal,* January 12, 1886, 6.

152. "Dots from Dallas . . .," *Galveston Daily News,* January 2, 1886, 5; "Waxahachie," *Forth Worth Daily Gazette,* January 12, 1886, 6; *Galveston Daily News,* January 12, 1886, 8; "Waco . . . Those Dizzy Blondes and Brunettes," *Fort Worth Daily Gazette,* January 12, 1886, 6.

153. "Waco," *Fort Worth Daily Gazette,* January 13, 1886, 4; "Waco . . . A Street Fight . . .," *Fort Worth Daily Gazette,* January 14, 1886.

154. "Pencillings," *Sporting Life,* January 20, 1886, 2.

155. "The Sporting World," *Oswego Daily Times,* January 20, 1886.

156. "Imperial Cadets," *San Antonio Daily Light,* January 28, 1886, 4.

157. "Rays of Light," *San Antonio Daily Light,* February 1, 1886, 4; "The Bayou City's Budget: . . . Female Ball Players," *Galveston Daily News,* February 14, 1886, 6; "Houston Happenings . . . Lovely Ball Tossers . . .," *Galveston Daily News,* February 15, 1886, 3; "Female Base Ballers," *Brenham Weekly Banner,* February 25, 1886, 3; "Base Ball," *Brenham Weekly Banner,* February 25, 1886, 3; "The City: Flotsam and Jetsam," *Galveston Daily News,* March 1, 1886, 7.

158. "Notes and Comments," *Sporting Life,* May 12, 1886, 3. See also, "Odd Items From Everywhere," *Boston Daily Globe,* May 4, 1886, 8; *Stanford (Ky.) Semi-weekly Interior Journal,* May 4, 1886, 4; "Personal Gossip," *Rocky Mountain News,* May 5, 1886, 4; *Abilene (Kan.) Reflector,* May 6, 1886, 5; *Cherokee (Iowa) Times,* June 1, 1886, 2; *Omaha Daily Bee,* June 9, 1886, 7; *St. Joseph (Mich.) Herald,* July 31, 1886, 4; *Thomas County (Kans.) Cat,* August 19, 1886, 2; *Spirit Lake (Iowa) Beacon,* December 3, 1886, 1. Even newspaper published months after-the-fact listed the date of the game as "last Sunday." The *New Orleans Daily Picayune,* April 26, 1886, establishes the date as Sunday, April 25.

159. "Freeman in Bondage: The Manager of the Female Base Ball Club Punished as a Vagrant," *New Orleans Daily Picayune,* May 5, 1886.

160. "Frolicking Freeman: The Man who was in Galveston with Female Base-ballers 'Detained' in New Orleans as a Dangerous Character," *Galveston Daily News,* May 7, 1886, 15.

161. "Last of a Female Base-Ball Club," *Chicago Tribune,* May 5, 1886, 5; "Freeman in Bondage," *New Orleans Daily Picayune,* May 5, 1886; "NYSPCC People's Brief."

162. "The Female Base Ball Fakir [sic]," *New Orleans Daily Picayune,* May 10, 1886; "Municipal: Freeman Leaves Escorted by Police," *Daily Picayune,* May 15, 1886.

163. See details in chapter 5.

164. "NYSPCC People's Brief," 5; *Boston Daily Globe,* August 16, 1891. See esp. "A Big String of Dupes. Christian Wilson's Many Victims in Kansas City. King and Nunnelly About His Equals—Associated With the 'Okolona States' Man—A 14-Year-Old Philadelphia Girl Represented as His Daughter," *Kansas City Star,* August 18, 1891, 1.

165. O. P. Caylor, "Minor Mention," *Sporting Life,* May 26, 1886, 1.

166. Local newspapers and the "NYSPCC People's Brief" chronicle Wilson's time in Kansas City. See esp. "A Big String of Dupes. Christian Wilson's Many Victims in Kansas City. King

and Nunnelly About His Equals—Associated With the 'Okolona States' Man—A 14-Year-Old Philadelphia Girl Represented as His Daughter," *Kansas City Star,* August 18, 1891, 1.

167. Months after Gutmann's teams played in their area, the *Daily Alta California* reminded readers how Gutmann had scammed local audiences with his "catch-penny schemes." "Victor E. M. Gutmann: An Account of the Ramifications of the Champion Dead Beat . . ." *Daily Alta California,* August 11, 1886, 2.

168. "Baseball," *Daily Alta California,* February 8, 1886, 2; "The Girl Ball Tossers," *Daily Alta California,* February 12, 1886, 2; "Amusements," *Daily Alta California,* February 12, 1886, 1; "Female Baseball Players," *San Francisco Daily Evening Bulletin,* February 13, 1886, 2; "Sporting in Central Park: Practice Games of Lacrosse and Remarkable Score of Female Baseballists," *Daily Alta California,* February 15, 1886, 5.

169. "Female Ball-Tossing: A Large Crowd Soon Gets Satisfied with the Performance," *Sacramento Daily Record-Union,* February 22, 1886, 3.

170. "Female Base-Ballists: The Latest 'Fake' Proposed for Los Angeles," *Los Angeles Times,* August 29, 1888, 1.

171. "A Mesmeric 'Stiff.' Prof. Johnson Mesmerizes Himself, Becomes Rigid, and the Faculty and Students of Rush Medical Center Sit on Him," *Chicago Daily Tribune,* April 25, 1883), 8; "The Girls and Boys Play Ball: A Victory for the Former, Though the Score Doesn't Show It," *Chicago Tribune,* July 5, 1887, 1; "The Ga-Lorious Fourth. . . . A Close and Interesting Base-Ball Game Between the Boys and Girls. . . .," *Chicago Tribune,* July 5, 1887, 1.

172. Emmett Dedmon, *Fabulous Chicago: A Great City's History and People,* (1953), October 1, 2012, describes the directory and the Chicago vice district of the era. Google eBook.

173. "Amateur Base-Ball," *Daily Inter Ocean,* June 9, 1889, 11; *Daily Inter Ocean,* June 21, 1889, 3.

174. "Some Straws," *Sporting Life,* July 3, 1889, 4.

175. *Daily Inter Ocean,* July 16, 1889, 4.

176. "Base Ball Notes," *State Republican* (Lansing, Michigan), July 27, 1889, 4; "A Great Game: The Young Ladies' Base Ball Club; Good Players Among Them—A Great Crowd Present—The Good Plays and Notes on the Game, *Young Ladies Athletic Journal,* September 13, 1889), 1; "Midland Matters," *Midland (Mich.) Republican,* August 8, 1889, 5; "Ball Tossing Maidens: A Crowd of Nearly 5,000 Men Witness a Travesty on the National Game—How the Girls Pitched, Caught and Slid Bases—The Male Players Defeated," *Cleveland Plain Dealer,* August 12, 1889, 8.

177. Wilson made this claim in an advertising flyer he produced in 1890 to promote his new Young Ladies Base Ball Club. Local newspapers in Chicago in 1889 do not support his claim.

178. "Base Ball Girls: The Travels of a Chicago Club—History of the Game," *Brooklyn Eagle,* September 8, 1889, 11; *Rochester Post Express,* September 9, 1889, 8; "Female Ball Players: They Entertained a Crowd at Windsor Beach Yesterday," *Rochester Union and Advertiser,* September 9, 1889, 1; "Female Base Ball Players: They Don't Play Ball But the Crowd Enjoy the Fun—A Legal Dispute Over the Management of the Club," *Oswego (N.Y.) Daily Times,* September 10, 1889, 4; "Female Base Ballists: They Made Their Appearance at Richardson Park Yesterday Before Eight Hundred People," *Oswego (N.Y.) Palladium,* (September 10, 1889; "Ladies to the Bat," *Syracuse Evening Herald,* September 6, 1889, 8; "Bulletined News," *Auburn Bulletin,* September 11 and 12, 1889, 1; "It Will be a Dizzy Game," *Havana (N.Y.) Journal,* June 15, 1889.

179. "Girls to Play Ball: A Team Composed of Pittsburg Young Ladies Being Organized; Good Material to Select From; Many of the Girls Enthusiastic Over the Open Air Pastime; Glad to Escape From Indoor Work," *Pittsburg Dispatch,* September 23, 1889, 5. For an example of a player advertisement, see *Pittsburg Dispatch,* September 21, 1889, 3.

180. "Little Locals," *Lock Haven (Pa.) Evening Express,* September 28, 1889, 1.

181. Wilson's Young Ladies' Base Ball Club of Philadelphia was scheduled to play at the "Colored Agricultural and Industrial Fair" in Richmond in September of 1891, but the game may not have taken place. Wilson was in jail by that point. "The Colored People's Fair: An Outline of the Programme That Has Been Arranged," *Richmond Dispatch,* September 20, 1891, 8.

182. "Young Ladies' Ball Club: Manager Franklin Will Bring Them Here during the Fair," *San Antonio Daily Light,* October 21, 1889, 15; "Females at Base Ball," *New Mexican,* October 21, 1889, 3.

183. *Shenandoah (Va.) Herald,* October 25, 1889, 3.

184. "Personal and Other Items," *Biblical Recorder* (N.C.), October 30, 1889, 2.

185. "Local News," *Goldsboro (N.C.) Headlight,* October 30, 1889, 5.

186. "The Ball Game: A Big Crowd Out to Witness the 'Girls' Play Ball," *Knoxville (Tenn.) Daily Journal and Journal and Tribune,* November 7, 1889, 3; "The Ladies Defeated Them," *Daily Journal and Journal and Tribune,* November 8, 1889, 8; "Greeneville," *Daily Journal and Journal and Tribune,* November 10, 1889, 2.

187. "A Female Baseball Club Disbands," *New Orleans Daily Picayune,* December 8, 1889, 14. Quoting *Atlanta Constitution* article, December 3, 1889.

Chapter 5. New Women, Bloomer Girls, and the Old Ball Game

1. "Girls and Base Ball: A St. Louis Lady Enters Her Protest Against the Newly Organized Ladies League—And She Hopes That Organization Will Not be Allowed to Display Itself in Any of the St. Louis Parks—A Most Entertaining Article," *Sporting News,* September 20, 1890.

2. Quoted in: "Indian Maiden Sprinter: Michigan Has Developed a Girl Who is a Record-Breaker," *Omaha Daily Bee,* May 17, 1896, 19.

3. Gladys E. Palmer, *Baseball for Girls and Women* (New York: A. S. Barnes, 1929).

4. "The Fat Men Take Their Turn," *Marquette Daily Mining Journal,* August 19, 1889, 8.

5. See the epigraphs and notes 1 and 2.

6. The term "New Woman" is used in a generalized way as it applied to white, native-born, upper- and middle-class women. There was no universal model of new womanhood, nor was there universal acceptance of the concept. New Womanhood pitted rich against poor, social conservatives against progressives, white against black (and other ethnicities), men against women, and women against women. For an excellent overview of the complexity of the New Woman ideal, see Martha H. Patterson, "Introduction" in *Beyond the Gibson Girl: Reimagining the American New Woman, 1895–1915* (Urbana: University of Illinois Press, 2005), 1–26.

7. Patterson, *Beyond the Gibson Girl,* 7–8. The influx of girls and women into schools, colleges, the workforce, and progressive reform organizations during the 1890s has been well documented by scholars. See, for example: Hunter, *How Young Ladies Became Girls;* John L. Rury, *Education and Women's Work: Female Schooling and the Division of Labor in Urban America, 1870–1930* (Albany: State University of New York Press, 1991); Rosalind Rosenberg, *Beyond Separate Spheres: Intellectual Roots of Modern Feminism,* (New Haven, Conn.: Yale University Press, 1982); Lynn Gordon, *Gender and Higher Education in the Progressive Era,* (New Haven, Conn.: Yale University Press, 1990); Kathryn Kish Sklar, *Florence Kelley and the Nation's Work: The Rise of Women's Political Culture, 1830–1900* (New Haven, Conn.: Yale University Press, 1995), Louise W. Knight, *Jane Addams: Spirit in Action* (New York: W.W. Norton, 2010). For a contemporary perspective, see Joseph Dana Miller, "The New Woman in Office," *Godey's Magazine,* January 1896, 132 and 787.

8. Miller, "New Woman," 132.

9. Charles Dana Gibson was a popular graphic artist whose illustrations appeared regularly

in books and periodicals like *Life, Harper's Weekly, Scribners,* and *Collier's.* During the 1890s his visual rendering of the "New Woman" became so iconic the ideal became known as the "Gibson Girl."

10. Bernarr Macfadden, "Erroneous Ideas of Muscle," *Physical Culture* 1, no. 4 (June 1899): 82, cited in Jan Todd, "Bernarr Macfadden: Reformer of Feminine Form," *Journal of Sport History* 14, no. 1 (Spring 1987): 68.

11. Todd notes that Macfadden's publishing empire (including *Physical Culture*) was so vast by the early 1930s that its circulation of publications exceeded those of William Randolph Hearst and Henry Luce. Todd, "Bernarr Macfadden," 73.

12. Quoted in "Women's Sports: Up To Date," *Chicago Daily Tribune,* August 21, 1895, 6.

13. Patterson, *Beyond the Gibson Girl,* 7–8. See also Nan Enstad, *Ladies of Labor, Girls of Adventure: Working Women, Popular Culture, and Labor Politics at the Turn of the Twentieth Century* (New York: Columbia University Press, 1999); Peiss, *Cheap Amusements*; Rury, *Education and Women's Work.*

14. Todd, "Bernarr Macfadden," 74.

15. *Rolla (Mo.) New Era,* March 4, 1893, 1. Article originally appeared in *Harper's* magazine and was reprinted across the country.

16. See appendices for details. It is impossible to provide a definitive number for teams because not every team was mentioned in contemporary sources, and countless teams remain to be discovered as new sources are digitized. This tally represents research done through 2014.

17. "Time Tower Talk: About What the Watch Makers are Doing in the Mill," *Rockford (Ill.) Morning Star,* August 16, 1891, 1; Rockford newspapers began publicizing the fund raiser as early as May 11. They carried dozens of articles including: "Fares Please: Trolley Day Set for Saturday, June 4, By the Ladies' Aid Society," *Daily Register Gazette,* May 11, 1898, 3; "Play Ball For Charity: Ladies will Essay National Game on Trolley Day; Two Captains are Named; Mrs. W. F. Barnes and Mrs. J. Stanley Browne to Lead the Teams—None But the Fair Sex Will Be in the Game," *Morning Star,* May 15, 1898, 9; "Fair Ones in Game: The Ladies Who Will Play on Trolley Day; Have Plenty of 'Subs;' Not a Horrid Man to Participate—Two Umpires and a Scorer Named—Practice Game to Be Played Daily—The Line Up," *Morning Star,* May 24, 1898, 8; "Belles of the Ball: Dramatic Rendition of a Fantastic on the Diamond for Charity," *Daily Register Gazette,* June 4, 1898, 7.

18. "Celebrating the Fourth: Negro Women Play Base Ball at Brisbane Park," *Columbus (Ga.) Daily Enquirer,* July 5, 1894, 1; "Base Ball: Girls and Base Ball; A Girlish Description of a Game by Girls; An Umpire in White Lawn—A Home Plate Concealed by the Catcher's Petticoats, Etc.," *Sporting Life,* September 10, 1892, 11; "Girls Who Play Baseball: How Some Young Women at Lenox Amuse Themselves," *New York Times,* September 3, 1893, 12, and "Lenox is Still Gay. Outdoor Sports Claim the Attention of the Younger Set: Events at Pittsfield," *New York Herald,* September 3, 1893, 26; "Lively Times at Fox Lake," *Chicago Tribune,* August 18, 1895, 14; "A Notable Game of Baseball," *New York Evening Sun,* May 22, 1897, 4; "Field Day Sports: University Notes," *Grand Forks (N.D.) Herald,* May 7, 1893, 4; "Nubs of News," *Grand Forks Herald,* May 13, 1893, 8.

19. The *Denver Evening Post,* July 20, 1897, 4 reported that a baseball team in Texas had a "pretty female pitcher." Lizzie Arlington gained significant fame, particularly in the Philadelphia area, after she signed a contract to pitch for men's minor league teams. Details follow in this chapter.

20. Sylvester Wilson used male players disguised as women on his teams but usually only when he could not find enough women to play. The Bloomer Girl teams of the 1890s and 1900s made "toppers" a regular feature of their teams—particularly in the early twentieth century.

Some of these players, like Smoky Joe Wood and Rogers Hornsby, went on to become stars of major league baseball. Jim Swint, "Don't Forget 'Smoky' Joe Wood You Were Some Kind of Ball Player," http://www.funvalleysports.com/history/smokey _joe_wood.shtml; "Here's Joe Wood, Boston's Best and A Giant Killer; He Started His Career As A Bloomer Girl in Kansas Wilds." *Fort Wayne Daily News,* November 16, 1912, 7; Wood identified Rogers Hornsby as a Bloomer Girl player in his autobiographical article: "Not Far From Slumgullion Gulch" published in Charles Einstein's *The Third Fireside Book of Baseball* (New York: Simon and Schuster, 1968).

21. Examples of positive comments: "Female Baseballists: The Score Yesterday Afternoon 2 to 6[?] in Favor of the Bloomers," *The State* (Columbia, S.C), August 15, 1895, 8.; "It Was Not a Ball Game: A Big Crowd Watches Bloomers Play the Butte Team; Only One Girl Player; And She Was All Right—the Rest of the Boston Beauties Were in the Game to Chase the Ball— Butte Wins the Game," *Anaconda (Mont.) Standard,* September 7, 1897, 5. (Despite the rather disparaging title, the article notes: "More than 2,000 people went to the ball grounds to see the Boston Bloomers play the Butte team, and everybody seemed to enjoy it.").

22. Examples of negative press: *Little Falls (Minn.) Weekly Transcript,* September 20, 1895, 2; "Bloomerites Frowned On: The Mayor of Duluth Forbids a Ball Game," *San Francisco Chronicle,* September 22, 1895, 15; "Telegraphic Notes," *Decatur (Ind.) Daily Republican,* September 25, 1895, 6.

23. "Belles at the Bat: Society Girls Play Base-ball, with a Preacher Acting as Umpire." *Daily Inter Ocean,* July 13, 1891; "Had a Parson for an Umpire: The Belles of an Ohio Town Play Base Ball with Their Lovers," *Chicago Herald,* July 13, 1891, 6; "Society Girls Play Ball: The Men Play with Left Hands—The Umpire a Minister," *Macon Telegraph,* July 14, 1891, 1; "A Sensational Ball Game," *Knoxville Daily Journal and Journal and Tribune,* July 14, 1891, 1; "Women in Base Ball: Respectable Ladies to Spoil Their Hands at the Sport," *Sporting Life,* July 18, 1891, 1.

24. "Base Ball," *Utica Saturday Globe,* August 2, 1890, 2; "Sporting: Base Ball," *Utica Saturday Globe,* August 29, 1891, 6.

25. Dean A. Sullivan, ed., introduction to *Early Innings: A Documentary History of Baseball, 1825–1908,* by Benjamin Rader (Lincoln: University of Nebraska Press, 1995), xviii. See also Rader, *Baseball,* 81.

26. *Atchison Daily Globe,* August 23, 1892.

27. "Topics of the Times," *Sioux County Herald,* September 2, 1891, 6.

28. "Current Comment," *Columbus (Ga.) Daily Enquirer,* May 20, 1893, 2. Reprint from *Chicago Times.*

29. "Girls and Base Ball: A St. Louis Lady Enters Her Protest Against the Newly Organized Ladies League—A Most Entertaining Article," *Sporting News,* September 20, 1890.

30. *Cedar Rapids Evening Gazette,* August 4, 1892, 5.

31. "A Novel Game of Ball," *Dorchester (Md.) Democrat-News,* May 27, 1893.

32. *Denver Evening Post,* August 24, 1895, 4.

33. Article was reprinted in numerous newspapers like *Lincoln Evening News,* October 7, 1896, 7; *Waterloo Daily Courier,* October 9, 1896, 6; *Winona (Minn.) Daily Republican,* October 13, 1896, 2.

34. "Base Ball in Bloomers: The Female Freaks Pull But a Few Pants Legs in Quincy," *Quincy Herald,* October 3, 1895, 1.

35. Reprinted in "At a Disadvantage," *Newark Daily Advocate,* June 10, 1895, 5.

36. "Were Too Polite to Win," *The Penny Press* (Minneapolis), July 18, 1895, 3.

37. "The Female Aggregation Who Came from Goodness Knows Where and Stopped Over at Rockford to Play a Game of Alleged Base Ball: Features of the Game and 'Cracks' From the Grand Stand," *Daily Register Gazette,* July 27, 1892, 3.

38. Article from *Des Moines Register* (1892) was reprinted in: John Zeller, "A Century Ago Today, 'Lady Champs' Hit Town," *Des Moines Register*, August 13, 1992.

39. "Played at Baseball," *Tacoma (Wash.) Daily News*, September 24, 1897, 4.

40. A. F. Groebl, "Who Would Doubt That I'm a Man?" Music by A. F. Groebl, words by M. Straube. Sheet music. (Cincinnati, c.1895). Library of Congress. http://www.loc.gov/item/ihas.200033458/.

41. See, for example, Charles Dudley Warner, "Give the Men a Chance," Chapter 4. *As We Go* (New York, 1893) and "The Feminization of Harvard Professors," *Public Opinion: A Comprehensive Summary of The Press Throughout the World on All Important Current Topics*, Vol. 27, July–December 1899 (New York, December 28, 1899), 823. Throughout the decade, numerous groups conducted studies to identify areas where "feminization" was occurring.

42. Alpheus Hyatt, "The Influence of Woman in the Evolution of the Human Race," *Natural Science: A Monthly Review of Scientific Progress* 23, no. 66 (August 1897): 90–92. Hyatt was a Harvard-educated zoologist, biologist, and paleontologist. He defined "virified" as "having acquired manly habits and character as tending to become mannish without being necessarily a degenerate being either physically or mentally."

43. "The Significance of the Frontier in American History," a paper read at the meeting of the American Historical Association in Chicago, 1893. Reprinted in: Frederick Jackson Turner, *The Frontier in American History* (New York: H. Holt, 1920), 1.

44. G. Stanley Hall, *Youth: Its Education, Regimen, and Hygiene* (New York: Appleton, 1906), 103–4. Reprinted in Amy Kaplan, *The Anarchy of Empire in the Making of U.S. Culture* (Cambridge, Mass.: Harvard University Press, 2002), 112.

45. For insights on the rise of professional coaches and physical educators, see Robin Lester, *Stagg's University: The Rise, Decline, and Fall of Big-Time Football at Chicago* (Urbana: University of Illinois Press, 1999), esp. 1–64.

46. "Notes and Gossip," *Sporting Life*, September 9, 1890, 4.

47. "National Game . . .," *Haverhill (Mass.) Bulletin*, July 23, 1891, 2.

48. "Women in Baseball," *Newtown (N.Y.) Register*, April 21, 1892.

49. "Short Skirts or No Game: Capt. Arlington's Reply to Bloomfield's Citizens' Committee," *New York Evening World*, May 6, 1893, 2.

50. "Girl Baseball Players: They are Fond of the Sport and Wear Nice Costumes," *Grand Rapids (Mich.) Press*, August 11, 1894, 7.

51. Ruth Egan was a standout player on boys' and men's teams and mixed-sex Bloomer Girls teams in and around Kansas City, Missouri, beginning in 1905; Myrtle Rowe became a local celebrity in and around Pittsburg in 1907, and Alta Weiss gained a national following for her exploits pitching for the Vermilion (Ohio) Independents in 1907 and her own Weiss All-Stars in 1908. Many more women followed their example in the ensuing decades.

52. The *Denver Evening Post* mentioned the "pretty young female pitcher" on a Texas baseball team (July 20, 1897), 4. This was likely a men's team; it would not have been newsworthy if she pitched on a female team.

53. Numerous books and articles have referred to Lizzie Arlington as Lizzie Stroud. This is incorrect. See Barbara Gregorich, "A Champion for All Seasons," *Pennsylvania Heritage* (Summer 1998): 4–9.

54. Gregorich, "A Champion," 5. "Girls Want to Shoot," *Mount Carmel (Ind.) Daily News*, January 27, 1900, 1.

55. The Reds were in direct competition with Wilson's Chicago Black Stocking nine that summer as both teams traveled in the same region of eastern Pennsylvania.

56. *Mahanoy City Tri-Weekly Record*, June 18, 20, 23, and 25, 1891, 4. Thanks to John Kovach for sharing these articles.

57. *Bedford (Ind.) Mail,* July 8, 1892, 3; John Kovach e-mail to author, November 2014. After years of research, Barbara Gregorich discovered that Maud Nelson's real name was Clementine Brida. Barbara Gregorich, "The Girls of Summer," *New City: Chicago's News and Arts Weekly,* May 2–8, 1996, 9–11.

58. John Kovach discovered Brida's immigration information and located other Bridas in Mahanoy City censuses. Gregorich believes Brida likely worked for the Stride family. E-mails to author from Kovach and Gregorich, September 1 and 2, 2014. No one knows for sure exactly when Brida was born. Her death certificate says February 15, 1874, her social security card says November 17, 1881, and her tombstone lists her lifespan as 1879 to 1944. Kovach believes Brida was born in 1873 based on her immigration records.

59. "The League Will Continue," *Richmond Dispatch,* July 13, 1898, 2.

60. The exact terms and date of the contract is unknown. By July 3, 1898, the *Philadelphia Inquirer* was identifying Conner as the one who had signed Arlington to a contract for $100 per week.

61. See, for example, *Sporting News,* July 10 and 17, 1897, 7.

62. "Miss Arlington's Tour: The Girl Pitcher to Twirl Against Professional Teams," *Philadelphia Press,* July 1, 1898, 10. Most secondary sources only mention Barrow when they discuss Arlington's signing of the first professional contract for a female ballplayer. Yet, the article in the *Philadelphia Inquirer* on July 3 makes it clear that Conner was Arlington's promoter at this time, and the article in the *Philadelphia Press* on July 1 makes it clear that Arlington was also going to pitch in other leagues that summer. If Barrow had signed Arlington on his own, it is unlikely he would have made plans to allow her to pitch in other leagues. On the other hand, I have found no evidence that Arlington ever did play for either of the other leagues so, perhaps, Barrow bought Arlington's contract from Conner at some point.

63. "Norristown's Female Pitcher," *North American* June 25, 1898, 3.

64. "A Woman in the Box: Lizzie Arlington Who Played in Two Games at Norristown Yesterday, Will be the Attraction," *Reading (Pa.) Times,* July 5, 1898, 1; "Ball Notes," *Reading Daily Times and Dispatch,* July 5, 1898, 4; "Allentown Goose Egged: Rank Errors in the Field Result in Defeat at Reading," *Allentown (Pa.) Daily Leaders,* July 6, 1898, 4; "A Woman in the Box: Lizzie Arlington Twirls the Ball in the Ninth Inning. Only Two Hits Were Made Off Her Delivery but Did Not Do Any Damage. Allentown Shut Out—All the Runs in Two Innings," *Reading Daily Times and Dispatch,* July 6, 1898, 4.

65. "Women Players in Organized Baseball," SABR. http://research.sabr.org/journals/women-players-in-organized-baseball.

66. For details on some of Arlington's achievements as a sportswoman and baseball player, see: "At the Traps," *Brooklyn Daily Eagle,* July 15, 1898, 11; "Sporting Notes," *Philadelphia Times,* July 9, 1898, 6; "Miss Arlington To Pitch," *Richmond Dispatch,* July 13, 1898, 2; "Take Another Game. . . . The Female Pitcher Gives an Exhibition. . . .," *Richmond Dispatch,* July 16, 1898, 6; "Another Defeat: Allentown Was An Easy Mark for Richmond Yesterday," *Allentown Leader,* July 16, 1898, 4; "Radiant Richmond: Satisfied That Lancaster is the Only Club to Be Feared," *Sporting Life,* July 23, 1898, 17; "Pitcher's Peculiarities: A Philadelphia Woman Demonstrates the Possibilities of Her Sex," *Winnipeg Tribune,* August 9, 1898, 7; "And a Woman Pitched," *Altoona (Pa.) Tribune,* July 28, 1898, 1; "Saturday's Double Header . . .," *Reading Daily Times and Dispatch,* July 25, 1898, 4; "Ball Notes," *Reading Daily Times and Dispatch,* July 30, 1898, 4; "Reading Radiant Over Her Greatest Week Since She Got an Atlantic Club," *Sporting Life,* August 6, 1898, 17.

67. Examples: "Ninth and Arch Museum," *Philadelphia Sunday Item,* April 30, 1893, 10. On page 11, the paper announced "Another New Innovation!!! Female Sprinting Race." The

same year in San Francisco, an athletic trainer recruited women from Canada, England, and the United States to form two football (soccer) teams. He expected their exhibitions would draw huge crowds. "Novel Football Game: Two Female Teams to Play Under Association Rules," *San Francisco Evening Call,* November 6, 1893, 3. The popular press and newspapers noticed the shift in attitudes toward female athleticism. Examples: "The Athletic Girl," *Philadelphia Sunday Item,* December 24, 1893; W. Bengough, "The New Woman, Athletically Considered, *Godey's Magazine,* January 1896, 132 and 787; "Out-Door Sport," *Harper's Bazaar,* July 28, 1894, 606.

68. "Coming," *Maysville (Ky.) Evening Bulletin,* May 12, 1890, 3; "A Female Aggregation," *Sporting Life,* May 31, 1890, 7; "City News," *Logansport Pharos,* June 9, 1890, 4; "Base Ball Girls," *Logansport Reporter,* June 13, 1890, 4; "City Brevities," *Titusville Morning Herald,* July 16, 1890, 4; "City and Vicinity," *Watertown Daily Times,* August 2, 1890; *Norwood (N.Y.) News,* August 5, 1890; "A Disgraceful Move: Introducing Females Into Professionalism; A Speculator's Proposal to Organize a League of Female Baseball [Teams]" *Sporting Life,* August 30, 1890, 8; " 'Lady Champions' at Ball: Disgraceful Sunday Exhibition With the Allertons at Monitor Park, Weehawken," *New York Herald,* September 1, 1890, 6; "Wanted, Girls to Play Base Ball," *New York Clipper,* (c. September 2, 1890). Randall Brown files.

69. The origin of Clyde and Bey's team is inferred from the article: "How One of the Female Ball Nine Deserted Husband and Babes—Stuck on Being an Actress—She Tagged the Runner and He Hurt Her Arm," *Quincy Daily Herald,* June 8, 1894, 8. Dateline of article is St. Louis, June 8. Article details how managers lured a young mother away from home to play baseball.

70. Note: Bruckner's name is spelled "Buckner" and "Brucker" in articles in 1892, but he is identified as Joseph Bruckner in official government correspondence related to the international incident his American Female Base Ball Club sparked in Cuba the following year.

71. At least seven of the players on the New York Champion team, including Maud Nelson, had played for the Cincinnati Reds in 1893; there is no record of a Cincinnati Reds team in 1894.

72. *Sandusky (Ohio) Daily Register,* May 9, 1890, 4; Ren Mulford Jr., "Ohio Fans' Conundrums . . . Seasonable Observations," *Sporting Life,* May 24, 1890, 10. Dateline was May 20.

73. *Sporting Life,* August 30, 1890, 8.

74. Ibid. The ad promised to pay qualified individuals ("young, over 20, good looking and good figure") $5 to $15 per week plus expenses, and to guarantee them year-round employment. Applicants within the city were to report to "Mr. Franklin" at the Dramatic Agency at 1162 Broadway or at his residence at 158 West 50th street between 8 and 10 P.M. Those outside of the city were to send a photograph.

75. Papers across the country carried the story. "The Female Figures: Are Pinched for Playing Ball on Sunday; Likewise the Local Team is Taken In and All Are Fined," *Danville (Ill.) Weekly Press,* June 11, 1890, 1. "Serves Them Right: Female Ball Players Arrested and Fined in Illinois," *Sporting Life,* June 14, 1890; "Pick-ups," *Rochester Democrat and Chronicle,* July 15, 1890, 7.

76. Attendance figures are available for only eleven of the thirty games. Wilson is the source of statistics for five of the games. If his (likely exaggerated) totals are excluded and only the average of 750 to 1,500 spectators for the other seven games reported in the media are applied to the remaining nineteen games, the total exceeds twenty thousand.

77. Name appears in an undated advertisement, c. September 2, 1890. Randall Brown files.

78. "A Disgraceful Move," *Sporting Life,* August 30, 1890, 8.

79. Ibid.

80. Ibid.

81. Roster for the Weehawken game: May Howard, Nellie Williams, Kitty Grant, Annie Grant, Angie Parker, Effie Earl, Alice Lee, Mamie Johnson, and Maggie Marshall. The first seven appear in the photograph; Maggie Marshall was arrested with the team in Danville on June 8 and

Mamie Johnson appears on a roster (as Laura Johnson) at least as early as July 17 in Titusville, Pennsylvania.

82. Murphy had been a talented player in his youth and stayed involved with the sport as he worked his way up the ladder in New York City's political machine; he was unofficial "chief lieutenant" for the eighteenth district when he and Wilson staged the game in Weehawken. For background on Murphy's association with baseball see Nancy Joan Weiss, *Charles Francis Murphy, 1858–1924: Respectability and Responsibility in Tammany Politics* (Northampton, Mass.: Smith College, 1968), 22.

83. "'Lady Champions' at Ball . . ." *New York Herald,* September 1, 1890, 6.

84. "Base Ball," *Yenowine's News* (Milwaukee), September 7, 1890, 7. In 1890 the Brotherhood of Professional Base-Ball players organized the Players' League—an 8-team circuit that survived only a single season.

85. Adam Forepaugh operated a series of circuses from the mid-1860s until 1889 when he liquidated his assets. He and P. T. Barnum were on-again, off-again partners and rivals throughout much of the 1870s and 1880s.

86. "A Female Base Ball Manager Employed a Fifteen Year Old Girl as a Mascot," *Syracuse Courier,* August 15, 1891, 1. A Female Ball Player: The Trouble She Has Brought to an Amusement Manager," *Rochester Democrat and Chronicle,* August 15, 1891, 1; "In Jail at Last: A Disgrace to Base Ball Probably Now Ended—A Notorious Manager of Female Base Ball Clubs Now at the End of His Rope," *Sporting Life,* August 22, 1891, 5.

87. "NYSPCC People's Brief."

88. Most of the details on the troupe's travels during this period are from the broadside Wilson produced circa September 13, 1890. See also "Wanted, Girls to Play Base Ball," *New York Clipper,* c. September 2, 1890. "The Gouverneur Fair," *Northern Tribune,* September 6, 1890); "Notes," *Gouverneur Press,* September 10, 1890, 2; "Women Wield the Bat: A Crowd at Capitol Park Cheer a Novel Game of Baseball; Local Players Play Incog[nito]; The Females Defeated After a Spirited Struggle by the Score of 15 to 10. . . . *Washington Post,* October 4, 1890, 6; "Batting Order," *Newark Daily Advocate,* October 10, 1890, 1.

89. "Notes," *Lebanon Daily News,* April 30, 1891, 1.

90. Wilson wore this style of facial hair for years. "Got Sylvester Wilson Again: Female Baseball Team Man Tries Basketball: Indicted For Abduction, a Crime for Which He Has Already Done Five Years—If Convicted This Time He May Get 20—He Has Been in Many Jails," *New York City Sun,* June 28, 1903, 3.

91. Examples: "Sylvester Wilson's Trial, *Syracuse Daily Standard,* September 12, 1891, 1; "Wilson Discharges Howe: The Manager of Female Base-ballists Creates a Sensation in Court," *North American,* October 13, 1891, 6; "Wilson on the Stand: He Denies That His Relations With Libbie Sunderland were Improper," *Utica Morning Herald,* October 14, 1891, 1. Richter's articles included: "Deserved Punishment: Wilson, the Female Base Ball Manager, Put Away For Five Years," *Sporting Life,* October 24, 1891, 1; *Sporting Life,* October 31, 1891, 3.

92. "In Jail at Last: A Disgrace to Base Ball Probably Now Ended—A Notorious Manager of Female Base Ball Clubs Now at the End of His Rope," *Sporting Life,* August 22, 1891, 5.

93. "Baby farm" was slang for homes where employees nursed the children of unwed mothers for a fee. They also housed unwed mothers and helped them arrange adoptions. Some were licensed; many were not. Annie Long played for Mark Lally's Cincinnati Reds the year after Wilson's arrest, appearing on a roster with Lizzie Arlington, Maud Bradi (Nelson), and Flossie Atwood, who was living with Wilson and Sunderland when he was arrested for Sunderland's abduction. *Bedford Mail,* July 8, 1892, 3.

94. Ibid.

95. "Libbie Sunderland's Abduction: More Witnesses Pile Up Testimony Against the Female Base-Ball Manager," *North American,* October 10, 1891, 4. The lengthy appeal filed by Wilson's new attorney confirms the details of the testimony and includes many other examples from other witnesses. NYCMA.

96. Though trial transcripts are unavailable, newspapers indicate that Sunderland's testimony mirrored the official deposition she gave to Police Justice C. W. Meade, on August 17, 1891. *The People &c., on the Complaint of William A. Finn vs. Sylvester F. Wilson, Police Court, 5th District, August 17, 1891."* NYCMA

97. "In the New York Supreme Court, General Term—First Department. *The People of the State of New York, Respondents, vs. Sylvester F. Wilson, Appellant.* Transcript of appeal prepared by Attorney James R. Stevens. (undated, c. late 1891, early 1892). NYCMA.

98. Sunderland detailed her sexual relationship with Wilson in her official deposition to C. W. Meade on August 17, 1891. In court she testified that Wilson had treated her "as a father and furnished her a home." "Female Baseball Player: A Trial in New-York Discloses Interesting and Shameful Details," *Buffalo Express,* October 1891, 2.

99. "Wilson on the Stand: He Denies That His Relations With Libbie Sunderland were Improper," *Utica Morning Herald,* October 14, 1891, 1.

100. "NYSPCC People's Brief" includes testimony from fifteen-year-old Margaret Dean about the first time Wilson forced her to have sex with him. Dean described how one of her teammates, Ray Garton, explained why she was bleeding and instructed her how to "syringe" herself and how veteran players cautioned new girls not to be caught alone with Wilson. Mary Engel, age sixteen, described how she had thwarted Wilson's plans to have sex with her on numerous occasions by refusing to go to his room when summoned. Wilson repeatedly told her that she was the only girl who was refusing to cooperate with him and he offered her $500 and marriage if she would relent. She refused. *N.Y. General Sessions, The People Against Sylvester F. Wilson.* NYCMA.

101. Some papers reported that the jury had taken three minutes; others said ten. "An Abductor Convicted," *Winnipeg Free Press,* October 17, 1891, 1. "Wilson Found Guilty: The Abductor of Libbie Sunderland Awaits His Sentence," *New York Times,* October 17, 1891, 2; "The Jury Convict in Ten Minutes," *North American,* October 17, 1891, 4; "Guilty of Abduction," *Bismarck (N.D.) Daily Tribune,* October 18, 1891.

102. "Wilson Convicted," *New Orleans Daily Picayune,* October 20, 1891, 4.

103. "Wilson's Story Denied," *New York Times,* October 20, 1891, 5. Wilson's and Giles's divorce had been finalized in 1887 after New Jersey had exhausted its attempts to get Wilson to respond to her charges. The following year, Giles married the thirty-three-year-old Hunt, a Harvard graduate who practiced medicine in Camden.

104. "Sylvester Wilson Sentenced: The Ex-Manager of Female Base-Ball Nines Sent to Prison for Five Years," *North American,* October 22, 1891, 5; "General Review of the World's Happenings for a Week . . ." *Southern Argus* (African American paper), October 29, 1891, 2; "Took His Breath Away," *St. Paul Daily Globe,* October 22, 1891, 1; "Was Thunderstruck," *Dallas Morning News,* October 22, 1891, 2.

105. *Sporting Life,* October 31, 1891, 3.

106. Wilson's legal strategy influenced new legislation drafted by New York District Attorney DeLancey Nicoll in February 1893 to end the practice of Supreme Court justices in one county issuing stays or overturning verdicts in trials from other counties. "A Judicial Evil," *Syracuse Evening Herald,* February 18, 1893, 2.

107. "Wilson Done For: The Female Club Manager Must Go to Sing Sing," *Sporting Life,* December 31, 1892; Koster & Bials was a popular haunt on 23rd Street famous for its vaudeville

shows and illegal alcohol. (New York City prohibited serving alcohol at theaters.) "Arrested For Abduction," *Poughkeepsie Daily Eagle,* December 24 1892; "Bad Egg in Sing Sing: Base-Ball Sylvester Wilson Lugged Off to Durance Vile," *Syracuse Herald,* December 25, 1892, 1.

108. Wilson's Sing Sing intake record. Sing Sing Prison Inmate Admission Registers, Box 10, Volume 28, p. 29. New York State Archives.

109. Court records at the NYCMA contain multiple letters and appeals written by Wilson and supporters between 1896 and 1898 as they tried to win his release from the Ludlow Street Jail. The NYSPCC People's Brief also includes details.

110. "NYSPCC People's Brief." The *Twenty-Fifth Annual Report* of the NYSPCC summarized Wilson's activities following his release from Sing Sing, noting that Society officials had received several complaints that Wilson was "engaged in schemes requiring the services of young girls" and that two of the girls had provided the Society with letters and other evidence of his criminal behavior. Before they could arrest him Wilson moved to Philadelphia. "August 20.—(Case No. 126,592)," *The New York Society for the Prevention of Cruelty to Children: Twenty-Fifth Annual Report, December 31, 1899* (New York: NYSPCC, 1900): 40–41. George Sim Johnston Archives of the NYSPCC. (GSJA, NYSPCC).

111. "Again in Trouble: Wilson Who Managed a Female Base Ball Nine," *Elmira (N.Y.) Daily Gazette and Free Press,* August 17, 1899, 5.

112. NYSPCC, *Twenty-Fifth Annual Report,* 40–41. GSJA, NYSPCC.

113. Copies of the ads were appended to testimony provided by the NYSPCC to the New York Court of General Sessions, August 18, 1903. Wilson, 1903 trial records. NYCMA,

114. Wilson had used similar wording in ads he placed in May 1899 to find players and investors for the first baseball team he organized after his release from Ludlow Street Jail. He had used the name Frank Watkins, but NYSPCC officials quickly confirmed their suspicion Watkins, Frank W. Hartright, and Sylvester F. Wilson were the same man.

115. Fourteen-year-old Augusta Messinger testified that Wilson had shown her photographs of a man and woman having sexual intercourse while he was molesting her. "NYSPCC People's Brief." *Court of General Sessions of the Peace in and for the County of New York. The People of the State of New York against Sylvester F. Wilson, Otherwise called Frank W. Hartright.* Wilson 1903 court files, NYCMA. "Gets Nine Years for Abduction: S.I. [sic] Wilson, Promoter of Women's Baseball Teams, Had Pleaded Guilty to Charge," *New York Tribune,* August 22, 1903, 11.

116. These efforts are detailed in Wilson's 1903 trial files at the New York State Archives. See, for example: Letter from Frank E. Perley to the Hon. William Travers Jerome, January 9, 1905; Letter from Hon. William Travers Jerome, to the governor's office, February 8, 1905; Letter from Hon. William Travers Jerome to the Governor of the State of New York, February 24, 1905.

117. The 1910 and 1920 Federal Censuses both show Sylvester F. Wilson as a "patient" at Dannemora, where mentally ill prisoners were kept.

118. *Journal of the Assembly of the State of New York at Their One Hundred and Fifteenth Session* (Albany, N.Y.: James B. Lyon, State Printer, 1892), 785. "The Excise Bill: The Assembly Committee Reports A Compromise Bill . . ." *Auburn Bulletin,* March 4, 1892), 1. McCormick represented Orange County but had ties to Libbie Sunderland's hometown of Binghamton where he had been admitted to the bar forty years earlier. Will L. Lloyd, *The Red Book; An Illustrated Legislative Manual of the State, Containing the Portraits and Biographies of its Governors and Members of the Legislature; Also the Enumeration of the State for 1892, with Election and Population Statistics, and List of Postmasters.* (Albany, N.Y., 1892), 144–45.

119. Entry for Friday, March 25, 1892: *Journal of the Assembly of the State of New York at Their One Hundred and Fifteenth Session* (Albany, N.Y., 1892), 1326.

120. "Wanted: A Female Base Ball Club," *Sporting Life,* February 18, 1893, 16. An official government dispatch identifies Laborde as a resident of Havana who helped Bruckner organize the tour.

121. Some historians credit Nemesio Guillo, the son of a wealthy Cuban planter, with bringing baseball to Cuba with him in 1868 when he returned from attending college in the United States. See Will Blackwell, "Competidores en Diamante de Béisbol: Cultural Exchange Between Cuba and the United States Through a Shared Love of Baseball," *The Sextant* (Summer 2007), publication of Christopher Newport University.

122. Ibid.

123. Livingston had played for Sylvester Wilson in 1890 and 1891 and had had a child fathered by him. It is unknown which team(s) Gordon (Myers) had played for, but the counsel general who took her testimony after the riot in Cuba noted her real name, address in Philadelphia, and the fact that she was a professional baseball player.

124. Enclosure #2 to Dispatch #1818 from U.S. Consulate General, Havana, Cuba to Assistant Secretary of State, William F. Wharton, Washington, D.C. National Archives, Volume 226 of "Enclosures," 498–501. (This volume has severe water damage, but enough text remains readable to provide firsthand details of the verbal testimony of player Mattie Myers to Ramon Williams, the U.S. Consul General.)

125. Enclosure #2 to Dispatch #1818, 6 March 1893.

126. Ibid.

127. Ibid.

128. "A Female Base Ball Club in Danger: Attacked by a Cuban Mob and One of the Players Hurt," *Brooklyn Daily Eagle,* March 6, 1893, 10. Portions of the *Daily Eagle* story were reprinted in dozens of newspapers across the country in the ensuing days and weeks. See, for example: "Mobbed the Girls: Warm Reception Tendered a Female Base Ball Club in Cuba; Spectators Think They Are Not Getting Their Money's Worth; For Once the Umpire Escapes and the Players are Mobbed; Police Required to Rescue the Alleged Athletic Young Women," *St Paul Daily Globe,* March 7, 1893, 1; "A Riot in Havana: An American Base Ball Team Causes a Fight," *The Salt Lake Herald,* March 7, 1893, 1; "The Female Twirlers: Women Base Ball Players Warmly Met in Cuba," *Sporting News,* May 11, 1893; "Mobbed the Players: Cubans Object to Poor Base Ball Playing by the American Female Club," *Northern Vindicator,* March 16, 1893, 2.

129. Dispatch #1818 from U.S. Consulate General, Havana, Cuba to Assistant Secretary of State, William F. Wharton, Washington, D.C. Available at the National Archives. I am indebted to University of Miami graduate student J. Camilo Vera for translating Williams's letter to the governor general for me.

130. Untitled, *Salt Lake Herald,* March 26, 1893, 4. The paper erroneously reported that the team was from Chicago. It was organized in New York City.

131. "Didn't Like the Females," *Dallas Morning News,* March 14, 1893, 2; "Will Sue Spain: The Female Base Ballists File for Damages For Their Treatment in Cuba," *Middletown (N.Y.) Daily Press,* March 15, 1893, 4.

132. "Want Damages," *Fresno (Calif.) Morning Republican,* March 15, 1893, 1. The same (or similar) articles appeared on this date in the *Salt Lake City Herald* (p. 8), the *San Francisco Morning Call* (p. 1), the *St. Paul Daily Globe* (p. 1), and in the *Rocky Mountain News* and *Galveston Daily News.* All had a dateline of New York, March 14.

133. "Riot and Outrage: As Pictured by the Manager of a Women's Base Ball Club Just Back From Cuba," *Sporting Life,* March 18, 1893, 1.

134. "The Story False," *Rocky Mountain News,* March 17, 1893. The story reads: "Havana,

March 16.—The statement made since the return from Cuba to the United States of the American Female Base Ball club, that during the disorder which broke out on March 5 at Almendares, an American flag was torn down and destroyed, is here declared untrue."

135. "No Insult Offered the Flag: A Cuban Paper Denies the Charge of American Female Ball Players," *Omaha World Herald,* March 24, 1893, 1.

136. "Not a War Cloud: No International Complications Likely to Arise Out of the Female Base Ball Club Trouble," *Sporting Life,* March 25, 1893, 1.

137. "It Would Be Risky: Anson Would Take No Chances With His Colts in Cuba," *Sporting Life,* April 15, 1893, 4. Quoted in the *Chicago Herald.*

138. Maud Nelson and Margaret Nabel are just two of the sportswomen who managed Bloomer Girl teams in the early twentieth century.

139. The term "Bloomer Girl" originated during the cycling fad of the 1890s. Robust, bloomer-clad women undermined stereotypes about women's physical and mental weaknesses and polarized debates over women's proper role in society. "I stand and rejoice every time I see a woman ride by on a wheel," wrote the aging Susan B. Anthony, "I think it has done more to emancipate women than anything else in the world." Others fumed. "I think the most vicious thing I ever saw in all my life is a woman on a bicycle," wrote one critic in 1891 from Washington, D.C. "I had thought that cigarette smoking was the worst thing a woman could do, but I have changed my mind." "The Woman on a Bicycle," *Sunday Herald* (1891), quoted in Adrienne LaFrance, "How the Bicycle Paved the Way for Women's Rights," *The Atlantic* Web site. Posted June 26, 2014.

140. Newspapers in California touted the arrival of The Bloomer Girl Big Burlesque and Minstrel Company for shows in March and April 1897. The troupe played multi-night engagements at indoor theaters and attracted crowds by staging street parades featuring "sixteen charming young ladies of *the new woman type* led by their own bicycle band" (emphasis added). "The Bloomer Girls Will Be The Next Attraction at the Barton," *Fresno Bee,* March 3, 1897, 2. See also "Local Brevities," *Fresno Morning Republican,* March 12, 1897, 3; *Fresno Bee,* March 14, 1897.

141. Reprinted in *Henderson (N.C.) Gold Leaf,* April 20, 1899, 3. Other examples of complimentary articles include: "The Bloomer Girls," *New Orleans Daily Picayune,* April 17, 1899, 8; "Batting Base Ball at Belt Line Park," *Lexington Morning Herald,* May 1, 1899, 7.

142. See, for example, *Arkansas City Daily Traveler,* September 12, 1892, 5; "Cincinnati 'Frauds'—They Play at Ball," *Camden Advance-Journal,* September 17, 1891, 3.

143. "Bloomer Gals Beaten. The Beantown Aggregation Throws up the Sponge in Five Innings," *Rock Island (Ill.) Argus,* August 4, 1895, 4

144. *Little Falls Weekly Transcript,* September 20, 1895, 2.

145. "The Female Baseballists," *Raleigh News and Observer,* August 6, 1895, 6; "Bloomer Girls on the Diamond: The San Francisco Athletics Succumb to the Boston Aggregation; Base hits, Runs and Errors Piled Up in a Most Bewildering Manner; Fully One Thousand People Witness the Performance at Sixteenth and Folsom Streets," *San Francisco Call,* October 25, 1897, 6.

146. "Notes About the State," *Philadelphia Inquirer,* June 21, 1891: 2; "A Baseball Fiasco: an Amusing Exhibition of Feminine Ball Playing," *Little Falls Evening Times,* August 15, 1891, 3; "Petticoats Playing Base-Ball," *Watertown Daily Times,* September 3, 1891, 8; "Camden," *Rome (N.Y.) Roman Citizen,* September 12, 1891.

147. "Girl Ball Tossers: Tame Playing, But One of Them Badly Injured," *Cheyenne Daily Sun,* June 28, 1892, 3; "The Female Ball Club," *Cedar Rapids Evening Gazette,* June 20, 1894, 8.

148. "A Bloomer Girl 'Kills' A Pitcher," *Lexington Morning Herald,* May 18, 1899, 8.

149. "Fell Dead on the Ball Field: Crossing Bats with the 'Bloomer Girl' Team Was Too Much for Winder," *Denver Evening Post,* July 10, 1898.

150. "Fair Ones Play Ball: The Ladies Aggregation Entertains 1,500 People; The Score Nine to Seven. The Girls Afraid to Play Ball Very Hard Because They Might Spoil Their Clothes—They Drink Oatmeal Water and Carry Sponges," *Topeka State Journal,* July 12, 1892, 3.

151. *Atchison Daily Globe,* August 26, 1892.

152. "Telegraphic Notes," *Decatur (Ill.) Daily Republican,* September 25, 1895, 6.

153. "The Field Day: Some Fair Records Made Yesterday; Interesting Bicycle Races; The Female Baseball Club a Fake; The Deception Severely Criticized," *Fresno Morning Republican,* May 31, 1894, 3.

154. "Lady Base Ball Players," *Wichita Beacon,* September 3, 1892, 4.

155. "Various and All About," *Newberry (S.C.) Herald and News,* April 4, 1899, 3; "The Bull Fighters and the Feminine Baseball Club," *Statesville (N.C) Landmark,* April 14, 1899, 3; "They Skipped the Town," *Henderson (N.C.) Gold Leaf* April 27, 1899, 3; "Boys Beat Boston Bloomer Girls: Twas A Tame Game Hits And Errors Many," *Lexington Morning Herald,* May 3, 1899, 7.

156. A study based on the census of 1900 found that almost a quarter of all working women were servants or waitresses. Textile workers and farm laborers made up the next largest groups. Department of Commerce and Labor, Bureau of the Census, *Statistics of Women at Work* (Based on Unpublished Information Derived From the Schedules of the Twelfth Census: 1900) (Washington, D.C.: Government Printing Office, 1907). Thanks to M. Ann Hall for bringing this source to my attention.

157. Meyerowitz, *Women Adrift,* 34–37. "Those Girls In Bloomers. Big Crowd of Sioux City People Sees Them Play Ball. Had Fully 2,000 Spectators. It was the largest Attendance in the History of Boyer's Park—The Pitcher Is a Crackerjack and the First Base-'man' a Good One—A Successful Tour," *Sioux City Journal,* August 30, 1895, 3.

158. Nelson (Clementine Brida) was from the Austrian Tyrol. In June 1896, another (presumably) Italian female baseball player was one of the featured attractions at the annual Italian picnic at Rockaway beach in Syracuse. "Great Day for Italy: Big Finale and Athletic Events Held at Rockaway Beach," *Syracuse Daily Journal,* June 30, 1896, 10.

159. Newspapers occasionally reported on the daughters of wealthy families running away to join female barnstorming teams, thus implying that this was out of the ordinary; most players came from the working class. One New York–based barnstorming team showed its class solidarity when it played a charity game against a group of clerks in Natick, Massachusetts to support striking lasters at J.W. Walcott & Co. "Girls Help Strikers," *Boston Journal,* June 14, 1894, 7.

160. "Novel Football Game: Two Female Teams to Play Under Association Rules," *San Francisco Evening Call,* November 6, 1893, 3. "Football" is the European term for soccer.

161. Wilson made several trips to Canada with his teams. M. Ann Hall notes that even though the Canadian press labeled these teams frauds and fakes, the teams still influenced the organization of numerous female baseball teams in urban centers and small communities across Canada. M. Ann Hall, *The Girl and the Game: A History of Women's Sport in Canada* (Toronto: University of Toronto Press, 2002), 37–38. See also Colin Howell, *Northern Sandlots: A Social History of Maritime Baseball* (Toronto: University of Toronto Press, 1995), 74.

162. In addition to reporting on the travels of the Boston Bloomer Girls in 1895, the local Cherokee newspaper was carrying articles about barnstorming female baseball teams at least as early as June 1890. See, for example, "Condensed News," *Weekly Cherokean-Democrat* (Iowa), June 18, 1890.

163. "In Central New York: All Around Us," *Ostego (N.Y.) Farmer,* April 29, 1898, 1; "Diamond Dust," *Richfield Springs (N.Y.) Mercury,* May 5, 1898.

164. "Biographical Sketch of Mrs. Harry S. Truman," Harry S. Truman Library and Museum Web site. http://www .trumanlibrary.org/bwt-bio.htm. Bess Truman was born in 1885 in

Independence, Missouri. She was the oldest of four children and the only daughter. Truman's daughter, Margaret, recalled her mother's exploits on the boys' team in Jean Ardell's *Breaking into Baseball*, 36.

165. Goodridge Wilson, *A Brief History of Marion College* (Class of 1948 and Alumnae Association in Commemoration of the Seventy-Fifth Anniversary of the Founding of the College, 1948), 37.

166. *New York Times,* November 14, 1896; A photo of a female baseball team at Mrs. Hazen's School taken in 1896 is available at: Blake A. Bell, "Baseball in Late 19th Century Pelham," *Pelham (N.Y.) Weekly* 13, no. 17, April 23, 1904, 8. http://historicpelham.blogspot.com/2010 /02/photograph-of-only-known-19th-century.html. The Smith College Archives has photos of female baseball players at the Mary A. Burnham School c. 1894–95. (School was renamed Miss Capen's School in 1909.) Edith Naomi Hill Papers, Box #867, Folder #2, "Capen School Photo Album."

167. The Chestnut Street Female Seminary leased Cooke's estate until 1916. https://www .libraries.psu.edu /psul/digital/ogontz/estate.html.

168. In addition to the two photographs from 1890, the Penn State Abington Library (PSAL) has another team photo from 1893 plus rosters and game results dating from 1898 to 1933 in its Ogontz School collection.

169. "The Month," *Ogontz Mosaic,* April 1895, 12. PSAL.

170. Walker apparently also taught physical education. It was not unusual for high school teachers to be dual hatted as physical education teachers.

171. Milo S. Walker, "Indoor Base Ball for Women," *Spalding's Athletic Library Official Indoor Base Ball Guide* (New York: American Sports Publishing, February 1903). http://www.lostcentury .com/1903-womens-softball.html.

172. *National Police Gazette,* March 16, 1895. Thanks to David Block for bringing this to my attention.

173. Walker, "Indoor Base Ball for Women."

174. J. R. Street, "A Study in Moral Education," *Pedagogical Seminary* 5, no. 1 (1897). Street was a Fellow at Clark University. Average age of respondents was seventeen to twenty-one years of age, which means that the female respondents who played baseball would have done so well before 1895 when they were still in school.

175. Abolitionist and women's rights advocate Sarah Grimké sometimes closed her letters with the phrase, "Thine in the bonds of womanhood." Grimké likened the onerous bondage of southern slaves with the unrelenting overt and covert pressure on women to submit to subservient roles in society. Young girls growing up in the nineteenth century understood that, while they might enjoy the latitude to explore many "masculine" activities as children, they would have to abandon those pursuits as adults if they wished to maintain society's approbation. Nancy F. Cott, *The Bonds of Womanhood: 'Woman's Sphere' in New England, 1780–1835* (New Haven, Conn.: Yale University Press, 1997).

176. *The (Bryn Mawr) Lantern* (1897), 11. Bryn Mawr College Archives (BMCA).

177. Millicent Peirce Potter, "Athletics at Wellesley," *American Athlete* 1, no. 1 (April 1897): 1.

178. Potter, "Athletics at Wellesley," 1; the Smith College archives includes team photographs and letters from students mentioning baseball in the 1890s; "Athletic California Girls in the Rain. A Sprightly Account of a Game Played on the Quiet—Bloomers and All the Paraphernalia—They Slide Bases in the Mud," *Kansas City Star,* February 14, 1897, 7; the Mills College Archives includes a team photograph from 1898; "Territorial News," *Weekly Phoenix Herald,* March 24, 1898, 4; "How Women's College Girls Play Ball," *Cleveland Plain Dealer,* May 7,

1896, 5; Converse College (opened 1890) began producing yearbooks in 1897. The yearbooks include photographs of the class baseball teams.

179. *(Mount Holyoke) Class Book*, [1891], 16. The students also mentioned baseball in the first issue of the college newspaper, *The Mount Holyoke* 1, no. 1 (June 1891). MHCLA.

180. "Field Day Sports: University Notes," *Grand Forks Herald*, May 7, 1893, 4; "Nubs of News," *Grand Forks Herald*, May 13, 1893, 8.

181. "Freshman Banquet," *Kalamazoo Gazette*, May 13, 1893, 1.

182. "College Cullings," *The (Olivet College) Echo* 9, no. 11 (April 20, 1897), 114; "Umpire Safe Here. Olivet College Girls Will Play Base Ball. And Falling Hairpins or Untied Shoe Laces Will Not Stop the Game," *Grand Rapids Press*, May 15, 1897, 7. Olivet College Archives (OCA).

183. Joan S. Hult, "The Philosophical Conflicts in Men's and Women's Collegiate Athletics," In David K. Wiggins, ed., *Sport in America: From Wicked Amusement to National Obsession*, (Champaign, Ill.: Human Kinetics, 1995), 301–17.

184. Rosenberg, *Beyond Separate Spheres*, 14.

185. "The Game of Battle Ball. It is the Invention of a Boston Doctor," *Kansas City Star*, April 21, 1894, supplement; "Harvard. An Athletics Shake-Up—Battle Ball With Annex Girls," *New York Herald-Tribune*, May 20, 1894, 22; "Female Foot Ball. Boston University Fair Ones Play Battle Ball . . . ," *Boston Journal*, January 26, 1895, 1.

186. "Trained to Bend Oars; Dimpled Arms of Fair Collegians for Rival Crews. The New Game of Baseball; It is Called Lang and Was Designed Solely for Feminine Players . . . ," *Washington Post*, April 12, 1896, 19.

Conclusion

1. The term "official" is used here to distinguish baseball and softball from precursor bat and ball games. "Official" implies the existence of an organized body that writes and promulgates rules of a sport and that governs (either formally or informally) and promotes the sport. Though historians trace the origins of softball back to the late 1880s, the "official" sport did not emerge until the mid-1930s when representatives from the United States and Canada established the Joint Rules Committee on Softball to standardize its name and rules.

2. Zane Grey, "Inside Baseball," *Baseball Magazine* 3, no. 4 (August 1909): 11.

3. William A. McKeever, *Training the Boy* (1913), 13; quoted in Michael S. Kimmel, "Baseball and the Reconstitution of American Masculinity, 1880–1920," in *Sport, Men, and the Gender Order: Critical Feminist Perspectives*, ed. Michael A. Messner and Don Sabo (Champaign, Ill.: Human Kinetics, 1992), 61.

4. Quoted in Fields, *Female Gladiators*, 20.

5. Fields documents the intensely emotional, gendered rhetoric generated by the lawsuits brought by teenage girls against Little League Baseball's ban on female players. See esp. pp. 21–32.

6. Quoted in Fields, *Female Gladiators*, 25.

7. Baseball For All: http://www.baseballforall.com; Girls Play Baseball: http://girlsplaybaseball.ning.com; USA Baseball Women's National Team: http://web.usabaseball.com/womens_national_team.jsp. Little League Baseball lifted its ban on female players in 1974 after a series of successful lawsuits forced its hand. The group immediately created a Little League Softball program and steered girls into it, but it has also accommodated the girls who want to play baseball.

8. Detroit River Belles Ladies Vintage Base Ball Club. https://www.facebook.com/pages/Detroit-River-Belles-Ladies-Vintage-Base-Ball-Club/171453793041731. Vintage Base Ball Association. http://vbba.org/Main /Ladies%20Vintage %20Base%20Ball.htm.

Selected Bibliography

This bibliography provides only a sampling of primary and secondary sources. It contains few newspaper articles; many are included in citations. A list of helpful digital resources is included.

Primary Sources (Non-Newspaper)

American Gynecological Society. *Transactions of the American Gynecological Society for the Year 1900*. Vol. 25. Philadelphia: Wm. J. Dornan, 1900. Google Books.

"The Athletic Girl," *Philadelphia Sunday Item*. December 24, 1893.

Austen, Jane. *Northanger Abbey,* Vol. 2. London, 1818. Google Books.

Austin, Harriet N. "Women's Present and Future." *Water-Cure Journal* 16 (September 1853): 57.

Babcock, S. Review of *The Young Lady's Home,* by Louisa C. Tuthill. *New York Review* 5 (1839): 246.

Bailey, James M. "The Female Base Ball Nine." In *Mark Twain's Library of Humor,* 126–29. New York, 1888.

Ballintine, Harriet I. "The Value of Athletics to College Girls." *American Physical Education Review* 6 (June 1901): 153–55.

Beard, Daniel Carter. *Outdoor Games for All Seasons: The American Boy's Book of Sports*. New York, 1896.

Beard, George Miller. *American Nervousness: Its Causes and Consequences ; a Supplement to Nervous Exhaustion (neurasthenia)*. New York, 1881.

Bengough, W. "The New Woman, Athletically Considered." *Godey's Magazine* (January 1896): 132 and 787.

Bigelow, Anne Marie Boren. "Memoir." (circa 1900). http://webpages.charter.net/joekuras/townball2.htm.

Bingham, Norman Williams. *The Book of Athletics and Out-of-door Sports: Containing Practical Advice and Suggestions from College Team-captains and Other Amateurs, on Bicycling, Swimming, Skating, Yachting, etc.* Boston, 1895.

Blackwell, Alice Stone. Journal Entries, 1872–1874. Reproduced in: *Growing Up in Boston's Gilded Age: The Journal of Alice Stone Blackwell, 1872–1874,* edited by Marlene Deahl Merrill. New Haven, Conn.: Yale University Press, 1990.

Blaine, Delabere P. *An Encyclopaedia of Rural Sports; or a Complete Account, Historical, Prac-*

tical, and Descriptive, of Hunting, Shooting, Fishing, Racing, and Other Field Sports and Athletic Amusements of the Present Day. London, 1840. Google Books.

Brown, Dr. John MacMahon (Physician, New York County Jail). Letter to Hon. Thomas J. Dunn, Sheriff, New York County. July 22, 1898. NYC Municipal Archives (NYCMA).

Carver, Robin. *Boys & Girls Book of Sports*. Boston, 1843. William L. Clements Library, University of Michigan.

Casa Borromeo Color Image of Fresco. http://www.storiadimilano.it/Arte/giochiborromeo/giochiborromeo.htm.

Chadwick, Henry. "The Ancient History of Base Ball." *Ball Players' Chronicle* 1, no. 7 (July 18, 1867): 4.

———. [No Title]. *Ball Players' Chronicle* 1, No. 8 (July 25, 1867). Cited in: Federal Writer's Project, Illinois: Work Project Administration. *Baseball in Old Chicago*, 8–9. Chicago: A.C. McClurg, 1939.

"Chats with Correspondents." *Ballou's Monthly Magazine* 50, no. 4 (October 1879): 393.

Checkley, Edwin. *A Natural Method of Physical Training: Making Muscle and Reducing Flesh Without Dieting or Apparatus*. Brooklyn, 1892.

"Court of General Sessions Minutes." (June 1879). Roll #41, p. 36, NYCMA.

Cowles, B. "History of Niles." *Berrien County Directory and History*, 1871, pp. 40–65.

Crane, Rev. J. T. "Popular Amusements, Part I." *Ladies Repository* 27, no. 7 (July 1867): 406–9. Making of American Journals (MOAJ).

———. "Popular Amusements, Part II." *Ladies' Repository* 27, no. 8 (August 1867): 476–79. MOAJ.

"The Cricket Mania," *Harper's Weekly*, October 10, 1859, 658.

Cust, Lionel. "The Frescoes in the Casa Borromeo at Milan." *Burlington Magazine for Connoisseurs* 33, no. 184 (July 1918): 8, 10–11, 13–14.

Cutler, Susan Rhoda. "Base-Ball for Girls." *Women's Journal*. May 24, 1890, 162.

"Doings Current." *The Letter Box* 2, No. 5 (May 1859), in *The Letter-Box*, 37. Vols. 1 and 2, 1858–59, edited by Harriet N. Austin and James Jackson. Dansville, N.Y., 1859.

Dudley, Gertrude, and Frances A. Kellor. *Athletic Games in the Education of Women*. New York, 1909.

D'Urfey, Thomas. *Wit and Mirth: Or, Pills to Purge Melancholy ; Being a Collection of the Best Merry Ballads and Songs, Old and New, Fitted to All Humours, Having Each Their Proper Tune for Either Voice, or Instrument*. Vol. 1. London, 1719.

"Editors' Table: Waifs." *Hamilton Literary Monthly* 3, no. 2 (September 1868): 69. Hamilton College Archives.

"Elizabeth Smith Miller on Dress Reform." New York Public Library. Elizabeth Smith Miller Collection. Accessed February 24, 2010. http://www.assumption.edu/whw/Smith_Miller_on_dress.html.

Elizabeth Smith Miller Diary, 1856–1868. Madison County Historical Society.

Emily Howland Scrapbook, 1868. NAWSA Collection, Section XVI, no. 2. Library of Congress Rare Book and Special Collections Division.

"The Errand Boy." *The Child's Friend* 9, no. 4 (January 1848): 157–76.

"Female Athletes: The Daughters of Senators and Congressmen Learning Gymnastics." *Sioux County Independent* (East Orange, Iowa). February 22, 1882.

Frost, Helen. *Basket Ball and Indoor Baseball for Women*. New York: C. Scribner's Sons, 1920.

Frothingham, Octavius Brooks. *Gerrit Smith: A Biography*. New York, 1878.

Gage, Frances Dana Barker. "Muscle Looking Up." *The Letter-Box*, 99. Vols. 1 and 2, 1858–59, edited by Harriet N. Austin and James Jackson. Dansville, N.Y., 1859

Gilder, Jeannette L. *The Autobiography of a Tomboy*. New York: Doubleday, Page, 1900.

"Girls Worth Having: What Muscular Evolution Has Done for the Development of the American Young Woman; The Delicate Pipestem Belle of 1840 Superseded by the More Robust Maiden of 1885; A Movement in Favor of the Physical Culture of Woman—The Good Results; . . ." *St. Paul Daily Globe*, September 6, 1885.

Glidden, Annie. Letter from Annie Glidden to John Glidden. April 20, 1866. Glidden Papers. Vassar College Special Collections.

Guiwits, Francis. "Correspondence." *Harper's Weekly* 11, no. 5, November 5, 1859, 707.

Hale, Sarah Josepha. *Woman's Record; or Sketches of all Distinguished Women From "The Beginning" Till A.D. 1850 Arranged in Four Eras With Selections From Female Writers of Every Age.* New York, 1853.

Hall, Benjamin Homer. "The College Customs of Harvard College, Anno 1734–5 as Transcribed by Richard Waldron, Class of 1738." A Collection of College Words and Customs. Accessed April 20, 2012. http://www.fullbooks.com/A-Collection-of-College-Words-and-Customs5 .html.

Hall, Henry. *The Tribune Book of Open-Air Sports.* New York, 1887.

Hamilton, Gustavus, James Neele, and Josiah Neele. *The Elements of Gymnastics, for Boys, and of Calisthenics, for Young Ladies: Illustrated by Forty-three Engravings.* London, 1840.

"Hannah Lyman," *Vassar Encyclopedia.* http://vcencyclopedia.vassar.edu/matthew-vassar/ hannah-lyman/index .html.

Hart, Livinia. "A Girl's College Life." *Cosmopolitan: a Monthly Illustrated Magazine* 31, no. 2 (June 1901): 188–195.

Hartwell, E. M. "Physical Training in American Colleges and Universities." *Circulars of Information of the Bureau of Education.* Washington, D.C.: Government Printing Office, 1886.

Hill, Lucille Eaton, ed. *Athletics and Out-Door Sports For Women.* New York: MacMillan, 1903.

Hurd, Charles W. "Letter from Charles W. Hurd to Charles H. Berry," April 8, 1869. http:// cgi.ebay.com/EARLY-ANTIQUE-HISTORIC-LETTER-1869-T206-OLD-JUDGE- /140434365961?pt=Vintage _Sports_ Memorabilia#ht_1754wt_1139.

Journal of the Assembly of the State of New York, at Their One Hundred and Fifteenth Session, Begun and Held at the Capitol, in the City of Albany, on the Fifth Day of January, 1892. Albany, N.Y., 1892.

Kate Wilson vs. Sylvester F. Wilson Divorce Records. In Chancery of New Jersey, October 14, 1887. New York State Archives (NYSA), Wilson files.

Kenealy, Arabella. "Woman as an Athlete." *The Nineteenth Century* 45, no. 266 (April 1899): 636–45.

———. "Women as an Athlete: A Rejoinder." *The Nineteenth Century* 45, no. 268 (June 1899): 915–29.

Leonard, Fred E. *Pioneers of Modern Physical Training.* Physical Directors' Society of the YMCA of N. Am., 1915.

Lepel, Mary. *Letters of Mary Lepel, Lady Hervey With a Memoir, and Illustrative Notes.* London, 1821. Google Books.

Leverson, Dr. Montagne R. Letter to the Honorable Joseph E. Newburger [sic], Judge of the Court of General Sessions of the City of New York. July 22, 1898. NYCMA.

Lewis, Dio. *Our Girls.* New York, 1871. Google Books.

———. "Physical Culture" 13, no. 10 (October 1860). *The Massachusetts Teacher: A Journal of School and Home Education,* 375. Vol. 13. Boston: Massachusetts Teachers Association, 1860.

Lloyd, Will L. *The Red Book, an Illustrated Legislative Manual of the State, Containing the Portraits and Biographies of its Governors and Members of the Legislature; Also the Enumera-*

tion of the State for 1892, with Election and Population Statistics, and Lists of Postmasters. Albany, N.Y., 1892.

Marcet, Jane. *Conversations on Natural Philosophy; In Which The Elements of That Science Are Familiarly Explained, and Adapted To The Comprehension of Young Pupils.* London, 1822. Google Books.

Mitford, Mary Russell. *The Works of Mary Russell Mitford.* Philadelphia, 1841. Google Books.

New York Society for the Prevention of Cruelty to Children. *Seventeenth Annual Report.* New York: NYSPCC, 1892.

———. *Twenty-Second Annual Report.* New York: NYSPCC, 1897.

———. *Twenty-Fifth Annual Report.* New York: NYSPCC, 1900.

———. *Twenty-Ninth Annual Report.* New York: NYSPCC, 1904.

Newbery, John. *A Little Pretty Pocket-Book, Intended for the Instructions and Amusement of Little Master Tommy, and Pretty Miss Polly.* London, 1744.

O'Loughlin, Daniel. Letter to His Excellency, Governor [Francis] Black. May 26, 1898. NYCMA.

"Our Letter Bag." *Oliver Optic's Magazine; Our Boys and Girls,* October 2, 1868, 605.

"Out-Door Sport." *Harper's Bazaar* 27, no. 30, July 28, 1894, 606.

Palmer, Gladys E. *Baseball for Girls and Women.* New York: A.S. Barnes, 1929.

Paret, Jahial Parmly. *The Woman's Book of Sports: A Practical Guide to Physical Development and Outdoor Recreation.* New York: Appleton, 1901.

People v. Sylvester F. Wilson. Witness Deposition, John W. Morrison. Court of General Sessions Indictments, Box 451, Folder 4157. NYCMA.

People v. Sylvester F. Wilson. Police Court, 5th District, New York City. August 17, 1891. Microfilm of Police Court Docket Books. NYCMA.

People v. Sylvester F. Wilson. Motion to Remit Fine. Court of General Sessions. September 10, 1891.

People &c v. Sylvester F. Wilson. Court of General Sessions of the Peace, County of New York. Petition of the Central Labor Union in the Matter of the Remission of the Residue of the Fine of Sylvester F. Wilson. August 2, 1898. NYCMA.

People of the State of New York v. Sylvester F. Wilson. Appellant's Points. Prepared by James R. Stevens. (c. 1892). NYCMA.

People v. Sylvester F. Wilson otherwise called Frank W. Hartright. No. 43345. Court of General Sessions of the Peace In And For The County of New York. "A True Bill." NYCMA.

People Against Sylvester F. Wilson. Brief for the People. N.Y. General Sessions. [undated, c. 1903]. NYCMA.

Peverelly, Charles A. *The Book of American Pastimes: Containing a History of the Principal Base-Ball, Cricket, Rowing, and Yachting Clubs of the United States.* New York, 1866.

"The Playground: Our National Game." *Oliver Optic's Magazine; Our Boys and Girls,* September 19 1868, 605.

Powell, E. M. "Physical Culture at Vassar College." *Herald of Health and Journal of Physical Culture.* New York, 1869.

"Puck's Exchanges." *Puck.* August 27, 1879, 376.

Richardson, Sophia Foster. "Tendencies in Athletics for Women in Colleges & Universities." *Appleton's Popular Science Monthly,* February 1897, 1–10.

Sargent, Dudley A. *Physical Education.* Boston and New York: Ginn, 1906.

Sing Sing Admission Record of Sylvester F. Wilson. December 24, 1892. Series B0143–80, Box 10, Volume 28, p. 29. NYSA.

Sing Sing Admission Record of Sylvester F. Wilson (Inmate #54383). August 21, 1903. Book 35, p. 416. NYSA.

Skene, Dr. Alexander Johnston Chalmers. *Education and Culture as Related to the Health and Diseases of Women*. Detroit, 1889. Google Books.

Sports and Games: A Magazine of Amusements for All Seasons. Vol. 1. Boston: Adams, 1870.

Sports and Pastimes for In-Doors and Out with Additions by Oliver Optic, Embracing Physical and Intellectual Amusements for Young People, the Family Circle and Evening Parties. Boston, 1863.

Stanton, Elizabeth Cady. "Editorial Correspondence." *The Revolution* 2, no. 5 (August 6, 1868): 65–66.

———. "Editorial Correspondence." *The Revolution* 2, no. 7 (August 20, 1868): 97–98.

State of New York in Assembly. No. 1063, Int. 940 "An Act to Prohibit Female Base Ball Playing." March 4, 1892. NYSA.

"Stool-ball or the Easter Diversion." *The London Magazine, or, Gentleman's Monthly Intelligencer* 2 (1733): 637.

Strutt, Joseph. *The Sports and Pastimes of the People of England: Including the Rural and Domestic Recreations, May Games, Mummeries, Shows, Processions, Pageants, & Pompous Spectacles, from the Earliest Period to the Present Time*. London, 1801.

Taylor, E. L. Letter from E. L. Taylor to Gerrit Smith. August 17, 1868. Gerrit Smith Papers. Special Collections Research Center, Syracuse University Library.

Tuthill, Louisa C. *The Young Lady's Home*. New Haven, Conn., 1839.

Voarino, Signor. *A Treatise on Calisthenic Exercises: Arranged for the Private Tuition of Ladies*. Printed for N. Hailes, 1827.

Williams, Ramon G. [Consul General, Havana]. Dispatch #1818 from U.S. Consulate General, Havana, Cuba to Assistant Secretary of State, William F. Wharton, Washington, D.C. National Archives. (Vol. 226, "Enclosures,"): 498–501.

———. [Consul General, Havana]. Enclosure #2 to Dispatch #1818 from U.S. Consulate General, Havana, Cuba to Assistant Secretary of State, William F. Wharton, Washington, D.C. National Archives. (Vol. 226, "Enclosures,"): 498–501.

———. Letter from U.S. Consulate General to the Governor General of Cuba. Havana. March 10, 1893. Translated by J. Camilo Vera, University of Miami.

Wilson, Sylvester F. Letter to Asa Bird Gardiner, Esq., District Attorney of the City of New York. July 14, 1898. Ludlow Street Jail. NYCMA.

———. Letter to the Honorable Joseph E. Neuburger, Judge of the Court of General Sessions of the City of New York. July 15, 1898. NYCMA.

———. Letter to the Honorable Judge Cowing, Court of General Sessions of the City of New York. August 18, 1903. NYCMA.

———. "The Truth Asks a Hearing. A Short History of the Case [of] the Malicious Persecution of Sylvester Franklin Wilson upon the False and Never Legally Proven Case of 'Abduction' Instigated by the Blackmailing Gerry Society of New York, Condensed From the Details of Over 500 Pages." To His Excellency Frank W. Higgins, Governor of New York. February 20, 1906. NYCMA.

Secondary Sources

Adams, Rachel. *Sideshow U.S.A.: Freaks and the American Cultural Imagination*. Chicago: University of Chicago Press, 2001.

Ainsworth, Dorothy S. *The History of Physical Education in Colleges for Women as Illustrated by Barnard, Bryn Mawr, Elmira, Goucher, Mills, Mount Holyoke, Radcliffe, Rockford, Smith, Vassar, Wellesley and Wells*. New York, 1930.

Allen, Robert C. *Horrible Prettiness: Burlesque and American Culture*. Chapel Hill: University of North Carolina Press, 1991.

Allman, Jean. "The Disappearing of Hannah Kudjoe: Nationalism, Feminism, and the Tyrannies of History." *Journal of Women's History* 21, no. 3 (Fall 2009): 13–35.

Altherr, Tom. "Coed Cat Games in Wisconsin in the Early 1850s." *Originals* 4, no. 1 (January 2011): 2.

Ardell, Jean Hastings, and Ila Borders. *Breaking Into Baseball: Women and the National Pastime.* Carbondale: Southern Illinois University Press, 2005.

Bailey, Peter. " 'A Mingled Mass of Perfectly Legitimate Pleasures': The Victorian Middle Class and the Problem of Leisure." *Victorian Studies* 21, no. 1 (October 1, 1977): 7–28.

Banner, Lois W. *Women in Modern America: a Brief History.* New York: Harcourt Brace Jovanovich, 1974.

Beadie, Nancy, and Kim Tolley. *Chartered Schools: Two Hundred Years of Independent Academies in the United States, 1727–1925.* New York: Routledge, 2002.

Bederman, Gail. *Manliness and Civilization: A Cultural History of Gender and Race in the United States, 1880–1917.* Chicago: University of Chicago Press, 1995.

Berlage, Gai I. *Women in Baseball: The Forgotten History.* Westport, Conn.: Praeger, 1994.

Block, David. *Baseball Before We Knew It: A Search for the Roots of the Game.* Lincoln: University of Nebraska Press, 2005.

———. "The Story of William Bray's Diary." *Base Ball: A Journal of the Early Game* 1, no. 2 (Fall 2007): 5–11.

Boydston, Jeanne. "Gender as a Question of Historical Analysis." *Gender & History* 20, no. 3 (November 2008): 558–53.

Brown, Randall. "Blood and Base Ball." *Base Ball: A Journal of the Early Game* (Spring 2009): 23–43.

Bryson, Lois. "Sport and the Maintenance of Masculine Hegemony." *Women's Studies International Forum* 10, no. 4 (1987): 349–60.

Buhle, Mari Jo, and Paul Buhle. *The Concise History of Woman Suffrage: Selections from the Classic Work of Stanton, Anthony, Gage, and Harper.* Urbana: University of Illinois Press, 1979.

Cahn, Susan K. *Coming on Strong: Gender and Sexuality in Twentieth-Century Women's Sports.* New York: Free Press, 1998.

Chudacoff, Howard P. *Children at Play: An American History.* New York: New York University Press, 2008.

Clark, Daniel A. *Creating the College Man: American Mass Magazines and Middle-Class Manhood, 1890–1915.* Madison: University of Wisconsin Press, 2010.

Clifford, Geraldine Joncich. *Lone Voyagers: Academic Women in Coeducational Institutions, 1870–1937.* New York: Feminist Press at City University of New York, 1993.

Cohen, Marilyn. *No Girls in the Clubhouse: The Exclusion of Women from Baseball.* Jefferson, N.C.: McFarland, 2009.

Cott, Nancy. *The Bonds of Womanhood: "Woman's Sphere" in New England, 1780–1835.* New Haven, Conn.: Yale University Press, 1977.

Cronon, William. *Nature's Metropolis: Chicago and the Great West.* New York: W. W. Norton, 1992.

Danziger, Lucy. *Nike Is a Goddess: The History of Women in Sports.* New York: Atlantic Monthly Press, 1999.

Davis, Janet. *The Circus Age Culture and Society Under the American Big Top.* Chapel Hill: University of North Carolina Press, 2002.

Dulles, Foster Rhea. *America Learns to Play: a History of Popular Recreation, 1607–1940.* New York: D. Appleton-Century, 1940.

Durant, John, and Otto Bettmann. *Pictorial History of American Sports.* 1st ed. Philadelphia: A. S. Barnes, 1952.

Dyer, K. F. *Challenging the Men: The Social Biology of Female Sporting Achievement.* St. Lucia: University of Queensland Press, 1982.

Elias, Robert. *The Empire Strikes Out: How Baseball Sold U.S. Foreign Policy and Promoted the American Way Abroad.* New York: New Press, 2010.

Enstad, Nan. *Ladies of Labor, Girls of Adventure.* New York: Columbia University Press, 1999.

Evans, Sara M. *Born for Liberty: A History of Women in America.* New York: Free Press, 1989.

Farnham, Christie Anne. *The Education of the Southern Belle: Higher Education and Student Socialization in the Antebellum South.* New York: New York University Press, 1995.

Felshen, Jan. "The Status of Women and Sport." In D. Stanley Eitzen, *Sport in Contemporary Society: An Anthology*, 412–20. New York: St. Martin's Press, 1979.

Fidler, Merrie A. *The Origins and History of the All-American Girls Professional Baseball League.* Reprint. Jefferson, N.C.: McFarland, 2010.

Fields, Sarah. *Female Gladiators : Gender, Law, and Contact Sport in America.* Urbana: University of Illinois Press, 2005.

Flexner, Eleanor. *Century of Struggle: The Women's Rights Movement of the United States.* New York: Atheneum, 1974.

Goldstein, Jonathan P. "Gender in American Tobacco Cards, 1880—1920: The Role of Coercive Competition." *Review of Political Economy* 24, no. 4 (2012): 575–605.

Goldstein, Warren. *Playing for Keeps: A History of Early Baseball*, 20th Anniversary Edition. Ithaca, N.Y.: Cornell University Press, 2009.

Goodsell, Willystine. *The Education of Women: Its Social Background and Its Problems.* New York: Macmillan, 1923.

Gordon, Ann D., ed. *The Selected Papers of Elizabeth Cady Stanton and Susan B. Anthony: In the School of Anti-Slavery, 1840 to 1866.* Vol. 1. Annotated edition. New Brunswick, N.J.: Rutgers University Press, 1997.

Gordon, Lynn. *Gender and Higher Education in the Progressive Era.* New Haven, Conn.: Yale University Press, 1990.

Gorn, Elliott J. *The Manly Art: Bare-Knuckle Prize Fighting in America.* Updated Edition. Ithaca, N.Y.: Cornell University Press, 2010.

Green, Harvey. *Fit for America.* New York: Pantheon Books, 1986.

Green, Jennifer R. *Military Education and the Emerging Middle Class in the Old South.* New York: Cambridge University Press, 2008.

Gregorich, Barbara. *Women at Play: The Story of Women in Baseball.* San Diego: Harcourt, 1993.

Grover, Kathryn, ed. *Fitness in American Culture: Images of Health, Sport and the Body, 1830–1940.* Amherst: University of Massachusetts Press, 1989.

Guttmann, Allen. *A Whole New Ball Game: An Interpretation of American Sports.* Chapel Hill: University of North Carolina Press, 1988.

Halttunen, Karen. *Confidence Men and Painted Women : Study of Middle Class Culture in America, 1830–70.* New Haven, Conn.: Yale University Press, 1986.

Hardy, Stephen. *How Boston Played: Sport, Recreation, And Community, 1856–1915.* Knoxville: University of Tennessee Press, 2003.

Hargreaves, Jennifer A. "Playing Like Gentlemen While Behaving Like Ladies: Contradictory Features of the Formative Years of Women's Sport." *British Journal of Sports History* 2, no. 1 (May 1985): 40–52.

———. "Where's the Virtue? Where's the Grace? A Discussion of the Social Production of Gender Relations in and through Sport." *Theory, Culture & Society* 3, no. 1 (February 1986): 109–21.

Harris, Barbara J. *Beyond Her Sphere: Women and the Professions in American History.* Westport, Conn.: Greenwood, 1978.

Harris, Dorothy V. "Femininity and Athleticism." In Gunther Luschen and George H. Sage, *Handbook of Social Science of Sport,* 274–94. Champaign, Ill.: Stipes, 1981.

Higginbotham, Evelyn Brooks. "African-American Women's History and the Metalanguage of Race." *Signs* 17, no. 2 (Winter 1992): 251–74.

Hise, Beth. *Swinging Away: How Cricket and Baseball Connect.* London: Scala Publishers, 2010.

Holliman, Jennie. *American Sports (1785–1835).* Durham, N.C.: Seeman Press, 1931.

Horowitz, Helen Lefkowitz. *Alma Mater.* 2nd ed. Amherst: University of Massachusetts Press, 1993.

———. *Campus Life: Undergraduate Cultures from the End of the Eighteenth Century to the Present.* Chicago: University of Chicago Press, 1987.

Howell, Reet A., ed. *Her Story in Sport: Historical Anthology of Women in Sport.* Champaign, Ill.: Human Kinetics, 1987.

Huizinga, Johan. *Homo Ludens : a Study of the Play-element in Culture.* London: Routledge & K. Paul, 1949. Google Books.

Hult, Joan S. "The Philosophical Conflicts in Men's and Women's Collegiate Athletics." In *Sport in America: From Wicked Amusement to National Obsession,* edited by David K. Wiggins, 301–17. Champaign, Ill.: Human Kinetics, 1995.

Hunter, Jane H. *How Young Ladies Became Girls: The Victorian Origins of American Girlhood.* New Haven, Conn.: Yale University Press, 2003.

Jenkins, Keith. *Rethinking History.* London: Routledge, 2003.

Kaplan, Amy. *The Anarchy of Empire in the Making of U.S. Culture.* Cambridge, Mass.: Harvard University Press, 2002.

Kasson, John F. *Amusing the Million: Coney Island At the Turn of the Century.* 1st ed. New York: Hill & Wang, 1978.

Kelley, Mary. *Learning to Stand and Speak: Women, Education, and Public Life in America's Republic.* Chapel Hill: University of North Carolina Press, 2008.

Kelly-Gadol, Joan. "The Social Relation of the Sexes: Methodological Implications of Women's History." *Signs* 1, no. 4 (Summer 1976): 809–23.

Kendall, Elaine. *"Peculiar Institutions": An Informal History of the Seven Sister Colleges.* New York: Putnam, 1976.

Kerber, Linda K., Alice Kessler-Harris, and Kathryn Kish Sklar. *U.S. History As Women's History: New Feminist Essays.* Chapel Hill: University of North Carolina Press, 1995.

Kerber, Linda K. "Separate Spheres, Female Worlds, Woman's Place: The Rhetoric of Women's History." *Journal of American History* 75, no. 1 (June 1, 1988): 9–39.

———. *Toward an Intellectual History of Women: Essays by Linda K. Kerber.* Chapel Hill: University of North Carolina Press, 1997.

Kern, Kathi. *Mrs. Stanton's Bible.* Ithaca, N.Y.: Cornell University Press, 2001.

Kibler, M. Alison. *Rank Ladies: Gender and Cultural Hierarchy in American Vaudeville.* Chapel Hill: University of North Carolina Press, 1999.

Kirsch, George B. *Baseball and Cricket: The Creation of American Team Sports, 1838–72.* Urbana: University of Illinois Press, 2007.

Knight, Louise W. *Jane Addams: Spirit in Action.* New York: W.W. Norton, 2010.

Kovach, John M. *Women's Baseball.* Charleston, S.C.: Arcadia Publishing, 2005.

Langum, David J. *Crossing over the Line: Legislating Morality and the Mann Act.* Chicago: University of Chicago Press, 1994.

Leitner, Irving. *Baseball Diamond in the Rough.* New York: Criterion, 1972.

Lerner, Gerda. *Why History Matters: Life and Thought.* New York: Oxford University Press, 1996.

Lester, Robin. *Stagg's University: The Rise, Decline, and Fall of Big-Time Football at Chicago.* Urbana: University of Illinois Press, 1999.

Levine, David O. *The American College and the Culture of Aspiration, 1915–1940.* Ithaca, N.Y.: Cornell University Press, 1986.

Mahoney, Kathleen. "American Catholic Colleges for Women: Historical Origins." In *Catholic Women's Colleges in America,* 25–54. Baltimore: Johns Hopkins University Press, 2002.

Manchester, Herbert. *Four Centuries of Sport in America.* New York: Derrydale Press, 1931.

Mangan, J. A., and Roberta J. Park, eds. *From Fair Sex to Feminism: Sport and the Socialization of Women in the Industrial and Post-Industrial Eras.* 1st ed. New York: Routledge, 1987.

May, Ann Mari. *The Woman Question and Higher Education: Perspectives on Gender and Knowledge Production in America.* Northampton, Mass.: Edward Elgar, 2008.

McDonagh, Eileen, and Laura Pappano. *Playing With the Boys: Why Separate Is Not Equal in Sports.* New York: Oxford University Press, 2009.

McDonald, Mary, and Susan Birrell. "Reading Sport Critically: A Methodology for Interrogating Power." *Sociology of Sport Journal* 16 (1999): 283–300.

Messner, Michael A. *Out of Play: Critical Essays on Gender and Sport.* Albany: State University of New York Press, 2007.

———. *Taking the Field: Women, Men, and Sports.* 1st ed. Minneapolis: University of Minnesota Press, 2002.

Messner, Michael A., and Don Sabo, eds. *Sport, Men, and the Gender Order: Critical Feminist Perspectives.* Champaign, Ill.: Human Kinetics, 1992.

Meyerowitz, Joanne J. *Women Adrift: Independent Wage Earners in Chicago, 1880–1930.* Chicago: University of Chicago Press, 1988.

Miller-Bernal, Leslie. *Separate by Degree.* New York: Peter Lang, 2000.

Mills, Dorothy Seymour. *Chasing Baseball: Our Obsession with Its History, Numbers, People and Places.* Jefferson, N.C.: McFarland, 2010.

Morris, Peter. *Baseball Fever: Early Baseball in Michigan.* Ann Arbor: University of Michigan Press, 2003.

———. *A Game of Inches: The Story Behind the Innovations That Shaped Baseball.* Chicago: Ivan R. Dee, 2010.

Mrozek, Donald J. *Sport and American Mentality, 1880–1910.* Knoxville: University of Tennessee Press, 1983.

Murphy, Cait. *Scoundrels in Law: The Trials of Howe & Hummel, Lawyers to the Gangsters, Cops, Starlets, and Rakes Who Made the Gilded Age.* New York: HarperCollins, 2010.

Nash, Margaret A. *Women's Education in the United States, 1780–1840.* New York: Palgrave Macmillan, 2005.

Nathan, Daniel A. *Saying It's So: A Cultural History of the Black Sox Scandal.* Urbana: University of Illinois Press, 2005.

Nichols, John. "Women in Medieval Sport." *Journal of Sport History Proceedings,* North American Society for Sport History Conference, 1992.

———. "Women in Sport: Images From the Late Middle Ages." Web page, c. 2001. http://sru-faculty.sru.edu /john.nichols/research/womensport.htm.

Ogilvie, Bruce C. "The Personality of Those Women Who Have Dared to Succeed in Sport." In *Sports, Games, and Play: Social & Psychological Viewpoints,* 149–56. Hillsdale, N.J.: Lawrence Erlbaum, 1979.

Oglesby, Carole A., ed. *Women and Sport: From Myth to Reality.* Philadelphia: Lea & Febiger, 1978.

Ogren, Chris. *The American State Normal School: "An Instrument of Great Good."* New York: Palgrave Macmillan, 2005.

O'Reilly, Jean, and Susan K. Cahn. *Women and Sports in the United States: A Documentary Reader.* Boston: Northeastern University Press, 2007.

Oriard, Michael. *Reading Football: How the Popular Press Created an American Spectacle*. Chapel Hill: University of North Carolina Press, 1998.

Pace, Robert F. *Halls of Honor: College Men in the Old South*. Baton Rouge: Louisiana State University Press, 2004.

Palmieri, Patricia A. "From Republican Motherhood to Race Suicide: Arguments on the Higher Education of Women in the United States, 1820–1920," in *Educating Men and Women Together: Coeducation in a Changing World*. Urbana: University of Illinois Press, 1987.

Park, Roberta J. "Physiology and Anatomy Are Destiny!?: Brains, Bodies and Exercise in Nineteenth Century American Thought." *Journal of Sport History* 18, no. 1 (Spring 1991): 31–63.

———. " 'Embodied Selves': The Rise and Development of Concern for Physical Education, Active Games and Recreation for American Women, 1776–1865." In *Sport in America: From Wicked Amusement to National Obsession*, edited by David K. Wiggins, 69–93. Champaign, Ill.: Human Kinetics, 1995.

Parratt, Catriona. *More Than Mere Amusement: Working-class Women's Leisure in England, 1750–1914*. Boston: Northeastern University Press, 2001.

Pascoe, Peggy. *What Comes Naturally: Miscegenation Law and the Making of Race in America*. New York: Oxford University Press, 2009.

Peiss, Kathy. *Cheap Amusements: Working Women and Leisure in Turn-of-the-Century New York*. Philadelphia: Temple University Press, 1986.

Pemberton, Cynthia Lee A. *More Than a Game: One Woman's Fight for Gender Equity in Sport*. Boston: Northeastern University Press, 2002.

Pope, S. W., ed. *The New American Sport History: Recent Approaches and Perspectives*. Urbana: University of Illinois Press, 1996.

Pruter, Robert. "Youth Baseball in Chicago, 1868–1890: Not Always Sandlot Ball." *Journal of Sport History* 26, no. 1 (Spring 1999): 1–28.

Rader, Benjamin G. *Baseball: A History of America's Game*. 3rd ed. Urbana: University of Illinois Press, 2008.

Radke-Moss, Andrea G. *Bright Epoch: Women and Coeducation in the American West*. Lincoln: University of Nebraska Press, 2008.

Riess, Steven A. *City Games: The Evolution of American Urban Society and the Rise of Sports*. Urbana: University of Illinois Press, 1991.

———. "Sport and the Redefinition of American Middle-Class Masculinity," *International Journal of the History of Sport* 8, no. 1 (May 1991): 5–27.

———. *Sport in Industrial America 1850–1920*. Wheeling, Ill.: Harlan Davidson, 1995.

———. *Touching Base Professional Baseball and American Culture in the Progressive Era*. Westport, Conn.: Greenwood, 1980.

Ring, Jennifer. *Stolen Bases: Why American Girls Don't Play Baseball*. Urbana: University of Illinois Press, 2013.

Rosenberg, Rosalind. *Beyond Separate Spheres: Intellectual Roots of Modern Feminism*. New Haven, Conn.: Yale University Press, 1983.

Rosenzweig, Roy. *Eight Hours for What We Will: Workers and Leisure in an Industrial City, 1870–1920*. Cambridge, U.K.: Cambridge University Press, 1985.

Rossi, Alice S. *The Feminist Papers: From Adams to de Beauvoir*. Boston: Northeastern University Press, 1973.

Rotundo, E. Anthony. *American Manhood: Transformations In Masculinity From The Revolution To The Modern Era*. New York: Basic Books, 1993.

Rury, John L. *Education and Women's Work: Female Schooling and the Division of Labor in Urban America, 1870–1930*. Albany: State University of New York Press, 1991.

Ryan, Mary P. *Cradle of the Middle Class: The Family in Oneida County, New York, 1790–1865.* Cambridge, U.K.: Cambridge University Press, 1981.

———. *Mysteries of Sex: Tracing Women and Men through American History.* Chapel Hill: University of North Carolina Press, 2006.

———. *Women in Public: Between Banners and Ballots, 1825–1880.* Baltimore: Johns Hopkins University Press, 1990.

Scott, Anne Firor, Susan K. Cahn, Sara M. Evans, and Elizabeth Faue. "Women's History in the Millennium: A Conversation across Three 'Generations': Part I." *Journal of Women's History* 11, no. 1 (1999): 9–30.

———. "Women's History in the Millennium: A Conversation across Three 'Generations': Part II." Journal of Women's History 11, no. 2 (1999): 199–220.

Seymour, Harold, and Dorothy Seymour Mills. *Baseball: The Early Years.* New York: Oxford University Press, 1989.

———. *Baseball: The People's Game.* 1st ed. New York: Oxford University Press, 1991.

Shattuck, Debra. "Bats, Balls and Books: Baseball and Higher Education for Women at Three Eastern Women's Colleges, 1866–1891." *Journal of Sport History* 19, no. 2 (Summer 1992): 91–109.

———. "Women's Baseball in the 1860s: Reestablishing a Historical Memory." *NINE: A Journal of Baseball History and Culture* 19.2 (2011): 1–26.

Shaulis, Dahn. "Pedestriennes: Newsworthy but Controversial Women in Sporting Entertainment." *Journal of Sport History* 26, no. 1 (Spring 1999): 29–50.

Sklar, Kathryn Kish. *Catharine Beecher: A Study in American Domesticity.* New York: Norton, 1976.

———. *Florence Kelley and the Nation's Work: The Rise of Women's Political Culture, 1830–1900.* New Haven, Conn.: Yale University Press, 1995.

———. *Women's Rights Emerges Within the Anti-Slavery Movement, 1830–1870: A Brief History with Documents.* New York: Bedford/St. Martin's, 2000.

Smith, Lisa, ed. *Nike Is a Goddess: The History of Women in Sports.* New York: Atlantic Monthly Press, 1999.

Smith-Rosenberg, Carroll. "Beauty, the Beast, and the Militant Woman: Sex Roles and Sexual Standards in Jacksonian America." In *Women, Families, and Communities: Readings in American History, Vol. 1: To 1877,* edited by Nancy A. Hewitt, 124–38. Glenview, Ill.: Scott, Foresman/Little, Brown Higher Education, 1990.

———. "The Female World of Love and Ritual: Relations Between Women in Nineteenth-Century America." *Signs* 1, no. 1 (Autumn 1975): 1–29.

Solomon, Barbara Miller. *In the Company of Educated Women: A History of Women and Higher Education in America.* New Haven, Conn.: Yale University Press, 1985.

Somers, Dale. *Rise of Sports in New Orleans.* Baton Rouge: Louisiana State University Press, 1972.

Stanton, Theodore, and Harriot Stanton Blatch, eds. *Elizabeth Cady Stanton: As Revealed in Her Letters, Diary and Reminiscences.* Vol. 2. New York: Harper & Bros., 1922.

Sullivan, Dean A., ed. *Early Innings: A Documentary History of Baseball, 1825–1908.* Lincoln: University of Nebraska Press, 1995.

Thorn, John. *Baseball in the Garden of Eden: The Secret History of the Early Game.* New York: Simon & Schuster, 2011.

———. *The Game for All America.* Charlotte, N.C.: Sporting News, 1988.

Todd, Jan. "The Classical Ideal and Its Impact on the Search for Suitable Exercise, 1774–1830." *Iron Game History* 2, no. 4 (November 1992): 6–16.

———. *Physical Culture and the Body Beautiful: "Purposive" Exercise in the Lives of American Women, 1800–1870.* Macon, Ga.: Mercer University Press, 1998.

Twin, Stephanie. *Out of the Bleachers: Writings on Women and Sport.* Old Westbury, N.Y.: The Feminist Press, 1979.

Tygiel, Jules. *Past Time: Baseball As History.* New York: Oxford University Press, 2001.

Vaught, David. *The Farmers' Game: Baseball in Rural America.* Baltimore: Johns Hopkins University Press, 2012.

Verbrugge, Martha H. *Able-Bodied Womanhood: Personal Health and Social Change in Nine-teenth-Century Boston.* New York: Oxford University Press, 1988.

Vertinsky, Patricia A. *Eternally Wounded Women: Women, Doctors and Exercise in the Late Nineteenth Century.* Urbana: University of Illinois Press, 1994.

Voigt, David Q. *American Baseball: Vol. 1, From the Gentleman's Sport to the Commissioner System.* Norman: University of Oklahoma Press, 1968.

Von Drehle, David. *Triangle: The Fire That Changed America.* New York: Grove Press, 2003.

Woody, Thomas, *A History of Women's Education in the United States.* 2 vols. New York: Science Press, 1929.

Digital Newspaper Resources Utilized

Ancestry.com. http://www.ancestry.com/

Brooklyn Public Library. http://eagle.brooklynpubliclibrary.org/

Chicago Public Library. http://www.chipublib.org/images/examiner/index.php

GenealogyBank.com. http://www.genealogybank.com/gbnk/

Georgia Historic Newspapers: Atlanta. http://atlnewspapers.galileo.usg.edu/atlnewspapers /search

Georgia Historic Newspapers: South Georgia. http://sgnewspapers.galileo.usg.edu/sgnewspapers /search

Kansas Historical Society. http://www.kshs.org/p/kansas-digital-newspaper-program/16126

The Library of Congress: Chronicling America. http://chroniclingamerica.loc.gov/

National Endowment for the Humanities. http://www.neh.gov/us-newspaper-program

NewspaperArchive.com. http://newspaperarchive.com/

The New York Times. http://query.nytimes.com/search/sitesearch/

Old Fulton New York Post Cards. http://fultonhistory.com/Fulton.html

XooxleAnswers. http://www.xooxleanswers.com/free-newspaper-archives/us-state-and-local -newspaper-archives/

Other Digital Resources Utilized

BaseballLibrary.com. http://www.baseballlibrary.com/chronology/

DVRBS.com. http://www.dvrbs.com/people/CamdenPeople-SylvesterFWilson.htm

Five College Archives Digital Access Project. http://clio.fivecolleges.edu/

Fold3. http://www.fold3.com/browse.php#43|

LA84 Foundation. http://search.la84foundation.org

The Library of Congress: Newspapers & Current Periodical Reading Room. http://www.loc .gov/rr/news/topics/bloomergirls.html

Making of America. http://quod.lib.umich.edu/m/moagrp/

Net54baseball.com. http://www.net54baseball.com/forumdisplay.php?f=5

19th Century Baseball. http://www.19cbaseball.com/field-10.html

Protoball. http://protoball.org/

SABR / Baseball Reference Encyclopedia. http://sabrpedia.org/wiki/Main_Page

Vassar Encyclopedia. http://vcencyclopedia.vassar.edu/

WorldVitalRecords.com. http://www.worldvitalrecords.com/default.aspx

Index

Bachs, 123

Bailey, James M., 60, 247

ballparks/playing grounds: Agricultural Park (Sacramento), 130; Asbury Beach (Asbury Park, N.J.), 113, 202; Beach Park (New Orleans), 128; Brisbane Park (Atlanta), 216; Central Park (New York City), 216; Central Park (San Francisco), 130; Dexter Park (Chicago), 74; Jumbo Park (Philadelphia), 119; Madison Avenue (athletic grounds), 83; Maroon Park (Chicago), 132; Meadowland Park (Bismarck, N.D.), 201; Merritt Grounds (Camden, N.J.), 119; Monitor Ball Park (Weehawken), 156; Monumental Park (Baltimore), 122; Oakdale Park (Philadelphia, Pa.), 86; Oriole Ball Ground (Baltimore), 119; Outing Park (Natick, Mass.), 216; Relief Grounds (Cincinnati), 186; South Side Baseball Grounds (Chicago), 131; South Side Park (Rockford, Ill.), 217; Sportsmen's Park (New Orleans), 123

Baltimore Canaries, 68

Bangor, Maine, 203

Bardstown, Ky., 220

Barnum, P.T./Barnum Circus, 67, 82, 132, 157, 270

base ball: British, 19, 24, 98; Massachusetts game, 14, 32, 206, 239, 243; New York version, 11, 13–14, 27, 30, 32, 233, 237

baseball creed/culture of baseball, 4, 6, 11, 14, 28, 34–35, 60–61, 115

Battle Ball, 178

Bayfield, Mich., 192

Beatrice, S.D., 209

Belfast, Maine, 194

Belles of the Bat (1883), 119, 198

Belles of the Bat (1890), 153

Belles of the Bat (1891, Caledonia, N.Y.), 210

Benicia Young Ladies' Seminary, 25, 184, 236–37

Benicia, Calif., 25, 184

Bey, Robert, 154, 269

Binghamton, N.Y., 158, 160, 272

Bismarck, Dakota Territory, 113, 201

Bismarck Female Base Ball Club, 113, 201

black female players, 113, 138, 204, 216, 238. See also Captain Jinks; Dolly Varden No. 1; Dolly Varden No. 2

Black Stocking Nine (fictitious), 101

Black Stocking Nine/Black Stockings (Sylvester Wilson team), 101, 153–59, 203, 209. See also Young Ladies' Base Ball Club No. 1

Blackwell, Alice Stone, 49–50, 188–89, 194

Blackwell, Henry, 49, 188

Blair, Neb., 210, 212

Blondes and Brunettes (1875, Springfield, Ill.), 73–80, 91, 97

Blondes and Brunettes (1879, New York City), 80–84, 86, 193. See also English Blondes (1879)

Blondes and Brunettes (1883, Almond, N.Y.), 198, 206

Blondes and Brunettes (1883, Philadelphia), 198

Bloomfield, N.J., 147, 214

Blue Stockings (1875, Frank Myers team), 76

Blue Stockings (fictitious team), 46

Blue Stockings of San Francisco (1886), 130, 201

Blunt, Dakota Territory, 113, 199

boating, 25, 51

Bordontown, N.J., 45, 185, 243

Boston Bloomer Girls, 142, 153, 167–71, 214–15, 217–20, 222–23, 225–27

Boston Red Stockings, 65–66

Boston, Mass., 12, 47, 67, 70–71, 74, 85, 89, 104, 158, 185, 188–89, 235, 244

boxing/prizefighting, 12, 32, 46, 67, 232–33

Bradi, Maud, 149. See also Nelson, Maud

Brady, Elizabeth, 130

Brenham, Texas, 128

Brida, Clementine, 149. See also Nelson, Maud

Bridgton Academy, 110, 199

Bristol, Pa., 80

Brock, Seth B., 75

Brooklyn, N.Y., 33, 73, 148, 156, 186, 191, 199, 204, 215–16, 240

Brotherhood of Professional Base Ball Players, 97–98, 157

Bruckner, Joseph, 154, 163, 165–66, 269, 273

Bryn Mawr, Pa., 213

Bryn Mawr College, 175, 213

Buffalo, N.Y., 78, 89, 121, 132

Buffalo Bisons, 65

Burdett, Hattie, 49

218, 227; Lawrence, Kan. (1895), 217; Leap Year Winners (1876, Virginia, Ill.), 57–58, 190; Lenox Cottages (1893, Mass.), 215; Longstockings (1875, Laporte, Pa.), 57, 190; Manistee, Mich. (1889), 115, 204; Marrieds (1870, Rockford, Ill.), 58, 187; McConnelsville, Oh. (1867), 185; Meade, Kan. (1897), 219; Mercersburg, Pa. (1878), 100, 192; Merry Maids (1890, Norwich, Conn.), 209; Morris, N.Y. (1898), 171, 221; Mount Washington, Md. (1889), 115, 205; Mrs. Jane Duffy Club, 197; Mt. Morris, N.Y. (1891), 211; Neodesha, Kan. (1877), 58, 191; Nevadaville, Col. (1890), 208; New Moorefield, Ohio (1886), 201; Niles, Mich. (1867), 34–35, 40, 184; North Edmeston, N.Y. (1881), 197; Norwich, Conn. (1886), 115, 201; Nyack, N.Y. (1888), 115, 202; Originals (1871, Elgin, Ill.), 188; Ostrich Feathers (1894, Rhinebeck, N.Y.), 216; Ovid, N.Y. (1892), 212; Paris, Ky. (1876), 191; Pensacola, Fla. (1867), 34, 40, 129, 186; Peterboro (Peterborough), N.Y. (1868), 37–43, 59, 101, 173, 185–86; Philadelphia, Pa. (1876), 190; Pittsburgh, Pa. (1871), 188; Pittsfield, N.H. (1874), 189; Plainfield, Iowa (1899), 223; Plymouth, Ind. (1868), 186; Pocahontas, Iowa (1889), 113, 203; Polka Dots (1890, Norwich, Conn.), 209; Pond Lillies (1894, Rhinebeck, N.Y.), 216; Providence, R.I. (1876), 191; Quincy, Ill. (1883), 198; Reading, Pa. (1875), 59, 190; Reds (1890, Staten Island), 209; Rhinebeck, N.Y. (1874), 189; Rochester, N.Y. (1878), 192; Romney, W.V. (1885), 200; Safford, Az. (1898), 220; Salamanca, N.Y. (c. 1897), 220; San Antonio, Tex. (1889), 113, 203; Saranac, Mich. (1867), 184; Sconset (Siasconset), Mass. (1892), 120, 213; Sedamsville, Ohio (1869), 186; Silver Creek, N.Y. (1882), 197; Singles (1870, Rockford, Ill.), 58, 187; Soquel, Cal. (1887), 202; South Side Stars (1895, Rockford, Ill.), 217; Springfield Female Baseball Club (1897, Kentucky), 220; Stars (1898, Rockford, Ill.), 222; Stowe, Pa. (1891), 210; Striped Stockings (1876, Manitowoc, Wis.), 190; Striped Stockings (1878, Jefferson, Wis.), 57, 193; Striped Stockings (1882, Quincy, Ill.), 113, 197; Stripes (1898, Rockford, Ill.), 222; Sun Flower Club (1889, McPherson, Kan.), 204; Tarboro, N.C. (1874), 189; Tekamah, Neb. (1891–1892), 210, 212; Thief River Falls, Minn. (1893), 214; unnamed black women's team (1894, Atlanta, Ga.), 138, 216; unnamed black women's team (1894, Fort Valley, Ga.), 138, 216; unnamed team (1872, Minnesota), 188; unnamed team (1880s, Ohio), 196; unnamed teams (1889, Kansas), 204; Utica, N.Y. (1888 & 1890), 115, 202, 209; Washington Courthouse, Oh. (1891), 138, 210; Westport Point, Mass. (1898), 221; Whites (1890, Staten Island), 209; Wichita, Kan. (1873), 189; Williamsburg, Ky. (1897), 219; Williamsport, Pa. (1877), 192; Woman's Suffrage Base-Ball Club (1869), 57, 186; Young Independents (1878, Syracuse, N.Y.), 57, 193

Civil War, 7, 27, 32

Clarke, Mame, 111

Clayton, Mich., 197

Cleveland Blues, 65

Cleveland, Ohio, 65, 68, 73, 132, 175, 211, 213, 218, 248, 253

Clifford, Lizzie, 120

club-ball, 19, 23–24

Clyde, William C., 154, 269

Colby, Kan., 113, 204

college/university teams (female) (by team name or location): Abenakis BBC (1866, Vassar College), 51, 184; Alabama Central Female College (1886, Tuskegee, Ala.), 201; Allegheny College (1889, Meadville, Pa.), 105, 107, 203; Bryn Mawr College (1892), 213; Converse College (1890s, Spartanburg, S.C.), 175–76, 219, 221–22; Diana Base Ball Club (Northwestern Female College), 53, 186 (*see also* Northwestern Female College); Earlham School (1881, Richmond, Ind.), 197, 205; Iowa State Agricultural College/Iowa State University (1890s), 56, 216, 226; Laurel BBC (1866, Vassar College), 51, 184; Mount Holyoke Nine (1880s & 1890s), 112, 199–200, 209, 218, 222; Normal School (1889, near Colby, Kan.), 113, 204; Olivet College (1890s, Michigan), 51, 177, 219; Ottawa University (1894, Ottawa, Kan.), 216; Precocious BBC (1867, Vassar College), 51, 184; Smith College teams (1880 & 1890s), 111–12, 196, 209, 212, 221–22; University of Arizona (1898), 175, 221; University of Michigan (1893, co-ed team), 214; University of North Dakota (1893), 51, 177, 214; Vassar College (1870s & 1890s, Poughkeepsie, N.Y.), 190–92, 218, 246; Wellesley College/Female Seminary (1880s), 105–6, 175, 199, 206; Whittier College (Salem, Iowa), 55, 189; Women's College of Western Reserve University (1890s, Cleveland, Ohio), 175, 218

Colorado, 109, 172, 202; Central City, 73; Denver, 73, 113, 142, 169, 199, 212; Nevadaville, 208

Colored Agricultural and Industrial Fair, 264

Columbus, Ohio, 39, 89–90, 239

Comstock, Anthony, 105

Concord High School, 110, 200

Concord, N.H., 110, 200

Connecticut, 11, 47, 88, 112, 172, 206; Danbury, 60, 192; Farmington, 184; Gilead, 61, 191; Norwich, 115, 201, 209

Converse College, 175–76, 219, 221–22, 227

Crawfordsville, Ind., 58, 188

cricket: female, 19–20, 22–23, 221, 235; male, 2, 9, 11, 15, 17, 19–20, 24, 36, 94, 98, 178

croquet, 44, 49, 51, 111, 115, 175, 185

Cuba, 163, 165, 214–15, 273

cycling, 67, 274

Dakota Territory: Bismarck, 113, 201; Blunt, 113, 199

Dallas, Tex., 127, 239

Danbury, Conn., 60, 192

Dansville Seminary, 25, 236

Dansville, N.Y., 25, 236

Delaware, 183

Denison, Tex., 127

Denver, Col., 73, 113, 142, 169, 199, 212

Denver Blues (1892), 212

Denver Female BBC (1892), 212

Detroit, Mich., 60, 89, 91, 128–29, 132, 187

Devilbiss, Sam, 131

Diamond Garters (1875), 75, 79. *See also* Blondes and Brunettes (1875, Springfield, Ill.); Lace-Top Stockings (1875); Myers,

Frank; Springfield Blondes and Brunettes (1875)

Diana Base Ball Club (Northwestern Female College), 53, 186. *See also* Northwestern Female College

Dolly Varden No. 1, 116–17, 171, 198

Dolly Varden No. 2, 116–17, 171, 198

Dooley, Charles, 152

Dowagiac, Mich., 184

Eagleswood School, 24–25

Earl, Effie, 154, 269

Easton, Pa., 122

East Tawas, Mich., 60, 189

Egan, Ruth, 148, 267

Elgin, Ill., 132, 188

Elgins (Elgin, Ill.), 132

Elmira, N.Y., 115, 202

Emerson, Pearl, 124, 130, 207, 261

Emerson, Ralph Waldo, 24

Emporia, Kan., 210

England, 10, 15, 19–20, 23–24, 149, 269

English Blondes (1879), 74, 80–84, 86, 193

Erie, N.Y., 191

Erie, Pa., 198

Evanston College for Women, 188

Evanston, Ill., 53, 55, 186, 188

Evanston, Wyo., 213

Evansville, Ind., 188

Everett, Edward E., 121–22, 206

exercise, 8, 12, 15–17, 19–25, 43–44, 46, 48, 51, 54, 57, 148, 171–72, 179, 183, 191

factory teams (female): Manayunk (Pa.) mill team (1878), 121, 193; Philadelpha shoe factory team (1883), 113, 197; Rockford (Ill.) factory team (1891), 138, 211

Fancy Stockings (1882, Quincy, Ill.), 113, 197

Farmington, Conn., 184

Favorites (1870, Cincinnati, Ohio), 48, 188

Fayetteville, Tenn., 33

Female Base Ball Club of New York (1879), 193

Female Base Ball Club of Philadelphia (1879), 193

Female Blue Stockings of Philadelphia (1879), 65, 86, 88–91, 99, 193. *See also* Female Base Ball Club of Philadelphia (1879)

Johnson, E.G., 131, 202
Johnson, Mamie (Laura), 269–70
Johnson, R.C., 217
Jolly Young Bachelors, 10
Joseph Medill High School, 173

Kalamazoo, Mich., 44, 185, 223
Kansas, 35, 81, 100, 124, 130–31, 140, 158, 167, 169, 207–10, 215–17, 225, 227; Argentine, 219; Atchison/South Atchison, 122, 127, 135, 209; Colby, 113, 204; Emporia, 210; Fredonia, 58, 191–92; Haddam, 113, 203; Hope, 113, 202; Kinsley, 58, 191; Lawrence, 217; McPherson, 113, 204; Meade, 219; Neodesha, 58, 191–92; Ottawa, 216; Severance, 127, 261; Wichita, 189
Kansas City Bloomer Girls, 167
Kentucky, 58, 89, 124, 190–91, 206, 222; Bardstown, 220; Paris, 191; Springfield, 220; Williamsburg, 219
kickball, 178
Kingston, N.Y., 121, 191, 259
Kinsley Free Booters, 58
Kinsley, Kan., 58, 191
Kirkwood, Ill., 200
Knickerbocker Base Ball Club, 10–11, 13–14, 36, 48, 237
Knoxville, Tenn., 134
Ku Klux Klan Club, 33

Laborde, Edwardo, 163
Lace-Top Stockings (1875), 75, 79. *See also* Blondes and Brunettes (1875, Springfield, Ill.); Myers, Frank; Springfield Blondes and Brunettes (1875)
Ladies Athletic Association, 81
Ladies' Baseball League (1890–91), 135, 141, 154, 156
Ladies B.B.C. of Hallsport (1867), 184
Ladies' Champion Baseball Club (1889), 134
Lady Nine of Baltimore (1879), 84–85, 193
Lady Nine of Boston (1879), 84–85, 193
Lafayette, Ind., 89, 190
Lally, Mark, 149, 168, 210, 270
Lampasas, Tex., 127
Lancaster, Ohio, 48, 188
Lang Ball, 178
Lang, John, 116–17, 198, 258

LaPorte, Pa., 190
Laurel BBC (1866, Vassar College), 51, 184
Lawrence, Kan., 217
Lawrence, May, 124, 261
Leap Year Winners (1876, Virginia, Ill.), 57–58, 190
Lebanon, Pa., 122
Lee, Alice, 154
leisure, 12, 15, 18, 32, 66, 71, 91, 95, 110, 115, 175, 243, 254
Lenox, Mass., 215
Little Falls, Minn., 168
Little Falls, N.Y., 169
Little League Association, 1
Livingston, Lottie, 159, 163, 226, 273. *See also* Long, Annie; Myers, Mattie A.
Lodi High School, 212
Lodi High School Unrivalled Female Base Ball Club, 212
Lodi, Wis., 212
Long Island, N.Y., 147
Long, Annie, 163, 270
Los Angeles, Calif., 73, 131, 203, 212
Louisiana, 206, 222; New Orleans, 18, 33, 84–85, 120–21, 123–24, 128–29, 193, 199–200, 239, 252; Spanish Fort, 128
Lowville, N.Y., 219
Lydia Thompson's British Blondes, 72–73

Magnolias, 10
Maine, 20, 110, 112, 175, 218; Bangor, 203; Belfast, 194; North Bridgton, 199; West Lebanon, 47, 186
Major League Baseball (MLB), 62, 104, 247
Manayunk, Pa., 121, 193
Manistee, Mich., 115, 204
marketing/marketing strategies, 64, 75, 82, 85, 95–96, 115, 138
Marrieds (1870, Rockford, Ill.), 58, 187
Mary A. Burnham School, 46, 172, 217
Maryland, 88, 109, 119, 122–23, 205–6, 260; Mount Washington, 115, 205
Massachusetts, 56, 175, 206, 212–13, 215–18, 238, 244; Ayer, 199; Boston, 12, 47, 67, 70–71, 74, 85, 89, 104, 158, 185, 188–89, 235, 244; Greenfield, 46, 189; Haverhill, 147, 208; Lenox, 215; Natick, 69, 216, 275; Northampton, 46, 172, 196, 209, 212, 217,

221–22; Pittsfield, 89–90, 110, 204; Sconset (Siasconset), 120, 213; South Hadley, 46, 112, 199–200, 209, 218, 222; Wellesley, 56, 105–6, 175, 199, 206; Westport Point, 221

Mather, Mary H.A., 111–12

Maximo Bloomer Girls, 167

McConnelsville, Ohio, 185

McPherson, Kan., 113, 204

Meade, C.W., 159, 271

Meade, Kan., 219

Meadville, Pa., 105, 203

men's teams/leagues: Allentown Peanuts, 151; Allertons, 156, 223; Almendares Club, 164–65; American Association (AA), 29, 95–97, 118, 139, 225; Atlantic League, 148, 151, 220; Bachs, 123; Baltimore Canaries, 68; Boston Red Stockings, 65–66; Brotherhood of Professional Base Ball Players, 97–98, 157; Buffalo Bisons, 65; Chicago White Stockings (White Sox), 65, 70, 99; Cincinnati Reds/Red Stockings, 32–33, 65, 68–69, 96; Cleveland Blues, 65; Elgins (Elgin, Ill.), 132; Forest City Club (of Cleveland, Ohio), 1; Forest City Club (of Rockford, Ill.), 31, 58, 187; Good Boys' Base Ball Club, 111, 199; Gothams/New York Gothams, 10, 99; Hackensack Giants, 142; Hartford Cooperatives, 151; Independents (1907, Vermilion, Ohio), 267; International Association of Professional Base Ball Players, 29, 71; International Baseball Federation, 181; Jolly Young Bachelors, 10; Kinsley Free Booters, 58; Knickerbocker Base Ball Club, 10–11, 13–14, 36, 48, 237; Ku Klux Klan Club, 33; Little League Association, 1; Magnolias, 10; Major League Baseball (MLB), 62, 104, 247; Mutual Base Ball Club (Jackson, Miss.), 123; National Association of Base Ball Players (NABBP), 14–15, 17, 20, 28, 34–36, 63, 69–70; National Association of Professional Base Ball Players (NA), 14, 28–29, 63, 66, 70–71; National League (NL), 29, 58, 65, 70–71, 91, 94–98, 139, 150; New York Gothams, 10, 99; New York State League, 151; New York Yankees, 151; Northwestern League, 97; Olympic Ball Club of Philadelphia, 11; Orions (of Philadelphia), 117; Philadelphia Athletics, 68; Players'

League, 97, 139; Providence Grays, 65, 99; Reading Coal Heavers, 151; Robert E. Lees (Galveston), 239; Stonewalls (Houston), 239; Syracuse Stars, 65; Troy Trojans, 65; Washington Nationals, 31–32, 58, 239; Washingtons (Long Branch, N.J.), 117; Western League, 151

Mercersburg, Pa., 100, 192

Merry Maids (1890, Norwich, Conn.), 209

Messner, Michael, 4, 13–14, 233, 255

Michigan, 11, 40, 60–61, 79, 124–25, 148, 222–23, 225, 238; Allen's Prairie (Coldwater), 35, 185; Ann Arbor, 177, 214; Bayfield, 192; Clayton, 197; Detroit, 60, 89, 91, 128–29, 132, 187; Dowagiac, 184; East Tawas, 60, 189; Kalamazoo, 44, 185, 223; Manistee, 115, 204; Niles, 34–35, 40, 184; Olivet, 219; Saranac, 184; Springport, 219

Michigan State University, 56

Miller, Elizabeth Smith, 38, 42, 235, 242

Miller, Gerrit Smith, 37

Miller, Nannie, 37–39, 185

Mills Seminary (Oakland, Calif.), 189, 195

Milwaukee, Wis., 125, 215

Minnesota, 37, 124–26, 172, 188, 211, 217, 222, 227, 238; Little Falls, 168; Thief River Falls, 214

Mississippi, 123, 183

Missouri, 21, 35, 75–80, 124, 127, 171–72, 190, 213; St. Louis, 71, 76–78, 80, 91, 120, 135–36, 141, 154, 171, 215, 239, 249

Miss Porter's School, 47, 184, 187, 203

Mitchell, Jackie, 254

Mitchell, Rose, 154

MLB. *See* Major League Baseball

Montana/Montana Territory, 109; Glendive, 113, 199

Moore, W.S., 252

Morris, Harry, 252

Morris, New York, 171, 221

Morse, Anna, 111

Mount Holyoke College/Female Seminary, 46, 112, 176, 199, 209, 218, 222

Mount Washington, Md., 115, 205

Mountain Maids (1870, Cincinnati, Ohio), 48, 188

Moyer, Carrie, 148

Mrs. Hazen's Suburban School for Girls, 172

Niles, Mich., 34–35, 40, 184
No. 7 Hose, 46. *See also* Blue Stockings
Normal School of Philadelphia, 118
North Bridgton, Maine, 199
North Carolina, 58, 133–34, 222, 238; Goldsboro, 134; Raleigh, 168; Tarboro, 189
North Dakota, 51, 109, 113, 177, 201; Grand Forks, 214
North Edmeston, N.Y., 197
Northampton, Mass., 46, 172, 196, 209, 212, 217, 221–22
Northwestern Female College, 53–54, 186. *See also* Evanston College for Women
Northwestern League, 97
Northwestern University, 54, 188, 194
Norwich, Conn., 115, 201, 209
novelty, 1, 3, 67, 75, 80, 115, 117, 138, 163, 219
Nyack, N.Y., 115, 202

Oakland, Calif., 189, 215, 219–20, 236
Oberlin College, 25
Ogontz School, 172–73, 208, 214, 220, 222. *See also* Chestnut Street Female Seminary
Ohio, 25, 34, 50, 68–69, 73–81, 124–25, 138, 172, 188–89, 196, 209–11, 217–18, 238–39, 250; Akron, 156; Cincinnati, 11, 48, 57, 69, 71, 81, 89, 120, 124, 128–30, 153–54, 156, 186, 188, 200, 206, 209, 239; Cleveland, 65, 68, 73, 132, 175, 211, 213, 218, 248, 253; Columbus, 39, 89–90, 239; Lancaster, 48, 188; McConnelsville, 185; New Lisbon, 100, 188; New Moorefield, 201; Rocky River, 89–90; Sedamsville, 186; Springfield, 74–80, 89–90, 98, 112; Tallmadge, 110, 200; Vermilion, 267
Oklahoma, 183
Olean, N.Y., 198
Olivet College, 51, 177, 219
Olivet, Mich., 219
Olympic Ball Club of Philadelphia, 11
One and Only Young Ladies' Baseball Club (1884), 121
One Old Cat, 22, 33
Oregon, 183
Originals (1871, Elgin, Ill.), 188)
Orions (of Philadelphia), 117
Oswego, N.Y., 122, 132, 196

Ottawa University (Kansas), 216
Ottawa, Kan., 216
Ovid, N.Y., 212

Packer, Annie, 55, 246
Paris, Ky., 191
pedestrianism/walking races, 15, 32, 67. *See also* walking
Pelham Manor, N.Y., 172, 218
Pennsylvania, 35, 98, 139, 148–49, 156, 158–59, 188–90, 206, 208, 213–14, 219–22, 238; Abington, 208, 214, 220, 222; Alinda, 214; Allentown, 122; Bristol, 80; Bryn Mawr, 213; Chester, 119, 121; Easton, 122; Erie, 198; Freeland, 149; Germantown, 219, 221; Gilmore, 113, 201; Glasgow, 211; Harmonsburg, 189; Harrisburg, 121, 184; Hazleton, 149; Laporte, 190; Lebanon, 122; Manayunk, 121, 193; Meadville, 105, 203; Mercersburg, 100, 192; Philadelphia, 11–12, 33, 71, 80–81, 84–86, 88–89, 95, 113, 116–18, 124, 127–28, 130, 142, 148, 159, 161, 171–73, 190, 193, 197–99, 211, 217; Pittsburgh, 59, 89, 132–33, 188, 267; Pottstown, 151, 211; Pottsville, 197; Reading, 59, 149, 151, 190; Ridgway, 59; Scranton, 197; South Chester, 198; Stowe, 210; Titusville, 270; West Philadelphia, 119; Williamsport, 133, 192, 203
Pensacola, Fla., 34, 40, 129, 186
Perth Amboy, N.J., 24, 183
Peterboro, N.Y., 37–43, 59, 101, 173, 185–86, 240–42
Philadelphia Athletics, 68
Philadelphia Female Baseball Club, 134
Philadelphia, Pa., 11–12, 33, 71, 80–81, 84–86, 88–89, 95, 113, 116–18, 124, 127–28, 130, 142, 148, 159, 161, 171–73, 190, 193, 197–99, 211, 217
Phillips, William, 121, 206
Phoenix, N.Y., 192, 196
pick-up/muffin teams. *See* civic/pick-up/muffin teams
Pittsburgh, Pa., 59, 89, 132–33, 188, 267
Pittsfield, Mass., 89–90, 110, 204
Pittsfield, N.H., 189
Pittsfield High School, 110, 204
Plainfield, Iowa, 223

Rhode Island, 238; Providence, 88, 99, 191

Richardson, Sophia Foster, 54–55, 245–46

Richmond, Ind., 197, 205

Richmond, Va., 101

Richter, Francis C., 95–96, 109–10, 119–24, 127–29, 132, 134, 139, 147, 156, 158, 161, 166–67, 255, 257, 270

Ridgway, Pa., 59

Robert E. Lees (Galveston), 239

Rochester, N.Y., 89, 113, 192

Rockport High School, 198

Rockport, Ind., 198, 205

Rocky River, Ohio, 89–90

Romney, W.V., 200

Rose Royal's Female Base Ball Club, 215

Rosette, Lewis, 75

Rotundo, E. Anthony, 12

Round Ball, 11, 13, 18

Round Cat, 33

Rowe, Myrtle, 148

rowing, 24–25, 36, 46, 48–49, 59, 176

Rush Medical College, 131

Sacramento, Calif., 25, 130, 236–37

Safford, Ariz., 220

Salamanca, N.Y., 220

Salem, Iowa, 55, 189

San Antonio, Tex., 113, 128, 133, 203

San Francisco, Calif., 25, 124, 130–31, 168, 171, 201, 237, 269

Santa Cruz, Calif., 204

Saranac, Mich., 184

school teams (female/co-ed) (by team name or location): Amazons (1878, Phoenix, N.Y.), 192; Argentine, Kan. (1897), 219; Benicia Young Ladies' Seminary teams, 25, 184, 236–37; Bridgton Academy (1884, N. Bridgton, Me.), 110, 199; Chauncy Hall School (Boston) teams, 189; Concord High School (1885, N.H.), 110, 200; Eagleswood School teams, 24–25, 183; Evanston College for Women (1871), 188; Favorites (1870, Cincinnati, Oh.), 48, 188; Galt High School (1887, California), 111, 201; Germantown Friends School (1897–1898), 219, 221; Good Girls' Base Ball Club (1884, Punahou School), 111, 199; Harris Grammar School

(1872, Boston), 49–50, 188; Haverhill Academy (c. 1890, Mass.), 208; Joseph Medill High School (1890s, Chicago), 173, 217; Kalamazoo, Mich. (1899), 223; Kentucky schools (1870s), 190; Lodi High School Unrivalled Female Base Ball Club, 212; Mary A. Burnham School (c. 1895), 46, 172, 217; Mills College (1890s, Oakland, Calif.), 215, 219–20; Mills Seminary (1872, Oakland, Calif.), 189; Miss Porter's School (1867 & 1889, Farmington, Conn.), 47, 184, 203; Mountain Maids (1870, Cincinnati, Oh.), 48, 188; Mrs. Hazen's Suburban School for Girls (c. 1896, Pelham Manor, N.Y.), 172, 218; Neodesha, Kan. (1877), 192; Ogontz School (1890s, Abington, Pa.), 172–73, 208, 214, 220, 222; Ohio school teams (1873), 189; Pittsfield High School (1889, Mass.), 110, 204; Prospect Hill School (1874, Greenfield, Mass.), 46, 189; Punahou School (1870s-1880s, Hawaii), 48, 189, 196, 199, 244; Rockport High School (1883, Rockport, Ind.), 198; South Junior Grammar School team (1870), 48, 188; South Senior Grammar School team (1870), 48, 188; Springport, Mich. (1897), 219; State Street grammar school (1897, Lowville, N.Y.), 219; Steuben County schools (New York), 183; Tallmadge High School (1885, Ohio), 110, 200; Tunxis Base Ball Club (1867), 48, 184; Walnut Lane Boarding School (1897, Germantown, Pa.), 219; West Division High School (1890s, Chicago), 173, 217; West Lebanon Academy, 47, 186; Westwood, N.J. grammar school (1891), 211

Sconset (Siasconset), Mass., 120, 213

Scranton, Pa., 197

Sedamsville, Ohio, 186

Seguin, Tex., 128

Seneca Falls, N.Y., 36–37

Severance, Kan., 127, 261

Sherman, Tex., 127

Silver Creek, N.Y., 197

Simmons, Frank, 75

Simmons, Lew, 248

Singles (1870, Rockford, Ill.), 58, 187

Smith, Ann, 38, 242

Wright, Harry, 66, 69
Wyoming, 37, 138; Evanston, 213

Yale College/Yale University, 25, 140
Young Independents (1878, Syracuse, N.Y.), 57, 193
Young Ladies Athletic Club of Cincinnati, 153
Young Ladies Athletic Club of Philadelphia, 203
Young Ladies Base Ball Club of Cincinnati, 153
Young Ladies Base Ball Club of New York (1894), 141, 149–50, 154, 168, 211, 214–15, 217–18, 220, 222
Young Ladies Base Ball Club of Philadelphia (1883), 198
Young Ladies Champions of the World Base Ball Club (1891–94), 149–50, 154, 215
Young Ladies' Base Ball Club, 99, 119, 122, 130, 153, 159, 170, 184, 198, 203, 207
Young Ladies' Base Ball Club No. 1, 153. *See also* Black Stockings (Frank Wilson team)
Young Ladies' Base Ball Nine of Chicago, 153

DEBRA A. SHATTUCK is Provost and Associate
Professor of History at John Witherspoon College.

Sport and Society

The University of Illinois Press
is a founding member of the
Association of American University Presses.

Composed in 11.25/13 Bulmer
by Jim Proefrock
at the University of Illinois Press
Manufactured by Sheridan Books, Inc.

University of Illinois Press
1325 South Oak Street
Champaign, IL 61820-6903
www.press.uillinois.edu